W9-AKB-651

LARGE
PRINT
EDITION

RANDOM
HOUSE

WALTER CRONKITE

A Reporter's Life

Published by Random House Large Print
in association with Alfred A. Knopf, Inc.
New York 1996

Library of Congress Cataloging-in-Publication Data
Cronkite, Walter.
A reporter's life / Walter Cronkite.
p.   cm.
ISBN 0-679-77414-9
1. Cronkite, Walter. 2. Journalists—United States—
Biography. I. Title.
PN4874.C84A3   1996
070'.92—dc20
[B]   96-36279
                                                              CIP

Random House Web Address: http://www.randomhouse.com/
Printed in the United States of America
FIRST LARGE PRINT EDITION

This Large Print Book carries the
Seal of Approval of N.A.V.H.

For the twenty-two million who were there Monday through Friday . . .

And for Betsy, who has been there every night

And for the children and grandchildren, who have made something very special of a reporter's life:

Nancy

Kathy and Bill, and their William and Jack

Chip and Deborah, and their Walter IV and Peter

ACKNOWLEDGMENTS

"Acknowledgment" isn't nearly a strong enough word to express the gratitude I owe all those who made this book possible.

Directly involved—those without whose help there would be no book—were, primarily, Shirley and Joe Wershba, two who are not only sterling newspeople but dear friends from my earliest days in television. Their tireless research and astute criticism were invaluable as was their never-failing encouragement.

My son, Chip, whose business is television production, turned out to have a flair for literary criticism that proved most helpful, as did the informal commentaries of Betsy, who, like others who suffer while spouses produce books, put up reasonably cheerfully with a lot of lonely nights and the sullen moods of unproductive days.

Equally tolerant, thank goodness, was my indefatigable and multitalented chief of staff, Marlene Adler. It fell to her lot to coordinate all the behind-the-scene details concomitant to getting a book published. I could not have asked for a greater devotion to the project, and I am thankful her marriage survived the long nights and weekends she put in on it.

Her faith in the book was a source of inspiration and it was she who named it.

Sandy Socolow, my closest associate at CBS and beyond for forty years, was there to help clear memories' cobwebs concerning many experiences we shared. Nancy Ramsey doggedly ran to ground some of the toughest research problems. Vincent Virga and Claudia Cummings were responsible for exhuming the ancient photos. The oral history that the University of Texas' Don Carleton extracted from me proved a valuable resource.

Thanks, of course, to my editor at Knopf, Ashbel Green. I not only deeply appreciate his expert guidance but am particularly grateful for his patience while I procrastinated for years in finishing the book. If he burned while I fiddled, there was no evidence in Ash to show it.

Those cited above were the hands-on helpers of inestimable value. There are others in the all-important television years on whose backs I was carried to fame. It is impossible to name them all—the correspondents, writers, camera people and film editors, and artists and makeup people whose skills were essential to the success of our broadcasts. Permit me to list a few to represent the many: the executive producers of the "Evening News" and our many specials—Don Hewitt, Bud Benjamin, Ernie Leiser, Les Midgley, Russ Bensley, Paul Greenberg and Socolow; and our score of writers through the years, best represented by three of the finest and longest serving, Charles West, John Mosedale and

Sandy Polster. They and our ever-vigilant and inspired editors, Ed Bliss and the late John Merriman, managed to remain loyal and steadfast despite occasional displays of what can only be described as my intemperate, irascible, irrationality. Hinda Glasser, Ann Whitestone and Carolyn Dorset, assistants and secretaries, were at my right hand to keep me out of trouble. To all of them and scores more, my gratitude knows no bounds.

And, finally, for their diligence, thanks to my long-time agent, Tom Stix, and my attorney, Ron Konecky. I owe them everything—including a share of the profits.

A Reporter's Life

CHAPTER I

IF, AS THEY say, the threat of the hangman's noose has a powerful way of focusing one's attention, the same can be said of pregnancy.

This truth came to me on an early March day in 1948. Through the frost that fogged the fortochka (double-hung) windows of our Moscow apartment, I could just make out that snow had fallen during the night. It reflected a bright sun with blinding intensity. The grime of Moscow's air had not yet darkened its glory.

Betsy had awakened earlier and gone off to her job at the American Embassy's United States Information Agency. Although my United Press salary wasn't exactly munificent, it wasn't the extra income that had attracted her to this job. It was more a matter of necessity to keep us fed.

The Soviet food ration was desperately small. Elsie, our elderly Finnish maid/cook, provided little supplementary food from the so-called free market. Goodness knows, the poor old lady tried, although clearly handicapped at the market. Her Russian was apparently as bad as her English, which was almost nonexistent. Betsy said she spoke no known language. In winter she braved the deepest cold and the worst blizzards. Wrapped in her sweaters and coats and layers of shawls and wearing her rubber-soled felt boots, she shuffled out of the apartment before dawn every day.

She joined the other babushkas (grandmothers) in a half dozen lines before she trudged home just before noon bearing the day's treasures in her little crocheted shopping bag: perhaps one or two potatoes, probably spoiled, with great black spots where they had frozen; maybe a hunk of gristle that was meant to pass for edible meat; with real luck an egg or two, also not infrequently spoiled.

Each month our government shipped into Moscow plentiful rations, including liquor, for the 110 or so Americans in the Embassy. The only other Americans living in Moscow were the eight news correspondents, but the State Department, in its bureaucratic wisdom, determined that it would somehow violate its sacred rules to include enough rations to take care of us as well. "You must understand," was their bureaucratically hidebound explanation, "there are other hardship posts around the world besides Moscow and we simply couldn't send food rations to all the nongovernment Americans at all of them." They could have if they had wanted to, but that would have destroyed the little privileges that gave them added stature—in their own minds.

So Betsy worked at the Embassy to get one American ration, which provided our daily minimum of calories, potassium, protein, and all those other things listed on cereal boxes. There were some supplements, of course, from the Soviet ration, from Elsie's pitiful contribution, and from a lot of dinner invitations from Western-nation diplomats.

On this snow-brightened morning Betsy called from her office to find out if I was staying in our apartment/office for lunch.

"I'll be there, and I've got a surprise," she said.

She was pregnant with our first child. Her joyful announcement did indeed focus my attention. The peripatetic life of a foreign correspondent no longer seemed appropriate.

The first order of priority, however, was to have the baby, and there was no question in our minds that as much of Betsy's pregnancy as desirable, and definitely the lying-in, would take place in the States, and that meant, to Betsy, back in Kansas City, which she still refers to as the Paris of the Middle West. Betsy cabled her parents that she was en route home pregnant, but the brevity of the message, coupled with our well-known problems with Soviet censorship and the fact that we had not conceived in eight years of married life, convinced the good folks in Kansas City that this intelligence must be a code for some other dire incident. They were thus totally unprepared for her arrival home some weeks later.

The foreshortened message was typical of Betsy's thrifty use of telegrams. Our four-year courtship somehow survived her habit of sending off telegrams ending with the minimum ten words whether she had conveyed the essential information or not. She avoided the per word surcharge for excess words with such truncated messages as: "Arriving 3:30 Monday Missouri Pacific Train 115 STOP Hope that." Or: "Sorry I havent written last two weeks but had to."

By the time she got the Soviets' permission to leave Moscow (an incredible imposition on citizens of other sovereign nations), Betsy was three months pregnant. It would be four months before I was able to join her in Kansas City, waiting for my UP replacement, waiting for the Soviets to play their little games with exit visa applications. At last I raced halfway around the world to be present at the accouchement, only to find that my services were not really required.

Nancy arrived, as babies seem to have a penchant for doing, in the immediate predawn hours of November 8, 1948. Delivery, I thought, was notably easy. It certainly seemed to be for me—a very short wait in the "Fathers' Room," barely enough time to tamp down the tobacco in my pipe.

The doctor who announced Nancy's arrival assured me that Betsy, too, had had a comparatively easy delivery and that the baby had the requisite number of limbs and digital extremities. I think the doctor even ventured an opinion that it was a beautiful baby, but he underestimated by at least half. She was gorgeous.

I left St. Luke's Hospital sometime in the early morning of that Indian summer day, a sparkling bright day, as bright as they seem to get only in Missouri in the fall. It was, to me, a day unlike any other that had dawned since the Creation. The revelation had come, the unveiling of the mystery of man's perpetual renewal. I looked back at the hospital and realized that there in swaddling clothes, up there on the fourth floor, was the reason for Betsy's and my being on earth.

Such self-oriented, navel-examining profundities do not come often to me, but apparently such is the effect of the birth of one's first child. As a matter of fact, I wondered that morning whether similar thoughts had occupied my father upon my arrival at Dr. Grey's Lying-In Hospital in St. Joseph, Missouri, thirty-two years before, almost to the day. What, I wondered, was in the mind of that rather handsome, medium-sized, impeccably dressed young dentist who crunched through the fallen acorns and up to the front porch of the modest two-story clapboard residence that Dr. Grey had converted into his medical establishment?

As he entered, a bell suspended over the unlocked door sedately tinkled notice of his arrival. Only slightly winded from his brisk hike up from the streetcar line that had brought him from downtown St. Joseph, he announced his intentions to the nurse who had answered the bell.

"I'd like to see Mrs. Cronkite."

"Of course, Doctor. And your little boy is adorable."

In reconstructing this scene, I just made up that last quote (as I will some others before this tale is done). My mother told me—sometime later—that I was an adorable child, so I feel it safe to assume now that the nurse would not have delayed in communicating this rather important intelligence to the infant's father.

As my father greeted my mother on that auspicious day just a year after their marriage, he must have remarked upon her appearance. With her light brown, naturally curly hair, her hazel eyes, her regular features and beguiling smile, she was indeed beautiful—beauty that blessed us right into her nineties.

We might also assume that, as my father gazed down at his newborn son in her arms, he stroked his blond mustache. It was closely cropped and neatly trimmed and it didn't require stroking to put it in order, but he did that all his life when he was admiring something—a piece of art, or a particularly arresting passage of prose or poetry, or a fine set of teeth he'd just finished fitting. He'd stroke first the right side of his mustache, with his index finger, three times, then the left side, and at the end of the third stroke on the left, his finger would pause at the corner of his mouth and stay there for another thoughtful minute or two.

Twenty years later I would grow a mustache just like that. The purpose: to look older. Long after it had outgrown its usefulness, fifty-five years later, I would still have it.

It is unlikely that my parents pictured me with a mustache at that exultant moment at Dr. Grey's.

Much more likely they were thinking of the immediate bliss ahead as, now a threesome, they began a new life together. World events weren't going to let them enjoy that life very long—a sort of harbinger of Baby Cronkite's years ahead.

On Baby Cronkite's third day, Dr. Cronkite left Dr. Grey's and stopped at the fire station on Frederick Boulevard. He patted the firehorses as he entered and, at the long plank desk, identified himself to the polling clerks to pick up his ballot. It took him only a moment to put an "x" in the box next to the name of Woodrow Wilson. It may have been the first Democratic vote ever cast by a Cronkite, but the young dentist liked Wilson's pledge to "keep us out of war."

That day's St. Joseph *Gazette* was still on the stoop of their bungalow when Dad got home. Its front page featured a great communications breakthrough by the *Gazette*. It had arranged with the power company to dim all the lights in the city three times if Charles E. Hughes was elected, twice if Wilson won. This imaginative promotion came to naught as Wednesday dawned with the election's outcome still awaiting a late count in California, a result that would make Wilson the surprise winner.

It also reported in another front-page story under a small headline the frightful slaughter on the Western Front in the Battle of the Somme. There were some alarmists who thought this Great War in France might suck the United States into its terrible maw, and there were powerful voices in the heavily

German Middle West warning against American involvement—and some even proposing that if we were to become involved, it should be on the German side. The *Gazette,* however, was solidly for the Anglo-French allies. Its headlines referred to the Germans as Teutons.

In the ethnic passions of the moment there was the potential for a split in the household of young Dr. Cronkite. The Cronkites were of pioneer Dutch stock. Old Hercks Seiboutzen Krankheidt, in fact, was one of the New Amsterdam colony's first grooms, long before New Amsterdam became New York. He married Wyntje Theunis on November 16, 1642.

The Cronkites never reached the prominence or wealth of other early Dutch settlers—the Vanderbilts, Rockefellers, Roosevelts and that ilk—but there was a moment early in this century when they broke into the papers. A genealogist began contacting Cronkites, by now of various spellings, with news of an astounding discovery. He claimed to have found a document establishing that there were vast riches in the Netherlands that had been left to the seventh son of the seventh son of some ancient named Cronkite. And, noted the genealogist, the time for the appearance of that fortunate individual was *now.*

My grandfather, otherwise a learned, well-read and sagacious man, was among those who swallowed the bait. He later said he had his doubts all along, but he did organize a Cronkite Heirs Association to pursue the alleged fortune. He placed advertisements in papers across the country and turned up a weird enough assortment of people to supply Barnum's freak show for a generation.

Of course, the self-proclaimed genealogist was a fraud. There was no such inheritance, but the legend lived and, with my television prominence, I received not a few letters from Cronkite heirs who seemed to suggest that perhaps I was living on the fruits of a hidden treasure.

A lot of the Cronkites spawned by the New Amsterdam pioneers intermarried with the English and Scottish to provide a classic American Anglo-Saxon mix.

Mother's grandparents on both sides had come from Bavaria in the great German immigration of the mid-nineteenth century. Grosspapa Fritsche had the first hotel in Leavenworth, Kansas; Grosspapa Renz believed that his cigar factory there was the first west of the Mississippi, and it might have been.

The possibility that conflicting "inherited" national loyalties would seriously disturb the Cronkite family's tranquillity during World War I thankfully never materialized. Mother may have been concerned, but she displayed an apolitical neutrality.

It was the greater cataclysm that shattered the bliss of the Cronkite household. Just five months after his "no war" election, Woodrow Wilson took America into the conflict, and young Dr. Cronkite was among the first to march off to training camp. Mother, with baby at breast, trailed along and took up residence and a temporary job in Sapulpa, Oklahoma, until the Thirty-sixth Division shipped out to France, with one young lieutenant as its dental surgeon and another commanding an artillery battery. The other fellow's name was Harry Truman.

To his credit, Dad, as far as I know, never claimed a close battlefield relationship with the thirty-third President of the United States, although, with a modesty probably meant to be becoming, he acknowledged having known the chap. Years later Truman, with probably more kindliness than honesty, acknowledged that he had known Dad.

It should not be inferred that, with these little manifestations of highly quixotic coincidence, History, so early in life, was brushing my cheek. But on the other hand, who is to say that they didn't leave some sort of postpartum impression that inspired a future passion for current events, history in the making, the stuff of journalism?

By the time I was six I already was taking to instant news analysis. The event was the death of President Harding. The newsboys had just come through the neighborhood hawking the Kansas City *Times* with the banner headline, so rare in the *Times*, and a nearly full-page picture of the newly deceased President.

In this day before radios were common, I could not wait to help spread the news. Clutching the paper, I went dashing down the hill to Albert Darling's house—a house considerably bigger than our bungalow. It passed for an upper-middle-class showpiece on Swope Parkway in Kansas City.

Back up the hill behind Swope Parkway was a more *middle* middle-class neighborhood, one whose reputation had recently been blackened by a raid that uncovered one residence as a major bootleg operation. The house was only a couple of doors from ours, and my mother watched with horror and I with fascination as the revenuers smashed hundreds of bottles in our neighbor's driveway. The spilled whiskey ran down the gutter in front of our house, and the heady aroma was enough to make the dogs giddy. My father breathed deeply and considered the destruction something akin to sacrilege.

Our hill overlooked, a half dozen blocks away, Electric Park, one of Kansas City's early amusement parks. One night after closing it burned in a spectacular fire. The Ferris wheel seemed to turn as the flames climbed up its sides. The grease caught fire on the two parallel tracks of the Greyhound Racer roller coaster, and twin blazes raced up and down with the speed of the cars that once followed the tortuous circuit. The fun house collapsed in a terrible shower of sparks.

For a child the scene was as horrible as it was spellbinding, and it left me with a lifelong fear of fire. I never check in to a hotel room without counting the doors to the fire exit—although it's unlikely I would remember the number in an emergency.

When I got down to the Darling house on that day of Harding's death, Albert was on the front porch, and I remember so well sitting in the swing with him explaining the importance of this moment in our history.

"Look carefully at that picture," I pontificated—
my first major pontification. "It is the last picture
you will ever see of President Harding."

I can't quite reconstruct today what led me to that
foolish conclusion, but I record it here to establish
my early predisposition to editorial work—the
ability to be both pontifical and wrong.

It was just about this time, or perhaps a year
later—I think I was seven by then—that I got my
first job in what later would become known as "the
media." I became a salesman of *Liberty*, a late-
coming rival of the *Saturday Evening Post* in the
weekly magazine field. It sold for a nickel. I got to
keep a penny from each sale, but even more important, for every five copies sold I got a green coupon,
and with each five green coupons I could get a
brown coupon, and with enough brown coupons, I
could get a pony. My mother wasn't too enthusiastic
about my going out alone around the neighborhood
with my *Liberty* sack over my shoulder, but I
assume she thought that there were some lessons in
self-reliance here—and besides, there was no hope
that I ever would amass enough brown coupons for a
pony to appear at our door.

Later, at the age of nine and a couple of years
after my retirement from publishing, I went into the
newspaper business. My mother was horrified and
frightened, as I suppose many mothers have been, or
should have been, when their children got into newspapering. Her fears were for my safety as I took the
streetcar down to the Kansas City *Star* every Saturday night and, carrying as many papers as I could,

caught the Troost streetcar back to the end of the line and peddled my papers there. I could carry about ten Sunday papers, and I netted, after streetcar fares, ten cents. But, as some sage once said in reference to another situation, it was a beginning.

There were other entrepreneurial excursions in my early life, although the earliest ones had a certain nepotistic coloring. By these years, the mid-twenties, Grandfather Fritsche had a drugstore on what was known in Kansas City as Hospital Hill. There were two large hospitals there on the rise above the Union Station and the railway freight yards—the city's big General Hospital and a fine private hospital whose name had been judiciously changed from German Hospital to Research Hospital during World War I.

The sprawling two-story plant of the Kansas City *Journal-Post* was also up there, and all in all, it was a nice hill. A sweeping lawn descended from the hospitals and surrounded the newspaper. From its height I could watch through its windows with rapture as the big presses rolled, and from there you could look across to the south side of Union Station Plaza, where on one side was Signboard Hill and on the other the prominence on which rose the imposing Liberty Memorial to the World War I dead. A little farther along that hill was Cyrus Dallin's bronze statue called *The Scout*. It depicted an Indian brave astride his horse, his hand shading his eyes as he stared intently from his vantage point out toward the plains of Kansas.

Signboard Hill was a spectacular display of the

latest in electrical outdoor advertising, the prairie's challenge to Times Square. And it was complemented by the memorial to the nation's war dead, the top of its 271-foot column crowned by a perpetual flame. It was dedicated to the soldiers' memory—but the nation hadn't even begun to count its heroes. There would be more to be remembered from World War II, Korea, Vietnam.

You could lie up on that hill in the daytime and watch the trains, ten or so at a time, being shunted through the yards, and the sleek expresses puffing into the bays of the passenger terminal. At night the fireboxes of their steam engines and the bright headlights patterned the tracks, and behind the lowered shades of the Pullman cars mysteries undoubtedly unfolded.

It appeared that America was on display from that hill—its history and its promise. The push west was there, in the figure of that Indian scout and in those endless freight trains moving the stuff of empire across the broad continent. The future seemed to wink out from those electrical signs. The memorial spoke of the cost of greatness.

The passenger trains were a transient panorama of human endeavor—glamorous movie stars, timorous migrant families, raucous traveling salesmen, vacationing adventurers destined for the wide-open spaces of New Mexico and Arizona, which barely a dozen years before had joined the Union.

When World Series time came, the lawn in front of the *Journal-Post* was packed with baseball fans.

In their straw boaters, their ties undone, their sleeves rolled up and jackets hung over their shoulders on an index finger, they came trooping up the hill before noon, refugees from whatever commerce they were supposed to be pursuing. Public school truants augmented their ranks.

The attraction was a great display that covered the side of the building. On it was depicted a baseball diamond. Along the base paths and in the field, appropriately placed lightbulbs could be activated to give a graphic picture of each play of the game. Inside the newspaper plant, a recruit from the sports department translated the telegraphed play-by-play for the electrical circuitry. And mingling among the assorted multitude was me—a sweating young lad in knickers buttoned below the knee, hawking soda pop from a galvanized pail sloshing with water and the remnants of ice that once had cooled it.

It was my idea that my cousin, Jack, at eight a year my junior, and I should become self-appointed World Series concessionaires. If I have not done so before, I now apologize to Jack. The pails were heavy, their handles cut our hands, and each trip back and forth along the two blocks to Fritsche's Holmes Street Pharmacy was roughly equivalent to Hannibal's trip across the Alps. The money was better, however, than the *Liberty* route.

When Graham McNamee took to the microphone at Forbes Field, Pittsburgh, on October 7, 1925, to broadcast by radio the meeting of the Pittsburgh Pirates and the Washington Senators for the baseball championship, the *Journal-Post* World Series Scoreboard was doomed. And barely more than a decade later, that soda pop kid would himself be broadcasting sports from a Kansas City radio station.

A snap compared to the soda pop operation were the regular deliveries from the drugstore—mostly cigarettes and ice cream to the hospital wards. Too poor for our services were the surrounding residences, many of which at that time still had outdoor plumbing and kerosene lamps. There was no customer like the motor repair shop a couple of blocks up Holmes Street. As far as I know, they never repaired a motor there. It was a front for a slot machine distributor. In a converted garage, behind the storefront blind, a dozen or so men worked at benches with the disemboweled innards of the slots. My grandfather, who I believe was innocent of the real nature of the establishment, never understood why deliveries to that address took so long. Little did he know that some kindly gentlemen were teaching me the intricacies of setting the cherries, plums and oranges to ensure a rational payoff.

The drugstore was a wonderful place. Grandmother and Grandfather lived upstairs in a warm apartment always bathed in the rich aroma of German cookies and with melodies a little lighter than Wagner spilling from the windup Victrola. They didn't have a phone, and when Grandmother received a call on the drugstore instrument, Grandfather summoned her by tapping on the ceiling with a long pole. She called him to meals by pounding on the floor with an old wood potato masher.

Weekends frequently were spent in dilettante employment at the drugstore, delivering or, joy of joys, helping Eddie behind the soda fountain and inventing glorious sundaes rich with marshmallow sauce, assorted fruits and nuts and nearly everything else at hand except cough syrup.

Grandfather was not beyond the occasional trick reserved for apprentices in every occupation. One very long Saturday morning was spent trying to fulfill his order for a tablespoon of powdered cork. Jack and I worked for hours at the mortar and pestle grinding away at our corks before it occurred to us that the task was impossible.

On the miserable winter days when Jack was not around, I showed an early proclivity for management, or perhaps for journalistic research, by timing the streetcars that ran under the apartment window—how long to the end of the line and back. I had a notebook full of my observations, in which virtually no one took an interest. That hobby wasn't as productive as manufacturing schoolyard trading material by flattening pennies under the streetcar wheels, nor did it have the excitement of a forbidden sport.

Grandfather was an old-fashioned pharmacist who never ceased venting his resentment at the growing number of retail items the drugstore had to carry, and he would go into periods of fearful rage when the subject of chain stores was raised. How difficult it was for the independent merchant was underlined by the price of cigarettes. The chain drugstores sold them cheaper than Grandfather could buy them wholesale. Katz Drugs limited each customer to two cartons, so Grandfather would send his four or five employees to Katz on numerous trips to buy his cigarette stock. There being no restrictions on juvenile customers, I was among the couriers.

Tobacco was an important commodity in the Fritsche family. Jack's father, Uncle Ed Fritsche, sold cigars wholesale, and one exciting summer I accompanied him on his rounds of nearby Kansas communities. He had a great smile and a store of stories, and he was welcomed everywhere as he swept into an establishment, surveyed the inventory, moved the cigar boxes around in their case until his brands were in front and his competitors' in the rear, and made out a new order list. And from his spiel I learned long before I could smoke them what made a good cigar: "A long-leaf wrapper and a short-leaf filler"—an incantation I remember to this day.

At our small-town hotel for the night, he introduced me to the unwritten manual of the 1920s traveling man. "Don't drink out of the glass; you don't know what people have used it for." "Wash the washbowl before you use it. Same reason." "Steam the wrinkles out of your coat in the bathroom—careful that the heat doesn't curl the paint." "Press your pants between the springs and the mattress overnight." "The socks you've just taken off will give your shoes a nice shine."

I think he knew every waitress in every restaurant on the route, and after he divorced, I suspect he dated a few of them.

Ed and his sister, my mother, were much alike—gregarious, amusing, handsome. They were typical of that live-it-up postwar generation, a definite part of the jazz age of which my parents partook with gusto, apparently undeterred by parenthood. Nevertheless, my folks were doting parents with their only child. Dad built my favorite Christmas presents. The absolute favorite was a perfect child-size fire engine complete with ladder and hoses, a bell and siren, all constructed on a coaster wagon.

They doted, but they did drink and they did party. Our house seemed to be something of a hangout for their crowd, which apparently enjoyed their hospitality despite a frequent command performance by a towheaded tyke in pajamas being ever so cute as he directed the orchestra music emerging from the old console stand-up Victrola. Occasionally I was privileged to accompany them in the early hours of a party, probably because of a no-show baby-sitter. I took pride in my folks' superb dancing. Others cleared the floor to marvel at their grace.

The happy years for them ended too early, when alcohol got the better of Dad. The dark days began not long after we moved to Houston, when I was ten. Dad never failed to appear at his office on time, and he always completed a long day's work, but before Mother picked him up in the car he had begun to secretly tipple. He became a solitary drinker and withdrew from nearly all social associations.

It was strange. He maintained an appearance of total sobriety. Only his conversation, fed by a runaway imagination, gave away his drunkenness.

There were tough nights at the dinner table, some of which live in my memory.

Lord Halifax, the British Foreign Secretary, was visiting Houston on one occasion, and at the table that night my father suddenly put down his knife and fork.

"Helen," he said, "how long has Lord Halifax been in town?"

"I don't know, Walter," she replied, as both of us held our breaths for whatever diatribe this was the prelude to.

"He's been here two days, Helen. I want to know why we have done nothing for him. Have you done anything? Have you invited him to dinner?"

Well, while we weren't exactly lower class and our duplex apartment was quite acceptable in a good middle-class neighborhood, we certainly weren't in the social circle of Lord Halifax' hosts. But Dad's tongue-lashing of Mother went on and on, with a long dissertation on her failure to promote the family socially—a matter that I feel confident never crossed his mind in his sober hours.

They divorced the year I went away to university. Dad had a very tough time, but he found a fine woman who straightened him out in his later years. He was sober for the last decade of his life, and we established a loving relationship. Silently but clearly, we told each other how much we regretted the years of lost companionship that alcohol had denied us.

Mother soon married an old beau, but it didn't

last. She enjoyed an active social life in Washington until her death at 102. From her young days as the belle of the ball at the U.S. Army's Fort Leavenworth Staff and Command School, she had many friends living in the Washington area—mostly retired generals. She was so frequently at the Army-Navy Club that I accused her of being a B-girl there, cadging drinks from friends to boost the establishment's sales.

With her almost perpetual youth and vitality, her only complaint was that her contemporaries were "so old."

"Why, Walter," she told me on one occasion, "General Gempel took me to the theater the other night and I had to slap his face."

"Gosh, Mom, General Gempel made a pass at you?"

"No, no, Walter. I thought he was dead!"

We danced at her 100th birthday party, but when I took her back to her table she was a little breathless and said: "Walter, I think I need my medicine."

Alarmed, I scurried for her nurse sitting outside. The nurse rushed to her side, and it took me a minute or two longer to get back through the crowd. Mother was sitting at the table, glaring at a pill in her hand.

"Walter," she greeted me, "who said I needed that?"

"You did, Mother. You said you needed your medicine."

And she replied: "I meant my martini!"

I have often wondered whether I should have

included "bartender" in my curriculum vitae. For a brief time when I reviewed movies for the Houston *Press*, I would read the biographies of the stars as supplied by the studios. In those days, when it still was considered a virtue to work for a living, they all claimed a long list of former occupations before they took to acting, which, by deduction, I assume they thought was not real work. I suspect that if the stars had indeed done any of the things their publicists claimed, their jobs in actuality were probably about as seriously pursued as were my many "occupations."

Cigar salesman back there with my uncle, for instance. Or, after we moved to Houston, cowboy, delivery boy, clothing salesman, short-order cook—none of great duration. And none really essential to sustenance of our reasonably well-off household. We were a long way from rich, but Dad did pass along to me his 1927 Dodge when I started high school at thirteen, no driver's licenses being required in Texas at that time. On weekends and during one summer I rode with the cowboys on the Bassett Blakely Ranch, a huge spread that, in the old Dodge over shell and dirt roads, was several hours outside Houston. Today it is part of the metropolis's western reaches. The rough but tolerant cowhands introduced me to a delectable dish that tasted a bit like very tender chicken breast. It was days before I discovered that it was only the by-product of our afternoon's endeavors turning yearlings into steers.

One summer I made pretty good hamburgers at a

little stand at Sylvan Beach, an amusement park on Galveston Bay outside Houston. I decided to leave that job after a slightly retarded curb hop choked me into unconsciousness while demonstrating what he said was a new wrestling hold. That was the summer I won second place in Sylvan Beach's yo-yo endurance contest. I kept mine going, up and down, up and down, nothing fancy, for a couple of hours. The job at Sakowitz' clothing store was a little more gentlemanly. I was twelve by the time I used my after-school hours and Saturdays to test the mercantile waters.

Mr. Barber, kindly head of the boys' department and known to every mother in Houston as the official outfitter to the Boy Scouts, was my mentor. My first hour at the store may have been my darkest up to then—excepting that portion spent in a wrestling-hold blackout, of course. Mr. Barber sent me to the first-floor hat counter to pick up a chauffeur's cap. I thought it was meant for me. The prospect of meeting my friends adorned in a chauffeur's cap left me weak with embarrassment. My strength returned as the clerk neatly boxed the hat and affixed a label bearing the name of one Mr. Roberts.

There were other embarrassing moments to come. Like the time approaching Christmas when Mr. Barber sent me to Kresge's for fifty cents' worth of assorted nuts. I reported back that they didn't have any, and three times an insistent Mr. Barber sent me back before I realized they weren't to be procured at the hardware counter.

Thirty years later I was at a party in New York given by Betty Furness, who had become famous in television's early years doing live commercials for Westinghouse and who later would become a consumer affairs consultant for President Johnson, New York's Mayor John Lindsay and NBC.

It was a typical Furness party—actors and actresses, writers and people from the fashion world. I found myself sitting on a divan next to Sydney Chaplin, then starring on Broadway in *Bells Are Ringing*.

"How did you like the big sailboat you got for Christmas in 1928?" I asked.

"My gosh," he said, "that was one of the greatest presents I ever got. I've still got it. How do you know about it?"

"I picked it out for you," I explained, also confessing that envy still ate at me. I had wanted that sailboat so badly—all four feet of her with a mast as tall as I was.

When a statuesque, raven-haired beauty came sweeping into our toy department at Sakowitz' that Christmas, I was assigned to help her pick out something for a boy about my age. The sailboat was my first recommendation and an instant sale. The woman was Sydney's mother, Lita Grey Chaplin, one of Charlie Chaplin's early wives and a versatile performer in her own right. She was appearing onstage at Houston's Majestic Theater that Christmas season.

The Majestic was one of those palatial movie houses of the twenties, famous in that part of the world for its "heavenly ceiling"—a blue canopy in which electric stars flickered. Rivaling that adornment was the Majestic's claim to being the first air-cooled theater in Houston—a feat accomplished by an array of fans on the roof blowing across great cakes of ice.

The Saturday morning show at the Majestic was a favorite pastime of the high school classes of the early thirties. Part of the ritual was the rhythmic foot stamping before the house lights were dimmed and the screen brightened with the first of three short subjects—newsreel, cartoon and continuing serial of the *Perils of Pauline* genre. Fortunately, these serials advanced their story line a little further each week than today's soap operas manage in a month. Otherwise the San Jacinto High School class of '33 might still be sitting in the balcony waiting for the last rescue of the imperiled Pauline. Classmates filled me in on the episodes that I missed through my occasional employment and other extracurricular activities, most of which I found more interesting than Hollywood's offerings. I learned early on that in the real world the masks of tragedy and comedy adorn the proscenium of every life.

I regret that my memory has lost the last name of Louis, for he should be remembered. He was one of the delivery boys at the West Alabama Pharmacy. He was one of the blacks who made deliveries by motorcycle to the more distant addresses. A couple of us white boys rode bicycles to the closer customers.

Louis was probably the oldest of the motorcycle

boys—I think he was in his early twenties. He wasn't very attractive and was totally uneducated. He had a muscular body and a leonine head with rather gross features and a strange fringe of whiskers that ran up along his cheekbones from just under his nose to his ears, an upside-down beard. He claimed that the higher one shaved, the higher hair would grow until eventually it would cover one's eyes. As a recent initiate to shaving, I was terrified by the prospect, until it seeped through that all the clean-shaven men in the world weren't growing hair over their eyes. This was an argument, however, that Louis could not grasp.

Louis had a musical talent that would be left undeveloped. He played haunting melodies that he made up on an ocarina, which he called a sweet potato. As we sat on our bench outside the drugstore, I heard for the first time blacks talk of their problems in a white world, a world then of total segregation, light-years away from the civil rights legislation of the sixties.

Already, a few years before during our first week in Houston, I had discovered racial discrimination. I am sure it existed in Kansas City as well, but there we saw few blacks and they seemed to move more freely in our white society. The discovery, then, came with brutal force.

Dad had been lured to Houston to teach at the dental college and share an office with a wealthy dentist, a leader of the community. I shall call him Dr. Smith because any relative who survives him today surely would be ashamed to be associated with this incident. We had been in Houston only a few days when we were invited to Dr. Smith's for dinner. He lived in River Oaks, Houston's first extensive, exclusive residential real estate development. After dinner we retired to the front porch for what to a ten-year-old was a welcome relief—ice cream and cake. Home freezers were still a few years away, and ice cream was ordered from the drugstore for immediate consumption.

It was pleasant out there on Dr. Smith's wide veranda, rocking gently in the wicker chairs, the air heavy with the aroma of fresh-cut grass and early spring flowers. The Spanish moss that draped the big oaks was still a wonder to a boy from the Middle West. Then the pop-pop of a motorcycle broke the calm of the deserted lane. A black delivery boy shined his flashlight along the curb and toward the sides of the house. Not finding an obvious path to the kitchen door and seeing us on the porch, he came up the walk from the street.

Dr. Smith stopped his monologue about the wonders of Houston for the first time that evening. He stopped rocking, too. With each step the delivery boy took up the walk, he leaned an inch farther forward in his chair. Now the tension was palpable. If this scene were being played in a film drama today, we would go to slow motion at this point. That is the way I remember it.

The delivery boy reaching the first step below the porch—holding out the brown sack and its carton of ice cream. Dr. Smith charging out of his chair. The boy taking one more step before Dr. Smith reaches him, a huge fist extended before him like a battering ram. The fist meets the boy's face, square at the tip of his nose. The boy goes flying backward to the lawn. The bag tumbles to the steps. And Dr. Smith shouts: "That'll teach you, nigger, to put your foot on a white man's front porch!"

Never before or after did I see my father in such a seething rage. As the bloodied delivery boy scrambled to his feet and back to his motorcycle, Dad said: "Helen, Walter, we're going now," and he escorted us down the front steps, followed by Dr. Smith's mystified entreaties.

Dad ignored Dr. Smith's offer of a ride and would not pause to call a taxi. We walked. And we walked. River Oaks was at the edge of town and sparsely settled then. We were lost along its winding lanes, at each turn of which we expected to see lights with the promise of a telephone. But we walked in the dark of this strange town until we came upon a busier street and a passing car that stopped for Dad's hail.

I did not fully understand then the import of the offense or of Dad's courageous response to it. Although fully dependent upon Dr. Smith to launch a new practice, he broke off the relationship and struck out on his own.

I couldn't have had a more searing example of racial injustice than this, my first brush with it. There was another confrontation not many weeks later, when my mother was warned that I should not play with a black boy who lived in a neighbor's servants' quarters down the block.

"You might do that up north, but that isn't the way we do things down here," she was admonished.

Again my father's indignation rose: "They turn over their infants to be wet-nursed by a colored woman and their children to be raised by them and then they won't let the children play together. Some system!"

Mother drove our maid the three long blocks from our house to the streetcar line at day's end, and invited her to share the front seat with her. Calley objected but yielded to Mother's insistence on what Mother considered this small social nicety.

As they drove up to the corner where other maids were waiting, several of them, with a look of considerable disapproval, flipped their hands over from palm down to palm up. Calley hurried out of the car, her embarrassment muffling her good-bye to Mother.

The next day, upon Mother's demand she explained that the hand flipping was the blacks' way of emphasizing the difference between the races. The back sides of their hands were black; the front sides white. The message was, according to Calley: "You'd better know your place and keep your place." Calley, they were saying, shouldn't share the front seat with Mother. The blacks, by the attitudes they had been forced to adopt to survive, helped to perpetuate the very segregation in which they were trapped.

Those who treated the blacks with at least some dignity called them "colored." That certainly was better than "nigger," although some Southerners of the period used even that term, so often pejorative, with occasional affection.

I never ceased to be surprised when southern whites, at their homes or clubs, told racial jokes and spoke so derogatorily of blacks while longtime servants, for whom they quite clearly had some affection, were well within earshot. It was as if the black servants were zombies entirely lacking in human feelings. It may be that after a lifetime of being treated that way, the blacks became impervious to the whites' insensitivity—but I doubt it. The enlightenment of this last half of our century has sharpened white sensibilities, but I am shocked to still witness on occasion this callous behavior.

Whites who are anxious to help eliminate racial bias have had some difficulty keeping up with the nomenclature the blacks themselves prefer. We went from "colored" to "Negro" to "black" and are now advised that the proper designation is "African-American." Even the most sympathetic among us must feel on occasion that the activists who perpetrate these changes do so with a certain pleasure in their power to make whites conform.

The culture shock for us Middle Westerners newly arrived in the South was augmented my first day in the fifth grade at Woodrow Wilson Elementary School. In Kansas City, aside from my propensity in the first weeks of first grade to slip away and go home, I had had a spotless record for conning my teachers into believing that I was a perfect angel.

Thus, when I raised my hand and answered my first question in Houston—something as simple as two-times-two—I was more than startled to hear Miss Jung say: "That is not the answer. What is the answer?"

I was certain I was right. "Four," I repeated.

"Come stand here in the front of the class until you think of the answer," Miss Jung hissed. There I was, in the best go-to-school clothes my mother could prepare for me, facing snickering classmates I hadn't even met yet, trying to will away the welling tears.

I dared not even look at Miss Jung, although her features in an hour had been fixed in my memory for a lifetime. Medium height, reddish brown hair worn in a boyish bob, and teeth scarred by drastic periodontal surgery. At last—had I been standing there a week? a month? a lifetime?—the bell rang for recess. And Miss Jung said in a tone as unkindly as only she could muster: "Now, then, have you thought of the answer?" When I confessed that I had not, she enlightened me: "The answer is: 'Four, ma'am.' "

That night Dad's indignation, still raw from the events at Dr. Smith's, burned furiously again. "You may say 'Yes, Miss Jung,' and 'No, Miss Jung,' but you won't say 'ma'am.' You go back and tell her that no son of mine will yield to this sectional ignorance."

That was easy enough for him to say. It was more difficult for me, and I was sent home at recess. Dad complained directly to the school board, and the case was compromised in his favor—but it was fortunate I had only two more months to endure the wrath of Miss Jung, who, I can now judge in retrospect, probably thought she was doing her part to maintain a fading southern gentility.

Or perhaps she just hated Yankees.

If America is a melting pot, so is each section of it, and we Northerners, flooding into Houston in the vanguard of its boom years, were accepted, gracefully by most of the natives, even as we preached some of our own values.

This was my background as, Miss Jung and Dr. Smith four years behind me, I sat with Louis and George and Tad outside the drugstore waiting for the next call. It went to Louis, and he rode off with a quart of ice cream for a distant address. It was the last I would see of him.

We didn't learn that night why he failed to return from that trip. No one from the police morgue took the time to call the drugstore. Only the next day did the police tell Mr. Wolf, the drugstore owner, that Louis had been shot.

All of us, but particularly George, the other black delivery boy, knew exactly what had happened. George and Louis had talked about the problem and their fears many times. Louis, George was certain, had looked for an alleyway or another path to reach the customer's back door. Finding none, he took the route he and George knew to be as dangerous as a Comanche trail. As he passed between the houses, the customer's next-door neighbor killed him with a single shotgun blast.

The neighbor said Louis was a Peeping Tom. The police and the newspaper accepted that—I don't believe the incident was even mentioned in the papers—and the neighbor was never charged. No white was ever indicted for assaulting, or even killing, a black.

It is not impossible, and it is even likely, that if there was something to see in the neighbor's house, Louis might not have averted his eyes. But that wasn't why he was there. He was following Dr. Smith's standards for the black man's conduct. Trying to avoid a punch in the nose, he lost his life. His executioner was excused by the unconscionable code of racial injustice. I was learning early the ways of the South, although in general they probably were different from those in the North only in their ingenuousness. My lessons on racial discrimination came early and had a lifelong impact, but at the time, of course, they were only incidental to the process of growing up in the South.

The usual boyhood/early teen activities, plus that compulsion to work at some gainful occupation, kept me busy: the Boy Scouts and DeMolay (the junior Masonic order), roller hockey and bicycle polo (except on those hot summer days when our wheels sunk in the goo of Houston's Tarvia streets), tennis and golf and swimming excursions to the beaches at Galveston and, occasionally, aquaplaning, the one-board predecessor to water skiing, on Clear Lake, the misnomer for the muddy body of water near which the Lyndon Johnson Space Center would be built.

There were minor triumphs. I probably was the best aquaplaner of our group, and I held the undisputed neighborhood championship for the longest leap with a bicycle off an inclined plane.

Briefly there were hunting expeditions with BB guns into the mesquite thickets that blanketed large undeveloped areas of the growing city, but after my first kill I never returned. I was unable to stifle the tears when I picked up that warm and still-living little sparrow and it looked at me. I don't know what it was thinking, but I know what I *thought* it was thinking. It didn't even seem to be reproachful—just disappointed in me, and that's as severe as a condemnation can get.

I haven't been hunting since, and I don't even like fishing.

My Grandfather Cronkite and Dad were great fishermen. They tried to teach me to cast, at which they were expert. I was six, I guess, when the lessons began at the end of the long pier in front of Grandfather's cabin on Wisconsin's Lac Courte Oreilles. They left me to practice as they returned to the cabin for the late afternoon iced-tea ritual with the ladies.

I got off a couple of reasonably successful casts,

but then, in a burst of uncontrolled enthusiasm, I somehow lost my footing and, still clinging to the rod, followed a mighty cast in a great parabola out into the lake. It wasn't deep enough to damage anything except my pride. As I waded back to shore, the laughter of adults and cousins from the porch set my determination never to cast again.

Actually, there were a few youthful fishing trips, but I never enjoyed the experiences, partly because I didn't like hurting the bait. There was a day when I was forced finally to yield to an oft-repeated plea by our girls, Nancy and Kathy, eight and six, respectively, to go fishing. Our venue would be the stocked pond at the club where we summered outside New York.

We drove into Carmel and bought bamboo poles and string and hooks and a can of grub worms—for this is the way I remember my rare boyhood excursions. The next morning, as we sat in a rowboat in the middle of the pond, it came time to bait the hooks. I took a grub from the can and the three of us sat there for some time admiring its big black eyes and the smile we thought we could make out on its tiny mouth.

When I explained the next step, there were screams of protest and I quickly agreed that we should put the worm back with his friends and, very possibly, family. So we tossed our hooks into the water without bait—a decision I secretly viewed with relief since it now seemed obvious that I wasn't going to have to contend with the catching of a fish.

This was not to be. A moment later Kathy had a bite. My heart sank. It wasn't much of a bite. She pulled up a baby something, maybe four inches long. Its gills worked frantically and its big eyes betrayed its panic.

"Let it go, let it go!" Kathy cried as I used my surgeon's hands—my mother always said I had surgeon's hands—to extract the hook. It seemed to come easily, and I tossed the little fellow back and reached forward to comfort Kathy. She stared at my right hand, horror distorting her pretty face. I followed her look. There on the end of my index finger was the fish's eye.

We rowed home, and raised grubs for the rest of the summer. But, knowing their fate, we couldn't bear to sell them.

My softheartedness knows no rational bounds. I once lifted a big black ant off my bed at our summer house and carefully released him (or her—it's hard to tell with ants) on the patio. The next day the tree man came to consult on our dying trees.

"This is going to be a pretty expensive job, even if we can save them," he reported. "They are full of these big black carpenter ants."

I spent a small fortune to kill thousands of associates and relatives of my little friend, and very probably him as well. But I was ruthless. After all, engaging the insect executioner was like sitting in a B-52 carpet bombing hundreds of an unseen enemy as opposed to bayoneting a lone soldier.

The new mores of the sexual revolution that liberated men to cry was a relief to me. I always have had great problems in the theater, tearing up at the slightest offense against animals and people, notably the very old or the very young. I used to be bothered when old people's feelings were hurt, but as I have aged, I have come to realize that the pain isn't that great. Now I cry when the young are hurt. I must have forgotten that that, too, is survivable. So, instead of hunting and fishing, I found other pursuits.

At least one of those was dictated by my mother— piano lessons. From about six I was one of that legion of children forced to endure a certain amount of practice and the torture of regular trips to the piano teacher. I once arrived on my foot-pedaled scooter at Mrs. Wallace's with my arm in a sling. I informed her that I had broken it. When she called my mother to confirm and, if true, sympathize, all hell broke loose.

I was good enough on the piano to take second prize in the Kansas City Conservatory of Music's junior competition when I was nine. My mother insisted I would have won first place if my hands had not been frozen during the long streetcar ride to the conservatory. The winner, of course, had come by private car. Mother recited this probably fictional excuse on the frequent occasions right up to her demise when she chastised me for not keeping up with my piano playing.

I acknowledge today that I might have been the life of a few parties if I had. I might even have saved a small fortune by having people buy me drinks. Instead, when we moved to Houston, I persuaded the folks to let me take up the saxophone and clarinet instead. I finally played them just barely well enough to get into the high school band—assigned the E-flat alto part on the saxophone, which consists mostly of single notes played on the offbeat with an occasional run of a dozen notes or so and long periods trying to count the bars at rest without moving one's lips.

My acceptance into Cliff Drescher's Cowboy Band really didn't count. Mr. Drescher was a model for the Music Man, the leading figure in Meredith Willson's wonderful show of that name. He not only taught you how to play, but he sold you the instrument and then the cowboy uniform to participate in his marching band, which was much in demand around the Southwest.

My fondness for band music never abated, nor did the desire to lead a band. To this day I can be lured to almost any charity function by a promise that I can lead the orchestra in the role of a "celebrity conductor." I'm pretty good at it, the key to success being the least number of milliseconds after the band hits a note that you can pretend you directed them to do it.

As a boy, my constructive hobbies included building a telegraph system connecting friends' houses around the neighborhood. We communicated by Morse code and were getting pretty good at it when it all ended abruptly. The telephone company took what we considered to be unnecessary umbrage at our use of their poles to string our wires.

That brush with authority wasn't nearly as dramatic as the time a fire lieutenant angrily threatened to send me up for arson. I felt he overreacted to the brush fire I had set in the vacant lot next door while experimenting in digging a tunnel with firecrackers. If he hadn't stunted my enthusiasm, I might have grown up to help build the Lincoln Tunnel or, at least, be a pyrotechnics guru like George Plimpton.

There was something I learned about myself in those years, but the lesson didn't sink in until later in life: I am one of that number who have an aversion to the slightest hint of regimentation or group conformity, although I carry an antigen of distaste for challenging authority or conspicuous nonconformity.

The first trait was evident when I resigned within days of joining a high school ROTC unit and later, although perhaps subconsciously, when I steadfastly marched north while the rest of the fellows reversed smartly and marched south, thus costing our De-Molay drill team a state championship.

On the other hand, until a painful muscle injury nipped in the bud my career skimming the high hurdles, I was a promising member of the track squad, where individual effort was more important than team coordination. I've often wondered since if it isn't this burning necessity for independence that leads a lot of people into journalism, where regimentation and conformity are dirty words.

Of course, girls provided an interesting diversion—girls and dances and end-of-evening rendezvous at the drive-in Pig 'n' Whistle. There were not a few nights when we were forced to practice a little zero-based budgeting even before that term was invented. Then a little necking in Herman Park and a root beer on the porch of the lady's parents' house wasn't a bad substitute for more expensive pursuits.

It was one of those nights when, with the girl of the moment beside me, I wheeled the old Dodge into a filling station to spend my last quarter on one gallon of gasoline, which would get me to her house and home. For my quarter I expected six cents change.

"A gallon," I said to the filling station attendant.

"Stop!" The scream was from my own throat as I realized that the pump was running past the four-gallon mark.

"I said 'a gallon.' "

"Oh," responded the attendant, "I thought you said 'eight gallons.' "

I left my watch as security for the fifty-one cents my quarter wouldn't cover.

Although the formal educational process was not my forte, I was a voracious reader. My mother sold *The World Book Encyclopedia*, and as a small child I spent hours poring through it. Today I still find it difficult to look up something in the *Encyclopaedia Britannica* without being waylaid by neighboring articles about subjects that a moment before I had neither knowledge of nor, I thought, interest in. I think I was always curious, seeking new information, but I found most classroom routine and homework boring. Since I wasn't exactly a dunce, I blame uninspired teachers for that.

Most depressing was the way history was taught. I was not lucky enough in either high school or college to have a teacher who seemed willing, or perhaps able, to portray the conflict of fascinating personalities that underlies nearly all the critical moments of human experience. Reducing this great drama to the rote of names, dates and places ought to be treated as a punishable crime. Let the tens of thousands of students who get their diplomas thinking that history was the dullest subject of their high school years be called as witnesses as we put the offending teachers in the dock.

History must share with reading, writing and arithmetic first rank as the most important subjects in the curriculum. Understanding the issues on which citizens of a republic are expected to vote is impossible without an understanding of the past. Those who have the opportunity but fail to impart that lesson can be accused of sabotaging the democratic process.

And another thing—geography! They don't even seem to be trying to teach it anymore. Maybe, now that we are homogenizing the world via television and the airplane, knowing where you are and where you're going and what the place and people are like wherever you are isn't considered as important as it once was. But surely this knowledge is fundamental

to understanding our place on this planet, philo-
sophically as well as physically.

Perhaps, though, there are some of us who find
this more important than others. With me it is an
obsession. When I travel I am desperately unhappy
if I can't refer almost constantly to a map. And, on a
microgeographic scale, I am frantic if I become dis-
oriented in a strange city and am uncertain which
way is north. Actually, I've always prided myself on
some innate ability to instantly sort out directions, a
sort of built-in gyroscope.

This is not a trait of my wife's. Betsy skipped
third grade at Bancroft School in Kansas City, and
that's when they had geography. She has never
looked back—nor apparently cared very much what
was back there.

In the early years after World War II, our first two
transatlantic flights via piston plane took us over the
northern route with a refueling stop at Shannon, Ireland. On our third trip our flight followed the
southern route and the refueling stop was in the
Azores. We were chased out of the plane at first light
and herded across the tarmac toward a long, low
white building with a green roof where we were
expected to have coffee and buy souvenirs. It was
just like the Shannon experience—the same beastly
time of day, the same building, even the same fresh
breeze from a nearby ocean.

"Where are we?" asked Betsy.

"The Azores."

"Who owns the Azores?"

"Portugal."

"Golly," she commented, "I remember when the Irish had it and called it Shannon."

Shortly after John Glenn made America's first orbital space flight, I made a trip to our missile tracking stations all the way out to Ascension Island, that little pimple of volcanic rock in the middle of the South Atlantic, next to St. Helena, where Napoleon was exiled.

I was traveling so extensively in those days that Betsy barely listened as I described my destination. With her attention focused on bringing up three children, the question uppermost in her mind was how long I would be gone. So perhaps it did come as something of a surprise when our executive producer at CBS called her to say: "Betsy, Walter is in Ascension and he is all right."

"Oh, that's wonderful," she responded. "How many times has he been around?" Geography lessons might not have helped in that case.

CHAPTER 2

LIFE AND THE course we take through it are af-fected by many circumstances, some beneficial, some considerably less so. This is an observation that is unlikely to be quoted in any compendium of great philosophical thought. Others have even re-marked on the fact before me.

But I am inclined to these lofty terms when I think of those events that followed upon meeting Fred Birney, a rather slight man of unprepossessing mien who, despite his glasses, always wore a frown, as if he were looking for something beyond the range of his sight. He was an inspired teacher who directed the course of my life. He wasn't even a professional teacher, but he had the gift.

Fred Birney was a newspaperman who thought that high schools ought to have courses in jour-nalism. That was a highly innovative idea at the time, but by presenting himself as an unpaid volun-teer and the program as a virtual no-cost item, he convinced the Houston school board. He spent a couple of days each week circulating among Hous-ton's five high schools preaching the fundamentals of a craft he loved.

His arrival on the scene at San Jacinto was timed

as if decreed in heaven. That same year, suffering the disabling shin splints that kept me off the track team and realizing that I'd never make the football team at 110 pounds (and with distinctly limited talent), I had wangled the job of sports editor of the *Campus Cub*, our semioccasional school paper.

Adding to the happy confluence of events, I had just read an exciting short story in *American Boy* magazine. That publication was printing a series of fiction pieces featuring various occupations, a little push toward career guidance. None intrigued me as much as that on the newspaperman.

With my interest thus already piqued, I was a sitting duck for Fred Birney, missionary from the Fourth Estate. I sat enthralled as this wiry man, this bundle of energy, sat on the edge of the classroom desk spinning tales from the world of print. I devoured not only every book he assigned but every one on journalism and journalists that I could find in the library. This turned out to stand me in good stead.

That year he entered me in the newswriting competition of the Texas Interscholastic Press Association. We finalists sat at typewriters as a set of facts was printed on the blackboard. From them we were to write our thousand-word stories. The facts that were presented were from the notorious Leopold-Loeb murder case, in which two brilliant young scions of Chicago's wealthiest, most socially prominent families kidnapped and murdered fouteen-year-old Bobby Franks, another boy from their set.

The Chicago *Daily News* report on the case had become an entry in the 1924 edition of an annual compilation of the year's best news stories. Purely by happenstance, with no thought of preparing for the contest, I had just read that very story the night before. My competition didn't have a chance as I loaded my entry with descriptive matter that must have amazed, and puzzled, the judges. Always a fast typist since taking a junior high school course in the art, I ripped the last page out of my machine and delivered the completed story to the front of the room while most of the others were struggling with their leads. I won.

I take a certain pride in having maintained a reputation for fast copy throughout my newspaper career. Fast-breaking stories left my typewriter in a hurry. Not great literature, perhaps, but fast, and usually accurate.

I wasn't the only one in our class to catch Fred Birney's eye. Bill Bell would develop into a superb newspaperman, and David Westheimer would go on to Hollywood to write such classics as *Von Ryan's Express* and *Watching Out for Dulie*.

The next year I was editor of the *Campus Cub*. Birney put its publication on a regular schedule so we would learn something about editing against a deadline, and he took us to the printer's to teach us makeup and composing-room skills.

We were a small group, we student journalists, and maybe that was the secret of Birney's success. But I felt that those spectacles of his were magnifying for him every move I made. I suppose my colleagues felt the same. He led us through our copy, showing us how to tighten here, explain more there, use adjectives and adverbs with caution lest they imply editorial opinion. He suggested questions we might have asked our interview subjects, noted facts we might have developed to improve our report. And every criticism, every suggestion, made clear that there was a sacred covenant between newspaper people and their readers. We journalists had to be right and we had to be fair.

I had a sense whenever I was in his presence that he was ordering me to don my armor and buckle on my sword to ride forth in a never-ending crusade for the truth. Good journalism, journalism that would please Fred Birney, became our Holy Grail. He so inspired us that Charlie Dyer and I, unable to get our fill of journalism, even started what surely must have been one of the country's early unofficial high school newspapers, even before the term "underground" was used. We put out four mimeographed pages that we called *The Reflector*. It could not be called lofty. In fact, it was a scandal sheet, filled with probably libelous comments on the doings of San Jacinto school society. On occasion, it also dipped into the doings of the school administration. It turned out that its publishers had more gall than courage, and in the face of some rather specific threats to their life and limb, they wisely folded the paper after a few editions.

Birney applauded our enterprise. He frowned at our tabloid style.

Birney, as far as I know, was never taught to

teach. His strength was his deep practical knowledge of his subject, his love of it, and his intense desire to communicate that knowledge and that love to others. That must be the secret of all great teachers, and the shame is that there are probably thousands of them out there who are denied a chance to practice that talent because of crowded facilities, disciplinary overload and stultifying work rules imposed by bureaucratic administrations and selfish unions.

Birney was a pragmatist, as well. He encouraged us to seek summer jobs at the local newspapers, of which Houston had three at the time. I was lucky enough to get on at the morning Houston *Post*.

Actually, thanks to the benevolence of the *Post* staff, or perhaps because of their shorthandedness, or both, I was allowed to be more of a cub reporter than a copy boy. They let me cover luncheon clubs and civic affairs for which they could not spare, or which did not warrant sending, a staff reporter.

The luncheons were the only payment they gave me, but I required nothing more. The occasional paragraphs that I got in the paper were worth more than any gold they might have bestowed upon me. Just the chance to hang around the newsroom was payment enough.

I found myself bridging two generations. Even as I was working in the *Post* city room, I was delivering the paper every morning along a route near my house. As far as I know, there were no other journalists delivering the morning paper with their very own compositions inside.

I suppose that those dedicated to most crafts take pleasure in the sights and sounds and smells peculiar to them, but I can't imagine any being as exciting as the heavy odor of printer's ink and pulp paper and melting lead, the unique clanking of the old Linotype machines, and the building-shaking rumble of the big presses.

Of course, most of that is gone now. Photocopying has done away with the Linotypes and the hot lead, and there isn't much rumble to offset printing. The newsroom used to be a wonderfully noisy, dirty place of only partially organized chaos. Toward edition time its floor was almost invisible underneath a layer of earlier editions, discarded publicity releases and crumpled early drafts of that day's history, testimony to the poor wastebasket marksmanship of frustrated writers. Deafening was the din of clacking news service printers and a score of typewriters, of rewrite men shouting into old stand-up telephones, of reporters and editors calling for copy boys, and of editors calling for reporters to come forward for assignment or perhaps to explain obtuse language or doubtful facts. God, how I loved it!

Additionally, there were the characters, and on the *Post*, city editor Ed Barnes was their spiritual leader. In the midst of deadline pressures he would extract from his desk drawer a large hand mirror and carefully examine his tongue. I don't believe he found whatever it was he was looking for. At least I'm reasonably certain he didn't die of it.

My days coincided with a period of frequent turn-

overs in the upper reaches of the *Post* hierarchy, and
we came in one afternoon to find a banner stretched
across one end of the city room. It said: "Be Kind
to the Office Boy. He May Be Managing Editor
Tomorrow."

I swore then, and I reaffirm now, that I had
nothing to do with it. I wasn't about to endanger the
start of a newspaper career just like the one in
American Boy.

Despite my commitment to journalism, there were
a couple of temptations along the way. Mining engineering, for instance. That also was inspired by
an *American Boy* short story. At that time, we in
Houston were sitting on one of the greatest oil
domes discovered up to then. The whole city was
oil-crazy. It is typical of my lifelong sagacity that I
should think, not of petroleum engineering, but
mining engineering, for heaven's sake. Whatever
lingering inclination I had in that regard disappeared
during first-year physics at the University of Texas
when I couldn't understand how a pulley works. I
still don't understand it. Why, simply because you
run a rope across a block of wood, does it gain in
lifting power? Doesn't make any sense at all. At any
rate, I was smart enough to appreciate that if one
could not understand how a pulley works, it might
be best not to go down in a mine. My physics professor, a good, decent, kindly man named Dr. Boner,
agreed with me and sealed his agreement by flunk-
ing me.

Interesting people I covered in my cub newspaper

days had undue, if momentary, influence upon me. There was a brief period during which I thought of the Episcopalian ministry—this inspired by the admiration I felt for the learned members of that denomination's House of Bishops, whose conclave I attended for the Houston *Press*. I admired the lawyers in the criminal trials I covered, so much that I thought briefly of the law. Only long enough to contemplate the boredom of returning to the class-room measured against the thrill of the city room.

There was the charismatic Britisher who was bringing a sensational thrill ride to the Texas Centennial Exposition in Dallas. He sought to recruit me to be, as he put it, in charge of public relations for his attraction. Even after he explained that my principal duty would be as a barker, the job still sounded glamorous, but not quite as glamorous as journalism.

That conviction was confirmed by Richard Halliburton's arrival in town. He was a daring adventurer-journalist and best-selling author, as devilishly handsome as a movie star. He had just returned from Africa, where he had been with the Ethiopian emperor as his spear-wielding army was valiantly but hopelessly resisting the modernized forces of Mussolini's Fascist Italy.

Halliburton commanded his audience with superb theatricality. The house lights dimmed and only a spotlight illuminated him as he confided: "And there, as the Italian troops were besieging the very edge of his capital, Haile Selassie, so small of stature, so large of heart, declared again that his people, once so bitterly divided, had rallied around him to defeat the invader."

Now the spotlight contracted until only a pinpoint of light illuminated Halliburton's face. "In that half dark, half light of an Ethiopian midnight Selassie said to me: 'Here's to Benito Mussolini, the man who gave me back my empire.' "

There was one occupational temptation in those days of uncertain youth that would not go away—radio. It had intrigued me from the time in the early twenties when Dad got the newest miracle of the moment, a crystal set. Wearing earphones, you maneuvered a small whisker-like needle over a crystal about the size of a shirt button. When you made contact with a certain spot on the crystal, you "brought in" a particular station.

The process took more skill than most people wished to apply. The programs were primitive and sparse and so were the listeners. One attempt to expand the audience was reasonably successful. Some genius brought out an aluminum horn that had a pair of cups at its base. By placing the radio earphones over the cups, the sound was magnified and more than one person in the room could listen to the program. We all agreed that this was a major scientific advance.

Radio listening in the crystal days had something of a cult quality to it. One could tell a wireless faddist. He or she was the one whose eyes were rimmed with dark circles from having stayed up all night, when reception was the best, bringing in distant stations. The first order of conversation among them each morning was the boasting about the number of stations received. I remember a vaudeville routine of the time:

"I got San Francisco on my wireless last night," bragged one comic.

"That's nothing," responded his partner. "I stuck my head out the window and got Chile."

That sort of thing promoted radio—and killed vaudeville.

Then, around the mid-twenties, there came along something called the "superheterodyne." It was a radio set with an array of tubes and a built-in amplifier. It was still a long way from today's printed circuit miniatures, but it represented another major advance and really opened the way for the radio revolution that would change the world's social patterns. Families began staying home together to enjoy the best in music and entertainment.

The best in music and entertainment—but a long way from the best in information dissemination. The early network newscasters were selected more for their entertainment qualities than their news abilities. Their information was taken mostly from the newspapers, and their scripts were heavy with feature stories and personal opinion delivered in parenthetical, snide asides.

They spoke like actors playing a part. The stranger the speech pattern, presumably the more attractive the network executives thought they would be. One,

Boake Carter, had a heavy British accent; another—
the flamboyant war correspondent Floyd Gibbons—
spoke so rapidly that it was almost impossible to
absorb what he was telling you.

In Houston a sports reporter named Kern Tips
imitated the Gibbons style in his newscast on
KTRH. He read so fast that he couldn't turn the
pages of his script quickly enough to keep up with
himself, so he devised the novel approach of pasting
the pages together into a continuous scroll, which he
then read standing at the microphone.

During my high school years Dad bought a fancy
console radio with record player that had a primitive
recording device on it. On aluminum disks the size
of the 78-rpm acetate records of the day, one could
record a scratchy soundtrack.

I interviewed most of my schoolmates until they
fled the house if I even moved toward the record
player. When alone, I imitated the announcers I most
admired. Right hand cupped to my ear to catch my
own resonance, just as they did, I mimicked those
fellows who did the dance band remotes that filled
the late night airwaves.

It is strange, but I don't remember pretending to
do news broadcasts. However, despite the short-
comings of mid-thirties radio news, which I only
later understood, I thought it to be glamorous. I was
destined to bounce between it and print journalism
for the next several years.

My first appearance before a microphone was
during my college years in Austin. A major local sta-

tion was KNOW, which until its privatization had been the university station, KTUT—"Kome to the University of Texas," a nifty slogan even if the misspelling didn't do anything to enhance the university's reputation as a citadel of education. Its program manager was a chap scarcely older than myself named Harfield Weedin. I persuaded him to take this total neophyte and put him on the air with a daily report on sports scores.

The only problem was that the station had no press service facilities to supply such information. My expedient was to tap the resources of a Sixth Street smoke shop, right down the alley just a block from the studio. It was a somewhat rough establishment with a clientele of overalls-clad, sombrero-topped men of no identifiable profession who sat around small tables playing dominoes and drinking what passed during Prohibition for beer. The place had a Western Union sports ticker. Like the old-fashioned stock tickers, under its glass dome a printer typed out on tape the day's sports results. Occasionally the bartender chalked up on a big blackboard the story the tape was telling—a running box score during the baseball season.

Every day I dropped into the smoke shop, bought some pipe tobacco and a beer and sat there at a table pretending to read the afternoon Austin *American-Statesman*. What I really was doing was memorizing those blackboard scores. There were just sixteen teams in the major leagues at that time, and night games hadn't been invented to destroy forever those wonderful indolent afternoons at the ballpark. So I had just eight games to memorize—who pitched and for how many innings, who got extra-base hits and who scored.

Five minutes before broadcast, I got up to leave with all the casualness I could muster. I checked the ticker for the latest scores that the bartender hadn't yet chalked up. Then, once out of sight of the smoke shop, I ran at breakneck speed back to the studio and typed out my daily sports intelligence before it fled my memory. I had an inkling that what I was doing might be illegal and that the bartender might throw me out of the joint if I took notes from his blackboard in full view. If I had leveled with him in the first place, there possibly would have been no repercussions, but on the other hand, if he had said no, there would have been no job.

This concern about legality has always plagued me. My mother and father drilled honesty into me until I became a wimp when confronted by authority. I don't think I could pass a lie detector test if I were accused of something as far-fetched as murdering Hitler. I carry such a guilt complex about things I've never done that a cop approaching to sell a ticket for the policemen's ball paralyzes me with fear.

It is a wonder, then, that my short sports-reporting stint at KNOW led to another brief occupation. The KNOW job ended with the baseball season, and I failed an audition for a job on the regular announcing staff. Harfield was kind enough about it: He just said that I'd never make a radio announcer. He hired another student, Nelson Olmsted, with whom I had appeared in one play at the University Curtain Club, *The Ninth Guest.*

I played the serious role of a doctor, and Nelson had the comedy lead. Because I was also working on the *Daily Texan,* the director permitted me to arrive late and participate in the dress rehearsal without donning makeup. The next night at the show's premiere I was daubed with greasepaint and rushed onto the stage, where, in order to read a telegram for my opening line, I snapped on a pair of pince-nez. To my horror, I felt the glasses creeping off my grease-slick nose. Those glasses were equipped with small springs that are supposed to keep them firmly on the nose. With a coating of greasepaint underneath, they acted instead like a pair of little catapults. As the glasses hurtled from my nose, I reached out and, wonder of wonders, snatched them from midair. The performance brought down the house, as indeed it should have.

The trouble was that this established me as the comedy lead and every serious line I delivered the rest of the evening drew a great laugh. Poor Nelson, with all the laugh lines, got none. Nelson went on to become a successful Hollywood writer and performer. Weedin and I remained good friends, and he became the West Coast vice president of CBS Radio.

Just as the KNOW job was ending, I was approached at the station by a sharp-faced little man in a checkered suit the likes of which was seldom seen in Austin. He didn't talk like a Texan either—a fast monotone out of the side of his mouth was his style. His name was Fox, he said, and he was opening a sports club—that's what he called it—and he wanted to know if I'd be interested in reading the sports results to his members for four hours every afternoon.

The job sounded a little peculiar, and so did the money—$75 a week, equivalent to $872 in 1996. I doubted that my dad made that much. It was enough to pay my tuition for a semester and my room and board at the Chi Phi fraternity house for two and a half months. When I told other, more worldly members of my set about my great fortune, they reinforced my growing suspicion that Mr. Fox's "club" was a bookie joint and probably illegal.

Suspicions as to the nature of the enterprise were confirmed when I went to work the following Monday. Any doubts about its legality were also put to rest. It was as illegal as they got. It was on the second floor of a run-down office building, and to gain entrance one was identified through a sliding panel in the door. My job was to sit in front of a tele-type machine over which came the vital information from the horse race tracks around the country. I was to relay this information by public-address system into the smoke-filled hall where my rough-looking colleagues in Mr. Fox's establishment would post the odds, results and payoffs on a blackboard.

I lasted just $150 worth of ill-gotten gain. I spent a sleepless two weeks imagining the inevitable raid, the handcuffs, Mr. Fox and the rest of us being led to the paddy wagon, the photographs in the next day's paper, the probable death of my parents from acute mortification. I didn't tell Mr. Fox I was quitting. I just didn't show up. I was terrified that he'd shoot me on the spot to keep me from squealing. For weeks I lived in dread that he or his evil cohorts would hunt me down. I learned that crime paid pretty well but was impossible to live with.

I often think of that when I contemplate those children in our city slums whose pockets bulge with the proceeds of narcotics peddling. In their case, crime does pay, for there is neither parental disapproval nor peer pressure to make it difficult to live with.

After my brief experience on the other side of the law, I went legit. I was fascinated by politics and spent idle hours in the galleries of the state legislature listening to the debates. I was fortunate enough to be introduced to a large courtly gentleman named Vann Kennedy. He was a sterling example of a type of journalistic entrepreneur to be found in most state capitols. Where a buck could be made in legitimate journalistic enterprise or any of its immediate offshoots, there Kennedy was likely to be.

He had wangled from friendly state-government types some space amid the rafters of the Capitol dome. There he presided over a two-man empire that published a political monthly and wrote speeches for politicians and advised them on policy and election strategy. The empire suddenly expanded as he managed to cajole Hearst's International News Service into establishing a bureau in Austin. This required a modest increase in staff, and I was it—office boy and cub reporter.

Vann and his cohort, Paul Bolton, were great teachers. They knew state politics, which is to say all politics, inside out, and they knew how to report and write it. And they patiently shared their knowledge with me.

The Vann Kennedy job may have been one of the best breaks of my life. But it was also the beginning of the end of my college education, a matter I have regretted ever since. At the time, though, I found the Texas legislature and the newspaper business far more fascinating and, I rationalized, far more educational than anything I was learning at UT.

For me the most exciting professors were those who, in some fashion at least, were dealing with current events. Professor Montgomery, for instance. He taught economics with a decidedly liberal slant. In fact, with his bushy hair and sharp features, he looked a little like those bomb-tossing Bolsheviks in the Hearst cartoons. He was either more progressive or less cautious than most of the faculty and was regularly called in by the legislature or the university administration to explain his leftist views.

He was far from alone in blaming the Republicans for the depression we were enduring, but he was far more outspoken. Montgomery was the master of the professorial sotto voce. In the midst of a lecture he would interrupt himself in mid-sentence. He would look out the window for a moment and then, in a voice barely audible, deliver a stunning one-line commentary.

He was speaking of President Hoover's Secretary of the Treasury one day. He paused, and along came the punch line: "Andrew Mellon. Ah, Andrew Mellon. The greatest Secretary of the Treasury since Judas Iscariot."

My professors, on the rare occasions when I attended class, would question me about the inside of arcane moves at the Capitol. This was flattering but hardly an endorsement of academia. I slowly dropped classes to pursue full-time journalism and sort of slipped out of school. Oddly, no one, including my parents, made much of a protest. It may have been that, in the throes of the Great Depression, nearly everyone valued a job in the hand more highly than an education in the bush.

The Depression affected Houston far less than it did other sections of the country, bolstered as the city was by the area's newly discovered oil fields and its recently completed ship channel. For the most part it escaped the depositors' panic that set off an epidemic of bank failures across the nation. But the city was hit by President Roosevelt's "bank holiday." He temporarily closed *all* banks in order to provide some breathing room in which, he hoped, he could restore the people's confidence in the banking system. Like just about everybody else's, Dad's cash flow suddenly dried up. The corner grocer was so frightened of the future that he cut off all credit.

Over the next eight days our pantry slowly emptied.
My mother denied it to her last breath, but I am posi-
tive that I remember her making hamburgers out of
the dog's last can of food. The banks opened the
next day and Lady and the rest of us survived.

The Depression still held the nation in its grip
when Vann lost me to a full-time job and a little
more money with the Scripps-Howard bureau in
the Capitol. The Houston *Press* was one of three
Scripps-Howard papers in Texas, and the two-man
bureau represented all of them. The two "men" were
husband and wife Dick and Eleanor Vaughan, and
they were wonderful tutors. They taught me everything, including how to keep one's mouth shut when
harboring a professional secret. When Governor
Jimmy Allred had the audacity to nominate a woman
for a state court judgeship, the more conservative
legislators rebelled. The fight for confirmation in
this early equal-rights matter became the year's
biggest political battle. On such nominations, the
senators protected their political futures with a
secret ballot.

The press was locked out, but Dick and Eleanor
got the results and the Scripps-Howard papers
printed the way each legislator voted. The storm that
broke over their heads threatened to wash the
Vaughans right out of the press room.

Dick was brought before the bar of the Senate on
contempt charges. No threats were drastic enough to
get him to yield his source or sources. His spirited
defense of the public's right to know overwhelmed

the senators' wrath. A weak warning was his only punishment. The Vaughans' protection of their source extended to the third man on their team. I never found out how they did it, although I, like others, suspected a Senate clerk.

The woman was confirmed and went on to a long and highly successful career on the bench. Her name was Sarah Hughes, and it was she who, after President Kennedy's assassination, administered the presidential oath of office to Lyndon Johnson on the plane at Dallas.

Covering Texas politics and particularly the state legislature was an excellent journalistic training ground. Texas was still a one-party state, but the party was split a dozen constantly shifting ways by the numerous interests across its broad geographical area. Oil, sulfur, cotton, timber in the east, fishing in the south, the new ocean commerce in Houston and the financial and insurance interests in Dallas, ranching in the west and livestock in Fort Worth and farming everywhere—it was a vast and diverse state, and the fight for dominance and privilege in Austin was never-ending.

It was a fertile field for lobbyists. They sat in the House and Senate galleries to be sure that the legislators they had bought stayed bought. They filled the hotels during legislative sessions, and they didn't restrict their activities to the foyers of the Capitol building. Scarcely a day went by that some legislator, in one house or the other, offended perhaps because he had missed the gravy train, would not point to the lobbyists lounging in the gallery and shout: "And there sits the third house of this legislature."

One of the most prominent lobbyists was Vance Muse, a towering figure both physically and intellectually. He represented various far right organizations, most of them of his own devising. He quoted Shakespeare and Dickens frequently, and usually aptly, and was a splendid drinker whose parties were legend.

After one particularly lively day when several legislators had found cause to castigate the power of the lobbyists, Muse and I pushed our way into an already overcrowded Driskill Hotel elevator. So packed in were our fellow passengers that we found ourselves facing the rear, and there, across the heads of the rest of us, standing in the back was a man the equal of Muse in physical stature.

I seem to remember that his name was Tom Holland, or something close to that. He had a great booming voice. It was said that when he shouted "aye" in the House, the vote was recorded across the Capitol's broad rotunda in the Senate. Holland was something of a populist and the most persistent critic of the lobbyists. Naturally there was no love lost between him and Muse. And so Muse found cause to note in stentorian tones for all of the crowded elevator to hear: "Well, if it isn't my old friend Tom Holland, the man with the biggest voice and the smallest brain in the legislature."

Holland did what any red-blooded Texan is supposed to do in such circumstances. He tried to raise his fists to fighting position. But so packed were we that he couldn't get his huge arms free. As he tried to thresh them upward, the whole elevator compacted with a concerted whump of expelled air. The contretemps came to no resolution by the time we stepped off at our floor and the elevator doors closed on a still-blustering legislator.

The Houston *Press* recruited me from the Austin bureau to come to work for it in Houston. I had a feeling that I had reached the pinnacle of journalistic success. I had a desk in the city room just like the big fellows, and I was dragging down fifteen dollars a week.

With a portion of my first check I went out and bought a Kaywoodie pipe on which I had long had my eye. I still have the old relic today, although the habit, which at one time kept a fire stoked just beyond my nose from rising to retiring, has long been abandoned. Now I only fall off the tobacco wagon when another sailor lights up on a long cruise. The pipe went more as a concession to public opinion than to prolong my life. As the antitobacco campaign took hold, more letter writers complained that I was setting a bad example by lighting my pipe at the end of each news broadcast. I finally took the hint. That first Kaywoodie, however, served me well as the new boy on the *Press* staff. It gave me a sense that I somehow looked like a writer.

Whatever I looked like, I got the usual freshman assignments. I did obituaries. I was the church editor and wrote the whole weekly church page—a feature, the digest of a couple of sermons, and the notices of extraordinary ecclesiastical events. And I was privileged to review the lesser movies to which our theater editor chose not to go.

The movie passes, the occasional sports passes and the police badge with "Press" embossed upon it assured me the social success I had not quite achieved in my high school years. Girls who at that time had preferred the company of football players finally began to recognize my virtues.

Flashing the press badge not only got you free passage on the city buses, but if done ostentatiously enough, I imagined, won you the admiration of your fellow riders. Sitting on the bus and watching others reading my story or stories of the day was one of life's great pleasures.

The year on the *Press* was a learning time. Perhaps my first lesson came at the end of my first week, when I put in an expense account for a dollar or two. Carefully itemized were several phone calls at a nickel each. "What are these doing on here?" city editor Roy Roussel demanded as he waved the account under my nose. "Don't you know how to make a phone call? Harold, show the kid how to make a phone call!" So Harold took me downstairs to the lobby pay phone and showed me. He had two straight pins inserted into the underside of his coat lapel. He removed them and stuck one pin in one of the pair of twisted wires leading into the phone box, and one into the other. Holding them together, he made the connection. The telephone company got wise to this a short time later and, always the spoilsports, put all the wires in impenetrable cables. It must have nearly broken Scripps-Howard.

I learned, too, the serious lessons of daily journalism. The need for accuracy, for instance. We competed in the afternoon with the Houston *Chronicle*, and we each published several editions a day. At press time each paper had a copy boy standing by the loading dock of the opposition to grab several copies literally hot, or at least warm, off the press. He then ran the eight blocks to his paper to breathlessly drop copies on the desks of the key editors.

Roy Roussel spread the *Chronicle* out on his desk and stood over it, flipping the pages, exclaiming when he thought we had bested them, frowning when the shoe was on the other foot—frowning until his heavy, graying brows almost covered his eyes.

Then, if there was hope of catching up in the next edition, he'd get the reporter on the phone or in front of his desk for a hurried conference. The cry from the city desk had a different tenor, though, when Roussel found what he thought might be an error. The call penetrated the clatter of the city room.

"Cronkite!"

The barely-innocent-until-proved-guilty hastened to the dock.

"The *Chronicle* spells this guy's name S-m-y-t-h. We've got it i-t-h. Which is it?"

Or: "The *Chronicle* says it was at 1412, we say 1414 Westheimer. Who's right?"

He was a stickler for that kind of accuracy, but

most editors were in those days. They understood a fundamental truth about newspapers and how the public perceived them. One mistake—"y" or "i," "1412" or "1414"—standing alone didn't make that much difference perhaps. But for each such mistake there was a given number of readers who recognized the error and whose trust in the paper was diminished thereby. And each of them probably told their friends, and the circle of doubt grew.

Regrettably, there isn't that sort of accuracy today. There can't be, and that may be a contributing factor to the distrust in which a portion of our population holds the press. There can't be because competitive newspapering is dead. Only in a few and diminishing number of American cities are there newspapers going head-to-head, edition by edition. Elsewhere, no matter how devoted to accuracy the editors may be (and most of them are), they have no mechanism with which to monitor the accuracy of their reporters. The Roussels of today don't have the luxury of spreading the competition out on their desks and checking item by item. Clearly the transitory broadcast competition is a useless resource for fine-tuning a printed report. The result is a generation of reporters who have escaped the discipline of accuracy and have left the rest of us with newspapers just a little less reliable, in this regard at least, than they used to be.

There was a frightening day when Roussel called me to his desk and there was no *Chronicle* spread out in front of him. The matter concerned the previous day's bank clearings, for which I was responsible.

We carried a little two-line item on the front page of each day's final edition under a standard head: "Bank Clearings." The item simply said: "Today's Houston bank clearings were"—for instance— "$3,726,359.27."

"You had the bank clearings wrong yesterday," the city editor said. The brows were hanging very low, the strong jaw was clenched.

"You said 27 cents. It was 17—17! What happened?"

A ten-cent mistake on a multimillion-dollar number? Surely he was kidding. His countenance warned me that I had that assumption wrong too. I returned to my desk in a blue funk of despondency—afraid that perhaps I was not going to make it in this profession I had chosen.

My mood was not alleviated by the older reporters' comments:

"Kid, you're in the soup now."

"How you going to fix this one, kid?"

"Have you thought about getting out of town?"

The whole thing bore heavily on me as I dropped into the *Press* Lunch for the end-of-the-day beer. Paul Hochuli, clever writer and local columnist, greeted me.

"Where's your bodyguard, kid?"

My frustration—and my innocence—burst forth.

"What's this all about? A ten-cent crror on a three-million-dollar number! What's the big deal?"

Paul and the others around him looked at me in amazement—an amazement that quickly turned to pity.

"Kid, don't you know why we print those bank clearings? Do you think anybody really cares about *bank* clearings? Kid, the numbers racket pays off on the last five numbers of that figure. They paid off yesterday on a bad number—and they don't much like the idea that somebody might be tampering with their numbers."

The next few weeks were a fear-filled time. I know what it is like to be a marked man. If there had been a witness protection program available, I would have applied. Every car that paused alongside my jalopy at a stoplight was filled with hoods casing me for the hit. Kid Cronkite was about to die at an even earlier age than Billy the Kid.

There was one genuine brush with the underworld in Houston. Our ace police reporter was one Harry McCormack. Harry was straight out of Ben Hecht and Charlie MacArthur's classic story of Chicago newspapering, *The Front Page*. He was from the same mold as their hero, Hildy Johnson.

Harry looked a little like Bogart, a ruggedly good-looking tough guy. The felt hat was cocked back on his head whether he was outside or inside, its band showing signs of wear at the point where he jammed in his press card when out on a story. A cigarette frequently dangled from the corner of his mouth.

I was the "second man" at police headquarters, when needed, and every afternoon after the home edition had gone to bed I stood by in case anything broke for the last two editions. So I did my best to imitate the great Harry McCormack. I mastered the art of picking up one of the then-standard upright telephones. To show that you were a member of the press, you grabbed it from the desk in a sweeping motion that catapulted the earpiece from its cradle. With the left hand you casually retrieved the hurtling earpiece in midflight and proclaimed: "McCormack." (This was not terribly effective if your name was Cronkite.)

This was at a time when a lot of the day's news was reported and called in by so-called leg men in the field and composed by so-called rewrite men at the office. My imagination was never quite up to matching Mac's use of the phonetic alphabet for spelling proper names for rewrite. It was an art form in itself. Mac could spell the name "Smith" so that every letter was represented by a different dirty word—and frequently the entire name would end up in a pornographic acrostic of soaring imagination.

He lives in my memory—hurrying into the headquarters pressroom, snatching up the *Press*'s private line, shouting to our switchboard operator: "Give me the desk, baby," and dictating the latest details of the hottest running story.

Mac was helpful to his cub protégé, but he didn't have much time in his busy life for the social conventions—or what passes in a police environment for social conventions. So I was mightily flattered the afternoon he suggested a beer after I got off.

I imagined I would be with my hero at the best table in the police headquarters' hangout, Ed's Good Eats Grill. But it was not to be.

"I'll pick you up in front at five-thirty," Mac advised. In his car we started on a route away from downtown.

"We're going to a little speak I know out by the ship channel," Mac advised. "Now listen, kid, and listen real careful. I'm going to meet somebody out there. I want you to not say a darned word . . . no matter what. Just sit there and listen and enjoy yourself. Got that?"

So ours was a business date—news business or monkey business. Frequently there is a close kinship. On a back street behind the channel we pulled up at a small frame building on whose flyspecked show window you could hardly make out the fading letters of a sign that had once said "Grocery."

Mac parked behind the building and we went in a back door. Four linoleum-covered tables, two of them occupied by some laboring types in overalls. A hefty woman of indeterminate age and almost indeterminate sex greeted Mac as we pulled up a couple of old kitchen chairs. Without our asking, she put a couple of drinks, without ice, in front of us. Rotgut—genuine, straight-from-the-bathtub rotgut. Mac contained his enthusiasm, just touching his drink to his lips.

I was pleased to perform my monkey-see, monkey-do act. We sat there a long time, perhaps a half hour. Very little conversation, Mac frequently checking his watch. And then a fellow walked in, through the door that led to the grocery. He had on a felt hat and the blue overalls that were virtually a uniform in this part of the world.

Mac waved a greeting and the newcomer pulled up a chair at our table. Mac and he exchanged a few words. A brief discussion of the weather and other inanities, and the guy left. We followed within a few minutes.

"Well, how about that?" Mac asked.

"About what?"

"How about Ray there?"

"Ray who?" I asked.

"You didn't recognize Ray? You didn't recognize Ray Hamilton? You didn't recognize Ray!"

Mac's voice was rising. A hint of apoplexy maybe.

Well, let's put this in context. The year was 1935. One of the biggest stories gripping the nation's attention in that prewar depression time had been the depredations and flight of a trio of desperadoes, Clyde Barrow and his cigar-smoking partner, Bonnie Parker, and their occasional sidekick, Ray Hamilton. They roamed the Southwest robbing banks and other targets, murdering lawmen who stood in their way and virtually thumbing their nose at the authorities, who seemed hopelessly inept in tracking them down.

But on a May day in 1934, in the bayou country of Louisiana, a carefully arranged police ambush caught Bonnie and Clyde. They were shot in a fusillade of fire worthy of Gettysburg. Hamilton was not with them, and the hunt for him over the next months narrowed to a small corner of southeastern Texas and Louisiana—roughly between Houston and New Orleans.

From out of those headlines Ray Hamilton had stopped in to see Harry McCormack in a sleepy ship channel speakeasy. And I hadn't even recognized the fugitive whose picture was in every paper in the land almost every day. McCormack was incredulous— and that may be an understatement.

"All right, kid. But here's what you've got to do: You don't ever, ever mention that you saw me with Hamilton here tonight. Ever! It'll go hard on both of us if you do. We've been consorting out here with a criminal. We could be in real trouble. So you don't ever say a word! Unless I need you to. I could need you to say that I met with Hamilton tonight. I'll tell you if I do. But otherwise, not a damn word!"

Naïveté played only a small part in my bewilderment. Nero Wolfe couldn't have imagined the deep plot that McCormack of the *Press* was spinning.

It began to unfold a few days later. Mac told the desk he was leaving headquarters to meet some anonymous informant at a designated street corner in the Houston Heights area. Shortly thereafter the desk got a call from police saying they had received an alarm that a man who looked like McCormack had apparently been forced into a car at gunpoint in the Heights. They had no leads.

Mac was missing for twenty-four hours until a

farmer a few miles outside Houston found a car in his fields. In it was Mac, bound hand and foot, his mouth taped. As the farmer untaped him, Mac's first words were: "Don't touch the windshield, don't touch the windshield."

When the sheriff's deputies arrived, Mac told them he had been kidnapped by Ray Hamilton and, to prove his story, pointed out that Hamilton had left his fingerprints on the windshield. Mac's tale was that Hamilton had kidnapped him because he wanted somebody to record his true story—the usual invented saga of the underprivileged Robin Hood. The story was spread across the front pages of the Houston *Press* for several days thereafter. It was, of course, a sensation, and Harry McCormack was the journalist hero of the hour.

Mac stuck with the fiction, even to me, that he had had no part in framing his "abduction." But clearly my role was to be his witness should the story break down for whatever reason and the need arise to establish that he had a relationship with Hamilton. Mac was probably better prepared in his own mind to admit to consorting with a criminal than to having his story doubted. It never came to that, and my testimony, thank goodness, was not needed. It was just weeks after Mac's coup that Hamilton was caught and executed.

In 1967 a hit movie was made of the Clyde Barrow–Bonnie Parker legend, and Parker was played by Faye Dunaway. Hollywood exercised the full extent of its literary license with that casting. Parker

was no beauty by anybody's standards. Shortly after
the film's release I was introduced to Miss Dunaway
at a small party. She was stunning. I palpitated, and I
couldn't wait to get a chance to tell her of my personal acquaintance with Ray Hamilton. She was
overwhelmingly underimpressed. But then I was
married anyway.

The newspaper competition was hot, heavy and
healthy in Houston, and in our daily effort to beat
each other, there were no holds barred. We resorted
to all the dirty tricks ever devised in the game.

There was the day that screaming sirens brought
Bill Collyer, my *Chronicle* opposition, and me to the
open window of the police pressroom. We watched
as two ambulances approaching on different streets
met at the corner in a horrendous collision. From the
back of one the gurney, with a patient aboard, flew
out and went rolling at considerable speed halfway
down the block before upending as it hit the curb.
One of the ambulances smashed into a storefront.
The other turned over. It was a dandy wreck.

As Collyer and I grabbed phones to our offices, he
said: "Hey, don't say you saw this thing. If you do,
you'll end up in court as a witness the rest of your
life."

The advice seemed well taken, and I took it. My
story was strictly a routine third-person report. Collyer's first-person, eyewitness report was spread all
over the *Chronicle*'s front page.

Newspaper competition led to a little practice
called picture snatching. The idea was to get a pic-

ture of the victim by whatever wiles one could employ. Families were frequently reluctant to loan out photographs of loved ones at their time of bereavement, and, perhaps having given a photograph to one paper, they had none to spare or they weren't inclined to let their last picture out of the house.

In Houston this was a particular problem for us on the *Press*. The *Chronicle* was the old-line, conservative paper. We were more flamboyant newcomers and owned by a distant—and *northern*—chain.

I was rather honored to get the picture-snatching assignment from time to time. I assumed that this was in recognition of my resourcefulness, but, upon later reflection, I'm afraid that the attributes from which my city editor was profiting were youthful innocence, a certain touch of diplomatic blarney and a willingness to engage in larceny in the splendid cause of the people's right to know.

I was remarkably successful, partly because I reached the home of the victim faster than the opposition man from the *Chronicle*. This was achieved through breakneck driving that would rival the kind seen in one of—*any* of—today's television films.

My success was also achieved, usually, by convincing the grieving that a picture in the *Press* was just as prestigious as one in the *Chronicle* or the morning *Post*.

But sometimes other methods were called for, and it was an imaginative use of these that caused my downfall. A young lady had died in an automobile crash with a prominent married citizen whose wife she did not happen to be. Upon arrival at her modest cottage home in one of the city's poorer sections, I found no one there. In keeping with the law-abiding nature of the times, the front door was unlocked. Through the screen door I could see on the mantel a picture of a young woman. If I left it there, the man from the *Chronicle* would surely filch it. Defensive journalism was called for. So I filched it and a delighted city desk made over the home edition to splash it on the front page.

There was just one little hitch. I had gone to the wrong address. The picture was of a next-door neighbor. Surprisingly, I was not arrested or fired for the incident. I deserved both.

I survived long enough to take my first paid vacation. I collected my two weeks' pay, all thirty dollars of it, and was on my way. Actually, I was on my way to Anna, Illinois, where I intended to test whether my affection for a high school sweetheart had survived her move there a couple of years before. I planned only a brief stopover in Kansas City to visit my grandparents. It was a fateful stop.

The first day there, sitting in the swing on the Fritsche front porch, I read a brief item in the Kansas City *Star* announcing that a new radio station was just coming on the air. Opportunity beckoned. I appeared the next morning at the rather spartan offices of KCMO and presented myself as a likely candidate for their news staff. I was received by the station manager, who, it turned out, was the first of a series of radio management types for whom I'd work, all of whom seemed to have been named by Charles Dickens. The KCMO boss was a Mr. Schlicker. (Later I would work for a Mr. Grubb and a Mr. Bonebrake.) August Schlicker hired me not as a member of the news staff but *as* the news staff, *and* the sports staff, *and* the news announcer, *and* the sports announcer.

The station, as far as power went, was as small as a radio station could be—100 watts' split time, which meant that it was licensed to operate with the minimum strength assigned by the government, and only between 6 and 9 a.m., noon and 3 p.m., and 6 and 9 p.m. My grandparents lived less than a mile from the transmitter and they had difficulty picking it up—if they could remember when it was on.

But Schlicker paid me a grandiose twenty-five dollars a week and I was in what, compared with the Houston of 1936, was a metropolis, Kansas City, the wild, wide-open gateway to the Southwest. Kansas City had the aura of a big city. It was thoroughly corrupt, run by one of the most successful of that era's big-city bosses, Tom Pendergast. Maybe the casinos weren't exactly wide open, but if you stood outside certain "bars and grills" and listened carefully, you could hear the calls of the croupiers, the rattle of the chips and even, at a particularly still moment, the riffle of the cards.

And the nightclubs. There were even a couple of restaurants, known as the Chesterfield and the Winnie Winkle, that featured nude waitresses—at

lunch! Nightlife centered on Twelfth Street. The
joints were shoulder-to-shoulder, and there wasn't
any closing hour. There were girls in most, transvestites in a few and, the street's real glory, great jazz in
many. A lot of the genre's most notable artists graced
Twelfth Street on their way up—Ellington, Cal-
loway and Count Basie among them.

If there was anything comparable in Houston, it
had certainly escaped my attention. I was nineteen
when I hit Kansas City. The visits to Twelfth Street
and the brief associations with its denizens helped
me grow up in a hurry. It was the sort of town that
practiced the old political-machine custom of voting
right and voting often. KCMO was owned by a good
friend of Boss Pendergast's and his handpicked
senator, Harry Truman, and it came as no surprise
when the federal government in a barely decent
number of years granted it as much broadcast power
as any station in the country.

During my year there I was at my desk on Election Day when two uniformed police walked up.
"You haven't voted yet, have you?" one asked.

I hadn't lived in Kansas City long enough to vote,
and besides, I wasn't old enough. I had lied about
my age to get the job. I wasn't about to admit that,
so I simply said that, yes, I had voted.

"No, we don't think so," the cop said.

"No, really I have, really."

"I don't think you understand us. You haven't
voted, and we're ready to take you down now to
do it."

They escorted me to the police car downstairs and most affably chatted about this and that as we drove down toward the heavily Italian north end. Just before we got to the polling place, one of them handed me a piece of paper and said: "That's who you are, fellow. We'll take you back when you're through."

I went in to the desk. A nice little lady and gentleman looked up.

"Your name?" they asked.

I read it from the paper: "Anthony Lombardo."

They found the name on the register and handed me a ballot.

"All right, Anthony," they said with perfectly straight faces.

I cast my vote and the police drove me back to the radio station. They would come back late in the day and, this time, simply note that my vote was needed. No pretense now of suggesting that I hadn't voted before.

The voting laws and democracy itself had been grossly violated, of course, but if any small drop of legality could be found in the process, it was that the police did not tell me *how* to vote. Since I worked for KCMO, they assumed that I knew that my civic duty lay with the Pendergast interests.

While the city's wide-open reputation attracted conventions, enhanced tourism and extended the stay of most of those cattlemen who brought their livestock to Kansas City's huge packinghouses, it also brought embarrassment to the righteous portion of the citizenry. They eventually prevailed. Boss Pendergast was indicted for income tax evasion, his machine collapsed, a reform government was voted in—and Twelfth Street faded away.

As is not unusual with reform movements, the followers frequently know little of the conditions they seek to reform. Take those transvestites, for instance. The homosexual community was quite extensive. Those of us who covered police activity were aware of frequent violence in the apartment houses where many lived in the seedier parts of the North Side. But it wasn't reported in the staid Kansas City newspapers and radio broadcasts. How innocent most Kansas Citians were of this shadow community in their midst was brought home to Betsy and me only many years later.

Danish doctors, in what was then a pioneering operation, catapulted an American, George Jorgensen, into fame by turning him into Christine Jorgensen. Upon returning to New York, Jorgensen had pretended to be publicity shy, but Millie Considine, wife of the popular Hearst columnist Bob Considine, scored something of a social coup. She was the first to get Jorgensen to a cocktail party.

A highlight was the moment when Jorgensen was introduced to Gypsy Rose Lee, who had made an art form of the striptease.

"Honey, when you get into show business—" Gypsy began.

Jorgensen protested that she had no intention of going into show business.

"No, honey, you will," Gypsy advised, "and when you do, take it from me, save your money. Invest it. Buy a boardinghouse. You can always keep it full with men hoping to get a look at you in the bath."

At this time Betsy's mother was visiting us in New York. She stood only four feet eight or so, and she was almost round. Eva Maxwell was of Scottish heritage and good Kansas prairie stock. Her first husband was an Indian agent. Betsy was the product of her second marriage, late in life.

So this dear little lady, well into her eighties but bright and vivacious, was at our dinner table as Christine Jorgensen again, as on so many recent days, became the subject of conversation. Eva finally spoke up: "I don't understand what this is all about. Would somebody please explain it to me?"

So Betsy and I undertook to try to explain in simple but acceptable terms the operation Christine Jorgensen had undergone. When we finished, Eva, folding her napkin, said: "Well, no wonder I didn't understand it. We don't have that problem in Kansas City."

CHAPTER 3

Kansas city was a good newspaper town. The Kansas City *Star* and its morning edition, the Kansas City *Times*, dominated, but it had lively competition from the afternoon *Journal-Post*. Radio wasn't yet a really major news source in the mid-1930s, but two network stations and a couple of independents did a pretty fair job.

For me at KCMO, the fact that the station had no news wire was only slightly bothersome. It was not unusual in those days for the news staffs at even much larger radio stations to simply rewrite the local newspaper, and at KCMO that's what I did. I made as much of a stab at doing some original reporting as a one-man news operation could. I made the regular telephone calls around to the police and fire dispatchers and hospital emergency rooms. And occasionally I'd try to amplify a newspaper story by calling the source.

As proud as I was of my effort, no one at the station seemed to pay much attention. And with our limited power, there weren't many listeners paying attention either. Few people had heard of Walter Wilcox. That was the name Schlicker had given me. There was a conceit at radio stations then that their talent might skip to another station. To prevent them from taking their fame with them, the station "owned" their name.

As Walter Wilcox I was also the sports department. Here we did make something of a splash locally. We subscribed to a quite remarkable service provided by Western Union. Any radio station could purchase virtually any college football game that the networks weren't broadcasting. Western Union sent a lone telegraph operator to the game's press box, and from there he tapped out in Morse code a running report on the game.

I never figured out where Western Union got all these football-knowledgeable operators. But they were good. They sent in their play-by-play reports in a tightly abbreviated form. In the radio studio at the receiving end, another Western Union operator translated the Morse code and typed out the cryptic message. It might read something like "Brown 3 LT Smith." We play-by-play announcers then let our imaginations run. My report on this play, for instance, would go something like "So, the ball's on the Trojans' 43, second and eight. Notre Dame's back in the huddle. They break. It's a shift to the left. A handoff to Brown, who hits a solid wall there. He didn't make much on that attempt to get back through that hole at left tackle. Maybe a yard or two. They're coming out of that pileup. It looks like Eddie Smith made the tackle. That boy is having some game today. Notre Dame picked up two—well, it looks like three yards on the play. So Notre Dame's on Southern Cal's 40—third and five."

The announcer's skill at doing this, and the phony

excitement he could generate on demand, were the keys to success. I was aided and abetted by a brilliant but slightly screwball announcer, Moreland Murphy, and some extensive research with which we backed up our broadcasts.

We took every Notre Dame game that wasn't on the nets. Kansas City had a big Catholic population, and a fair number of local fans made the trek to South Bend by special trains for major games. We checked on who was going and found out from their wives what they were wearing.

We got from the colleges in advance the description of their halftime shows and what the band would be playing. At halftime Moreland and I described Kansas Citians in the stands and all of the halftime color while Moreland, at the studio console, played the band recordings. During the game Moreland was brilliant at the sound effects. For the kickoff, he blew a whistle and slapped a football with a stick that was a pretty good imitation of a kicker at work. And his recorded sound effects of cheering crowds were highly effective.

We did such a good job that the Federal Communications Commission suggested to Schlicker that perhaps we should give a few more notices than required that our broadcasts were by telegraphic reports. Schlicker, of course, used the letter in a flyer to advertisers pointing out how good our broadcasts were.

The Western Union service was nearly flawless, except on those occasions when the wire would go down. These were rare, and of short duration—a couple of minutes, tops. I filled in by simply calling a time-out. Who, I figured, was counting? When the wire came back, the sending operator quickly filled us in on anything that had happened on the field. No problem. Except one day—and it was the all-important Notre Dame–Southern Cal game.

The wire went down. Two minutes passed, three minutes passed, four minutes passed. The wire stayed down. It was too long for a time-out, too long for a couple of player substitutions. I decided there was nothing to do but resume the game. The Irish had the ball when the wire went down. So I moved them down the field in gentle increments.

Now they were getting near the Southern Cal 20-yard line and I knew I couldn't get them inside the twenty. *That* would make the papers the next day and expose my fictional game. Nor could I have any sensational plays for the same reason. So I kept the two teams moving back and forth as nearly mid-field as I could, and with absolutely nothing of interest happening.

That wire was down almost a half hour. When the wire came back, the operator in California gave me a quick fill-in to bring me up to date. It turned out that Southern Cal had scored. At the moment, I had Notre Dame with the ball. I had to get the ball back in Southern Cal's possession and then down the field for the score. It was the longest and dullest quarter in the history of organized football. Only some Super Bowl games of recent years have had duller quarters, but at least they didn't last as long as ours.

About the same time I was doing football at

KCMO, there was a fellow doing telegraph baseball reports in Des Moines. His name was Ronald Reagan. Many years later, at some occasion at the White House, President Reagan and I were exchanging stories and I told him of my long game.

A year or so after that, I was chatting with some group about that Trojan-Irish broadcast and one of my listeners said: "Hey, you know I was at the White House a couple of weeks ago and President Reagan tells a story just like that about having to fill in when the wire went down during a baseball broadcast."

I won't say the President of the United States stole my story, but . . .

Among the characters at KCMO was a young writer of advertising copy, Harry Bailey, a man of sometimes startlingly quixotic humor. We took an apartment together, and the time came when I began getting frequent calls from women who seemed to have gotten the idea that I was available. I even got a few from angry males who suggested that I was a menace to society. One or two particularly irate men even threatened a drastic cure to what they seemed to believe was my unfettered sex drive. As I fielded these strange calls, Harry would be looking across his book at me with a stern, disapproving glare.

It was only months later that I caught him at his dastardly game. The state of Missouri had recently adopted the sales tax, and at first it was in mills—in tenths of a cent. The sales tax tokens were cardboard caps such as those used in milk bottles. They were blank on one side. Harry was opposed to the sales tax and calculated that it cost the state more to print and distribute those bottle-cap tokens than they could make out of the tax. So, he reasoned, if we all saved the caps, we could break the state. He had a drawer filled with them at his KCMO desk. He spent his idle moments during the day carefully lettering the backs of the tokens with little advertisements, all of which carried roughly the same message: "Hey, Girls. For a Good Time, Call Walter"—with our phone number, of course. From the fifteenth-floor window, which commanded a sweeping view of Kansas City, he sailed his finished work, to be carried by the wind to the farthest corners of downtown.

Actually, those advertisements of which I was the innocent victim might have been productive if I had been interested. But I was not. That first summer at KCMO I had met Betsy Maxwell. This incredibly beautiful redhead came to work for KCMO straight out of the University of Missouri School of Journalism. She was hired on as an advertising writer. I find it hard to recognize myself in my memory of that first couple of days after her arrival, but I was so stricken that I was afflicted with a shyness that is hardly my hallmark.

Now, in those early days of radio, tape had not been invented and not many commercials were on records, so local stations wrote and performed many of them. When it came time to broadcast a commercial that required more than one voice, Robert Simmons, KCMO's program manager, simply grabbed any employees within sight, pushed them in front of the microphone and handed them the copy they were to read. Usually within minutes and without rehearsal, they were on the air.

Our staff was so small that occasionally Simmons, without ceremony or explanation, would shanghai visitors to the studio. So swift was the maneuver, and the commercial, that they were back in the reception room before mike fright had a chance to set in.

The third day after the arrival of the redhead, I still had not managed to meet her, but this would be the fateful day. Simmons grabbed me for a commercial. At the studio's mike there stood the redhead and Moreland Murphy. Simmons passed out the scripts.

"You, Wilcox, are 'Boy.' She's 'Girl.' Morph's the announcer. Here you go."

We're on the air.

> Announcer: A scene at Twelfth and Walnut. Boy meets girl.
> Boy: Hello, angel, what heaven did you drop from?
> Girl: I'm no angel.
> Boy: Well, you look like an angel.
> Girl: That's because I use Richard Hudnut.
> Announcer: Richard Hudnut, the cosmetic that [blah blah] . . .

Betsy and I went from the studio to lunch, and from lunch to dinner. And from KCMO through life together.

Our love-at-first-sight relationship almost produced a marriage-at-first-sight. Within a couple of months we were seriously considering the idea. Betsy thought her folks wouldn't approve and we decided on a secret marriage. We could accomplish that, we thought, by getting married in Independence, the county seat—then a twenty-minute drive out Fifteenth Street. So we took a lunch-hour break. We figured twenty minutes each way would leave us twenty minutes to get the license and get hitched by the county judge. By the time we got to a parking place in front of the Jackson County Court Building, we were beginning to have doubts. For twenty minutes we sat immersed in searching debate. When one was ready, the other was seized with uncertainty. At the end of twenty minutes, we finally reached agreement—that we had to get back to work.

Our courtship would last another four years before I finally got Betsy to the altar. Four years and forty-five minutes—but let me hold that story for a little later.

My KCMO job ended rather precipitously in a few weeks.

Simmons rushed to my desk shouting: "Flash it, flash it! City Hall's on fire. The new City Hall's on fire. Three people have jumped. They're dead. Get it on the air! My wife just called me. We live across the street. Get it on the air."

I reached for the telephone.

"What are you doing?" Simmons queried. "Get on the air, get on the air."

I was calling the fire department to confirm the story, I explained.

"You don't need to confirm it. My wife's watching the whole thing."

I went ahead with my phone call. Simmons left, and a moment later, just as I'm getting the fire dispatcher on the line, I hear him broadcasting a bulletin with his wife's version of the fire. Even as he's blabbing away, the fire dispatcher is telling me that it isn't much of a fire. Some scaffolding on the new building had caught fire, it was under control and just about out, and, no, there hadn't been any injuries.

The little contretemps that followed ended in my being fired. In the fashion of radio stations of the times, it wasn't the violation of responsible journalism that bothered the bosses, even to the extent of putting a highly erroneous story on the air. The sin I committed was daring to question management's authority.

I had never been out of a job before, nor have I since. My unemployment lasted a couple of months, long enough for me to have been inoculated with a lifelong appreciation of that terrible state. The Roosevelt New Deal had not yet brought the benefits of unemployment insurance, my savings were minuscule and soon exhausted, and I was ashamedly bumming most of my meals at my grandparents' or the Maxwell household, neither of which could afford an extra mouth without a little strain.

The KCMO experience had cooled any thought I

had that radio might be an interesting medium in which to practice journalism, and I limited my job search to the newspapers and the press services. I landed at the United Press.

The Kansas City bureaus of both the United Press and its larger rival, the Associated Press, were big and important. In those days the teletype circuits that carried the day's news report to client newspapers across the country all terminated in Kansas City. The services were nearly identical in their operations. State wires connected the newspapers and press service offices in a given state. Items selected for their regional interest were then condensed and filed on regional wires. Stories from these wires, selected for their even broader interest, made it onto national wires, one for the eastern United States, one for the west. These two national wires fed into Kansas City, and so did regional wires from the Midland and Southwestern states. In the Kansas City offices, large staffs of us reedited, condensed and sometimes rewrote the stories for the other sections of the country. In effect, we were helping set the agenda, helping select the stories for newspapers across the nation. Banks of teletype machines clattered twenty-four hours a day, an insatiable maw demanding sixty words of copy every minute.

Our competition across the street, the AP, was doing the same thing. Our job was to write better than they, and get our copy to the newspapers first. It was a blistering, relentless battle. It was said that somewhere in the United States or among our worldwide clients, there was a paper going to press every minute. It meant that we faced a dead-line every minute.

Unlike our brethren on the newspapers, we didn't have the luxury of only one deadline—or in the case of the bigger papers, a few deadlines—a day. We couldn't spend much time in contemplation. We wrote fast, and because our client newspapers al-ways compared our stories with the opposition's, fact by fact, we had a powerful incentive to be right.

I haven't the slightest doubt that at least a period of press service apprenticeship should be mandatory for anyone who pretends to a career in journalism. It will be valuable in their future careers to know how the wholesalers work.

Of course, there are aberrations in any business. Our regional manager, Jacques D'Armand, was no-torious for his lack of attention to small details, like arranging vacation relief for Jim Downing, who ran our one-man bureau in Tulsa. An exasperated Downing finally sent a message to Kansas City that he was leaving on his vacation on Saturday and assumed that there would be somebody there to take his place. D'Armand put me on a bus Saturday morning. By the time I got to Tulsa, Downing was long gone. He had left a clipboard in the office with each day's routine on it. It wasn't too hard to follow: File American Association baseball scores in the morning and, through the day, dictate to a number of small newspapers in the area a brief digest of the day's news report.

And, of course, cover whatever news might break in the neighborhood. My most exciting story was the attempted comeback of the great St. Louis Cardinals pitcher Dizzy Dean. He started for the Tulsa Oilers after a few of his usually quotable brash promises of a performance unparalleled by any other human who had ever stepped to the mound. He flopped miserably in that first game of the planned comeback. The comeback never developed and he became—what else—a radio announcer, thus setting a pattern that continues to this day.

I was following that clipboard routine. Monday went well. So did Tuesday and Wednesday. Thursday I was doing the duties, hour by hour as dictated by the clipboard, when suddenly I ran across "File 400-word oil column on overtime wire." When I read that, the overtime wire to Kansas City had already been running for an hour and had less than another hour to go.

As in almost every press service office, there was a great untidy stack of so-called exchanges in the corner. These were newspapers from the region that we were supposed to regularly peruse for possible news leads. I dived for the exchange pile and frantically searched for any news of the oil industry. I came upon a copy of the Chicago *Journal of Commerce*. I had no idea why it was among the Tulsa bureau's exchanges, but I thumbed it quickly. There was an oil column! This was my meat. I hastily rewrote the *Journal*'s oil column and got it onto the overtime wire in the nick of time.

The following week I had no concern about the

oil column. I could always rewrite that excellent column in the *Journal*—and I felt sure that eminent paper wouldn't mind my spreading its fine words a little wider than its readership might otherwise reach. It was the practice for wire services to pick up clients' material without attribution.

With the usual pressures in a one-man bureau, I didn't dig through the exchanges for the *Journal* until the last minute. Out it came and I flipped with confidence to the oil column. The oil column was mine. No byline, of course, but there it was. The column exactly as I had written it . . . or rewritten, as the case was, from the *Journal*'s column of a week before.

It was too late. There was nothing for it now but that I should rewrite again the column that I had rewritten the previous Thursday from the *Journal* column of the previous week. This time I was not nearly as sanguine as I filed the column on the overtime wire. I waited for the blast from Kansas City headquarters when my perfidy was discovered. It never came.

Back in Kansas City the next week I got a brief note with an enclosure from the UP headquarters in New York. The note said simply: "Congrats. Well done." The letter was to the big boss in New York praising the recent oil columns as the best in some time. It was from the Chicago *Journal of Commerce*.

Shortly thereafter I was sent to Dallas to temporarily relieve a personnel shortage. I had been there only a couple of days when the New London school in East Texas blew up. I was the editor of the state wire, and it was just coming upon three o'clock, when the wire was to be closed down for the night. Three bells rang on the machine and a coded message came across from Houston. The code was simple, but I hadn't had much reason to use it in my Kansas City duties, so, rather than take time to translate it right then, I went ahead with the procedure for closing down the wire. Now the bell rang frantically and, in the clear, came a message from Houston: "Don't close this wire!" That's what the coded message had said, too, and the reason became obvious within a minute or two.

Houston filed the first bulletin reporting that oil field sources had said there had been an explosion in the consolidated school at New London and requesting all the ambulances the area could send. The Dallas bureau manager and I took off immediately for New London, a good four hours away. We had to find it on the map, but our only delay was a slight detour so he could visit his bootlegger.

There weren't car radios then. We had no idea how bad the explosion had been until we reached Tyler, twenty-five miles from New London. There was a funeral home on the main road, and for blocks around it there were ambulances and hearses and pickup trucks, all unloading bodies.

We hurried on to New London. We reached it just at dusk. Huge floodlights from the oil fields illuminated a great pile of rubble at which men and women tore with their bare hands. Many were workers from the oil fields, but among them were office workers and what appeared to be housewives. Many were parents, others volunteers, searching desperately for children still buried in the debris. Before they were through, they would bring 294 shattered, crushed bodies out of what had once been a two-story building, only four years old and considered one of the most up-to-date school structures in Texas.

The architect had reinforced the building with vertical rows of tiles. The building was heated with residual gas from the oil fields, gas so volatile and unstable that it is usually burned off in the flares we see around most oil fields. The gas is odorless and invisible. It leaked somewhere in the subbasement of the school building. It filled those vertical columns of tiles. The school was a bomb waiting to explode. Two minutes before classes were to be dismissed for the weekend, a student in the basement woodworking shop switched off a band saw. The spark did its work.

To add to the horror, the Parent-Teacher Association was meeting in the school's gymnasium, just yards away. The mothers were there from the start of the frantic search for the few survivors. When we got there, the school superintendent, William Shaw, superficial cuts from the explosion bleeding across his face, was still wandering through the ruins. "There are children in there, there are children in there," he kept muttering. His own seventeen-year-old son was somewhere under the debris with two of his cousins.

A news reporter's duty can sometimes be difficult. It is not easy to approach someone in such distress to seek answers to the questions that need asking. It was never a problem that bothered the public until television came along. But now that reporters at the scene of a disaster can be seen asking those questions, the public asks its own questions about what it perceives as journalists' total insensitivity.

There is a perfectly rational excuse for the news-persons' seeming callousness: Stories change with each retelling. Even a person really trying for the most faithful recital of events is almost invariably susceptible to slight modifications, certain little embellishments, with each recital. Accuracy of a story is in direct relation to how soon after the event it is recorded, and how frequently the story has been retold.

Thus, I talked to the superintendent. I didn't know about the school's use of the highly dangerous residual gas. But he told me about it. He wept as he told how he and the school board had decided to tap into those gas lines. The use of the gas was illegal, but nearly everybody in the small towns adjoining the oil fields did it. The New London school simply was terribly unlucky.

On one tottering wall a blackboard carried an ironic message: "Oil and natural gas are East Texas' greatest mineral blessings. Without them this school would not be here and none of us would be here learning our lessons."

The world press poured into the little town of New London and its slightly larger neighbor, Overton. The United Press sent down Delos Smith from New York, one of our fastest and best writers and editors, to head up our staff, which consisted of Tom Reynolds, a top Washington correspondent who later, and for years, would be the UP's White House man; and, to handle the feature stories, Henry McLemore, our top sports writer.

Early Sunday morning, after some forty-eight uninterrupted hours on the job, Delos suggested I get some sleep. It was midnight when he sent me off to the Overton Hotel, a one-story structure with a single hall, off of which were the rooms. In Texas they call that a "shotgun" building, meaning you could fire a shotgun down the hall and hit everybody in the place.

"You won't need a key," Delos said. "Our room is the first one past the men's room on the right. McLemore's there right now. He brought some stuff to us. There's shaving stuff and toothbrushes. There are a couple of extra shirts in his bag."

So I stumbled down to the Overton, located the room and fell into the twin bed opposite McLemore, whose snoring was of classic dimensions. Delos had sent me off at midnight with instructions to "get a good night's sleep," noting that he would have someone wake me up at six. Some night's sleep!

I was awakened by the sun forcing its way through the cracks in a window shade too tired to keep out the rays. It was eight o'clock. I was grateful to Delos for giving me a little bonus. Mac was up and out. I found a toothbrush, borrowed the razor and shaving cream and stumbled to the shower. Slightly more awake upon my return, I realized that Mac was even more of an eccentric than legend had it. He had arrived in New London directly from the baseball spring training camps in Florida, but, my gosh, to come to a two- or three-day assignment like this and decorate the room with framed pictures of baseball players? Wild. And when I went into his bag for that clean shirt, there were baseballs there.

In my clean shirt I appeared back at our head-quarters. Delos looked up and, without any notable early morning cheerfulness, said: "Well, that's a young buck for you. You don't sleep for two nights, you get a few hours off, and you go shack up with some broad somewhere."

I was stunned. I protested.

"Cronkite," said Delos, "don't give me that. I sent for you at six o'clock and you weren't in the room. I sent down there at seven and you still weren't there."

He was right. I hadn't been in the UP room. I had shared the room of the manager of the area's semi-pro baseball team. I never met him. I still don't know who he thought it was sleeping in his other bed that night, or if he missed the shirt.

The UP sent me to Austin to cover a special ses-sion of the legislature to rescind pari-mutuel horse race betting, and from there to El Paso to organize a new United Press bureau. It turned out I was a pawn in a typical early skirmish between the print press and radio. It would be years before the United Press had a wire serving radio stations, but D'Armand had sold an El Paso station, KTSM, on subscribing to the UP's regular newspaper wire.

The editor of the Scripps-Howard El Paso *Herald Post* screamed bloody murder. Ed Pooley, who it happens had been my managing editor in Houston, saw the radio station as a serious competitor for his advertising dollars, and he viewed the UP action as tantamount to treachery.

So I was there, not to cover the news, although that would be expected as well, but to rewrite the news wire so that KTSM would not be getting the same reports, at least in the same words, as the paper. The whole exercise was part of the struggle that would span the decade just before World War II, when the newspapers realized the threat to their advertising revenue from the rapidly growing broadcasting business.

The United Press and INS saw radio as a new source of revenue but had to tread carefully lest they step on the toes of their newspaper clients. The AP had the same problem with its member papers. They faced occasional threats from upstart news service like Trans-Radio Press. Trans-Radio was vastly underfunded. So thin and frayed was its shoestring that, in the business, it provided more laughs than news. It signed up a client or two in Texas, and so sent one young fellow down to cover and service the largest state in the Union (circa 1937).

The new man apparently had not been out of Manhattan. He arrived in Texas—by bus, of course—

in full safari gear, complete with boots and a pith helmet. This appeared to be his only outfit. He wore the costume for the remaining months before Trans-Radio folded.

I had been in El Paso only a week or two when a phone call came from Oklahoma City. The man on the other end talked so fast that I had to ask for frequent repeats. There scarcely had been the formality of a "hello" when he plunged in: "Gayle Grubb, WKY. Hear you're a great football announcer. We've just signed the University of Oklahoma to the first exclusive radio contract for all their games—at home and away. Kellogg cereal is the sponsor. I want you to come up here for an audition."

I really wasn't that interested in getting back into radio, and I sure as shooting didn't know whether I could do a live football broadcast. The KCMO reconstructed games hardly qualified. On the other hand, I had been battling a sense of loneliness and isolation in El Paso. It was the farthest west I had ever been. In a whole different time zone from Kansas City. And I feared it was far too far to keep the romance with Betsy alive.

So I got a weekend off to take the train as far as Dallas, where Mr. Grubb and his commercial manager, Matt Bonebrake, would audition me. In a bare studio they stood me in front of a microphone, retired to the control room and directed: "OK, broadcast a football game."

Well, that little order was right down my alley. I gave them an imaginary five minutes of an imaginary game. They came out rubbing their hands and asked how much I wanted and when could I start.

Not wanting a job very much does all sorts of wonders for strengthening one's bargaining ability. So I tripled my UP salary and asked for a big seventy-five dollars a week. I was dumbfounded when they agreed on the spot—dumbfounded that I was dumb in more ways than founded. Clearly I should have asked for even more.

WKY was a first-class operation. It was owned by the *Daily Oklahoman and Times*, the state's preeminent newspaper, was an affiliate of NBC and did a lot of fine local programming. There were still a couple of months to the football season, and they suggested I might like to live on the university campus at Norman to get more familiar with the team.

And, they asked, what assistance did I feel I'd need for the broadcasts? I felt I would need a lot of assistance, but I tried to hide my concern. I suggested an electric board that would have little lights for each of the positions as the teams lined up for play. I would have a spotter for each team, and they would press buttons to light the bulbs that would indicate who carried the ball and who made the tackle. From there on out, I reasoned, it would be no more difficult than those telegraphed reports.

The first game was the traditional opener against Tulsa. All the Kellogg brass was there from Battle Creek and the ad agency people from New York. There was a big party the night before—the broadcast executives and the University of Oklahoma officials. It really was a shame we couldn't have adjourned right then and there.

The broadcast was a disaster. My spotters weren't worth a darn and the electric board was worthless. I was trying to get the numbers off the jerseys as the plays progressed, refer to the program and finally deliver some sort of report of the play, which by then had unfolded some minutes before. The cheers for that play had long since died down and were being succeeded by the cheers for the next play before I had identified the players in the first one. I was hopelessly behind.

Grubb stood behind me in the booth. After the first few plays he started mumbling something. The mumbles got louder and more frequent until I had no trouble getting the drift. "Jesus," he was saying. A long exhale. And another "Jesus."

The mumbles got so loud toward halftime that I was sure my microphone must be picking them up. Bathed in perspiration, I was certain that the whole booth and the whole radio audience for my much-advertised debut was probably keeping company with Grubb in this—what was it, prayer, comment or exhortation?

When the game came to its merciful end and, as they say, shadows were lengthening over the playing field, Grubb invited—no, commanded—me to sit next to him in the top row of seats outside the radio booth. We sat there for some time in silence. Finally he said: "All right. I'll see you in the office the first

thing Monday morning. I don't know about you—
I'm not going to the sponsor's party tonight." And
he just got up and left, a man who clearly thought
that his presumably bright career, along with mine,
had ended up there in that Tulsa radio booth.

I was not quite dressed yet Monday morning
when the phone rang. "Grubb," said the voice. "Mr.
Gaylord wants us in his office at eight-thirty. I'll
meet you downstairs."

Mr. Gaylord was the big boss, the biggest boss
of the entire *Oklahoman* empire. That he wanted to
see me at all, but particularly with Grubb, was as
ominous a signal as a funnel-shaped cloud on the
horizon.

A huge shadow of trepidation accompanied
Grubb and me into Gaylord's office. I had never met
him before. He could have stepped out of a *New
Yorker* cartoon: the absolute epitome of the big
boss—a little on the heavy side, wire-framed
glasses, balding, a frown that creased most of his
extended forehead. He motioned us to chairs.

"Well, I thought you fellows did pretty good," he
nodded. "The folks I've talked to thought it was
good. I liked it. A few little things I know you're
going to fix up, but I just wanted you to know that
we liked it around here."

He practically had to invite us to leave. Relief had
frozen Grubb and me in our chairs.

Needless to say, we fixed up the "little things." I
had learned a lesson that would prove highly valuable as the years went on. Never again would I be

caught without having done whatever research was possible for whatever it was I was going to cover. For the football games, along with the color announcer Perry Ward, who selflessly volunteered to be my spotter, I learned the name and number and positions and hometown, height and weight and record of every member of each squad of every game we broadcast.

He and I memorized alone until Thursday night. That night we sat for hours throwing numbers or names back and forth for the other to fill in the details. And we continued that drill with extended hours all day Friday with a quick review before the game Saturday.

That next game was vastly different from Tulsa. I hardly needed Ward's spotting. Just by watching the game unfold, if I could see the players' numbers, I knew who they were and all about them. We had a wonderfully successful season.

There was only one game that gave us a problem. The Nebraska game was played at Lincoln, which, already a football power, had the biggest stadium in the conference. The radio booth was three decks away from the action. It was tough to follow the plays even with binoculars. But even that became impossible as a driving snowstorm totally blanked out the field below. There were a few minutes there when I was tempted to invoke my imagination and repeat the KCMO "long quarter." My own reason prevailed, and within minutes our engineers had tapped us into the coaches' telephone circuit at the sidelines. The assistant coach's dry recitation of the events on the field did require a little of the old telegraphed-report buildup, but I never heard any complaints.

With the football season over, I was assigned to the WKY news staff. The station had a widely held reputation as a superior news operation, but the lack of original reporting—most of the broadcasts were simply rewrites of *Oklahoman* material—and the brevity of the reports still left me feeling incomplete as a journalist. My heart was still with print.

So I was ready to move on when a friend who was public relations manager for Braniff Airways suggested that I should join the new airline. He was being promoted and I was to take his job. This wasn't journalism, but it sounded more interesting than WKY.

I am proud to say that WKY, already preparing the promotion for the next season's football broadcasts, was disappointed with my decision. I thought I might have to swallow my pride and ask for my job back when I appeared at Braniff for my first day's work. The line's general manager, Chuck Beard, guarded the headquarters' front door from his desk just inside.

"Hi, Walter, what are you doing here this hour of the morning?" he greeted me.

"Coming to work, Mr. Beard."

"Doing what, in heaven's name?"

"Well"—my answer now just a touch timorous perhaps—"Bill Beattie said I was going to be the public relations manager."

"Hell's fire," said Beard. "Beattie's going to be the public relations manager as well as reservations manager. He'd better help you find something else."

The whole thing surprised Beattie as much as it did me, but he maneuvered things so that I would be trained as a traffic manager and would be assigned to Kansas City (back with Betsy!), with additional duties as his public relations assistant for the north end of the line.

"Traffic manager" was a misnomer. The job consisted of selling tickets and handling reservations, usually out of a downtown ticket office. So new was air transport that a large part of the job was calling on potential clients to convince them that they should travel by plane instead of by train. With the airline struggling in its early days, the job sometimes involved participating in emergency maneuvers.

Our Kansas City operations manager was the sort of Cool Hand Luke you would expect in that job in air transport's infancy, when life-threatening emergencies were not rare. Bill Cunningham was the kind you found in the movies, in the control tower talking that distressed plane down through the fog. But this day even he seemed a little agitated as he asked how many passengers we were putting on Flight Three, our afternoon flight from Chicago en route to Wichita, Oklahoma City and Dallas. And could I get in touch with them?

It turned out there were three, and I did have phone contacts for them all. He wanted me to bring them to Fairfax Airport, not let them go to the Municipal Airport. Fairfax was just across the Missouri River from Municipal, a smaller field on the Kansas side of the river. Cunningham said he had no time for explanations, just get them there.

I rounded them up and took them to Fairfax. There Cunningham met me at the tiny terminal building. He took me aside and said that when our flight landed in a few minutes, it would taxi to the end of the runway and we would take our passengers out there and pick up the passengers destined for Kansas City. Still he had no time for explanations.

The passengers, naturally, had a few questions of their own. Cunningham answered them all with: "Technical problems. No danger. Everything's all right. Just technical problems."

The plane landed, and taxied to the end of the runway, and we exchanged our passengers. When they all were on their way, Cunningham literally wiped his brow: "Well, we got away with it that time. The Jackson County sheriff was after us. We owe a little fuel bill. Oklahoma City said the money's on the way, but he threatened to attach the airplane. I'll get him paid off or calmed down by Flight Four. Don't worry about it."

I scored only one publicity coup in my year with Braniff. Sally Rand had won fame dancing nude behind a fan at the Chicago World's Fair. She had moved on to using a bubble to hide her charms. The opaque quality of the bubble, actually a huge balloon, enhanced the titillation considerably. Personally I was confident that she wore a very thin leotard. But that's neither here nor there.

My point is that she was appearing at the Follies Burlesque in Kansas City. We had a flight to Chicago that left Kansas City at 3:30 a.m., obviously not a trip on which I could sell many tickets. Except Saturday morning. The burlesque show changed each week after the Friday night performance, and most of the comedians and strippers, anxious to get on into Chicago, were my pigeons.

I approached Sally with the idea for a publicity picture. I would have the airport weatherman show her the balloon with which he tested winds aloft. She agreed and I posed them on the airplane steps. I suggested how Miss Rand should hold the balloon. She fixed me with a withering look and said: "Sonny boy, are you telling Sally Rand how to hold a balloon?" I was withered, but the picture made the papers.

Just a few months later, anxious to return to newspapering, I landed back at the United Press and I found good feature-story material backstage at the Follies. We weren't in the war yet, but possible shortages of strategic materials were being discussed, so I found myself asking some questions of Hinda Wassau, a strip queen who earned a place in the history of burlesque by being the first to use the proscenium arch as a sex object. She concluded her act by caressing the pillar at the edge of the stage, doing a few bumps and grinds against it and finishing with a clenched fist waved at the audience with the dedication: "And one for the boys in the balcony!"

What would the strippers do if there was a zipper shortage, I wanted to know. This brought a tirade from Miss Wassau.

"I guess you haven't seen my act, big boy," she said. "I don't use zippers."

"Oh, you use hooks and eyes," I ventured.

"Not that either. Library paste." She waved to one of those big schoolroom-size jars of Carter's library paste on her dressing room table.

"I paste my costume on. Press it down for a minute and it's just tacky enough to hold. And then I just peel it off—nice and ladylike."

I saw that story sort of slipping away, as it were. So I pressed on. "What do you think, Miss Wassau, will be burlesque's part in maintaining wartime morale?"

She grabbed me by my coat lapel. I wouldn't come across that gesture again until Lyndon Johnson.

"Let me tell you something. The morales behind a burlesque stage are just as good as the morales at Radio City!"

Chances to do that kind of significant reporting were rare in Kansas City in those days. At the time I left Braniff, the news reports from overseas were filled with the prewar clichés: "War clouds gathered over Europe today"; "Lights burned late in the chancelleries of Europe tonight."

As Hitler swallowed Austria, and British Prime Minister Neville Chamberlain at Munich served him Czechoslovakia with the declaration that he had ensured "peace in our time," only the most irrationally hopeful felt that war could be avoided.

At the UP I was back in the world in which I felt I belonged. These were days and nights filled with eminently satisfying work and heady prospects.

The backwaters of Europe's troubles began to lap at us in Kansas City. I had a nice story about an ice skater caught in a diplomatic Catch-22. She was a lovely blond world champion from Czecho-slovakia appearing in the Ice Capades. I learned from the press agent that she was devastated and deeply troubled. She had refused to skate before Hitler at Berlin's 1936 Olympics. Fearing retribu-tion, she had fled Prague when the Germans seized Czechoslovakia. Now her U.S. visitor's visa had expired and she was threatened with deportation back to Czechoslovakia and a highly uncertain fate.

An apparently unsympathetic State Department maintained that the quota for Czech immigration was full and it could do nothing. The day after my UP story appeared in papers around the world, I had a telephone call from a government bureaucrat in Washington. He refused to give his name but, practi-cally whispering, said he knew how "that young lady" could get into the States. His solution was simply that she apply for her visa in Alaska. It was still a territory and had a visa quota of its own, and there were openings for Czechs. That's how Vera Hruba got into the United States to become a movie star.

And I had a little scoop with what probably was the world's first aerial hijacking. Some fellow had pointed a revolver at a pilot at St. Louis' airport and forced him to take him aloft. They disappeared flying west. I had an avid amateur's interest in aviation at the time. There was the Braniff background, and Betsy and I had been taking flying lessons. So I calculated how far that plane might go with the gas it could carry, and at our UP wall map, I drew a circle representing the area in which I figured it would have to land.

I began phoning airports in the circle. On the second call I hit bingo. The airport reported, with understandable excitement, that the plane had just landed there. The culprit had shot the pilot but had landed safely and been caught, and I had a nice beat on the opposition.

Alf Landon, defeated by Roosevelt in the 1936 election, lived in Topeka, Kansas, and, as the most recent Republican standard-bearer, was grist for our mill. We were occasionally requested to contact him for comment on one story or another. I had never interviewed such an internationally recognized figure before the day I was asked to get his opinion on some arcane economic story. He was gracious enough during our telephone conversation until, having gotten the material I needed, I proffered a "thank you and good-bye, sir."

Whereupon Landon said: "How long have you been a newspaper reporter, young man?"

I mumbled something about four or five years, whereupon he said: "Well, if you had more experience, you might have asked me what I think about Roosevelt running for a third term. I think it is a darned fool idea that can cause all sorts of trouble. Good-bye."

It wasn't a major revelation. He had been quoted on the matter before. But it did teach me that once you've got a news source on the phone, don't let go until you've tested for every possibility.

Occasionally I would serve as night editor. Many of us from the *Times* morning paper, the AP and UP got off at one or two in the morning and spent the rest of the night in rapt, if not raucous, attendance at the nightclubs. Sometimes the evenings ended with a spirited hopscotch contest on the nearly deserted Armour Boulevard out in front of our apartment. These sometimes ended with a smiling admonition from the occupants of a cruising police car.

The Bainbridge Apartment also counted among its guests several ballplayers from the New York Yankees' American Association farm club, the Kansas City Blues. Downstairs from me lived Gerald Priddy and Phil Rizzuto, on the way up to greatness.

With my future settled, I felt, for some distance into our tomorrows, I convinced Betsy that our long courtship might indeed be ripe for marriage. An interesting coincidence was discovered during the preparations for the nuptials. Betsy's mother was sewing a satin cover on a small Bible that Betsy had acquired in her Sunday school days. My mother was visiting and Eva Maxwell showed her the Bible. My mother opened the Bible to the flyleaf and gasped: "This was given to Betsy for graduating from Lin-

wood Presbyterian Church Sunday School. Walter
was in the same class; he's got the same Bible with
the same inscription."

Indeed, it was so. That class for five-year-olds
wasn't that large. Surely we had known each other
all those long years earlier. Perhaps there is something to this thing called Destiny.

Betsy was beautiful as she carried that Bible
down the aisle of Grace and Holy Trinity Episcopal
Church on March 30, 1940. Frankly, she would have
looked pretty good to me if she had shown up in
overalls. Until she made her appearance, I wasn't
sure I was ever going to see her again.

It was a big wedding. My best man and ushers
were mostly up from Houston, old school chums and
fraternity brothers. We were gathered in the sanc-
tuary, somewhat uncomfortable and self-conscious
in our rented cutaways and tails. The church filled,
and at the appointed hour the organist played, as
requested, "I Love You Truly."

At that point there arrived a runner from out front.
Betsy, it seemed, had not arrived.

The minister was reassuring: "I've seen them as
much as five, even ten minutes late. There could be
traffic, anything. Don't worry, Walter."

His allotted five minutes, and ten minutes, passed.
Now the minister was more nervous than I. My
emotion was more one of annoyance. Meanwhile
the organist, to whom my contribution had apparently been only adequate for one song, kept punching away at "I Love You Truly." The audience

was stirring, none of its number more than my Uncle Ed, who, I learned later, had to go to the bathroom during most of the wait. There may have been others who were not so frank about the problem.

That wait, it turned out, lasted forty-five minutes, or approximately twenty-one and a half renderings of "I Love You Truly." When Betsy finally appeared, most of our relatives and the audience were relieved. The minister was pale and shaken but bravely carried on. The organist's fingers were cramped into sort of permanent "I Love You Truly" claws. I was writhing somewhere between relief and disgust, like a parent whose lost child has reappeared.

It turned out that Betsy's brother had burned up her new lingerie along with the gift wrappings, and she would not hear of any substitute. Brother Allen had to go downtown and fetch the exact replacement.

But we did the "for better, for worse, in sickness and in health" thing, Betsy agreed with me that I would never have to hear "I Love You Truly" again, and we have made it work, ecstatically some of the time, pleasantly most of the time, for fifty-six years at this 1996 writing.

I attribute the longevity of our marriage to Betsy's extraordinarily keen sense of humor, which saw us over many bumps (mostly of my making), and her tolerance, even support, for the uncertain schedule and wanderings of a newsman.

We didn't know as we left the church that we had less than two years before World War II would sweep us into that long separation which so many of our generation would endure.

CHAPTER 4

BETSY'S and my salad days lasted eighteen months. Soon after the great performance at Grace and Holy Trinity, she finally realized the dream for which she had studied at the University of Missouri's famed School of Journalism. She was hired on as the women's editor of the *Journal-Post*.

The job included writing an advice-to-the-lovelorn column, "Ask Hope Hudson." The new Hope Hudson at this point was all of twenty-four years old and, given the mores of the times, about as sophisticated in affairs of the heart, love and marriage as a puppy dog. The letters seeking guidance from the romantically stricken and underprivileged turned out that winter to be the stuff of social success for the Cronkites. There were few gatherings of our fellow newspeople that did not feature Betsy's reading from her bag of mail and an outpouring of suggested answers, most decidedly irreverent and definitely unprintable.

The paper was in the old tradition before college degrees became de rigueur in the city room. It was staffed with characters, one of whom was an assistant city editor who was sober most of the time but was inspired to theatrical heights by touring schoolchildren. As they came through the door, he would extract a bottle from his drawer, take a healthy swig of its alcoholic contents, jump onto the desk and scream "Stop the presses!" The presses were actually stopped a couple of times before he could be persuaded to tone down his performance.

John Cameron Swayze, who would go on to fame and fortune as the first anchorman of NBC's evening news, was an editor of the entertainment page. Early on he was stricken by the broadcast bug, and each morning he did a live newscast from the city room for a local radio station. The city room was on the third floor, just across the hall from our UP bureau. As overnight editor, one of my duties was to spike a carbon copy of our overnight report for Swayze's use. Habitually late, Swayze would come puffing up the stairs with minutes, sometimes seconds, to spare before broadcast time. He would dash in, snatch the copy from the spike and, catching his breath as he dashed for the hall, ask me for the headlines.

I would accompany him across the hall reciting the lead stories as I remembered them. Swayze would swing into his chair, lean into the microphone with a cheery "Good morning" and then repeat what I had told him. Then, during the first commercial, he would sift through the carbon copies and be ready for the rest of his fifteen minutes. He was a marvel at making it sound so easy.

The *Journal-Post* folded that year. Although its continued existence always was tenuous, the end came suddenly with a publisher's announcement between editions. The staff did not react well. They trashed the place—all except those (like Betsy) who were out on assignment. They threw typewriters through the big arched windows. They overturned desks. Sin of all sins, they emptied many of the file drawers that contained the day-to-day history of the region. And they smashed on the floor the huge paste pots with which editors had made up their pages.

The stench of that rotting paste and the wind through those broken windows—and the rats that thrived on the paste—made life almost unbearable for us at the UP, who remained as the lone occupants of the building. We were busy, though, editing and transmitting the growing clichés from Europe.

Betsy and I enlisted in the Civilian Pilot Training Program, an effort to train the pilots who would be needed for the 50,000 planes Roosevelt later promised to build each year, a promise that garnered universal skepticism. She got her pilot's license. I was washed out with the discovery that I was color-blind (as far as I knew, my ties had all matched up to then). And I was besieging New York for a foreign assignment. Betsy, with her journalistic training, was approving but fearful.

I was on the desk the night the bells on the tele-type machines rang out the signal for a flash: "Germany invades Poland."

The war was on. In a few weeks I would be summoned to the foreign desk in New York.

The great conflagration that engulfed Planet Earth in the fourth decade of the twentieth century is popularly known as World War II. Actually, it was the War of Failure. The most extensive and costliest war was the result of "civilized" man's failure once again to resolve differences without resorting to violence. As long as nations cannot learn to live cooperatively, there must be conflict. As long as there are aggressors, there will be resisters.

From the end of the War to End War, as World War I was delusively described, the nations proved that the lessons of the bloody conflict had been lost upon them. This was no more apparent than in the United States Senate, where the American chauvinists, blindly jealous of meaningless sovereignty, rejected Wilson's dream of a League of Nations, a mild first step toward world government. Whatever chances that body had of preventing another war were diminished to near oblivion by the failure of the United States to join.

And so attempts at disarmament or even substantial limitations of armament were unsuccessful, and the nations raced to Armageddon fueled by the development of a pair of ideologies that were at opposite political poles but strangely alike in their application.

How alike were Communism and Naziism was exposed when the Soviet and German dictators suddenly forswore their presumed ideological enmity and agreed to a nonaggression pact. That Hitler could have so totally missed what he saw in the mirror and thus have trusted Stalin is a mystery that perhaps only a Freudian could untangle, but, believing his rear protected, he felt free to turn his attention to Europe, and we all know the consequences.

(That Soviet-German pact, of course, had another result: It was used in the United States as the litmus test of the depth of commitment of those judged to be sympathetic to Communism. Those who condemned the pact were generally excused as simply fuzzy-headed liberals, while those who still supported Communism after the pact were forever assigned to hell as hard-shell conspirators against our democratic system. The distinction became a matter of near life or death during the unconscionable witch hunts of the McCarthy era.)

So on September 1, 1939, Hitler unleashed his tanks and his Stuka dive-bombers against the horse-mounted Polish cavalry. The British and French declared war, but for eight months nothing much transpired on the Western Front while Germans and Russians carved up Poland. And then in April 1940 Hitler sent his forces crashing across northern and western Europe and the real war was on.

America tut-tutted with increasing alarm as the British on their tight little isle became the last bastion of democracy across the Atlantic. We listened with horror as Ed Murrow and others described the bombing of London and Canterbury and dozens of other places dear to our Anglo-American heritage. Voices were heard for American intervention—but others renewed the old philosophy of American isolationism.

Japan's war machine ended all that on a bright

December Sunday, the first Sunday in December
1941. It blew up a large part of our Pacific fleet in
Pearl Harbor in what was generally sold to the
American people as a "sneak attack"—a date President Roosevelt said would "live in infamy."

It later turned out that we had pretty good intelligence indicating that the fleet of Japanese aircraft
carriers was heading toward Hawaii. The responsibility for our lack of readiness at Pearl Harbor is still
a matter of controversy among historians. But the
version that seems most plausible to me is that,
rather than risk revealing that we had broken the
Japanese code, Washington did not specifically advise Major General Walter Short and Rear Admiral
Husband Kimmel, our commanders in Hawaii, that
their island was under threat of imminent attack. It
would have done nothing for the nation's morale to
have acknowledged that fact at the time, so Short
and Kimmel were left to twist slowly in the wind,
deliberately turned by the high command in Washington into scapegoats for "inadequate" preparations
for the "sneak" assault.

At any rate, we were at war, and the personal
aspect began coming home to the American people
as the draft was accelerated and khaki became the
uniform of the day. While tens of thousands were
being drafted, a few hundred were being selected out
of civilian life for specialized talents, and they were
suffering the same sort of embarrassing indoctrina-
tion as the lawyer in New York who was called to
come immediately to Washington. He was told by

telephone that he was being made a lieutenant commander in the Navy and was to report the next morning. In response to his proud but anguished inquiry, he was told he could get a lieutenant commander's uniform at Brooks Brothers in New York, and get moving. He called his wife in Greenwich asking her to bring to town his shaving kit, and he hurried to Brooks for the uniform.

Happily wearing it through Penn Station a few hours later, he was suddenly confronted with a sailor throwing him a salute. He overcame momentary panic and snapped back with the mandatory responsive salute. Only sometime later as he now confidently took his seat on the train, a full-fledged officer in his country's service, did he wither in embarrassment as it came to him that he had answered that sailor with his little finger crimped under his thumb—the Boy Scouts' three-finger salute.

My uniform problem was a little less acute when, a couple of months after Pearl Harbor, my United Press bosses sent me to Navy headquarters in New York for credentials to go to sea with the North Atlantic convoys—so far the nation's only combat role, except for getting what was left of our Pacific fleet out on rather flimsy early patrols.

The United States military was as unprepared for handling the requirements of the press as it was for meeting the enemy. It extemporized that civilian war correspondents would be given the privileges of officers and should wear officers' uniforms without insignia of rank or branch of service. And we would be identified as correspondents by a green brassard with a large white "C" to be worn on the left arm.

So adorned, I went off to war. My first assignment was to accompany the most valuable convoy assembled up to that time—a dozen of the world's great liners taking to England the nucleus of the American Air Force that would carry the war to Hitler's Germany.

The convoy commodore, Captain C. F. Bryant, had no directives for hosting a correspondent aboard his flagship. He solved the dilemma by assigning the chaplain to be my escort, and it was the good man of the cloth who introduced me around the old battleship *Arkansas* as she lay off Staten Island waiting for the convoy to form.

The officers in the ward room that evening seemed to me particularly dull. There was little conversation among them and scarcely any with me until one of them assayed a question: "Excuse me, sir, but what denomination are you?"

"Oh," said I, "a sort of jackass Episcopalian."

I intercepted a couple of hasty glances from under raised eyebrows.

"Do you have a church of your own?" the young officer pressed.

"Oh, sure," I answered, "I belong to St. Bart's in New York. But, I'm ashamed to say, I don't go very often."

Puzzlement was spreading through the *Arkansas'* officer corps.

"Well," one lieutenant finally piped up, "how did you happen to become a chaplain?"

Being introduced by their chaplain, wearing an Army uniform with no insignia of rank and just that big white "C" on my sleeve had proved a baffling camouflage for a leading backslider from the Fourth Estate.

Confusion spread in the British Isles, too. Few Americans had been seen on the Clyde side when our convoy reached there, and perhaps I was the first of us in uniform to drop into the so-called Casual Officers' Mess in Greenock. Only a pair of Scottish officers were there, one in kilts, the other in the close-fitting tartan trousers the Scots call trews.

I ordered a drink from the bartender, and the kilted one approached.

"I say, old boy [my first 'old boy']," he inquired, not without a touch of belligerence, "is it customary in your army for cashiered officers to drink with the gentlemen at the officers' bar?"

The lack of insignia and the big white "C" had done it again.

It would be another year before the military decreed that badges should be worn on the shoulder and breast pocket which clearly indicated our war correspondent status.

On the return with that early convoy to the United States, I had my first wartime scoop, handed to me solely because I was the only correspondent within a few hundred miles when one of the converted luxury liners was swept by fire. She was the former *Wakefield*, now bearing her wartime name of *Manhattan*. She was carrying home several hundred construction people and other civilians who had been helping the British during our neutrality. With incredible courage and seamanship the skipper of the cruiser *Brooklyn* put his vessel's bow against the furiously burning *Manhattan* to take off all the civilians and some of the crew. Most of the crew stayed aboard and successfully fought the fire to a standstill, and the *Manhattan* eventually was towed home to be rebuilt for further duty.

There was a brief sequel to this story that would foreshadow things to come. In my story I had quoted a Navy officer who blamed the fire on the careless disposal of a cigarette in one of the staterooms. I received an indignant complaint from the tobacco industry that I had accepted without proof an insidious presumption.

My story, by some miracle, got past the censors and made the banner headline in a lot of American papers. I had lucked into early recognition as a war correspondent, although there had been no other reportable drama on that convoy—brief excitement when our escorting destroyers picked up the blips of an occasional submarine, but there were no attacks.

By September I was en route with a sizable fleet from Norfolk to attack Morocco as part of the North African invasion. Our small task force, led by the pre–World War I battleship *Texas*, was to take the small town of Port Lyautey and the French arsenal there, said to be the biggest in North Africa.

There may be nothing more amusing than the Army afloat, except perhaps the Navy ashore. The Army put aboard the *Texas* a team of reservists and hastily converted civilians recruited by the Office of War Information to operate something they called "Clandestine Radio Maroc." Their sole function was to broadcast propaganda intended to persuade the army of France's puppet government to desert Hitler and come over to the Allied side. Their most important broadcast would be President Roosevelt's announcement of the invasion and his appeal for the colonials in West Africa to honor their French patriotism and join the Allied cause.

One of the team was the well-known radio announcer Andre Baruch, a junior officer in New York's terribly social cavalry reserve. He came aboard wearing his full uniform with boots and riding crop. Another was a former newspaperman and longtime between-the-wars habitué of Paris' Left Bank who by a strange set of circumstances had served for a few days as treasurer of the Loyalist forces during Spain's Civil War. A third was a Swiss native from the importing business. Apparently all they had in common was a familiarity with the French language.

The Navy assigned the radio team to bunks in the forecastle just forward of the officers' wardroom. Perhaps dictated by interservice rivalry or possibly accidentally, the hatch above their quarters was left open as the *Texas* reached the open sea beyond Hampton Roads. The first big wave poured down the hatch. The midnight watch had just changed and the wardroom was full as the Army contingent, their fancy civilian pajamas dripping with a goodly part of the Atlantic, came charging out of the forecastle led by the intrepid Captain Baruch, the only one of the team with even reserve military training.

He had his men halfway across the wardroom on the way to the boats as, in one of the grandest double takes since Mack Sennett, Baruch skidded to a stop upon realizing that, with the ship's officers at least, all was normal, with no indication that the *Texas* was soon to sink.

If that was a result of interservice rivalry, there was to be a more serious example as we hit the beaches of Morocco. A team of Army communications technicians had been put aboard the *Texas* to install clandestine Radio Maroc's transmission equipment. The proud Army types, possibly operating under orders of extreme secrecy, turned down the offer of the *Texas'* communications officer to help with the installation.

When, on that African D-Day, the *Texas* fired off its big fourteen-inch guns for the first time in anger, even the ship itself suffered the repercussions. It was as if, instead of disgorging the shells, she had been hit by them. She shuddered, she shook, she staggered. Ceramic bathroom fixtures shattered and some pipes burst.

And just as it was getting warmed up with President Roosevelt's message to the people of France, Radio Maroc was blown right off the air by the concussion.

"If they had asked, we could have told them how to prevent that," shrugged a Navy communications officer.

The firing of those big naval rifles is awesome and, to the uninitiated, frightening. The great belch of yellow flame threatens to engulf the ship herself, and the blast of heat sears the freshman war correspondent on the bridge. The gun blows its own great smoke ring and the shell can actually be seen disappearing toward the horizon through the middle of the doughnut. Whatever has been loose on deck is sent skyward, sucked into the vacuum the explosion has left behind.

As I stood there trembling with wonder, playing cards began raining from the heavens. One dropped on the back of my hand that was gripping the rail. It was the ace of spades.

The previous day Admiral Monroe Kelly had called me to his quarters. He noted that the men of the *Texas*, at least officially, had never been briefed on the ship's mission and now he was about to take care of that with a short speech over the public-address system. He allowed as how he would like to conclude his little talk with "something heroic, something memorable, something like 'Your country expects every man to do his duty.' "

"You're a writer, Mr. Cronkite, perhaps you could help me come up with something."

I regret to say that I failed to do my duty. I couldn't think of anything either heroic or memorable. The admiral's request did open a question in my mind. Was there by chance a public relations man along as Washington crossed the Delaware? And did he suggest, "General, it would look great if you would stand up in the boat"?

Not many minutes into D-Day it seemed that the *Texas* was about to undergo her baptism by fire. A flight of fighter planes came diving out of the clouds directly for her. We had been advised that the Vichy French were putting up some aerial resistance to the invasion, and every gun on the *Texas* opened fire. The sky above us was black with antiaircraft bursts as the fighter planes peeled off to escape the barrage, and as they exposed their wings, there were the big white stars identifying them as off the U.S. carrier down at Casablanca. Fortunately, none was hit, and a moment later a furious Captain Roy Pfaff was on the ship's public-address system.

"Men, there is nothing worse in war than firing at your own men. We've been drilling on aircraft identification ever since we left Norfolk. There is no excuse for this. I'm going to find the man who gave the order to fire and I'm going to have him before the mast.

"But, men, my God, if you're going to shoot at them, hit them!"

When Port Lyautey was secured, I went ashore with the *Texas'* gunnery officer, who was anxious to assess the accuracy of their fire as they attempted to destroy the French arsenal out behind the hills beyond the town.

As we approached the town center, a colonel in a jeep stopped us. "Lieutenant," he said, "one of your big shells landed in the town square and didn't go off. All our traffic is detouring around it. Could you get a party ashore to remove it?"

"Colonel," the lieutenant answered, "we've got an

old rule in the U.S. Navy: Once the shell leaves the muzzle of the gun, it doesn't belong to the Navy any longer. Good day, sir."

The *Texas'* big guns had spent the better part of two days pounding the arsenal, or so we thought. Our spotter planes were reporting that the shells appeared to be landing right on target, but through our binoculars we weren't seeing the sort of explosions that should have followed such marksmanship.

Now ashore, our jeep drove toward the arsenal, huddled under the seaside bluff. As we approached, the road became almost impassable. It was pitted with shell holes. To the side, rubble marked where houses had been. The last shell hole was right on the edge of the arsenal. It had blown down the gate and we passed through, to be hailed by an elderly French soldier. He limped toward us with his cane, his World War I medals neatly arrayed on his chest. He introduced himself as the arsenal superintendent.

"Ah, gentlemen," he said in quite good English. "I see you are from the Navy. From the battleship, perhaps? I am an artilleryman. Two world wars now. And, gentlemen, let me congratulate you. Never have I seen such shooting. You cut every road leading to the arsenal and not one shell inside to do any damage. You have left it intact for yourselves. My congratulations. Splendid shooting, splendid."

Our lieutenant returned his salute and, his reconnaissance completed with something less than satisfaction, ordered the jeep back to the beach.

Clandestine Radio Maroc was moved ashore along

with its crew. Its stay with the Navy had been an uneasy one. Much of the Navy, including its intelligence apparatus, had some trepidation about these civilians from the newspaper and radio business, particularly Jay Allen and his friendship with the Spanish Loyalists and their Communist supporters.

Admiral Kelly had been about as uncivil to him as he had been kind to me, so it was to me that Allen appealed for an audience with the admiral. He said he had to see him on a matter of the utmost importance. I escorted him to the admiral's cabin and the admiral waved us to a chair. Without ceremony Allen launched into his pitch.

"Admiral, you have to realize that, with this war and the recruitment and draft of all these young people, you have a heavy responsibility."

That opening didn't augur well for any chance my friend had of endearing himself to naval authority as represented by Admiral Kelly. Allen, oblivious to the admiral's stiffening neck, plunged on.

"You aren't only their military leader. You must take the place of their mothers and fathers, their teachers, their ministers. And one thing you must teach them is at least some basic principles of the language they are supposed to speak—English!"

He was fast losing both the admiral and me, but his intensity had a certain fascination—a little like an asp coming out of a basket.

"Admiral, I've been hearing it all over this ship. You simply have to tell these young men that there is no word in the English language, let alone a four-letter one, that can be used as a noun, pronoun, verb, adverb and adjective in the same sentence!"

Allen was a big man with an intellect to match, one of the more unforgettable characters of my experience. He was a part of the bohemian culture that marked Paris' Left Bank between the great wars. He was a good friend, and undoubtedly a welcome companion, of Ernest Hemingway's. When he needed funds, he worked as a newspaper reporter and was with the North American Newspaper Alliance covering the Loyalist side of the Spanish Civil War.

According to his story, that beleaguered government one day found itself without a minister of treasury and named him to the post—an appointment that apparently lasted only a day or two. Allen was not particularly forthcoming about his stewardship of the job.

The Clandestine Radio Maroc officers, a couple of reservists from Naval Intelligence and I were invited to breakfast each day in Captain Pfaff's quarters. We were barely past the fruit juice before something would remind Jay of an experience in his past, frequently of a sexual nature. To various degrees, all of us, except Captain Pfaff, seemed to find his stories amusing.

Each morning, as the stories became more raucous, Pfaff would excuse himself from the table. There came the morning that our captain was clearly determined to control his own breakfast table. He grabbed the conversational ball as we sat down and launched into what appeared to be a well-prepared soliloquy. He only got as far as: "I was on the *Panay* at the time and we docked at a little Chinese village up the Yangtze a way from Shanghai. It was called—"

Captain Pfaff only got that far. I'm not repeating the name of the town to protect the innocent, but when he mentioned it, Jay was out of the gate.

"I know the town. Great little town. Right up the hill there, over on the right side of the road, is one of the greatest little whorehouses in the world."

Pfaff choked briefly on his grapefruit and left the table, never to return to breakfast with us.

The landing at Port Lyautey had not gone well. French resistance was heavy; the port we had hoped to use for unloading heavy equipment was blocked by scuttled ships; and the sea conditions were not conducive to landing the stuff by small boat. I heard that the *Texas* was going to take its remaining unloaded ships down to Casablanca. The Port Lyautey story was finished as far as I was concerned, so I hitched a ride. But I had heard wrong. It turned out the *Texas* was bound for home, back to the States.

It seemed clear to me that my career as a war correspondent had crashed shortly after takeoff. While we correspondents assigned to the Navy had sworn that we would stay with our ship and not try to join the Army ashore, I had assumed (and I assumed that the Navy had assumed) that any red-blooded war correspondent was going to jump ship and stay where the action was. That had been my intention and, I was sure, would have been New York's orders if they could have reached me.

Now, however, I was on the way back to Norfolk, like it or not. I saw only one silver lining, as gossamer thin as it was: At least I would be the first correspondent *back* from the North African invasion. Perhaps I would be able to write some stories that might have been censored from the thirteen I had sent from the *Texas*. That was my only hope of getting back into the UP's good graces.

Admiral Kelly sympathized with my predicament, and he was almost as sad as I when he called me to his cabin one morning to report that the *Massachusetts*, the newest and fastest of our battleships, was also on the way home, to Boston. He knew that aboard was one of my competitors, INS's John Henry, and I knew, from what John had told me before we sailed, that he had planned all along to return with the ship.

The *Massachusetts* had spearheaded the action at Casablanca, helping to pummel into submission the queen of the French fleet, the battleship *Jean Bart*. John would have some great stories to tell, and there wasn't much doubt that the *Massachusetts* would beat us back home by days.

My despondency was shared by the crew until one of the Navy pilots, Bob Dally, came up with a brilliant suggestion. "If you can get the Old Man's approval," he said, "I could fly you into Norfolk and probably save a couple of days. Maybe you could still beat the *Massachusetts*."

The admiral did approve, and the minute we were within range of Norfolk, Dally and I climbed into the open cockpit of the little OS2U observation plane. These were the tiniest aircraft in the whole American arsenal. Almost midgets, they were biplanes fitted with pontoons to land and special gear for takeoff.

They nuzzled against a large catapult atop a short railway that ran the width of the battleship. The catapult was fired with one of the battleship's big fourteen-inch shells. This was as close to being shot out of a cannon as one could arrange without joining the circus. Dally revved up the engine to full speed, the cannon fired, my neck snapped, and the plane shot off the rail and dropped toward the water. Dally deftly skimmed the waves and slowly gained altitude. I was on my way to Norfolk.

The flight was uneventful until shortly before the mainland came into view. At that point Dally confided that our gas was low. His attempt at reassurance wasn't as comforting as he meant it to be. "I think it's okay," he said. "I think we'll make it."

We did, sputtering up to the dock on the tank's last drops. Security threw up all sorts of roadblocks to making telephone calls from the air base, and it turned out there was a Navy plane leaving immediately for New York. I skipped the phone call and hopped aboard.

At Floyd Bennett Field in Brooklyn, the same situation. A truck was on its way into New York City, so I skipped the phone call. Thus, I walked into the United Press office in the *Daily News* building unannounced. The teletypes kept pounding, but the rest of the normal background noise went dead. The typewriters had stopped. All faces were turned toward me. Mert Akers, as tough and as good an editor as they came, looked up from his desk. He leaped up and grabbed me in an embrace that may have been a first for him.

"My God, Cronkite, you're safe!" he exclaimed. The words scarcely having cleared his lips, he pushed me from him and added: "And where in hell have you been?"

It turned out I had been missing ever since sailing from Norfolk, almost six weeks. Not one of my dispatches had gotten through from the *Texas*. The ship had radioed them to the British navy's communications center on Gibraltar as instructed, but the British there had failed to relay any of them to our office in London. I later learned that this had happened to several of the American correspondents in North Africa, as the British military favored the dispatches from their own newspapers and press services.

My first question to Akers determined that my INS competition, John Henry, had not yet been heard from. Apparently we had beaten the *Massachusetts* back after all.

After the emotional telephone calls to Betsy and my mother in Kansas City, I sat down to rewrite my previous stories. They hit the wires with an editor's note saying that I was the first correspondent back from North Africa and these were the first uncensored stories from that historic landing.

The note was only half right. They certainly were the first uncensored stories, but I wasn't the first correspondent back. The *Massachusetts* had arrived in Boston a couple of days earlier, but Henry, confident, as were his editors, that I had stayed back in Africa as planned, had gone home for a couple of days' rest before filing.

My rest at home was fairly brief. Shortly I was off to England for, it turned out, the duration. I shipped over on an old Dutch passenger ship, the *Westernland*, that was so slow she was assigned to a convoy of freighters and tankers. She sat in the middle of scores of ships that stretched from horizon to horizon, her big stacks sticking up like a target for marauding U-boats. There were some attacks on the convoy's outskirts. We saw distant flames and heard explosions at night, but we made it to Glasgow unscathed.

The battle in Glasgow was almost as exciting as the one at sea. A couple of American sailors were in the men's room of the Central Hotel when two Scottish soldiers wearing kilts came in. Said one of the sailors to his buddy: "Stand back, this I want to see."

The Scots took umbrage with a couple of haymakers and the fight was on. The noise attracted nationalist partisans on both sides. The brawl filled the men's room, then spilled out into the halls and the lobby of the Central. It was the best fight I've ever seen off a movie screen.

The British Isles took some getting used to. That first day in Glasgow I was shocked to see the headline in the Glasgow *Herald*. "Knockers-Up on Strike," it said.

My immediate reaction was that, while I understood that Britain was a little ahead of us in the organization of labor, this was going too far. Upon inquiry, however, I learned that the knockers-up were indeed organized and were on strike, but that their occupation was not in the line I had imagined.

Few British laborers of that period, it turned out, had alarm clocks. So factories and mines employed people to go around and wake them up in the morning—or, as the British say, knock them up.

Getting used to London was difficult too. England was damp and cold, and relief was nowhere to be found.

Wartime scarcities severely limited the menu available at restaurants, although British cooking was never among the world's great accomplishments. There was a large brick building in the West End that called itself "Mrs. Bradford's School of Cookery." I maintained that it was the only four-story structure in the world dedicated to the art of boiling.

The London blackout was total. At times it was accentuated by the smog—the natural fog off the Thames thickened by the heavy coal smoke that hung over the city. In such complete blackness there was special duty for the girl conductors on the buses—clippies, they were called, in an allusion to their task of punching the tickets. In the impenetrable darkness they walked in front of the buses, guiding them along the street by flashlight.

As we males walked along Piccadilly in that darkness, we could hear the click of heels announce the arrival of a lady of the night. Wearing cheap perfume, she would run her hand along our pants leg. To the neophyte, this might have seemed to be an opening to a street corner mating dance.

Wrong. This was economic foreplay. By feeling the pants cloth, the experienced ladies could tell whether the male was in the American or British Army and was an officer or an enlisted man. On that determination hung the price at which she would open the bidding.

This was the environment into which the cream of American youth was plunged. Too many assumed that what they experienced was typical of England, just as the English assumed that the behavior of tens of thousands of young men barely out of adolescence, uprooted from home and family, was typical of American manhood.

Sometimes the contrasts and conflicts grated. The English, struggling with the rationing of food and fuel, their personal finances strained by the nation's economic squeeze, looked with barely concealed distaste on the apparently profligate American military, which shipped abundant food to their forces, stocked their post exchanges with tobacco, candies, cosmetics and all the appurtenances of the good prewar life and paid their soldiers far better than their British allies did.

And, of course, this comparative wealth proved a powerful attraction to the British girls. This led to the popular saying of the day: "The trouble with the Americans is that they are overpaid, overfed, over-sexed and over here."

The American soldier in World War II was a "GI" (for "government issue"), a self-deprecating term reflecting the dehumanization of military-enforced conformity that was intended to turn individuals into robots instantly responsive to command. (The even more descriptive "grunt," referring to an enlisted man, I believe, came only with the Vietnam War. It led to a serious misunderstanding with one of my television viewers. She wrote in high indignation that I had referred to our heroic boys in Vietnam as "runts.")

It is too bad that tens of thousands of GIs, restricted most of the time to their fully American-ized bases with only occasional forays into the British countryside to rub elbows with the British citizenry, had little opportunity to observe the strength of those remarkable people. Britain stood against the Germans not because of its military, which was ill-prepared, ill-supplied and too often ill-led, but because of the unyielding strength of the British civilians. They suffered with unbelievable stoicism the Luftwaffe's terrible bombing. They gathered together their children and went uncom-plaining into the dank, nearly airless subway stations and other air raid shelters. They came forth to find their cities and villages in ruins, but they picked up the pieces and carried on.

Never before in history, I believe, have any people so patriotically accepted economic dictation as did the British in responding to rationing. Of course there was a black market, but it was so despised that those who dealt on it, even for the most modest supplies, were shunned by friends and neighbors. They queued for everything—at the grocery, at the bus stop, at the restaurant, at the movies, which they called flicks. Only taxis were fair game for individual enterprise. Although few British could afford them, the battle for the limited supply clearly provided a release for accumulated frustrations.

We Americans had some problems with the language. The taxis, for instance. I left our UP office in Fleet Street many nights with the intention of going to Jack's Club, a prewar actors' hangout to which we war correspondents had gravitated.

"Fourteen Orange Street," I would direct the driver.

"Don't believe I got that name, governor," almost invariably came the reply.

I hoped throughout the war to win this one, and on each ride I proceeded through a little litany. I pronounced every possible variation of "Orange" I could think of.

"Beg pardon, governor," was the only response from drivers, who I felt were sincerely troubled by our inability to communicate through a common language.

Finally, before the cab was on an irreversibly

wrong course through London's one-way streets, I would give in.

"Orange Street," I would say, "between Leicester Square and the Haymarket."

"Ew, governor, Orange Street," the driver would answer, and I never detected the slightest difference between his pronunciation and mine. Fifty-five years later, I occasionally test my "Orange Street" against theirs, and even with the homogenizing influence of international television, I get the same result.

There were some sobering, and disappointing, brushes with England. For instance, the day, not long after my arrival, when I discovered my wallet, complete with precious passport, missing from my jacket, which I had hung in the UP cloakroom. The situation was dire, but here was an opportunity I hadn't expected so soon.

Into the phone on my desk I shouted to our operator: "Ring me through to Scotland Yard!"

The clerk who answered didn't sound like Sherlock Holmes or any of the great detectives of British fiction. He demanded my address.

"Just a moment, sir," he said. "I'll ring you through to the Snow Hill Station."

The plebeian touches were only beginning. The voice came on from Snow Hill Station. "Lieutenant Gooch here," it squeaked.

But Gooch of the Snow Hill Station and his meek and seemingly ineffective buddies solved the crime, catching a cat burglar whose Fleet Street depredations had been extensive.

Fleet Street, all the national newspapers crammed into a few blocks, the great pubs filled with journalists throughout their working hours, would be my home for almost two years, until the Allies were on the Continent.

I was lucky enough to be assigned to cover the American and British air forces. The air war was the only war in Europe during that long year of 1943 and those months of 1944 before the landings in Normandy. It shared the headlines at home with the island-hopping invasions in the Pacific.

Sizable numbers of the British four-engined bombers—the Lancasters and Halifaxes—had been carrying the war to the German homeland. British fighters—the doughty Spitfire heroes of the Battle of Britain, Hurricanes and Typhoons—had wrested control of the air over England from the Luftwaffe, and the bombing raids on London were far less frequent and less effective.

By the end of 1942 the American Eighth Air Force, including the four-engined Boeing Flying Fortresses and the Consolidated Aircraft Liberators, was still testing its strength against targets in nearby France. They were testing, too, their daytime strategy, which was based on a belief that well-armed aircraft flying in formation could spread across the sky a field of fire that would defy attacking fighters.

This proved to be wishful thinking. Luftwaffe Messerschmitt and Focke-Wulf fighters, particularly the crack squadrons in the distinctive aircraft with checkered noses, were taking a heavy toll. The

Americans called them "the Abbeville boys," for the French town where the Germans were first based.

The Ninth Air Force, the American force of fighters and medium-range twin-engined bombers, was just getting into action. None of the fighters, British or American, yet had the range to accompany the bombers past the European coast, and they were left alone to battle the full force of the German defenses—both the fighter planes and the heavy flak thrown up by the concentrations of antiaircraft guns that ringed every city.

Our coverage of the air war consisted mostly of interviewing the bomber crews as they returned from their missions. We watched them coming home from battle, most with at least some damage—a cannon hole here or there or the almost delicate lacework of holes left by a trail of machine-gun bullets.

Sometimes the damage was so great that the earth-bound airmen of the headquarters staff gasped in disbelief that the plane had made it back at all. Engines would be missing, tail surfaces almost shot away, wing tips crumpled. And too often, as those crippled ships cleared the edge of the runway, out from the radio operator's window would fly a red flare. Wounded aboard! The ambulances would follow them down the runway to bring what succor was possible the minute they rolled to a stop. Often that stop came more abruptly than planned, as the landing gear, damaged by gunfire, collapsed beneath them.

I watched one day as an aircraft flown by a friend

came gliding down to its landing. It appeared un-damaged, but the red flare burst over it. The ambu-lance was there at the end of the runway and then departed, apparently for the hospital. The open truck that ferried the air crews around the base came roll-ing back toward the debriefing shack and, to my an-xious but apparently hasty eye, all the crew seemed to be aboard. They drew closer and the scene changed drastically. There were only nine of them. There should have been ten. And to a man—or make that, to a boy—they were crying uncontrollably.

Their captain was one of the most popular men of the 303rd Heavy Bombardment Group. He was twenty-six, with a cowlick always adorning his fore-head under his crumpled officer's cap—a "twenty-mission cap" they used to call them when they took out the stiffening wire to give them that daring Air Force look. He had a beguiling smile for every-one and a hearty greeting for all. He planned to marry an Air Force nurse he had met in London. We had spent many evenings together at various London pubs.

His plane was hit by a single machine-gun bullet. It pierced the windshield—and his heart.

With my heart heavy, I wrote the story. I called it "Nine Crying Boys and a Flying Fort." Nine crying boys and a war correspondent who thought he was too tough to cry.

Those young Air Force crews quickly became veterans. One flight usually did the job. The bom-bardier of one of the first Forts over France came back full of wonder at what he called the amazing tactics of the German pilots.

"When they come in to attack, they flash these signals back and forth to each other."

What signals? an amazed debriefing officer asked.

"These red lights they have in the wings of their planes."

When he was told that those were not red lights, those were guns, he fainted.

For what seemed like most of the air war, we correspondents had to take the train back to London to file our stories. British security, with fears of a German invasion unabated, was so tight that we could not report by telephone until our copy was cleared by censors.

When the bombers were going out on a mission, we got a call at our London offices with some coded message from Air Force public relations—"we're going to have a poker game tonight," for instance—that sent us scurrying for the first train to air base country.

I had the joy of traveling with Homer Bigart, the New York *Herald Tribune* reporter who would garner a pair of Pulitzer Prizes in a distinguished career. Homer was plagued with a frightful stutter. The day came when British security lifted the telephone ban. The Air Force said that once a base intelligence officer had cleared our copy, we could use their field phones to dictate it to our London offices.

I dictated my story first, having great difficulty with a very poor phone circuit. Now it was Homer's turn. He stuttered his identification to his office and then turned to the sergeant who was keeping an eye on us in the intelligence office.

"Wo-wo-wo-would you mi-mi-mind re-re-reading this to my off-off-office?" he asked the sergeant.

The sergeant performed an almost impossible physical feat. He slouched *upward*, assuming a position nearly erect.

"Why can't you read it to them?" he asked.

"Da-da-da-dammit," replied Homer, "I'm de-de-de-deaf!"

Gladwin Hill was my AP opposition. He was a fine reporter and writer, erudite and a great story-teller, although inclined to be long-winded as he spun his monologues in a deadly monotone. On one of our railroad trips to the air bases, Gladwin was beguiling us with stories of the great correspondents of World War I, of whom he had apparently read considerably more than we had. After some time, Homer leaned over, tapped him on the knee, and said: "G-g-g-glad, if you're not d-d-d-damned c-c-c-careful, you're going to b-b-b-be the Gladwin Hill of W-w-w-world War Two."

The air forces had plenty of heroes. The war in the sky had plenty of glamour. And for a number of reasons, not least the maintenance of home front morale, there were the inescapable public relations campaigns.

The famed director William Wyler brought over Clark Gable to do a feature movie on Eighth Bomber Command. They were in the Air Force, and it was considered good politics as well as good public relations to get Gable an Air Medal. This required five combat missions. So they picked five milk runs to the nearby coast of France, and he was decorated with all the hoopla that Air Force public relations could muster.

Gable was a good guy. I saw him often during those days, and I thought he was just a little self-conscious about that Air Medal. He had good reason to be, but he was living the role assigned to him and doing it as graciously as possible.

In sharp contrast was Jimmy Stewart. Stewart had enlisted as we got into the war, and gone through flight training to become leader of a squadron of Liberators—among the first in England. He led his group on more than twenty combat missions, always on the toughest ones. And he eschewed any publicity whatsoever. He was a pain in the neck to the public relations people who were assigned to protect rather than exploit him. He even put his squadron off limits to the press until we explained that he was denying any recognition to his crews. He relented enough to let us do the hometown stories about them, but he remained unavailable.

Several of us war correspondents had been appealing for months for the right to accompany the bombers over Europe. The Air Force finally relented and chose eight of us representing the principal news organizations to prepare for flight. This consisted of sending us to something called a Combat Crew Replacement Center. These had been estab-

lished as the casualties over Europe began to out-
run the supply of air crews coming from the States.
The Army assigned infantry soldiers to the Air Force
and sent them to a CCRC to learn aircraft identification, aerial gunnery with a .50-caliber machine gun,
high-altitude survival and first aid and all the rest of
an arcane technology.

The courses lasted several weeks. It was decided
that we correspondents could learn enough for our
purposes in a few days. It became apparent, however, that the Air Force intended to train us as fully
qualified gun crews despite the Geneva Conventions, which, laughingly, were supposed to provide
rules for armies in combat. It stated that civilian correspondents should not carry arms on penalty of
possible execution if captured by the enemy.

Apparently the Air Force considered, rationally
enough, that once you bailed out of an airplane, the
enemy could scarcely know whether you had fired a
gun or not. And they figured that we might as well
be able to take the place of wounded gunners.
Before we left CCRC #11 at Bovingdon, we were
reasonably adept at taking apart and reassembling a
machine gun—blindfolded. This is not a talent I
have found much use for since.

And we were drilled in aircraft identification. A
wonderful little Yorkshireman displayed large sil-
houettes of the aircraft we were likely to encounter,
enemy and friendly. "This 'ere," he lectured, "is the
'Awker 'Urricane. A mighty nice aircraft. It helped
our troops when Rommel had them on the run in the

desert. It protected the boys getting out of Greece. And it was a big help getting out of Norway. The 'Awker 'Urricane, as a matter of fact, was essential in all our defeats."

We considered ourselves a pretty exalted group. An Air Force public relations man dubbed us "the Writing Sixty-ninth," a parody of World War I's legitimate heroes, the Fighting Sixty-ninth. My Writing Sixty-ninth comrades included Andy Rooney of the Army newspaper *Stars and Stripes* and Homer Bigart and Bob Post of *The New York Times*.

Our first mission was the Americans' second raid on Germany. The target: the submarine base at Wilhelmshaven. As we were being assigned to the bases from which we would fly, our public relations major, Bill Laidlaw, complained that we all wanted to go with the Flying Fortresses. We did. The Forts, just the name, had captured the public's imagination as the Liberators had not.

"Come on," Laidlaw said, "one of you has to go with the Liberators. Those guys deserve some recognition too."

It was Bob Post who spoke up with his cultured Ivy League accent: "I'll go with the Liberators. The *Times* doesn't care about headlines."

Bob's Liberator was shot down. He was lost—the only loss among the five of us who got over the target that day. Crews of other Liberators said they saw men bail out of Bob's stricken plane, but they came under heavy ground fire as they floated down.

It was a tough raid. Our fighter escort left us just before the coast of Holland, and over the Frisian Islands, we watched the Luftwaffe fighters taking off to intercept us. We were under constant attack for two and a half hours until we came back under our own fighter protection off the English coast.

And the antiaircraft fire was intense. Golden bursts of explosives all around us, dissolving into those great puffs of black smoke. As the flyboys said: "So thick you could get out and walk on it."

I was assigned to a gun in the bombardier and navigator's plastic nose. They had three guns between them. This was a handy spare. I fired at every German fighter that came into the neighborhood. I don't think I hit any, but I'd like to think I scared a couple of those German pilots. That was part of the job anyway—keep them at bay. I could hardly get out of the plane when we got back—I was up to my hips in spent .50-caliber shells.

Of the sixty-six Forts and Liberators that winged out of England that morning, thirteen didn't return— a loss of almost 20 percent of our force. Back on the ground on the way back to London, Bigart asked me what my lead was going to be.

"I think I'm going to say," I responded, "that 'I've just returned from an assignment to hell, a hell at 17,000 feet, a hell of bursting flak and screaming fighter planes, of burning Forts and hurtling bombs.'"

Homer, whose Pulitzer Prize–winning prose was never tinged with purple, looked at me a moment and finally said: "You—you—you wouldn't."

But my story got good play at home and led the British papers, which have always liked that purple stuff.

Far from winning any medals, I barely escaped being thrown out of England by the Air Force. It had to do with secrecy and censorship.

During wartime, of course, secrecy is a weapon. It was drilled into the troops. Posters warned the general population with signs such as "Loose Lips Sink Ships" or a simple "Hitler's Listening." Mail was censored, sometimes maddeningly so. Everything that even hinted at troop locations, movement, equipment, training, was cut out.

For us war correspondents the secrecy rules were a heavy burden, and tension with the authorities, particularly the censors, was a constant. For most of the war, while England was still under threat of invasion, any form of transmission of a story before the censors' approval was forbidden. We had to write our war stories in the physical presence of the censors in a large press room set up at the Ministry of Information.

Few hours passed there without a near violent scene as an indignant reporter argued with an unmovable censor. The key question at the heart of almost every argument was whether or not the Germans could reasonably be expected to have knowledge of the situation about which the reporter was writing. If the answer was yes and the censors still persisted in killing the story, the ready assumption was that either (1) the censor was stupid, or (2) he or she was covering up a purely political decision. Not infrequently both answers applied.

I got embroiled in a controversy about daylight bombing. At the Casablanca conference a courageous General Ira Eaker, commander of the Eighth Air Force, defying Winston Churchill, sought to persuade President Roosevelt to continue our daylight bombing. The British felt we would be more effective if we abandoned our attempt at high-precision bombing of military targets and adopted their nighttime tactic of area bombing. The pressure was intense. A lot of our missions had had to be aborted when the target area was covered by cloud, denying our bombardiers a clear look below. Of equal importance: Our bombers penetrating Germany in bright daylight were taking a terrible beating from the German defenses.

The British bombed by the so-called Pathfinder technique. They sent a few daring bombers in at low level under the clouds. They dropped the first bombs to light the target and sent up flares to help the following waves of bombers locate the area.

One of our UP reporters, Collie Small, found out that General Eaker had been training a squadron of Liberators in the Pathfinder technique. This was a big story, and Collie and I set up a watch for the break. It came with a raid on Emden, Germany. The Eighth Air Force for the first time bombed through the clouds using the RAF's Pathfinder technique.

I wrote the story expecting censor trouble. It came. The story was killed. I appealed to the chief

U.S. censor, an exceptionally bright colonel recruited from a New York law firm. I pointed out that
the Germans at Emden sure as the devil knew that
there was complete cloud cover through which those
bombs tumbled. Their fighters had flown over the
clouds to attack the Americans, and their antiaircraft
had fired through it. Who were we kidding? Who
were we keeping this story from except the American people?

The colonel agreed and cleared the story. When it
led the British press and the *Stars and Stripes* the
next day, it looked for a while as though it might be
my last story from the European theater. Multi-
millionaire Jock Whitney, an Air Force colonel, was
head of Eighth Air Force public relations. He
phoned early that morning to say he was coming by
my apartment to pick me up, that we had both been
summoned to Eaker's headquarters in the London
suburbs.

When we met, it appeared to me that the usually
unflappable Jock Whitney was near flapping. Eaker
was angry, very angry, he said. The only thing I
gained from the rest of that ride was a chance to end
the speculation among his officers and the press as to
what Whitney carried around in his ever-present
briefcase. The question was asked because it appeared to most of us that he had little active association with Air Force public relations and was more
concerned with fulfilling a sort of self-appointed, but
not unimportant, role as American armed forces
ambassador to British society. He opened the myste-

rious case at one point and I got a peek inside. The letterheads read: "Whitney Investments," "Twentieth-Century Fox," "Greentree Farms" (his racing stables).

Eaker's headquarters was in a prewar English country home, the standard for our high officers. As Whitney and I crossed the parquet floor into the general's office, our footsteps bore an unsettling resemblance to those of a condemned man approaching the execution chamber.

Eaker was more than angry. He was apoplectic with rage. I had violated security. I had ruined the Allied air strategy, possibly lost the war to the Germans. My war correspondent credentials were to be lifted. I was to be sent home in disgrace.

Of course, all of this was politically inspired. The Germans knew exactly what we had done at Emden. But this premature revelation scuttled Air Force plans to withhold the story from the American public and political leaders until after photo-reconnaissance pictures of bomb damage at Emden justified the new strategy. I've always believed, without ever being able to prove it, that Eaker could only have been so upset if he'd thought that Roosevelt himself had not been told—Roosevelt, whom he had persuaded at Casablanca to stand up to Churchill in defense of daylight precision bombing.

Perhaps Washington wasn't as upset as Eaker expected. At any rate, in London calmer heads prevailed and I was not thrown out.

There would be other, lesser air missions. At one

point I accompanied Mitchell medium bombers on a raid to a target on the Belgian coast just across the Channel. The Ninth Air Force told me it would be an interesting target, but they could not identify it until sometime in the future, when I would be glad I had seen it. It turned out to be a launching ramp for the pilotless bombs that the Germans would rain on England in 1944.

And there was the most miserable twenty-four hours I ever spent—riding an RAF Coastal Command flying boat on a submarine patrol along a box pattern out to Iceland and back. It was cold; the sandwiches were soggy and the coffee frigid. We dropped bombs on one suspected submarine that turned out to be a whale. The Geneva Conventions didn't protect whales any better than they protected humans.

That trip had started out badly. The flying boat base in Northern Ireland was even colder than most RAF bases. They apparently allotted one chunk of coal per night for each Nissen hut. I took a mystery story from the officers' lounge, donned my sheep-lined flying suit including hat, gloves and boots, and huddled in my bunk, picking out the book's words as best I could under the single lightbulb that hung halfway down the barracks.

As difficult as it was to turn the pages with those fleece-lined gloves, I finished the book. That is, I finished all that there was of the book. Just as the author was about to disclose the identity of the evil-doer, the book ended abruptly where some even more evil doer had torn out the last pages. (This was not an entirely unique event. Paperback books were particularly vulnerable during the wartime toilet tissue shortage.)

My final wartime adventure with powered flight would come on D-Day.

CHAPTER 5

M Y D-DAY assignment was to stay in London and help write the lead story. My reaction to not getting to accompany the troops was somewhat ambivalent, I'm afraid. I hated missing the experience, but on the other hand, landing on a beach in the face of the massed German armies could prove to be somewhat unpleasant.

The whole world knew that the invasion was imminent. The secret being guarded to the very death was exactly when and where.

I had just turned in when a knock at my apartment door and the following voice identified my midnight visitor as Hal Leyshon. He was an Air Force major in public relations and a good friend from many evening sorties in the pubs of London. Now he stood there in full uniform, dignified, official as all get out.

He demanded to know if my roommate, Jim McGlincy, was there. Jim was somewhere with the troops on the south coast. Was there anybody else there? He confirmed that there wasn't by personally poking his nose into all the rooms and closets. Finally he said: "Cronkite, you've drawn the straw to represent the Allied press on a very important mission. It will be dangerous. No guarantee you'll

get back. But if you do, you'll have a great story.
You can turn it down now, or you can come with me.
And security is on—you can't tell your office."

I dressed. I knew it had to be D-Day. I figured if I
made it, the UP would forgive me.

One squadron of heavy bombers had been ordered
at the last moment to bomb a heavy artillery em-
placement that commanded Omaha Beach. It would
go in just as the troops were landing, and, to ensure
accuracy, it would attack at low level—a maneuver
made difficult by its normal tight formation and one
it had never practiced.

The weather was lousy, but through the broken
clouds I had a good look at the unbelievable armada
of Allied ships. There didn't seem to be room in the
ocean for another vessel. And then, just as we approached the beach—blackout. The cloud cover was
total.

Our bomb bay doors were open, our bombs were
armed to go off on contact. But we couldn't see the
target. And we couldn't see our own planes flying in
close formation on either side. Any collision would
probably set off a chain explosion, wiping out the
squadron. Normally bombs would be jettisoned over
enemy country, but our orders forbade that. No one
knew in that first hour where our airborne had
landed or even how far ashore the landing troops
might have gotten.

Squadron leader Lewis Lyle led that potentially
explosive flight up through the clouds. When we
broke out, he planned to make a full circle and try

again for the target, but then he recalled that during his briefing he'd been told that there would be so many planes at so many altitudes that strict flight patterns had to be observed, and that meant returning home. We landed on a fog-shrouded runway with those bombs still armed. Now, *that* was a hairy landing.

A few days later I would return to Normandy for a longer stay. Intrepid Ninth Air Force engineers, under heavy fire, had managed to lay down a landing strip up on the bluff just behind Omaha Beach. Under pretense of covering the engineers' feat, I flew over for a closer look at the war. There I began to catch up with my colleagues and hear some of their hair-raising stories about their first hours on the beaches. I ran into Charlie Lynch, a redoubtable Canadian who had survived the landing while caring like a mother hen for a case containing three homing pigeons. His outfit, Reuters news service, had used pigeons to beat rivals to news of arriving ships in the days before the telegraph. Now they were up to their old tricks.

Huddled on the beach, he typed out his first dispatch on the special lightweight paper Reuters had supplied. He tucked the folded paper into a capsule on the leg of Pigeon No. 1. And he let the bird fly. It circled him twice and then flew direct as an arrow—toward Berlin. He had no better luck with the other two pigeons, which he damned as feathered turncoats.

My Normandy stay was a short-lived exercise, as

the UP summoned me back to London. I arrived there with my musette bag loaded with some of Normandy's famed Camembert cheese. In that first month or so, when our troops were still pretty well stuck in Normandy, the trademark of an officer returning to London from the front was unmistakable. The heady odor of Camembert stank up many a London elevator.

Not all Camembert survived the invasion, and some suffered an ignominious fate. While a non-English-speaking farmer pleaded, a non-French-speaking Army sanitary crew burned down his barn, certain that whatever it was that was ripening in there constituted a hazard to the health of our troops.

The UP asked whether I would like to be attached to our airborne forces for an upcoming mission. The mission turned out to be the most promising and exciting yet. We were to parachute into Rambouillet Forest north of Paris and take the French capital. With faces darkened, the troops were in the planes ready to take off when the signal came that the ground forces had broken through and were on their way to Paris, and therefore the Airborne would not be needed.

That's how I missed the liberation of Paris, and how we almost lost that beautiful city. We know now that Hitler had ordered the city burned rather than surrendered. The German commander was holding out against carrying out that awful order, but the pressure on him was building.

In this race against time, elements of Patton's Third Army, the U.S. Seventh Army and Montgomery's British forces were ready to enter the city when they were ordered to wait for General Jacques Philippe Leclerc's French Second Armored Division to come up. General Charles De Gaulle had insisted that the French should be the first into Paris, although eventually the Seventh Army's Fourth Division would share the honor. For two days the armies marked time. The Germans were literally lighting their torches when Leclerc finally marched in.

The liberation of Paris has been thoroughly documented, but I have seen no reference to a meeting of two equally famous correspondents and vastly different characters, Ernest Hemingway and Ernie Pyle. Hemingway proclaimed himself the liberator of Paris, and indeed he had, without benefit of military escort, taken a jeep and a couple of friends into the city some hours ahead of the armies. A hero to the younger correspondents, he was lionized nightly at the bar of the Hôtel Scribe, official press headquarters.

Pyle had spent his first days in Paris with the troops, but when he finally arrived at the Scribe he became the bar's magnet of the moment. The story goes that Hemingway appeared in early evening to find a large group around Pyle at one end of the bar. Hemingway's entrance went unnoticed as he took a place at the other end. He pounded the bar to get the bartender's attention. "Let's have a drink here," he commanded. "I'm Ernest Hemorrhoid, the rich man's Ernie Pyle."

Back in London I remained available for the

next airborne mission, and over the next couple of months there must have been eight or ten of them planned, only to be scrubbed when our speedy ground advance overran the drop zone before we could get under way. The war came to me in London, however. Shortly after D-Day the Germans unleashed their V-1s on the city. These were bombs to which they had attached wings, a gyroscopic piloting device and a little one-cycle engine. They were devilish weapons.

Ed Beattie of the UP and I saw the first one arrive in Bloomsbury as we left the nearby Ministry of Information one night. The air raid sirens had sounded, but in the absence of any obvious action, Beattie and I were outside looking for a cab when we heard this lone aircraft, its engine clearly malfunctioning, just clearing the housetops with flames pouring from its tail area. It crashed with a terrible explosion a few blocks away.

The government announced the next morning that the explosion had been the result of a gas leak. Beattie and I, and untold scores of others, who had witnessed the crash of that plane, knew that this was a lie. Our efforts to pierce the mystery, however, produced no information except some mysterious knowing looks from defense officials. A couple of days later the euphoria that Londoners had felt with the invasion of the Continent was shattered with the announcement that the desperate Germans had turned a new weapon against them.

Hundreds of the so-called flying bombs were

aimed at London from those launching sites on the Channel coast. Air raid sirens were screaming again, day and night. The people were told that they would probably have fifteen seconds to seek shelter after the bombs' engines quit. The bombing was so random and so frequent, however, that few people stayed for long in the shelters, despite the fact that the bombs exploded on impact and spread their death and destruction over wide areas.

It was the second week of the new attacks that I got mine. I lived on Buckingham Gate Road, a couple of blocks from Buckingham Palace and overlooking the Guards Barracks and the parade ground. It was a Sunday morning and I had just rung for our building's ancient servant, George, to order breakfast.

The air raid sirens went off, followed a moment later by the unmistakable roar of a flying bomb overhead. I ducked back from the window just as the bomb hit the Guards Chapel, a few hundred yards away. It was in the middle of the service and many high-ranking Allied officers, and some British wives, died there.

Our old apartment building didn't fare too well. The hall door with its glass pane blew off its hinges, the plumbing broke, and the dust of centuries shook out of the cracked walls, forming a blinding, choking cloud. In disasters like that there is eerie silence in the first moments. Ours was shattered by someone crunching through the splintered glass that covered the hall's tile floor. There was a knock on the torn door frame. There stood George, holding a towel over a bleeding eye. And, so help me, he said: "Did you ring, sir?"

By God, and thank God, there will always be an England.

George was my most unforgettable Englishman. There was another I met also during the V-1 attacks. The frontline against them was on the Dover-Folkestone coast, to which the British had brought practically every antiaircraft gun and barrage balloon in the British Isles. The guns behind their sandbag bunkers were shoulder-to-shoulder along the coast, with the cables from the barrage balloons draped behind them in the hope of catching the V-1s that escaped the concentrated antiaircraft fire.

Overhead, Spitfires flew constant patrol. Their pilots had developed a daring, potentially suicidal technique to bring down their pilotless enemies. They would fly alongside the comparatively slow-moving bomb, maneuver their wing tip under the wing tip of the bomb and tilt the bomb off course. Once the bomb tilted, its guidance system became terminally confused, and the bomb went off in a direction its Nazi masters had not intended—sometimes even back toward its launching site in Belgium.

Throughout the war the British towns on the Channel had been subject, from time to time, to rather desultory, usually ineffective shelling from the German-occupied coast. The constabulary, on those occasions, rolled out onto the main roads leading into town signs that were themselves representative of British understatement. They simply said: "Warning. Shelling in Progress."

The signs stayed out during the months of the V-1 battle. The friendly antiaircraft shells raining their debris on the coast, the stricken V-1s exploding overhead or crashing on the countryside, the never-ceasing roar of the Spitfires—it was a noisy and dangerous war.

My first night there I found myself, with a Canadian gun crew, huddled under my helmet and crouching against the sand parapet. I felt a tug at my trench coat and there, alongside me, was a chap of near midget dimensions. He was wearing a black bowler hat, a black overcoat, and carrying a furled umbrella. And he was shouting something to me.

I couldn't understand him and I was a little too preoccupied to care. But he persisted. More tugs. More shouts. Finally I leaned down to catch his message: "I'm the best piano player in Folkestone."

Later around the pub bar that night I was recounting this strange episode to a couple of other correspondents. I finished the story to a round of laughter when the bartender leaned over and said quite earnestly: "Oh, that's Professor Snodgrass. And he is the best piano player in Folkestone."

After the aborted airborne mission to liberate Paris, the combined airborne command in London grew increasingly nervous, overcome by a palpable fear that the war would end before they could get their forces into action—and collect the resulting ribbons and promotions. So they set up a number of missions of various sizes, only to have the ground forces occupy the landing zones before they could get their troops in the air.

I was assigned to one such mission, which was to land outside Brussels. It consisted only of a Polish battalion. I forget what the darned mission was, but it was a hair-raiser. For one thing, the Free Poles were a wild bunch. They were tough and mean and impatient to get back at the Germans—and the Russians, for that matter. Few of them spoke English, and we were going to land among not only German soldiers but French- and Flemish-speaking Belgians. The chances were good that I would be shot by someone in this Babelian hell.

This mission, as well, was called off, but it left me with a strange trauma. Back in my London apartment I had a frightful nightmare of being captured in battle by strange people speaking an unknown language. They were jabbing bayonets into me and demanding answers to questions I couldn't understand. I awoke in a cold sweat.

Thank God, it was only a dream. But the voices continued. They were subdued, but they were angry, and they were in some totally unintelligible language. They were coming from behind the closed door to my living room.

I did this James Bond performance. I turned the knob slowly and gently. I pushed the door open just a crack, so that, without alerting them, I could hear better these strangers in my home. With that, one of them lapsed into English: "You've been listening to the Welsh-language broadcast of the BBC."

The airborne call that counted came that fall. The operation was called Market Garden. The mission was to land three divisions of airborne troops to grab a road north through the Netherlands to the bridge over the Rhine, which the Dutch call the Maas, at Arnhem. The main body of the British army under Montgomery would then roll down this corridor, across the bridge, and turn east to invade the German homeland.

I was assigned to the U.S. 101st Airborne, ordered to land just outside Eindhoven to take the southern extremities of the road. I had no knowledge of any of this when the telephone call came on that morning in September '44, with the prearranged code to come along on "that picnic we'd been talking about."

I went to press headquarters in Grosvenor Square, decked out, as previously ordered, in full combat regalia. To my surprise, there was Stanley Woodward, star sports reporter of the New York *Herald Tribune*. I had not met him previously. He had just arrived in London, the *Trib* having finally yielded to his pleas for an overseas assignment. The man the paper had designated for the airborne mission, Ned Russell, was in Paris. When a message from the military was left on the *Trib* desk for Russell instructing him to show up at 20 Grosvenor, the dutiful Woodward appointed himself Russell's substitute without having any idea of the nature of the story.

Stanley was a little overaged for combat duty—overaged and somewhat overweight. His eyesight was extremely poor. He showed up at 20 Grosvenor in his dress uniform—khaki jacket, pink trousers, oxford shoes, and with a demand to know what this was all about. So tight was security that I did not know any of the details, nor did the public relations staff. I suggested to the baffled Woodward that he accompany me to our assigned base. Once in the car, I whispered to him that this was an airborne mission, that we would be parachuting into someplace, presumably behind German lines. It seems hardly adequate to say that he was astounded. He stared long and hard at me through his bottle-thick glasses.

At 101st headquarters we found the officers' mess in a fit of a mission-eve adrenaline rush—aided and abetted by a considerable infusion of alcohol. We were embraced, toasted and regaled with horror stories of the 101st's hairy landing in Normandy. Sometime midevening we were invited to General Maxwell Taylor's quarters for a private briefing. At this point Woodward could not be found. I had last seen him at the bar, the center of attention as he spun sports stories for an enthralled audience. I guessed that the 101st had discouraged him from attempting the landing.

Taylor's deputy gave me the bad news. I wasn't going by parachute. I was assigned to a glider. I had seen the fate of the gliders in Normandy—impaled on the stakes the Germans had planted, splintered to kindling by midair crashes, crumpled by hard landings. I would have refused the assignment if I had thought I could face my colleagues ever again. At least, I rationalized, with the tow plane a blissful couple of hundred feet ahead, it ought to be a nice quiet way to die—no roaring engine, just a nice silent glide into eternity.

I was wrong. Those American Waco gliders were built of aluminum tubing with canvas skins. The canvas cover beat against the aluminum, and it was like being inside the drum at a Grateful Dead concert.

Over the drop zone, the second surprise: The tow rope was dropped and down we went. No glide—a plunge almost straight down. I was muttering to myself that I knew these things wouldn't fly. Actually we had a great pilot, doing it just right. The technique was to dive, right up until the point just before the G-force would snap the wings off the plane—a mad dive to evade enemy ground fire.

For the same reason, our pilot didn't let us roll long once we were on the ground. As soon as he felt the ground was soft enough—the good loose black dirt of a potato patch—he nosed the glider in, totally oblivious to the danger he was facing right up there in front. The plane did a half flip, the dirt came pouring in, our helmets went flying off.

I was with a headquarters company of about fourteen men. We dug ourselves out of the dirt. I grabbed a helmet and slapped it on my head. There was some enemy fire. Gliders collided overhead, spilling their guns and human cargo around us. I crouched and ran toward what I thought was our rendezvous point—a drainage ditch at one side of the large landing zone. I glanced behind me, and there, apparently following me, were several men. One of them shouted: "Hey, Lieutenant, are you sure we're going in the right direction?"

I shouted back that I wasn't a lieutenant; I was a war correspondent. With a full GI vocabulary of unrepeatable words he advised me, rather strongly, that I was wearing a helmet with an officer's big white stripe down its back. It was the only chance I had to lead troops in the whole war. I didn't do badly. The drainage ditch was that way.

I don't recommend gliders as a way to go to war. If you have to go, march, swim, crawl—anything, but don't go by glider.

I got to that drainage ditch and was working my way toward the copse at the end. In that little woods was supposed to be the headquarters' company, and the radio transmitter that would get my story out. I stumbled on a heavyset fellow perched uncomfortably, implausibly, on the edge of the ditch. His helmet was pushed back on his head, which he held in his hands in obvious anguish.

"Stan?" I asked. "Is that you, Stan?"

Woodward looked up through bloodshot eyes, the picture of a man with a raging hangover.

"Nobody told me," he mumbled, "that it was going to be like this."

Soldiers in combat are scarcely paragons of fashion, but Stan's habiliment was ridiculous. It seems that he had passed out at the bar and the fun-loving officers who had become his drinking buddies, certain that he wanted to go along, had dressed him and placed him aboard the glider.

Finding combat clothing for his outsize frame had presented an insuperable challenge. The pants were at least four sizes too small. They wouldn't close at the fly and were held together at the beltline by a piece of rope. He had already split the jacket at the shoulders. Fortunately, the boots, at least, fit.

Stan turned out to be a good sport and one terrific correspondent in the few days he was at the front. Our greatest difficulty was at night, when he could not see at all, and our greatest challenge was navigating down the slick sides of the Zon Canal, onto a tiny raft made of empty fuel tins, and up the other side.

The Zon bridge was our first objective upon landing, but the Germans blew it up before we got there. A good part of the 101st had crossed the Zon on those rafts. The Germans had pulled back from Eindhoven, the city was undamaged, and the celebrating populace was out in force.

Some miles south of us, Montgomery's forces took two days longer than planned to get across the Escaut Canal. The 101st had secured its part of the road north, the 82nd had its bridge at Nijmegen, but the poor British airborne had landed on top of a division of German tanks on the move. The Germans pulverized them, and only a pitiably small percentage made it back across the Maas. British reinforcements arrived far too late to be helpful, and the Allied line would be anchored at Nijmegen for the winter.

But there would be a lot of action before that stalemate developed. At Eindhoven the British had to wait for a temporary bridge to be flung across the Zon. One smaller bridge had remained intact on a country road just outside the town. The 101st had left it alone, hoping the Germans would not destroy it before the British arrived.

The first patrol from the slowly approaching British reached Eindhoven. The 101st artillery commander, General Higgins, rushed to meet the convoy of three armored vehicles. He greeted a cheery young lieutenant perched in the turret of the lead vehicle. Higgins pointed toward the bridge and told the lieutenant to rush it from this side while Higgins ordered a coordinated attack by the 101st from the far side.

"I say, General," responded the lieutenant, "you know my chaps have been going since dawn and we haven't had our tea yet."

Higgins was reaching for the huge wrench, the tank tool, on the side of the vehicle. At that moment, the Germans blew up the bridge. They saved the lieutenant from a probably fatal beating.

Now the bumper-to-bumper parade of British vehicles, brought to a full stop, jammed the highway and the narrow streets of Eindhoven. At dusk the Luftwaffe hit this choice target. The fuel trucks burned. The ammunition trucks turned all of Eindhoven into a display of deadly fireworks.

My old UP friend Bill Downs, long since with CBS, had arrived with the British. I had joined him in his jeep, and when the bombers came, we were on the edge of the huge Phillips Park, part of Eindhoven's vast Phillips Electric works. We abandoned the jeep and leaped over a fence into the park. We huddled under the fallen trees, but somehow we became separated.

When the bombing was over and the sky was lit by the fires and the exploding ammunition, I began calling for Downs and conducting a somewhat tentative search for him. The Luftwaffe had taken to dropping butterfly bombs, small antipersonnel devices that floated down slowly enough to lodge in trees and bushes. I was thinking of them almost as much as I was thinking of finding Downs or his body.

Eventually I gave up and went back to the fence. An interesting phenomenon presented itself. Human beings are capable of extraordinary feats of physical prowess when under extraordinary stimulus. Downs and I had leaped that fence with no trouble. Now I discovered that there was no way I could clear its seven-foot height. No way, that is, had it not been for the bomb-blasted tree that served as a convenient bridge.

I found Downs' jeep where we had parked it, covered with dirt and tree limbs. On its back was his recording machine, a cumbersome device like a large record player. I didn't know how to operate it, but I dusted it off, pressed a button or two until the record spun, and then delivered a eulogy to Downs. I left it there in the hope that someone might find it and recover the recording. I never heard of it again.

I visited nearby bomb shelters looking for Downs among the frightened men and women and crying children. No luck. Downhearted and beginning to compose in my mind my letter to his family, I hitched a ride to Brussels and its wire facilities, where I would not be under the tight wordage restrictions of the 101st Division's radio.

I checked into the Metropole Hotel and, before going to my room, dropped into the bar. There stood Downs, immaculate in a clean dress uniform. My emotions seesawed from delight at his survival to anger.

"Damn, Bill, I spent all that time at risk of life and limb from those mines yelling for you, looking for you, and you just up and left me there."

He found his feeble excuse in the fact that the name Cronkite sounds like the German word for "sickness." "Walter," he said, "I figured the Germans were going to follow up that bombing with a ground attack, and I'll be damned if I'm going to wander through that park calling out 'Cronkite, Cronkite.' They would have figured I was sick and hustled me off to a hospital in Berlin."

Downs and I returned to Holland, and a few days later we were a little in front of our troops. We ran into some heavy small arms and mortar fire, scrambled from the jeep and took refuge in a ditch. We had been there a while when Downs, lying behind me, began tugging at my pants leg. I figured he had some scheme for getting us out of there, and I twisted my neck around to look back at him. He was yelling to me: "Hey, just remember, Cronkite. These are the good old days."

The 101st held that long sliver of road for some weeks before the British fanned out and secured the whole area. It was tricky, with the Germans occasionally sharing a few miles of the road for an hour or two at a time, usually under cover of night. Out on that road one night, my GI driver and I heard the clank of tank treads. Certain that there weren't any Allied tanks in the area, we pulled over to the side and held our breath. Five German tanks came lumbering down the road. They passed within feet of us, and a few of their drivers shouted a greeting. They apparently assumed we were German. They rumbled on and we breathed again.

As the front cooled down, we had a visit from royalty. King George paid his first visit to British troops on the Continent—a brief sortie of a few hours. British army public relations named a pool of correspondents to cover his arrival at Eindhoven Airport, and I was selected as the American representative.

I was still in the same airborne combat outfit I had been wearing for the past couple of weeks. As a matter of fact, I was rather proud of my airborne combat boots, my pants legs tucked into them in the best paratrooper fashion.

Before we were to be escorted to the airport,

Montgomery's press aide, a Brigadier Neville, came into the press room. Neville was some sort of civilian retread, but he affected the most lampooned of the British colonial service. He carried a riding crop that he whipped at his boots as he walked, as if to urge himself along.

"Pool correspondents," he announced. "Attention! Inspection!"

Ridiculous, pompous and unprecedented orders to a gaggle of civilian correspondents. But the subservient British press marched forward. I slouched after them. They passed Neville's inspection, receiving only some minor suggestions, but apparently the colonel was repelled by my appearance. He looked with particular disfavor on my boots.

"Get this man a pair of gaiters," he ordered.

Gaiters were the white leggings the British army wore over pants leg and boot top. I wasn't about to give up my airborne combat boots for those ugly wrappings.

"Brigadier Neville," I said, "we Americans dumped a helluva lot of tea into Boston Harbor in 1773 to avoid wearing those gaiters, and I'm not about to start now."

It may have been my finest hour. The British Empire wilted before my determination, and I met the King in my good American combat boots.

With Market Garden over, UP sent me to Brussels to cover increasingly tense civil unrest. The group that, since the German occupation in 1940, had been serving in London as the Belgian government-in-exile had returned to the capital to assume the reins of government. Conservatives all, they suspected the Belgian underground, which had been heroically harassing the Nazi occupiers, of being Communists, or at least of being heavily influenced by them. It ordered the underground to turn in its arms.

Many members of the underground resisted the order and threatened to march on Brussels. The government ringed the principal buildings with tanks, and there were a few small skirmishes. My AP counterpart had been on the ground for some time, he had good contacts, and he was giving the UP a good licking when I showed up.

That first day I pulled together what I thought was a usable story and cabled it off to New York. Within an hour or so I had a cable back: "Rocks [our code word for the AP] far superior for third straight day. Can you do anything?"

It was from Harrison Salisbury, our foreign editor. Time delays in transmitting cables made it impossible to determine whether his message had been sent before or after the arrival of my dispatch. At any rate, his cryptic message raised a question that has plagued me to this day. How was I to read that second sentence? The interpretation meant a great deal to my future, and my present. Where did the emphasis go?

"*Can* you do anything?"

"Can *you* do anything?"

"Can you do *anything*?"

I didn't dare query Harrison at the time, and in

later years he pretended to have no memory of the incident.

I was in Brussels covering Montgomery's Twenty-first Army Group when the sky fell in. On December 16, 1944, Hitler took his last big gamble. He unleashed Field Marshal Gerd Von Rundstedt, who sent a quarter of a million men crashing through the Ardennes Forest of Luxembourg. He hoped to advance through Belgium to the sea at Antwerp in an effort to split the Allied armies and perhaps win enough time for the Wehrmacht to organize the defense of the Third Reich.

The U.S. military leadership had recognized its weakness in the area. Only a few days before the German attack General Omar Bradley was briefing some visiting newspaper editors at his Luxembourg headquarters. One of them pointed to the thin American line through the Ardennes. Bradley acknowledged that this was "a calculated risk" but said it was the American opinion that no army would attempt to attack along the narrow roads through that thick forest in the dead of winter.

The offensive caught the 60,000 men of the four American divisions facing von Rundstedt by surprise. The attack sent them into headlong retreat, a new experience for U.S. forces in the European theater. Nineteen thousand Americans and 40,000 Germans would die in the ten-day Battle of the Bulge.

I was asleep in my Brussels apartment when I was awakened by the UP's First Army correspondent, Jack Fleischer. He was dirty, unshaven, obviously tired and considerably shaken. He had reached Brussels after being caught in the maelstrom of American men and vehicles fleeing the front in a disorganized retreat. He wrote a dispatch for me to try to get through the censors and remounted his jeep to return to the front. I filed the dispatch (it never went through) and sent another advisory to our Paris headquarters stating that I, too, was en route to the action.

Only later did a message from Paris catch up with me. It said: "Communications difficult. Can you coordinate coverage of front?"

Hell, communications weren't difficult, they were nonexistent. Coordinate coverage? The divisions and the armies themselves had lost touch with each other.

Fleischer would die later when a stray bomb hit near the First Army press camp. I was luckier. Fighting my way through that oncoming chaos of trucks, guns, tanks, marching soldiers—a retreat that was close to panic—I finally reached Luxembourg City. The center of town was oddly, eerily calm, seemingly almost oblivious to the terror on the roads outside. I checked into the Cravatt Hotel.

For the rest of the Battle of the Bulge, several of us who were fast enough to get ensconced there commuted from that fur-lined foxhole to the war each day, suffered through the snowstorms and the terrible cold that were bedeviling our troops, and returned each night to a bottle of champagne, a hot bath and a warm bed. If Episcopalians are supposed to suffer guilt from such selfish indulgence, I'm afraid I missed that day at Sunday school.

Our troops had been regrouped and the front was more or less stabilized by the second day. Then, like the cavalry of old, General George Patton's Third Army rode to the rescue. It had been facing the Germans across the Rhine down south, but Patton, in one of the greatest military feats of the war, turned it around in forty-eight hours and threw it into the battle.

So I joined the Third Army press camp that set up in Luxembourg. Patton came back from his first inspection trip to the front to meet the correspondents. There before him in a school auditorium was the usual assembly of thirty mostly unshaven, dirty newsmen. But in the front sat six beautifully coiffed ladies in hand-tailored uniforms. They were fashion writers whom the War Department had accredited to go to Paris. They had been on a little public relations trip to quiet Luxembourg, arranged by movie-handsome General Hoyt Vandenberg, commander of the Ninth Air Force, whose headquarters were there. They had been trapped by the same terrible weather that had grounded Vandenberg's planes and given Von Rundstedt cover for his offensive.

Patton, his guns strapped to his side, mounted the stage, looked down at the women and said, in his high, cracking voice, permanently strained by shouting over the din of too many cavalry horses: "Well, I didn't know there were going to be ladies present. Sort of cramps my style. What I was going to say was, what do you do when you got a monkey hanging by his tail in a tree? You cut his balls off. That's what I'm going to do to Von Rundstedt. Dismissed."

Patton was tough, brilliant. He was highly respected for his talent—and feared for his temper. His career had barely survived a pair of incidents in Sicily when he had slapped hospitalized soldiers he thought were malingering.

During preparations for D-Day, the Allies had devised an elaborate plan to trick the Germans into thinking the invasion was going to come not in Normandy, but at the far more obvious place, across the Channel at its narrowest point, the Pas de Calais. They assembled a decoy army in England with trucks and armor made of wood and balloons and a headquarters company presided over by Patton. They filled the air with phony messages intended to be intercepted by the Germans. There was a welcoming ceremony in one of the nearby British towns. The irrepressible, always bellicose Patton proceeded to tell the assembled townspeople that it was the destiny of America and Britain to rule the world. He added the Russians as an afterthought, but it was far from the most tactful of statements and the damage was done.

Washington was furious, and there were again demands that Patton be sent home. Some years later General Eisenhower told me what happened next. Ike's story went something like this:

"I thought I had no choice but to fire George and I

called him in. He came into my office wearing that crazy helmet liner of his, painted red with the big stars on it. He knew what was coming, of course. He stood at attention at my desk, looking straight ahead.

"I asked him to sit down. He said he preferred to stand. So I told him, 'Well, at least stand at ease.' And I began telling him all the reasons that he was in trouble again.

"Tears began welling up in his eyes. I was just getting to the final line, in which I was going to order him back home, when I realized that I simply couldn't do it. I needed him too much. I just kind of bit the bullet and said to myself, 'Dammit, I'll just take the licks if I have to on this one.'

"I got up and walked around to George and said: 'George, despite all that, I'm going to give you another chance.'

"Well, George let out a sob and threw his head on my shoulder. And the darned helmet liner came off and clattered across the floor. It was just so darned ridiculous, I laughed. When I did, George pushed me away and said: 'Thank you for that, and I'll stay, you son of a bitch.' And he stamped out."

Patton had earned his reprieve in the Ardennes. It was war in the worst of winter conditions. One of his fixations was that windshields should be kept lowered on all vehicles so that the sun's reflection would not help enemy gunners. In the Battle of the Bulge, that bordered on cruelty. The temperature was well below zero and the windchill factor, even at the slow pace we made along the crowded roads, was almost insufferably bitter. We wrapped our faces in our woolen scarfs and, resembling Washington's troops at Valley Forge, were almost indistinguishable one from the other.

On one of the early days after I joined the Third Army press camp we were caught briefly in a fire-fight in a Belgian hamlet south of Bastogne. We piled out of the jeep and I ducked into a doorway. There was a GI there, and every once in a while he'd lean out and take a potshot with his carbine at the Germans down the block.

Ever the reporter, I shouted: "What's your name? What's your hometown?"

He shouted the answers back over his shoulder, keeping a wary eye out the door.

"And what's your unit?" I asked.

Now he turned and gave me a long look.

"Hell, Mr. Cronkite," he said, "I'm your driver."

That was the day, as we were coming back from the front, that my helmet bounced off and rolled into a field. The driver stopped, but my mission of retrieval was short-lived. In that field were signs in three languages left by a trio of armies. They all said: "Danger. Mines." We resumed our trip with me helmetless.

One inviolable rule in Patton's army was, helmets at all times, and trouble was on its way down that road. Here came Patton's little entourage behind us—his outriding jeep with a flashing red light and siren, the general himself and another escorting jeep behind. They stopped just in front of us, blocking the urgent traffic of war like cops at a minor highway accident. Out of the general's jeep bounced a full colonel who came striding back to us.

"Okay, soldier," he shouted at me. He didn't need to shout. His face was a foot from mine. "Name, rank and serial number, and where's your helmet?"

I took the questions in reverse order. "My helmet," I said, "bounced off and is out in that minefield."

That raised a look of utter disgust. But I bravely continued: "And I'm not a soldier; I'm a war correspondent."

Disgust changed to a sort of frantic disappointment.

"Stay as you are!" he ordered, and returned to Patton's side. We watched him gesticulate, pointing to the field and then raising his arms in the universal sign for "what can I do?" hopelessness. Whereupon Patton uttered a single word that might have been an expletive well known among the troops. The colonel climbed in and they drove on.

The most dramatic part of the Ardennes battle was the effort to relieve my old mates, the 101st, who were surrounded in Bastogne. The world followed the dramatic fight as they held that road junction which was vital to von Rundstedt's progress.

It was there, of course, that General Anthony McAuliffe answered a German demand to surrender with a single-word response that will live in military lore and will always be exemplary of the 101st spirit. He handed this answer to the German courier: "Nuts!"

The drama at Bastogne offered a test of courage

that I flunked. Units of the Third Army, led by Lieutenant Colonel Creighton W. Abrams, Jr.'s Thirty-seventh Tank Battalion, were desperately trying to break through to them. I was at Abrams' forward command post on the morning when word came that one of his patrols had made it to Bastogne. Just minutes later General Maxwell Taylor arrived on the scene. He was the 101st's commander, but he had been back in Washington when his troops were thrust into the Ardennes fight. Taylor, despite the cold, was still scantily clad in the dress uniform he was wearing when he hastened from Washington.

He swept into Abrams' "office" in the kitchen of a half-destroyed farmhouse, took a quick look at the map, got a hasty briefing and came out to climb back into his jeep.

"Cronkite," he said, "I'm going to Bastogne. Do you want to come?"

The story would have been great—first correspondent into Bastogne. On the other hand, how would I get the story out? There was no communication link from Bastogne, and in the days before I had my story on the wires, those correspondents monitoring military communications on the outside would be reporting the drama.

That's the excuse I gave to Taylor, and tried to explain to myself. But I knew the truth—and I suspect he did: Taylor's drive to Bastogne could well have been a suicide mission. A lot of glory, perhaps, for a career officer; simply a sad footnote for a war correspondent.

The 101st and their other airborne colleagues were always somewhat amused by the world's concern about their being surrounded at Bastogne. As one told me when I finally got into Bastogne: "What was all the excitement? We were where we are trained to be—behind the enemy lines. We are *supposed* to be surrounded!"

Not quite as cowardly as the Bastogne choice was my decision not to be killed on Christmas Day. Instead I thought I might make use of the day to do a story I had been postponing about a new tactic used by the artillery. It was called T.O.T. for "time on target." By using barometric fuses that could be set to detonate at precise heights, and various ammunition from concrete-piercing to antipersonnel shrapnel, and by timing an entire artillery battery's fire to reach the target simultaneously, an entire village could be destroyed in one devastating blow.

This was all new and still secret when I went to a battery outside Luxembourg for the story. The colonel in charge was delighted to have some press attention.

"Let me show you how this would work," he offered. "This is our sector map. Pick a target."

I pointed haphazardly at a crossroads town. The colonel peered for a moment at the map and then called out the coordinates to a sergeant at a nearby telephone switchboard. The sergeant repeated the coordinates several times, presumably to various batteries. The colonel and I were in the middle of our chat when suddenly the countryside erupted with a violence I had hardly known before. I cringed.

"What was that?"

"That's the T.O.T. you ordered," the colonel answered. "That town's had it."

"But," I protested, "I thought you were just giving me a demonstration."

"That was the demonstration. Oh, don't worry about it. You picked a good target. We've had our eye on it for a while. It's going to take a lot of cleaning up before the Germans can use that crossroads again."

And they call it the fortunes of war.

Von Rundstedt got as far into Belgium as he did because the weather favored him. The snow and fog that covered his attack hung on for eight days. It grounded the Allied air forces. I was lucky enough to be at a Ninth Air Force forward control point the day the pilots' discouraging helplessness ended. The weather gave promise of breaking, and U.S. P-47 Thunderbolts were patrolling above the clouds, the battleground shrouded somewhere below them. At control we were listening to the occasional radio chatter between them when there came the flight leader's electrifying words: "Blue flight, blue flight. I think I see an opening down there. Let's go. . . . Follow me." And a moment later: "Jesus Christ, there's the whole goddamn German army, boys. Okay, follow me, follow me. Wow-ee!"

The rest of the Ninth fighter force would be following him in short order, as the weather continued to clear. In their own words, they "pranged the Germans good." The smoke from the burning tanks and trucks and guns they left behind was the funeral pyre of Von Rundstedt's army and Hitler's dreams.

The war in Europe would end a few months later. Just before the general surrender at Reims, the Germans in western Holland surrendered to the Canadians. A Canadian correspondent and I disobeyed the press officer's orders to take a place far back in the column that would enter Amsterdam. He said there might be mines and the army didn't know how the still-armed Germans would react to our arrival. We figured they just didn't want correspondents out in front spoiling their parade, so we took a back road around the troops and entered Amsterdam first.

From our open command car we took the salute of confused German troops lining the route and the unrestrained adulation of the thousands of Dutch who jammed the streets. They pelted us with tulips until our car was fender deep in them. Tulips are heavy flowers. In bunches they are dangerous. The only blood I spilled in the war was that day—hit by a bunch of tulips tied together with a piece of wire.

Our greatest difficulty was finding a place to relieve ourselves. The celebrating Dutch were everywhere, and the crowds were so thick that, once out of the car, we would never make it through to a men's room. But just outside Amsterdam, as we sped toward The Hague, there appeared an opening. No Dutch were visible. We took refuge behind a dike. We had hardly begun taking care of our needs when the Dutch arrived in force—men, women, children. They poured over the dike and swept us up in their arms, totally oblivious to the fact that we were, at least partially, exposed.

The residents of western Holland had suffered horribly in the long winter of 1944–45. With our airborne liberation of eastern Holland, they and their Nazi occupiers had been cut off from the German homeland. What little food there was, the German army took. We found the Dutch near starvation. They had been reduced to eating tulip bulbs. Their clothes hung on their gaunt forms. They looked like children in their parents' clothing.

That day of liberation I went around to where the UP office had been before the German occupation. And there, sitting on the front stoop, were three members of our rather large prewar staff—waiting for the UP correspondent they knew would be coming. Through their tears of joy they couldn't wait to tell me that they had a teleprinter available, that we could put the UP back in business. With incredible courage, they had disassembled one of our teletypes when the Germans entered Amsterdam. Each of them had taken a third of the parts to hide in their homes. If they had been caught, they would have faced certain execution.

Just as the UP gang in Amsterdam had risked their lives for the press service, there was the redheaded former employee of the English-language *Herald Tribune* in Paris who, throughout the German occupation, kept the paper's presses greased and ready to roll when liberation came. The Nazis never caught on, and when the first New York *Herald Tribune* war correspondent rolled up to that old Rue de Berri building, the self-appointed guardian of the presses switched her skirts coquettishly, made a slight bow and presented her prize.

The wire services' race to reestablish communications in Western Europe was on. The UP bypassed Amsterdam in favor of Brussels as our Low Countries headquarters, and there we won the race. Sam Hales, converted from a UP business salesman to a war correspondent, gave us a head start by seizing as our personal reparations two teletypes from the Siemens electric plant in Germany.

With one in Brussels and the other in Paris, we were scheduled to open the first leased wire link between the two capitals, and, by extension, Amsterdam. We had to do our own wiring of our offices. Although there had been delays since wire was purchased in small quantities from war-short suppliers, I was assured that the job would be completed in time for the scheduled opening day. Editors from the Brussels papers and a couple of government officials were on hand for the big moment. We were waiting for the first signal from Paris when the foreman of the crew that had been installing the wires appeared at the door. He wore a deeply troubled look. He reported that they were just thirty feet short of enough wire to finish the job. He shared my distress. But then he brightened. He slapped his head and said: "I just thought of something. I know where I can get the wire, but it is on the black market. It will cost."

I hated the black market and refused to deal on it, but this was an emergency that warranted an exception. I produced in Belgian francs the sizable tribute demanded. The foreman disappeared—he could not have gone farther than the floor below—and reappeared with the requisite wire. The ceremonial greeting from Paris appeared on time.

Only days later we received our first bulletin from Paris. In French it reported that the Americans had dropped on Japan a bomb the equivalent of 20,000 tons of TNT. Clearly, I thought, those French operators have made a mistake. So I changed the figure to 20 tons before sending the story along to our Belgian clients. With further adds on the story, my mistake became abundantly clear.

It also turned out that at that time the world's only known supply of uranium, out of which the atomic bomb was made, was the Belgian Congo, and Belgium's Union Minière company sat on all of it. I went around to the Union Minière's headquarters. Those officials in Brussels seemed to have no advance knowledge of the use to which their precious metal had been put. They were pale and almost trembling with fright when they heard the news that, thanks to their monopoly, they held the world's future in their hands—in war and, perhaps, in peace. The revelation seemed to have gotten their tongues. I might as well have tried to interview zombies.

The war in Japan was over, but there was still

some unfinished business in Europe. The Nazi leadership was being rounded up, as were their collaborators, who had helped rule the occupied nations. The Dutch had seized their quisling on the day of liberation. I had wangled an interview with him the following day. Cowering in his cell, Anton Mussert, revealing fat in the land of the starved, perspired profusely as I tried to question him. He claimed with every breath that he was no Nazi sympathizer, that he had pretended loyalty to the Germans only to try to protect his people. I got up to go and said good-bye.

This sniveling man got up and, so help me, said "Heil," the obligatory Nazi greeting. His right hand automatically flew into the straight-armed salute before he managed to pull it down and mutter, in English, "Good-bye, good-bye." He was executed.

Shortly I would be in the presence of Mussert's bosses. That fall the Allies put on trial in Nuremberg the top officials, civilian and military, of the Nazi regime.

There they sat in the dock before eight judges, two each from Britain, France, the Soviet Union and the United States—twenty-one of the archvillains of our time, or perhaps of any time. Twenty-one of them, side by side, sullying for all time, as surely as would atomic waste, the 250 square feet of space they occupied.

I wanted to spit on them. I don't recall that it had ever occurred to me to spit on anyone before. But this was what I wanted to do now. I had never thought before of what a precise mark of contempt that action is. I wouldn't spit on the street, but now I would spit on them, to show, subconsciously, I suppose, that I thought them lower than the dirt on the street.

I watched them as they watched films of the concentration camp victims. They buried their heads in their hands, they sobbed openly. And I couldn't help wondering whether they cried out of pity for the victims or out of fear of the retribution that society sought.

Almost as shocking as those films were the tales from the witness stand, notably those of a very ordinary-looking man who calmly told of supervising the deaths of three million persons as if he were telling a neighboring farmer of having to put down a sick cow.

Rudolf Franz Ferdinand Hoess (no relation to defendant Rudolf Hess) was for three years the boss of Auschwitz, the notorious extermination camp in Poland. He unemotionally described in excruciating detail the operation of his gas chambers.

"At least two and a half million victims were executed and exterminated by gassing and burning," he recited almost in a monotone. "At least another half million succumbed to starvation and disease, making about three million."

They had been men, women and children, most of them Jews, but also including political, military and intellectual leaders of the occupied countries.

Hoess was asked if he felt any remorse or even

had second thoughts about what he was doing. He replied: "Don't you see, we SS [the elite Nazi security force] men were not supposed to think about these things. . . . It was something already taken for granted that the Jews were to blame for everything. . . . We were all so trained to obey orders that the thought of disobeying an order would never have occurred to anybody."

Hoess was hanged in the Auschwitz compound next to the house where he had lived with his wife and five children.

The star witness was Hermann Goering, second only to Hitler from the beginning of the Nazis' rise to power. On trial for his life, he displayed on the stand all the arrogance with which he had once set out to rule the world.

Goering was on the stand for nine days. For the first three, under direct examination by his attorney, he read into the trial record what in effect was a new testament of Naziism. With diabolical cunning, Goering undoubtedly intended to use the Allied sense of fairness against the democracies. He calculated that the tribunal and subsequent historians would not tamper with the full transcript of the proceedings.

So he laid out in exquisite detail the Nazi philosophy and its program. He in no way apologized for any of it. He did apologize, however, for its mistakes, which he carefully outlined so that they might be avoided by a future generation of Germans intent on finally achieving a Deutschland über Alles. Goering fell just short of stating flatly that Naziism should be restored. Most of the courtroom was not oblivious to what he was doing. There were whispered conferences among the judges and at the prosecution tables, but the chief American prosecutor who would be cross-examining him, U.S. Supreme Court Associate Justice Robert Jackson, did not seem to catch on and registered no protests. Jackson, who, as much as anyone, was the father of the International Tribunal, had been brilliant in his advocacy of the procedure, and his four-hour opening statement was a masterpiece widely praised among lawyers. But he had virtually no experience in criminal law and totally lacked the bulldog tenacity of a skilled prosecutor. During three days of cross-examination Goering ran circles around him.

Although Jackson's table was piled high with the documents that conclusively established Goering's guilt, the defendant had only his astounding memory and a few notes in the lavender notebook his jailers had provided (undoubtedly with the snicker of junior high school pranksters). Thus armed, Goering parried many of Jackson's thrusts, frequently correcting dates and figures that Jackson misquoted from the documents in front of him. Jackson was totally unnerved by Goering's almost jovial impudence. To Goering's insouciance he could respond only with bluster and a posture reminiscent of the country lawyer he once had been.

Several of the judges in subsequent memoirs were critical of Jackson's performance, none more than

Britain's Sir Norman Birkett. In fact, he was critical of the Nuremberg proceedings as a whole. He was acerbic, acidic in his complaints about the slowness of the trial, which he blamed partly on his fellow judges but primarily on what he considered the far-too-methodical German lawyers.

He had come to Nuremberg already famous in London courts for his sharp wit. With his red hair peeking out from under his judicial wig, he once offered a minor criminal his last words before the bench.

"As God is my judge," said the man, "I'm innocent."

"He isn't, I am, and you aren't," replied Birkett.

There were many nights at the press camp bar in Nuremberg and later when I argued for the legitimacy of the Nuremberg trial, defending it against those who contended that it was built on the sand of ex post facto justice, on the basis of law that did not exist when the crimes were committed. For one thing, there *were* international treaties that Nazi Germany clearly violated—the Kellogg-Briand Pact of 1928, which outlawed aggressive war, and the Geneva Convention of 1897 and the Hague Convention of 1899, which defined the treatment of civilians and prisoners of war.

Although Justice Jackson put it somewhat more obliquely in many of his eloquent statements, I always believed the trial was justified by the necessity of establishing judicial precedent even before the establishment of the international law that it was meant to support. This justification was built on the basic truth that the world is unlikely to survive a third world war, which would almost certainly bring universal nuclear devastation. If we are to avoid that catastrophe, a system of world order—preferably a system of world government—is mandatory. The proud nations someday will see the light and, for the common good and their own survival, yield up their precious sovereignty, just as America's thirteen colonies did two centuries ago.

When we finally come to our senses and establish a world executive and a parliament of nations, thanks to the Nuremberg precedent we will already have in place the fundamentals for the third branch of government, the judiciary. This, to my mind, was the meaning of—and the justification for— Nuremberg.

Or perhaps its meaning came through even more clearly at the vast party stadium outside Nuremberg, the scene of Hitler's great annual rallies, one of which was so skillfully filmed by Leni Riefenstahl for her Nazi propaganda opus, *Triumph of the Will.* The American occupation authorities had put it off limits to the Germans, but the mayor of Nuremberg appealed for permission to use it for a peace rally marking the first anniversary of the war's end.

He was standing at the center of the vast review- ing stand where Hitler used to take the salute of his regiments of military, civilian workers and the Hitler Youth. At each end of the stand were huge marble and brass bowls from which great flames had burst during the rallies. Now children were climbing up their sides and playing in them. The mayor's first words—the first German words spoken in the stadium since the fall of Naziism—were "Will the children please come down from the sacrificial urns."

With the Fascists gone, the Nazis gone, only one of the twentieth century's major dictatorships remained: the Soviet Union. That was the next stop for Betsy and me.

CHAPTER 6

MY UNITED PRESS career almost ended on a dock in Helsinki harbor. Betsy and I came close to not making it to Moscow at all.

We took a ship from New York to Göteborg, Sweden, and the train on to Stockholm. We were alone in our compartment on the train as the Swedish immigration and customs inspectors came through. The customs man inquired as to how much foreign currency we were carrying. I declared my puny UP allotment—only a couple of hundred dollars. Betsy made a totally ineffectual attempt to whisper. "Twelve hundred dollars," she said.

I was shocked. We had never had that much money in our lives. There was no way she could have saved it from my income. I'm embarrassed even now to recall the terrible suspicions with which I was briefly assaulted.

Her embarrassment may have been even greater as she confessed that the money had been given to her by her father. She explained: "Father always has given me enough money to get home from a date."

She had the fare from Moscow almost literally pinned to her lingerie.

We took a Soviet ship, the *Sestoresk*, from Stockholm to Leningrad via Helsinki. In the Finnish harbor I got my first taste of Soviet efficiency. Betsy and I were topside to watch the midnight landing. The harbor was dark except for the lights at one end that marked the *Sestoresk*'s dock. It turned out to be more like the captain's target.

As we approached, the ship showed no sign of slowing down. On the dockside the greeting party of officials and workers fled for the hills. I grabbed Betsy and ran toward the stern. The *Sestoresk* hit the dock bow on at what seemed to be full speed. A huge piece of concrete was chewed from the dock, and part of its canopy came down. There appeared to be no damage to the ship and its ice-breaking bow. The captain calmly backed off and swung his ship around for a normal landing. Apparently this was the way he always docked.

Aboard with us was an acclaimed Swedish tenor, Jussi Björling, making his first postwar trip to Finland. We were due to sail for Leningrad at 2 p.m., and Björling insisted that we have lunch ashore with him. We went to a charming little restaurant; his other guest was the chief of police, adorned in black leather from head to toe.

The mutual toasting was unrestrained. The clock crept toward our sailing hour, but the chief assured us he would get us to the boat in plenty of time. He miscalculated. Despite the flashing red lights and the screaming siren, we reached the dock to see the *Sestoresk* retreating from the harbor. The ship had all of our possessions aboard, but far more important, it was the last means of entering the Soviet Union before our visas expired.

With a cavalier wave of the hand, the chief insisted there was no problem. He got on the radio and ordered the *Sestoresk* to stop. The Russians paid no heed, so the chief ordered up a police boat. Now, with our flashing lights and siren waterborne, we overtook the ship.

Police entreaties were ignored on the *Sestoresk*— except that it seemed to slow slightly and dropped a Jacob's ladder over the side. The deck seemed the height of the Matterhorn away, but there was nothing for it. Betsy went first and we climbed that swinging rope ladder with its wooden rungs, straight up and up and up. It was the hard way to get to Moscow, but perhaps no harder than the life we would find there.

In those days, scarcely a year after the war, the American "colony" in Moscow was made up of seven newspaper and radio correspondents and the wives of one or two of them. Except for the 110 or so personnel in the American Embassy, there were no other U.S. residents. The occasional touring official and the two or three fur traders who spent a fortnight in town every winter were our only personal contacts with the outside world.

Most of the correspondents lived in the Metropole Hotel, which shared Theater Square with the Bolshoi Opera House. Its once-proclaimed grandeur had long since faded under Communism and war. The rugs were unwashed and worn. Horsehair bayonets

pierced the upholstery. The drapes looked like used
blankets donated by a charity clinic. It didn't matter;
the pulls didn't work and they couldn't be opened
and closed anyway. As crummy joints go, it compared favorably only with certain welfare hotels in
New York.

This wasn't destined to be our home. Back in the
twenties, the Soviet Politburo declared a new economic policy. The private investment program was
intended to bring into circulation millions of gold
rubles and other treasures that wary Russian citizens
had squirreled away during the Revolution. One
scheme provided for private purchase of apartments.
With the serious housing shortage, this was a highly
popular program.

The UP correspondent at the time, Eugene Lyons,
must have had one of the most persuasive pens in
all of contemporary literature. He persuaded the
notably tight Roy Howard, head of the United Press,
to invest in an apartment. Once the Kremlin decided
it had uncovered all the hoarded gold it was going to
find, it abrogated the new economic policy and
seized the apartments. Howard was incensed, not at
the Kremlin's duplicity but at the fact that he had
been duped. He mounted such a campaign that the
powers didn't take the UP apartment. No paper ever
confirmed this arrangement; there simply was never
another bill tendered for the apartment or any of its
utilities. When we left Moscow in 1948, we hadn't
paid a cent for our two years there.

The five-story building was in a fine location, just

off the Arbat Square, not far from the Kremlin and the American Embassy. Its location was better than the structure. Its stucco exterior had peeled so badly it looked like a serious case of sunburn on the third day. Glass was missing from one of the front doors; the other hung by the thread of a hinge.

Our four rooms, bath and kitchen were interconnected by a large foyer that gave the apartment a sense of spaciousness which was partly illusory. It was luxurious, however, compared with the building's other apartments, which were shared by a minimum of four families—five if the foyer was occupied, as in most cases, or six families if the kitchen was inhabited, as in many cases.

You could tell which apartments had kitchen dwellers. The stove had been moved out into the hall. All six families shared it, which was no real trick considering the scarcity of food. Most stoves had on their burners a perennially boiling pot or two into which the residents dropped whatever meager offering they could obtain that day—a beet here, half a cabbage there, perhaps a carrot, on rare occasions a piece of meat. The oldest member of the household tended the stove, stirring this ever-developing mélange and parceling out a bowl on demand.

Meyer Handler, the number two UP man in Moscow, had warned us that Henry Shapiro, the number one man, with whom he had carried on a bitter feud for two years, had sold most of the apartment's furniture before his departure, and we had shipped some utilitarian pieces down from Stock-holm. But they had not preceded us to Moscow.

We assumed that we could get a room at the Metropole pending their arrival. It was our first major clash with the Soviet bureaucracy. No, we were told, we could not stay at the Metropole, since, in granting our visa, the government had ac-cepted our word that we had secured our own accommodations.

Succor came from Dick and Ann Hottelet. They had two rooms in the Metropole, one for his CBS office and one for living. We could sleep on the sofa in the office—just as long as we were up and out by the 9 a.m. start of Dick's busy day. Until his long day ended, we camped out in the lobby. We re-packed our two suitcases every morning to clear Dick's office, and unpacked them again at night.

We endured, with gratitude, almost three weeks of stiff necks and aching backs from that torture device that masqueraded as a sofa. While I was beginning to find out some of the horrors of reporting in a dic-tatorship, Betsy was strengthening her stomach for the long haul in Moscow. On her first attempt to visit the central market, she had to flee to fresher air to escape its dominant odor of open sewer.

The furniture finally arrived, but the trunks we had shipped from the States did not. Since the com-bination of Soviet bureaucracy and Soviet elec-tronics rendered the telephone system inoperable, I went daily to the incoming baggage counter at cus-toms. Each day an unsympathetic woman, skilled in bureaucratic discourtesy, went down the handwritten list of incoming shipments and reported that there was nothing there for "Cronkite."

Until the day that, watching her thumb through the several pages of her log on the other side of the counter, I saw it. From at least five feet away I could read "Cronkite" written in Russian. But, standing over it, she couldn't make it out.

The trunks had arrived—days before—but now a new contretemps developed, for which I could only partially blame the Russians. The trunks were locked and we had lost the keys. The Russian police had some very strong feelings about locks and keys. There were no locksmiths for civilian patronage in Moscow, and one was not permitted to receive keys mailed from abroad.

We obtained screwdrivers and pliers and, under the watchful eyes of the customs guards, pried open our trunks. The customs routine seemed to be going well until the inspector reached into a trunk and brought forth a golf ball.

"Shto eta? Shto eta?" she demanded. What was it?

I found it difficult in almost nonexistent Russian to explain a golf ball. It was a game. You hit it with a stick. There really wasn't much I could do with the story line. Finally I picked up the ball, intending to bounce it in what perhaps would be a meaningful demonstration. The woman ducked and threw her hands over her face. She screamed and other guards came. It seemed she thought I was going to explode this dimpled little white bomb. Although she found a dozen or more golf balls sprinkled throughout the trunk like mothballs, the crisis of understanding seemed to have passed—at least with the Russian authorities. I still needed to understand why Betsy had thought to bring them along in the first place.

"Well," she explained, "they told me in New York that you couldn't get golf balls in the Soviet Union."

Whereupon I explained that this was understandable: There were no golf courses in the Soviet Union. I had the good grace not to mention that she did not play the game and I hadn't played since before the war.

Those golf balls came in handy later. Golf balls were a very scarce and expensive commodity in England after the war, so when our friends in the British Embassy left for home after their tours of duty, we presented them with a ball or two. For years we basked in self-satisfaction over our clever largesse until Betsy recalled that one of the balls was a trick one, designed to fly in any direction rather than the one intended. Perhaps this accounted for the fact that we never heard again from one of our Moscow friends after his return to England.

Social life in Moscow was much more active than either of us had anticipated. The government extended only one privilege to foreign correspondents, but it was an important one. They gave us ambassadorial rank. This entitled us to buy at a diplomatic store a few items not available to the general public and, occasionally, to get seats at the ballet or opera.

Its greatest benefit, however, was that it put us on the diplomatic list for invitations to all of the embassies' parties on the nights of their national holidays.

And the benefit of that was, first, the food, and second, the company. The embassies served elaborate buffets, but the problem was getting anything to eat. While cocktails were being served, the doors to the dining areas always remained closed, perhaps bolted, for all I know, and the guests—mostly the Russians and Eastern Europeans—jockeyed for position in front of them. When the doors opened, it was the Oklahoma land rush. Men and women circled the buffet table and took their positions. With elbows flailing to guard their space, they ate whatever was within reach. If they were stuck by the radishes, radishes is what they had.

These occasions were just about the only opportunity we had to meet Russian government officials. They simply were not available to us at other times. Even the Foreign Office spokesman was unreachable except by letter. At the parties, however, we might see members of the Politburo and perhaps exchange just a word or two. Vyacheslav Molotov, the foreign minister, frequently was present; Stalin never.

Most communicative was Andrei Vishinsky, Molotov's deputy and, as Stalin's chief prosecutor, the man who had sent thousands to their deaths in the 1936–38 purges. His jovial mien belied his background. He spoke almost colloquial American English, and his sense of humor was keen. One night he recalled for a small group of us that he used to be a newspaperman himself. "And I found out," he said, "that it takes just two things to be a good news-paperman: a strong pair of legs and a very weak mind."

Except for one occasion, we saw Stalin only as he reviewed the May Day and October Revolution parades from the top of Lenin's tomb in Red Square, or as he opened sessions of the Supreme Soviet in the Kremlin. The one exception was when he appar-ently attended the Bolshoi Opera one night.

I must qualify that with "apparently." There was a great stirring behind curtains temporarily en-closing a box next to the stage; those in the front rows strained to see the occupants; and the singers seemed enthralled as they played to the box. At the end of the show the players and audience all ap-plauded toward the box, and there appeared, for just a second, a hand waving acknowledgment. I was told that I had seen Stalin at the Bolshoi.

I hoped he liked the program. There was a story that he had left Prokofiev's new *Romeo and Juliet* complaining that there was no tune he could whistle.

At the Supreme Soviet meeting I was amused that Stalin joined in the applause that greeted his arrival on the stage. I learned later that this was a Russian custom and that the honored one is, in reality, ap-plauding the audience, and not himself.

When I wasn't in white tie and tails for "national days," I was in black tie for what in any place other than an outpost of empire would have been just another night out. Our hosts were members of the diplomatic colony, almost exclusively from the democracies of Western Europe and South America. They, and the foreign service personnel at our embassy, were our social set, since all relations with the Russian people were circumscribed. It was a little like attending a cocktail party every night with fellow occupants of a submarine.

There were claustrophobic moments, but there were also memorable highlights featuring various ambassadors and career diplomats displaying their amateur talents, both practiced and improvised and abetted by vodka and champagne.

The ballet was one of the few entertainments available to us, and it inspired not a few after-dinner performances at embassy parties. An American first secretary did a magnificent *grand jeté* one night right through the open French doors of a second-floor balcony. A large bush below preserved him for an encore.

Elbridge Durbrow, later to play an important role in the early stages of our involvement in Vietnam, was counselor of our embassy. He and I were frequently called on for our ice-skating duet. That it was performed on Oriental rugs seemed to enhance the audience's appreciation of our delicate artistry.

For a couple of months one winter I was the star parlor entertainer in a rather passive performance. I had been saved from double pneumonia by an emergency shipment of penicillin from our occupation army in Germany. There was none of the comparatively new wonder drug in Moscow. At that time the drug was suspended in beeswax and injected by a horse syringe into the buttocks. The body absorbed the beeswax over a period of many days and slowly released the penicillin to do its best. It did its best for me and I soon recovered, except for a wad of beeswax the size of a baseball in each of my cheeks.

When I sat down it was touch and go whether I would tilt over like a round-bottomed Russian doll. Indicative perhaps of the high level at which we entertained each other was the nightly queue as the other guests felt my bumps with appropriate comments on their exceedingly slow subsidence. This was accompanied by the requisite hilarity until the night that, midway through the group grope, the realization ran through the group that among us was Madame Vijayalakshmi Pandit. She was destined to become the first woman president of the UN General Assembly.

She had just that day presented her credentials to the Kremlin as the first ambassador from the newly independent nation of India. As the sister of her nation's first native-born Prime Minister, Jawaharlal Nehru, she was not unacquainted with the formalities of the British foreign service. Surely the dinner up to now had met the expectations of this beautiful lady whose serenity bordered on severity.

Now, as if by secret signal—a whistle, perhaps, that only diplomats can hear—the buttocks-feeling hilarity turned to an awkward silence. The embarrassment hung there for just a moment, broken by the Ambassadress from India.

"May I?" she asked, and gamely, if a bit tentatively, joined in a feel.

There were no equivalent social highlights in our associations with the Russians. The official propaganda line, often repeated in the newspapers, warning the populace against friendship with foreigners, worked. Only two or three couples dared to invite us to their homes, and interestingly enough, they were all Jewish. I assumed their daring was in their genes, planted there by generations forced to defy czarist pogroms.

These invitations took the form of chapters from a spy novel. They were notes always placed directly in our hands, usually in front of our apartment, by people who were strangers to us but presumably trusted friends of our hosts. They instructed us to meet the messenger at a certain corner at an appointed time, to be led to our hosts, usually by a circuitous route down narrow streets and narrower alleys.

In their apartment a phonograph played at full volume to thwart any devices intended to listen in on our conversation. The only silence was when records had to be changed, at which point the host put his fingers to his lips.

Secrecy and fear were pervasive. They hung heavily over every transaction, every conversation in Moscow.

The UP office was in one room of our apartment—a small room intended for a bedroom, crowded with my staff. Madame Tarasova was my secretary-translator, a woman whose tiny bones, pinched face and sharp nose betrayed an upper-class heritage. A not-unattractive young college student, whose full round face, high cheekbones and widely set eyes spoke of an Oriental background in the distant past, was an assistant translator and messenger. The other messenger had stepped out of every painting of Russians at work, in the factories or the fields—the small eyes and the button nose, a face capable of an astoundingly large range of emotions from hearty good humor to desperate sadness, sometimes changing, frequently inexplicably, with the speed of a slide show.

They drove me crazy. So few Russians did I get to know in my two years there that I cannot testify whether they were typical, although the experience of other non-Russians seemed to confirm my impression. What I detested was the one trait they shared: They could not wait to try to prove their loyalty to me by citing the disloyalty of the others.

The moment one of them would leave the room, the others would shower me with allegations that their absent colleague had been seen going through my papers, or taking notes from my correspondence, or making mysterious telephone calls. The planting of suspicion seemed to be their entire raison d'être.

I came to the conclusion that this uncivilized behavior was a part of a national cultural heritage prompted by a history of one cruel dictatorship after another. A whole people had it drummed into them for generation after generation that the way to get along with authority in a secret society was to establish one's own loyalty by impugning that of fellow workers, neighbors or even family members.

And this, of course, was model behavior under Stalin and the Politburo.

The effect of the drumbeat of propaganda spread through a controlled press and radio was brought home to me by my driver, my principal source of the day's hottest rumor. There was always a rumor du jour. In a nation where, by government press policy, there are no accidents, no fires, no crimes, no illnesses, no government scandals, whispered rumor passes for the news of the day.

Alexander was a regular fifteen-minute newscast each day—tales of scores killed in a bus crash, dozens dead in an apartment fire, a murder in the Bolshoi dressing rooms. There was rarely any substantiation of his catalog of woe. On the other hand, the effect of propaganda on him was clear.

He had been a driver in the Soviet army and, during our first months together, he spent most of our conversation time praising the American "zheep," as he called it. To his mind, the jeep was the greatest technical achievement of the twentieth century, and the Americans, in developing it, had proved their technical superiority.

But Alexander was undergoing the brainwashing that the Kremlin propaganda masters had directed to wipe out such impressions left by American aid during the war. The propaganda was vicious and persistent. One of their most heinous lies was that the British and American air forces had deliberately bombed the working-class quarters in Germany in order to rid the nation of those most likely to be sympathetic to the Soviet Union.

We also, allegedly, delayed the second front in Normandy so that the Germans could kill more Soviet soldiers. And there were scores of little stones to go with these boulders of shameless falsehood. They claimed that Russians had invented every modern device, from the telegraph to the airplane. They reached the pinnacle of mendacity with the claim that they had invented baseball.

I thought surely that the people must find the official claims as ridiculous as I did. But I came to realize how effective lies can be when the truth is suppressed as I heard Alexander's tune change, day by day. Within months he was asking me, plaintively and with genuine disappointment, why we Americans claimed to have invented the "zheep" when we knew the Russians had. His plaint grew aggressive as the weeks wore on, until he was accusing us of deliberately changing the Russian nameplates with which the vehicles had originally been equipped.

It was this control that the Communist authority had over the minds of the people that laced their propaganda with real danger. The morning that *Pravda* published a letter "exposing" our colleague Robert Magidoff as a spy, we all shuddered with apprehension. The letter allegedly had been sent by his secretary, a young lady of Finnish-American background who seemed about as pro-American and anti-Soviet as one could be. Magidoff represented several U.S. business publications, and she cited letters from them asking perfectly reasonable questions about various financial and production matters in the Soviet Union. In any democratic nation these were the most innocuous and routine news inquiries. *Pravda* turned them into "proof" that Magidoff was involved in industrial espionage, or worse.

Magidoff was of Russian heritage; his wife, Nila, was a Russian citizen. We trembled for their fate— and for ours, since this could well be the opening of a campaign intended to either drive all of us correspondents out of the country or, worse, jail us indefinitely as examples of capitalist treachery.

The *Herald Tribune*'s Joe Newman and I hurried around to the American Embassy to seek counsel. What, we asked Ambassador Walter Bedell Smith, should we do if the secret police showed up at our door one night?

"You fellows were correspondents in the war," he answered. "You know the GI rules if captured. Don't tell them anything. When they interrogate you, just give them your name, rank and serial number."

We considered that all very well, but meanwhile, we asked, what was the Embassy going to be doing?

"Protesting," he said. "And we'll demand to see you. They might not let us do that, but we will deliver a strong protest."

"And that's all, Mr. Ambassador?"

"What do you expect Washington to do?" he answered. "We'll be very sorry, but you don't really think we're likely to go to war over a couple of jailed newspaper reporters, do you?"

He wasn't unsympathetic, just frightfully realistic.

Magidoff was expelled, but the Soviets showed a rare bit of humanity and permitted Nila to go with him. His secretary was never heard from again. The populace got the message regarding the sinister nature of foreign correspondents, and our difficult jobs were made even more difficult in the months ahead.

Incidentally, Bedell Smith became a great friend of ours. I wouldn't have given a plugged nickel for the chances of that happening. But I learned that Smith was a man of the highest integrity who played to the hilt the role to which the vicissitudes of a life-time of government service assigned him.

I had known him first as General Eisenhower's chief of staff in World War II. He played the black hat to Ike's white hat. Ike was the smiling diplomat who got along with all the Allied brass and politicians, no matter how unreasonable or difficult they might be. Bedell was the guy who came along in his wake with the real truth of the situation and the hard line to enforce it. Just when Ike would get going at a headquarters news conference, Smith would interrupt to call time and end the meeting. He wasn't a favorite of the press.

When I was planning at Nuremberg to go to Moscow, I saw one silver lining in an assignment that we recognized to be a dreary one, what with Soviet press restrictions, the overwhelming censorship and difficult living conditions. At least our ambassador, Averell Harriman, was a dear old friend from London days, and his daughter was a lovely hostess.

The very day that I learned in Nuremberg that my visa had been granted for Moscow, *Stars and Stripes* reported that Harriman was leaving Moscow and the new ambassador would be . . . Bedell Smith. The Russians *and* Bedell Smith. I damn near refused the assignment.

It turned out that Bedell could not have been more helpful and friendly in Moscow. That was the Ambassador's job, and he did it extremely well. He had doffed his black hat and donned a white one. When we all returned to the United States, we were frequent guests for dinner at the Smiths' in Washington, where he was serving as a deputy secretary of state. With his wife, Norey, we were waiting for him to arrive for dinner one night. He called and said he would be late, telling us to go ahead. He arrived soon thereafter, stuck his head in the dining room and said a perfunctory hello, and disappeared upstairs.

I had had my last friendly conversation with Bedell Smith. On that day he had been appointed head of the CIA, and as our top intelligence officer, he felt it unseemly that he should associate with a newsman. He had terminated our association.

Thank goodness for his friendship in Moscow, though. Not only was the Soviet government locked behind the crenellated walls of the Kremlin, every government building was, for us, an impregnable fortress. We correspondents were not even allowed to see the so-called official information people. Except for the foreign ministry's alleged spokesman, we didn't even know who they were.

The Western diplomats did not have much better luck in contacting their opposite numbers in the government. Their intelligence was almost entirely limited to interpreting the abstruse reports in the press and analyzing the meaning of the order in which the pictures of Politburo members were displayed on public holidays or where they stood and sat at public functions.

This, too, was the basis of almost all our reporting. First-person or descriptive stories not taken directly from the press were so heavily censored that they seldom made sense. Just before my arrival the correspondents had made a decision that I never fully understood. Because other systems had proven even more bothersome, they agreed to let their copy be sent to their offices after censorship without their seeing it again until after its transmission. No matter how seriously the censors had butchered the copy, even if they changed the meaning of sentences, there was nothing we could do about it. Attempts to send messages to our offices amending or killing the story would themselves be censored.

The censorship was so complete and so inane that when pneumonia laid me low, I could not advise my office that I was ill and out of action. For days they queried me on stories with no response until finally the Embassy advised them through the State Department of the problem.

Of course, the Kremlin's duplicity knew no bounds. The foreign ministers of the wartime Allies met in Moscow in 1947. Suddenly the Soviet Union seemed to be as open as the United States. Correspondents were welcomed and hundreds came. They could not have found a friendlier or more cooperative government.

What did they want to see—collective farms, automobile factories, the subway construction, the inside of the Kremlin? *Puzhalista*, please, step this way. Everything that had been totally off limits to us became a tourist sight for them. There were not a few of them who returned home questioning the complaints of their Moscow-based colleagues. They felt we either were paranoid, incompetent or had been brainwashed by the cynical Western diplomats with whom we consorted.

Among the things they got to see that had been denied us was the plant that produced the Soviet's top-end limousine. The burly manager with a big smile, from which gleamed his steel teeth, told of his apprenticeship in a Detroit factory. When asked how it was that his car seemed to resemble the American Packard, he said: "Oh, you know how we automobile executives are. We steal a little from one competitor, and a little from another."

The conference the visiting correspondents had come to cover was intended to address unified demands for German reparations, which in turn meant deciding questions concerning the occupation of Germany and the form of its postwar government. I have always considered the meeting, and its outcome, in a sense the formal declaration of the cold war.

Although it had been strongly hinted, the conference established that the Soviets had no wish to see a unified Germany and intended a permanent division between the occupying powers. There were virtually no diplomatic highlights to report, and few social ones to enjoy. Our Secretary of State, General George Marshall, gave the mandatory dinner at the Embassy, at which Betsy and I occupied a couple of seats by the salt. On one side of me sat Min Shepherd, the wife of the assistant military attaché and an old Army friend of the general's. Min was a favorite among the military, a warm hostess with a notoriously ribald sense of humor.

On her other side was the Cuban Foreign Minister. Earlier in the day he had held a news conference to detail his nation's reparation demands. He told us that Cuba had lost its entire merchant marine to the German depredations in the Atlantic. And how many ships was that? he was asked. His answer: both of them. Perhaps he misunderstood the question.

At the dinner there came one of those moments, said to be twenty minutes after and twenty minutes before each hour, when all conversation, by some mysterious mandate, comes to a halt. In the breach was heard the Cuban's heavily accented query to Min Shepherd: "And, madam, have you ever experienced a movement on the sidewalk?"

"We're talking about earthquakes," Min fairly shouted down the table to our austere Secretary of State.

The Soviet trick of extending privileges on special occasions to the visiting press which were consistently denied to the resident press was old hat by the time of President Nixon's second trip to Moscow. On that occasion I was a visitor and I took full advantage. I did a little commentary standing out in front of our old apartment building, which looked like the slum it was. I was drawing a somewhat favorable picture of the improvements in Moscow since those immediate postwar years.

"And today," I reported, "you see dogs on leashes and riding in cars. We saw none in the streets of Moscow right after the war. They had all been eaten."

The technicians at Moscow Television watched my report being transmitted and they raised Cain. They told the papers that I had insulted the Russian people, and the story spread quickly at the press bar that had been set up at one of the hotels. Young Russian reporters were raging about my story when a grand old man of the Soviet press, *Pravda*'s Yuri Zhukov, slammed down his glass and, in a voice calculated to command attention, proclaimed them all fools.

"Cronkite is right," he virtually shouted. "You children know nothing of the war. We Muscovites ate our dogs to survive."

In the long parade of depressing days in Moscow, perhaps one of the worst was when the Pulitzer Prize was awarded to my friend, but also my competition, Eddy Gilmore of Associated Press. It wasn't that

Eddy wasn't a good and diligent reporter and a clever writer, but the dispatches honored by that supposedly learned awards committee in New York had all passed, without correction, through those Soviet censors.

Despite the nagging from us in Moscow, none of our organizations ever saw fit to lead our dispatches with a small note stating that they had passed through censorship. The rationale of our bosses was that there were all sorts of censorship around the globe, some more blatant than others, and it would be impossible to define in a few words the extent of each. Thus, no notice was better than an incomplete one, they reasoned.

So the Pulitzer committee actually handed its award to Eddy Gilmore *and* the Russian censors. I lost a lot of respect for the Pulitzer after that.

An award should have gone to *The New York Times'* Drew Middleton. Without any suggestion of their source, he sprinkled his articles with quotations from *Alice in Wonderland* that indicated that the Russian official "facts" he cited were as imaginative as Lewis Carroll could have made them. The censors never caught on.

Before I left Moscow I did a piece about the changes in the city since our arrival two years before. Making a series of parallels, I tried to report on the progress in that time, limited though it was. But the fool censors mangled that, as well. At one point, for example, I had reported:

"Two years ago, everybody was in the felt boots

with rubber soles that they called valenki. Today one sees leather shoes on the people of Moscow."

That whole paragraph was reduced to "Today one sees shoes on the people of Moscow."

The secret police, notorious for their brutal tortures, imprisonment and exile, could be devilishly ingenious as well. Travel within the Soviet Union was restricted even for the Russians. They needed internal visas to travel outside their places of residence. As for us foreigners, it was rare that we could get such permission, but an undersecretary of our embassy, by some subterfuge, managed to get tickets for three couples to take the river boat to Stalingrad—a nearly three-week voyage down the Volga.

Betsy and I accompanied the two Embassy couples. We half expected to be stopped at the gangplank when we presented our tickets. Nothing was said and we found our "deluxe" cabins barely adequate but at least neat. The same was far from true of the public toilet we were required to use. It was so filthy that the women clinched to the point of imminent explosion.

The trip downriver was fascinating. The boat stopped at small landings for women, children, traders and farmers, packs on their backs and occasionally an animal at the end of a rope. At night they entertained themselves with accordion or balalaika music, a song or a dance.

One of the entries in my list of most unforgettable characters was a pleasant, gregarious older man who wore the tieless, buttoned-up shirt and leather-billed khaki hat of an old revolutionary. We played chess together and talked to the limit of our restricted vocabularies.

On our last day out before Gorki, where he would be disembarking, we stood at the rail and he pointed to the far bank and to a distant smokestack. That, he said, was where he worked. And what did he do? I asked.

"Oh," he said, "I'm one of the people who run this country. I'm a member of the KGB."

My dear new friend was a member of the dread secret police. It turned out, however, that he was in a nominally passive position as superintendent in a prison-camp shoe factory.

We, too, were disembarking at Gorki, where we were to change ships for the rest of the voyage to Stalingrad. Gorki was the city that would later be the exile home of Andrei Sakharov, who helped develop the Soviet atomic bomb before breaking with the regime, and later won the Nobel Peace Prize.

As we docked at Gorki, the ship at the wharf immediately ahead of us was identified as the one bound for Stalingrad. In a land without porters, we managed to get our luggage to its gangplank. And there we were told that the vessel was oversold and our tickets could not be honored. In response to all our protests and inquiries, we were told only that we could get the answers at the Intourist Hotel at the top of the hill.

Carrying all our luggage, we struggled upward to

reach what must once have been a splendid hostelry of almost universally typical resort architecture—broad verandas that overlooked the river and the limitless plain beyond. There wasn't a soul outside and, we found, there were no guests inside, but as we opened the door, there, lined up in order of importance, was the hotel staff—the majordomo, the bellman, the elevator operator, a couple of waiters, the chambermaids. Their uniforms were clean, neat and ironed but would not stand close inspection. They were in tatters, as if they had just been taken from trunks unprotected by mothballs. The linen runner over the worn rug was in similar shape, with enough holes to qualify as lacework.

The majordomo pleasantly beckoned us to the reception desk. The lone receptionist sat behind a cashier's wicket. Her less pleasant greeting carried a warning. "You should have told us you were coming. We could have prepared for your visit."

Our first question was about our boat passage to Stalingrad. If this boat, the first of the navigation season, was full, could we take the next one? She advised us that the next boat was full, as was the next one after that. In fact, there were no reservations left for any of the boats all summer.

We were beginning to get the drift. Could we, perhaps, get train reservations to Stalingrad? Not surprisingly, there were no train reservations available either. Then could we get train reservations back to Moscow? Unfortunately, none of those could be had.

"But," she said, "here are your airplane tickets back to Moscow. The plane leaves at six forty-five tomorrow morning. If you would like to go to the theater here tonight, *Uncle Vanya* is playing and I can arrange tickets."

If there was an airport at Gorki, that was not where we were taken the next morning. We were driven to a large field with no facilities. En route we were exposed to the only interesting sight of our Gorki visit—a field of German prisoners at work digging—digging what, we had no idea. But there were a lot of them, the first we had seen of an immense army for whom the Russians were refusing to account.

An old American twin-engine DC-3, the work-horse of World War II, sat at the end of our airfield. Standing at the foot of a ladder that substituted for a ramp was a woman in military garb. Unsmilingly, she helped us aboard and waved to the metal bench running down the plane's length.

The flight was not pleasant. Sitting in silence, each of us was highly apprehensive. We dared not voice our concern, certain that our conversation was being monitored. This special plane, the possibly secret airfield—it all seemed well within reason to conclude that we were being shipped off to a distant incarceration. There was no immediate relief when we landed.

We put down at what was clearly a military air-field. But instead of taxiing to a reception building somewhere, the pilot stopped at the end of the runway. The hostess, if that's what she was—we had not been offered even coffee, tea or milk—lowered the ladder, helped us and our luggage down, nodded a good-bye and reboarded, and the plane was gone.

We hiked down to a gate at the far end of the field expecting to learn our fate. The guard, his automatic weapon armed with a dazzlingly sharpened bayonet, saluted with a smile and waved us through. Our Embassy friends identified the landing field as a military base in suburban Moscow. Since no hostility was evident, they dared to ask the guard to borrow the phone, and they called the Embassy for a car.

We couldn't believe we had escaped so easily. Yet we hadn't. The diplomats received letters of reprimand from the Kremlin, but they weren't thrown out. The severest penalty was reserved for us.

We found our apartment ransacked. All of our clothes were gone. The jewelry boxes in which we had only memento stuff—fraternity and sorority pins—were gone. Madame Tarasova was in a tizzy. She had come in one morning to discover the robbery. My office files had also been gone through, she noted, but apparently nothing had been taken. She was a little too confident, in an apology fit for a servant of the state, that the thieves had only been interested in the material value of our things.

Madame Tarasova had notified the police. They had come and dusted the place for fingerprints and examined the door and windows for points of entry. Of course, they came up with nothing. Their only response was to warn us that this sort of thing could happen when an apartment was left unoccupied. Or, in other words, we shouldn't have left town on an unauthorized trip.

Eventually we had to fly out to Vienna to get reoutfitted, although, while waiting for the necessary visas, I had ordered a couple of suits from Wolff Brothers in Kansas City, the last place at which I had bought clothes. I sent off the measurements taken by the Russian tailor who serviced the Embassy, but I was confident that Wolff's would remember me.

The suits came back some weeks later. They would have fit the Cardiff giant. The measurements had been in centimeters, which Wolff's mistakenly took to be inches. They were so big that we displayed them as objets d'art in our bedroom.

Our bedroom was a meeting place for most of the diplomatic set. This was not a tribute to our charm, although Betsy's sense of humor was one of the colony's greatest assets. Rather, it had to do with the physical nature of the place. One of our bedroom walls was the common wall of the adjoining building, a wall in which the flue was encased. And the flue was clearly defective. That wall was as hot as a radiator and our bedroom was the warmest room in Moscow.

Occasional official visitors briefly enlivened our endlessly dreary existence in Moscow. None brought more excitement than the late President Roosevelt's second son, Elliott, and his bride, the former Faye Emerson. Faye was an actress who became one of the earliest of the "famous for a minute" television personalities, mostly because of her daringly revealing décolletage and what it barely covered.

They were enchanted with Moscow, a rare impression. Just a coat of paint, Faye proclaimed, and it would be prettier than Paris. She would have a hard time getting an endorsement of that opinion.

Far more important, of course, was their passionate approval of much of Soviet foreign policy. It caught the Embassy and the rest of us by surprise. At one party they held forth at great length about the Soviet right to the Dardanelles and a warm-water passage to the sea, a matter of great sensitivity in which we supported our allies, the Greeks and the Turks.

I thought their views were provocative enough to warrant an interview, in which they sounded off at even greater length about the "mistaken" American foreign policy, particularly with respect to our relations with the Soviet Union. Here was a piece with which the Soviet censorship had no quarrel, and it was spread across American newspapers. The reaction was immediate, including a disappointed but rather tut-tut admonition from Elliott's mother, Eleanor.

The young Roosevelts were in Leningrad when the story broke, and could not be reached for their reaction to the reaction. But I met their train upon their return to Moscow and accompanied them to their hotel, next door to the American Embassy. They ranted and they raved, mostly about our gov-

ernment and particularly our foreign service. At
one point Elliott pointed in the direction of the Embassy and delivered a scathing indictment: "Our
State Department is run by people whom my father
wouldn't trust to run his messages."

My story reporting the reaction to the reaction
created a reaction of its own, one of awesome pro-
portions. The Embassy, of course, was livid and, as
far as I was able to determine, had no further deal-
ings with the Roosevelts, who, in any case, departed
the next day.

The censors severely restricted what we could
report about distinguished visitors from other
nations, on either side of the Iron Curtain, but our
contacts with them, limited as they were, provided
important background for us.

Shortly after the Communists had seized power in
Prague, when there was still the shadow of a coali-
tion government, Jan Masaryk, the Foreign Minister,
visited Moscow. I had known this distinguished son
of one of the founders of the Czech Republic when
he was part of the refugee government in London
during the war. He was in Moscow only briefly, and
there were no parties for him, no diplomatic receptions, no public meetings with him at all. The rumor
was rampant that the Kremlin had outlined a dreary
future for Czech democracy, and had proclaimed
to him that Czechoslovakia was now a part of the
Soviet sphere.

This was not certain when I learned that Masaryk
was leaving on an early plane a couple of mornings

after his arrival. Dawn comes very late—hardly at all, as a matter of fact—on those long winter days in near arctic Moscow. The airport was in darkness, its few lights casting gloomy shadows, as I took up a lonely vigil at the gate through which distinguished visitors entered. No other correspondents, foreign or Russian, had bothered to come out.

The official party arrived. Three ZIS limousines stopped at the gate. Foreign Minister Molotov and Masaryk got out of one; the rest of the officials, Czech and Russian, tumbled out of the others. There was a comparatively paltry honor guard of Soviet militia, and the usual gang of brusque and ornery security agents seemed smaller than usual.

At any rate, Masaryk saw me standing to one side and he nodded a greeting. I took the signal as an invitation, whether he meant it as such or not, and I approached him. I got a few steps before two of the plainclothesmen began moving toward me.

I waved a hasty good-bye, and said: "Au revoir."

His reply was equally hasty as he was escorted away: "Oh, no, my friend," he said. "Farewell."

A few days after returning to Prague, on March 10, 1948, Jan Masaryk went out one of the windows of his apartment in the Foreign Ministry building. It was officially declared a suicide, although to this day there is deep suspicion that he was murdered by the Communists. I thought at the time of our "farewell" that Masaryk was simply confirming his gloomy awareness that the Iron Curtain was about to be lowered around Czechoslovakia, but I have wondered since whether his words bore a deeper significance.

Many times during the cold war and America's near hysteria over the Communist threat, I thought of Masaryk. And I thought a lot about the fervent anti-Communists' seldom questioned slogan: "Better Dead than Red." That sort of deeply patriotic sentiment, it seems to me, might have had some rationale in the days when wars had winners and losers. But does it stand up in the nuclear age, when a massive exchange of bombs would cause such great losses, even, perhaps, the destruction of life on earth as we know it?

It does not seem to me unpatriotic to offer the possibility that it might be better to be Red than dead, under those nuclear circumstances. We all know of the transient nature of governments and the philosophies that inspire them. The collapse of the Soviet version of Communism proves that point, but even if the Red dictatorship had lasted with all of its horrors for a couple of centuries, would that not have been preferable to a world altered forever by nuclear poison? Does any one country have the right to destroy humanity in its own national interest?

I think I would rather be dead than Red, but I'm not at all sure that my personal preference, or even that of a whole generation, should be a basis for sound foreign policy.

One of those Red horrors, by the way, was the class inequality practiced by those master hypocrites. It was evident in a thousand ways, but perhaps none more so than the parades through Red Square in the waning years of the 1940s. As they passed Stalin's reviewing stand on Lenin's tomb, the open cars of the generals seemed barely able to sustain the weight of their passengers, resting their ballooning stomachs on the seats ahead of them.

The colonels marched behind them, their midriffs hinting of a miraculous pregnancy. And then the majors and the captains, almost as trim as those joggers that fill the paths around the Pentagon at lunch hour. Behind them the troops, so emaciated it was a wonder they made it the length of the parade route.

We watched those parades with awe at the heavy equipment, the tanks and the great mobile guns they displayed, and we wondered about their nuclear capability. The Soviet inefficiency in all visible things made me doubt they had any.

When our apartment sink clogged up, we wrote the necessary letter to the proper authorities to get a plumber. (They didn't accept phone calls.) Within a matter of weeks a child showed up at the front door and announced he was the plumber. We ushered him into the kitchen. He took a look at the situation, extracted half a hacksaw blade from his pocket and asked if we could lend him a towel. This he wrapped around the blade as a handhold, and proceeded to saw the drainpipe in two. He bent the top half out and the bottom half in, and asked if we had a bucket. The bucket he placed under the top half so it would catch the drainage—and he presented the receipt for us to sign. Mission accomplished.

We didn't sign the receipt, but the authorities insisted until the day we left Moscow that the sink had been fixed, and denied us further assistance.

When I returned to the United States, I went out on a lecture tour. I was speaking in Omaha one night and got the usual question about whether the Russians would get the nuclear bomb. Citing my plumber story, I said I believed that if they couldn't fix a stopped-up sink, they couldn't develop an atomic bomb.

I walked from the hall to see the headline in the next morning's Omaha *Bee:* "Russians Explode Atomic Bomb."

I had missed the obvious: All their experienced plumbers had been recruited to build the bomb; none were left for civilian duty.

That night in Omaha was an important one, a turn in the road.

Back in Moscow, Betsy and I had come back to our apartment one night to find a dollar sign painted on our door. This anti-American stigma was the equivalent of the yellow star with which the Nazis branded the Jews.

Little did we know how that Russian graffiti artist would change our lives.

CHAPTER 7

W HEN I GOT to New York from Moscow, en route to my pregnant wife in Kansas City, the UP made the most of me, a correspondent just returned from the Soviet Union, which, with its strict limitation on visitors and information and its postwar posturing, was again proving to be, as Churchill put it, a riddle wrapped in a mystery inside an enigma.

They trotted me around to meet all the columnists who would garner an "inside story" or two from me—Winchell and Leonard Lyons and Earl Wilson and Louis Sobol and a lesser-known fellow named Ed Sullivan on the New York *Daily News*. And the UP sent me out to make speeches.

I returned to my hotel after that speech in Omaha to find a telegram from Earl Johnson, the UP's general manager in New York: "Explain please Leonard Lyons today."

That was the full text. Its meaning was obscure. Of course I knew Leonard Lyons, but explaining him? That might have been difficult even for Lyons.

Lennie was one of the nicest and hardest-working of the Broadway columnists. He eschewed gossip, the lifeblood of the others, in favor of anecdotes about the famous. He had picked a strange occupation, considering that he was a law graduate and his sense of humor was greatly underdeveloped. As a consequence, he was noted for stepping all over the punch line of the stories that filled his column. A favorite show-business game of the time was trying to guess the real punch line of the stories he recounted.

When we met in New York, the story of mine that had incited Lyons to attack his notebook concerned the growing anti-Americanism which the Soviet propagandists were inspiring in 1948. As evidence, there was that large dollar sign scrawled on the front door. I told Lyons: "When we saw it, Betsy said: 'If they had known we were newspaper people, they would have put a cents sign on the door.' "

Now, in Omaha with Johnson's cryptic telegram in my trembling hand, I scurried to the hotel newsstand, only to find that the Omaha *Bee* didn't print Lyons. I rushed to my room and did, for that period, the economically daring thing: I telephoned the UP desk in New York and had them read me the Lyons column. Lennie's version of that last paragraph was: "If they had known I worked for the United Press instead of the Associated Press, they would have put a cents sign on the door."

The UP was always sensitive about its pay scale, which generally was somewhat lower than its principal competition. Johnson had a right to be offended. I wired back that I had been misquoted, which, in the case of a Leonard Lyons column, was a more believable explanation than might otherwise have been the case.

It led to a discussion with Earl about the UP remuneration in general and mine in particular. I had believed that my next assignment was to be general European news manager based in London. This was to be a major step up the UP ladder and it pleased me in many ways. With the new baby, I was happy that we would be going to a civilized city, and London was my favorite of all the world capitals. The common language was a major factor, but the shared experiences of wartime also made me feel at home there.

London has been called "a man's town" and it was, and is. The men are better tailored than the women are dressed, and although, there as here, women are winning entry to the men's clubs, the fine old leather lounge chairs and the aroma of good cigars have not given way to chintz and Chanel No. 5.

Paris was more beautiful and the chic of the French women was dazzling, but the French themselves always seemed to me, well, distant. I want to say "arrogant" and "snobbish," but my considerable disabilities in handling the language may have something to do with that impression. I wonder if we Americans appear remote and unfriendly to those in our midst who speak our language with heavy accents and a garbled vocabulary.

Yes, London would have been great, but that was

not to be. When I asked Earl what raise I could anticipate in my new exalted managerial role, he looked at me in amazement—feigned amazement, I suspect.

"Why, Walter, there's no raise in this. You already are getting more than any of our other foreign correspondents." (I never established the veracity of this statement. At $127.50 a week it was possible, although there were other correspondents of far greater value than I.)

"Furthermore," Earl went on, "you ought to know that we are cutting out the cost-of-living allowance in London."

In the face of my clear disappointment, he grew avuncular. "How long have you been with the UP now—eleven years? Surely you must have learned by now how we operate. We take young men, train them, work them hard, don't pay them very much, and when they get good enough to get more money elsewhere, we let them go."

This was indeed true. For the half century until the mid-seventies, there certainly were more former Unipressers serving on the nation's newspapers, magazines, broadcast organizations and public relations firms than graduates of any other institution. We even had our own informal organization, called the "Downhold Club" in honor of the frequent abbreviated instructions from New York to hold down expenses.

Earl's reminder of UP's economic philosophy was sobering, but unbeknownst to him or me or any of the other players, the wheel of fortune was already spinning toward a stop at TV.

Soon thereafter and still on leave back in Kansas City, I found myself lunching one day with a good friend, Karl Koerper, who was the second in command at one of the city's leading radio stations, KMBC. Karl had graduated with a major in journalism from the University of Kansas and considered himself to be news-oriented.

These were the days when radio was enjoying its most successful period. The years of hectic growth were over, television wasn't yet a serious threat, advertising contracts were almost automatic, the money was rolling in.

On Madison Avenue and across the country, radio station operators lived a sort of pixieish, devil-may-care existence. Their offices usually featured a portable bar (disguised as credenzas in the Bible Belt). A humidor for expensive cigars graced their desks, the drawers of which were loaded with the tokens with which they paid their wages of sin—antacids and stay-awake pills and an assortment of prescription medicines.

The preluncheon martini was considered mandatory, and Karl and I were observing this protocol with religious fervor when he asked how Kansas City looked to me after my years in Europe. I told him Kansas City didn't seem to be the lively gateway to the Southwest that it used to be. I said I thought it was because it had become a one-newspaper town, that something goes out of the spirit of a city when that happens. I had noticed the same effect in Omaha and Des Moines. Newspaper competition seemed to be necessary in order to keep a community on its toes.

Warming to my subject, I went further and said it was radio's fault. "You guys have cut up the advertising dollar so many ways that only one newspaper can exist in a city," I charged. "And furthermore, you haven't done a darned thing to take the place of the missing paper."

"Wait a minute, wait a minute," Karl interjected. "Do you know how many people we have in the newsroom at KMBC?"

"How many?"

"Five," he boasted.

"And," I responded, "do you know how many people there are in the newsroom at the Kansas City *Star*?"

"Well, hold on a minute, that's their principal business."

I slammed the table so hard I thought I'd broken my watch. "You've just proved my point. News is their principal business. Your principal business is entertainment."

Karl wanted to know what I would do about it.

"The least you ought to do is put your own reporters out on the beats where the really important news is, where things happen that really affect the people—City Hall, the county courts, the state capitols, Washington.

"Those correspondents in Jefferson City and

Topeka, and particularly Washington, ought to be breaking down the day's news and telling the guy at Tenth and Walnut how it affects him."

It was pretty fundamental stuff—Journalism 101 in almost any communications school. But one month and two meetings later I would be on my way to Washington with a hefty salary to open a bureau for KMBC and a consortium of other Middle Western stations.

I got there in time for the 1949 inauguration of Truman, a story of particular interest to his hometown, where his haberdashery had failed and his county court judgeship had been undistinguished and where, therefore, there was considerable trepidation about the future of the nation when he first took office upon Roosevelt's death. By now, however, concern had been replaced by pride.

I also had a hand in the UP coverage of the election in which Truman had defied the polls to defeat the Republican candidate, Thomas Dewey. So certain were we all of Truman's defeat that the news services had set up a death watch at his modest home at the corner of North Delaware and a street then called Elm in the county seat of Independence, out at the end of Fifteenth Street from Kansas City, Missouri. It seemed likely that at some point during the evening, the President would appear at the doorway on the North Delaware Street side and would read a statement conceding and congratulating Dewey, and that perhaps he would answer a question or two.

Before the assassination of John Kennedy, presi-

dential security was rather loose and the small posse
of us reporters and a couple of newsreel cameramen
were permitted to wait at the edge of the Truman
lawn. Relay teams brought refreshment from a
nearby coffee shop to help ward off the early fall
chill as we shuffled through the thick deposit of oak
leaves and trampled the neighbors' browning grass.

It is hard to believe that as late as November 1948
few people had portable or automobile radios. We
got our election returns from the coffee-shop relay,
which brought the startling news that Truman had
taken an early lead. But NBC's H. V. Kaltenborn and
other pundits advised us that this would change
when the rural precincts were heard from. The
Chicago *Tribune* was so confident that it proclaimed
a Dewey victory with a banner headline in its early
edition.

By this time, a press aide assured us, Mr. Truman
had long since retired, so there would be no statement until morning. The lights went out and the
Truman house was dark. Our vigil continued, and
indeed there was proof through the night that our
President was still there. His bedroom was on the
Elm Street side, and several times the bathroom light
went on for a brief few moments. The older members of our press corps were able to interpret this
signal for us younger chaps.

Shortly after dawn messengers from our offices
began arriving with the word: Stand down. The
President would hold a news conference later in the
morning at the Muehlbach Hotel. Nothing would be

happening in Independence. Indeed, nothing would be. It turned out we had been hoodwinked. The President had slipped away in the early afternoon before our watch had begun, and had spent the night watching returns and sleeping at the Elms Hotel, a suburban retreat. A Secret Service man said he could not explain the bathroom light, but his eyes danced as he said it.

Years later, after we had become good friends, the President's daughter, Margaret Truman, who was home that night, denied that the family had indulged in any such gambit, but I thought her denial was a little tentative.

The Truman inaugural was the first and the last story of any major significance during the life of our Middle West radio bureau. I did six fifteen-minute commentaries a week with surprisingly little impact, considering that almost all of my ten stations were leaders in their markets.

I did learn some important lessons: for instance, that radio isn't a medium for great subtlety, sarcasm or irony. Paul White, a journalist who came early to CBS and practically invented radio news, used to point out that the flow of information to the ear was so transitory that every point in a broadcast story had to be repeated: "You have to tell them what you're going to tell them, tell them, and then tell them what you've told them."

That sort of thing can certainly defeat any attempt at subtlety. But I didn't know that at the beginning.

I found occasion to comment on the Daughters of

the American Revolution's disreputable refusal to let the great Marian Anderson sing at Constitution Hall in Washington simply because she was black. I identified the DAR as "this splendid group of ladies who have chosen to preserve our past by living in it." I waited with some trepidation for their reaction and that of our conservative station owners.

Only one letter came my way. It was from the national commander of the DAR, who happened to live in Missouri and had heard my broadcast. In her own hand on the engraved peach vellum of her stationery she wrote two pages expressing appreciation for my kind words, so different, she noted, from the treatment the DAR was receiving from the unpatriotic liberal press.

As far as the daily news coverage to my clients went, it turned out that the news editor at only one station had any idea how to use a Washington bureau. With a Washington correspondent to answer their queries, these stations could have customized their news reports to great advantage, but despite my urging, only Jim Borman at WMT in Cedar Rapids, Iowa, had the concept, knowledge or interest to do so.

I suspected that some of this disinterest had to do with the fact that many of the news editors weren't very skilled at their jobs, and some was just the result of sloth. But perhaps at least some was a result of the kind of show-business jealousy that plagues broadcast news. These local broadcasters simply were unwilling to share any of their glory with some Washington parvenu. There was not a great cry of rage, therefore, when the service came to a precipitous end and I was launched onto the network.

The Korean War did it. With the American commitment to the fight and my World War II correspondent buddies already on the way, I knew that was where I belonged, although Nancy was barely a year and a half old and Kathy was on the way. (We didn't know she'd arrive on the day General MacArthur made his daring end run around the North Koreans and landed at Inchon.)

Ed Murrow had tried to hire me during World War II, when we were both in London. I had accepted his offer and then reneged a few days later when United Press gave me a flattering raise with an equally flattering assurance that I would certainly rise far in the company. Now, hoping that Ed had forgiven me, I rapped out a telegram to him saying that, while I was one war late, I was ready to join CBS if they'd have me.

The answer was affirmative. The stations let me out of my contract on condition that I'd come back when the war was over. It was a nice safety net, although I don't think they were any more confident that this was a good idea than I was.

So I began getting my shots and attending the daily briefings at the Pentagon preparatory to going to Korea. And I was substituting for various of our Washington correspondents on CBS Radio. There was a lot of this work around. Several people had already been dispatched to the Pacific, and others hadn't yet been retrieved from vacation.

Eric Sevareid did one of our major broadcasts, the fifteen-minute news and analysis at 11 p.m. He was taken ill, and the manpower pool was so dry that they thrust me into the spot. Unfortunately, I had grown a little rusty on the techniques of fine-tuning a broadcast to the second, as demanded by the network. Those recordings for the Middle Western stations ran just fifteen minutes or so.

So when I went into the studio for the first Sevareid broadcast I was a little offended when the producer, known for his rather smart-alecky tongue, asked: "Do you want a watch?"

I thought he was making a snide remark about my freshman status, suggesting that I was ready for my retirement award. That wasn't it at all. He was asking the usual radio producer's question as to whether I would do my own timing or whether he should slide across to me a stopwatch showing the last minute of the broadcast as it counted down.

He seemed startled when I didn't appear to start a watch of my own but appeared to be timing the broadcast by the big clock on the wall. The result was a shambles. I ran over by untold seconds—at least a half minute. Red lights were flashing in the studio and bells clanging in the control room. My producer was in a paroxysm of anguish. No one in the Washington bureau, perhaps no one in the whole world of CBS News, had ever so violated the holy covenant of time.

So strapped was CBS for manpower that despite this start there was one substitution job after another that filled the days while I waited to go to Korea. The North Koreans had pushed the South Koreans and the United Nations—that is, American—troops back into the southeastern quadrant of the country behind something that had come to be known as the Pusan perimeter.

The fighting wasn't going at all well, and I was beginning to doubt my sanity in volunteering for war correspondent duty. The state of things was pointed up by a little vignette at Tokyo's Haneda airport late one night that summer.

Ed Murrow was coming in from the States for a look at the war, and Bill Downs, by now a veteran of World War II's European, Russian and Pacific fronts, was over from Korea to meet him. In those days the Japanese by the hundreds crowded the airport balconies all night long to watch the procession of planes shuttling through between Korea and the States.

As Murrow appeared at the plane door and began descending the stairs, the crowd was treated to the sight of Downs, in full battle dress, running across the tarmac waving his arms frantically over his head. He was shouting: "Go back, go back, you silly son of a bitch! This isn't our kind of war!"

At just about that time, there were fateful developments on the Washington front. Much earlier than expected, the government suddenly granted CBS permission to buy an existing Washington television station. The transfer was almost immediate, and the network was anxious to put the stamp of CBS News on its outlet in the nation's capital. They needed somebody to deliver the news, but when they looked around the radio newsroom, the cupboard was bare. The regulars were in Korea or had a full schedule of sponsored radio programs that they were unwilling to drop for a medium whose opportunities were still somewhere around the corner.

So I was asked to go out to WTOP-TV and do the six o'clock newscast. They sent along a young radio producer who knew scarcely more than I did about television. With a cameraman who doubled as our graphics director, we were the WTOP-TV news staff in Washington.

We learned fast with primitive equipment, no film except that which we shot locally, and a limited budget. Korea, of course, was the big story, and I covered that with a simple expedient. I had attended enough daily war briefings during World War II and lately at the Pentagon that I could do them blindfolded.

We put up a large blackboard with an outline of Korea and, drawn across it, the 38th parallel, which was supposed to divide North and South Korea. I extemporized a chalk talk with a description of that day's action, slashing great arrows and crosses across the board to depict the movement of troops and where they battled.

Of course, prompting devices were still a long way from the drawing board, and anyway, as new as television was and as little of it as I had seen (we didn't even own a television set yet), I had a gut feeling that television news delivery ought to be as informal as possible. I imagined the newspaper editor running down a list of the day's big stories when asked at home: "What happened today?"

I had early training to do that. When I was on the night desk of the United Press in New York in the early days of the war, our president, Hugh Baillie, used to call in from wherever he was, which most frequently was a high-level dinner party, to ask what was going on. He expected a seamless rundown of all the big stories on the wire—the newly breaking ones and the latest developments in the running ones. If he asked for more details, the deskman on the phone was expected to deliver them as if he had memorized them.

So the television ad-lib came easily to me, and I thought that this seemingly extemporaneous type of delivery fitted the concept of speaking to that single individual in front of his set in the intimacy of his own home, not to a gathering of thousands. My "script" consisted only of a list of the subjects on which I would report, proper names I would need to remember, and the occasional precise figure I might need. I crammed it all on a slip of paper I pasted behind the desk sign that identified the WTOP-TV News. We attempted some pretty dramatic effects, primitive though they were, to spice up the broadcast. As drought struck the Middle West, we went to an easel with a map of the United

States. Behind the easel stood a studio assistant with a powerful studio light. As I started the story, he pressed the hot light to the map behind Kansas and, lo and behold, a miracle of early television: Kansas began to smolder and smoke and the "drought" spread to neighboring states. The effect was rather unique, as was the arrival of the fire department summoned by the studio's automatic smoke detectors.

So sudden had been my assignment to television that I was severely deprived in the wardrobe department. Certain limitations of the early iconoscopic cameras dictated that only single-colored suits, shirts and ties should be worn—no patterns. I had none of the above, so I hastened to Woodward & Lothrop and asked for a hurry-up outfitting. They cooperated and delivered my suit the next day in time for a Sunday panel show on which I was to appear, my first network appearance.

I felt I was doing just dandy, and at one point even attempted a little of the old casual gentleman stuff. I thought I would emphasize my thoughtful attitude by sliding my hand into my jacket pocket. I tried but my hand wouldn't go. I fumbled a bit right there on camera before giving up. When I was off camera and had a chance to evaluate the situation, I found that the store had neatly bound all the pocket openings with white thread. When I scolded my colleagues and the director for not telling me of this wardrobe gaffe, they blandly said they thought that was the way I always wore my suits.

We learned a lot in those early television days, not least that our new medium had a powerful impact. In 1953 the Netherlands suffered a devastating flood and there were appeals from relief organizations for clothing and blankets. I had a brainstorm that veterans of the 101st and 82nd Airborne Divisions who remembered with fondness the help of the Dutch in the war's Arnhem operation might spearhead an American civilian effort to repay those valiant people.

A good friend, Rex Smith, vice president for public relations of American Airlines, offered to cooperate. Their ticket offices would be used as collection points for donations, and American Airlines planes would fly the material to Amsterdam. My old friend from the 101st days, General Anthony McAuliffe, the hero of Bastogne, agreed to go on the air to mobilize the veterans. Arthur Godfrey, whose CBS program was one of the nation's most watched, agreed to put McAuliffe on and said: "I'll switch you over to my writer for my lead-in," and he gave me to a gruff voice that barked: "Rooney. What have you got?"

It was my old World War II buddy Andy Rooney, of whom I had lost track entirely. After the war he had had a successful screenwriting career in Hollywood before becoming Godfrey's head writer. Neither of us could foresee then that he would go on to become a television personality in his own right.

The McAuliffe pitch went on Godfrey's show that very Tuesday night. I was awakened the next morning by Rex Smith. An exceedingly cool customer who in his earlier life as a longtime big-city managing editor had handled every sort of crisis, Rex was now, incredibly, near hysteria.

"What have you done to us?" he shouted. "Our ticket offices are inundated. Some of our people couldn't even get into their offices—stuff was piled in the doorways before they ever got to work. There isn't going to be enough cargo room on our regular flights to move all this stuff. What are we going to do?"

What we did was get the Association of American Truckers to organize their members and have them move the tons of material to a Hoboken pier from which we planned to ship it by sea to the Netherlands.

Smith's efficient American Airlines staff made all of these arrangements in the next few days while, I gather, Smith fought off American's other executives, including his old friend, American's president and founder C. R. Smith, who had a reasonable question as to how Rex had had the temerity to get the airline involved in such a massive venture without first clearing it with them.

The answer to that was, Rex and I agreed, simply that neither of us expected anything like the response of the public, airborne vets and others alike, to McAuliffe's appeal. This observation came as we met the following Tuesday for lunch at Rex's favorite watering hole, New York's "21" Club. Despite the problems, Rex and I were exulting in this new demonstration of the compassion for the unfortunate, and the spirit of volunteerism, that is such a hallmark of our American people.

But Rex added an observation. "What is really strange," he noted, "is the difference in that giving spirit between people in different parts of the country. The people on the West Coast just don't seem to have it. We got very little, practically nothing, from them."

We pondered that for a while when suddenly it hit me. In those early days before the coaxial cable stretched across the nation, all network programs were shown on the West Coast with a one-week delay. This was Tuesday, a week later, and the Godfrey program was about to be repeated throughout the West, and our whole experience of the previous week was about to be reprised as well.

For the second time in a week I saw the usually unflappable Mr. Smith begin to come apart. He hastened to one phone to warn his superiors at the airline, and I rushed to the adjoining booth begging Rooney to excise the Dutch relief bit from the repeat of the Godfrey broadcast. Rooney tried, but by then cutting McAuliffe and adding material to fill the hour was impossible. What he did manage for us was a quick note at broadcast's end saying that the need had been fulfilled and no further donations were required. That didn't stop the West Coast donations, but it kept them within acceptable bounds.

There was an unfortunate sequel to the story that demonstrates another thing about us humans—that sometimes political considerations can get in the way of humanitarian need. The Netherlands' Ambassador had made a very gracious little speech at the airport as the first planeload of donations had left Washington, and his staff had been profuse in their expressions of gratitude for our efforts.

Simultaneously, however, across the Atlantic a political brouhaha was developing. General Lauris Norstad, commander of the Allied Air Forces in Europe, in his deep concern for the flood victims, surveyed the damage by helicopter and immediately ordered help sent by American planes. The anti-American, left-wing Netherlands press seized this as an issue and complained that the Netherlands couldn't even have a disaster without the United States getting involved. It seemed perfectly silly at the time, and even more so in retrospect. The Dutch government, however, was so sensitive to the charge that I was coolly advised, by the Netherlands' Embassy which only two days before had been so grateful, that thank you very much but they didn't need any more help.

So now we had a warehouse full of old clothes and blankets that the Dutch government said it didn't want. American charities were the beneficiaries.

There was a lesson a day to be learned as we felt our way into the television age, about ourselves and our power to move people, and about the people we moved. And indeed about those who expected to profit by our ability to move people.

At WTOP-TV, within weeks of the inception of my 6 p.m. newscast, we had a sponsor and added an

11 p.m. broadcast, a local station pattern universally followed today. Our night sponsor was Hechinger's, "the World's Most Unusual Lumberyard"—unusual because it catered to "Harry Homeowner." A cartoon version of Harry was its logo. Whereas most lumberyards sneered at the would-be purchaser of anything less than 1,000 board feet, Hechinger's listened patiently as its suburban customers described with detailed imprecision that piece of lumber they needed: "About so long and so wide and about that thick." They made a fortune with their idea of personalized service.

With Hechinger's I had an early experience with sponsor discounts. I was assured that if I presented myself to the manager of Hechinger's Silver Spring store, he would give me the best employee price on the attic fan I needed. I was not too discouraged when the manager proved to have no idea who I was when he got the mysterious call from the head office. After all, even we still didn't have a television at that time.

Shortly thereafter I did buy a huge Magnavox cabinet that had a record changer and radio behind phony drawers in the base and, above them, a tiny screen that must have been about a ten-incher. We still had that set ten years later, when color was coming in. The box was so big and the screen so small that our friends assumed we had color. We let them think the color wasn't working.

The manager-without-the-television-set said: Mr. Hechinger says you want an attic fan, Mr. Cartwright."

"Cronkite," I corrected.

"Yeah, well here they are up on that shelf. I would recommend the Twin Vornado. People seem to like it."

And how much would it be to me? I inquired.

He picked up a nearby phone and dialed the home office. He then looked carefully over both shoulders. It was midmorning on a rainy weekday and there wasn't another soul in the store, but he appeared as if he expected to find spies ducking under the hardware counter and behind the paint cans.

With one hand cupped around the mouthpiece, he whispered: "I've got Mr. Conkwright here. He wants the Twin Vornado. Can you give me the employee discount on that?"

He wrote some figures on a notepad, hung up and held the pad so that none of those nonexistent spies could see it.

"That's the list price," he whispered again. "And that's what it will cost you."

The list price was $97.50, as I remember. The cost to me would be $82.85, which sounded good to me. I was grateful for my employee discount. I'd take it.

"You know what, Mr. Conkwright, maybe you don't want to do that."

He pointed to a big sign off to the side, which I had not noticed.

"We've got them on sale for $79.95."

I was so disillusioned that I haven't asked for a discount from a sponsor in forty years. It is a bad idea anyway, promoting an unhealthy coziness between the news and the advertising sides.

In those early years, when the number of sets was still comparatively small, there was a disconcerting anonymity for us on-air people. Chevrolet sponsored a weekly news summary that I did with Ernest Lindley, *Newsweek*'s Washington bureau chief.

Shopping for a new car, I found myself sitting at the desk of a salesman at Ourisman Chevrolet in Washington. Overhead was a huge banner stretched across the room with heroic-sized pictures of Lindley and me. It exhorted: "Watch Ernest Lindley and Walter Cronkite. Chevrolet Week-in-Revue. WTOP-TV Channel 9. Six p.m. Saturday."

The salesman was filling out an order form in case I decided on the car we had just seen.

"That name again?" he asked. After some difficulty and a couple of false starts he got it right.

"Now who do you work for?"

"CBS," I responded.

He stared for a moment at what he had written and finally asked: "Is that a government agency?"

Our six o'clock sponsor was the Esso Oil Company, which had had great success with local radio newscasts. Esso picked us as the first test market for a television version of "The Esso Reporter."

Esso was to become Exxon. It may have been among the first companies to change its name to a totally meaningless combination of vowels and consonants. I've never understood that corporate fad of later years, causing big companies with nice, respectable, old-fashioned names like United States Steel, Baltimore & Ohio Railroad and the like to

suddenly become USX and CSX and other unin-
spiring symbols.

Apparently the WTOP broadcasts were successful. At least we certainly seemed to please one
elderly man who unfailingly appeared at our station
every night, watched the eleven o'clock news on the
set in the lobby and then quietly disappeared into the
dark. Our receptionist told manager John Hayes,
who found the story rather charming—or at least,
and far more likely, marketable.

"Get his name," ordered Hayes of the receptionist.

The next day she reported back.

"He says his name is Hechinger."

Mr. Hechinger, the elder, was a self-made man—
up the hard way. As an immigrant youth he'd pushed
a wheelbarrow from one location to another around
Washington where old buildings were being demol-
ished. For whatever was discarded he found a customer until his savings permitted him to open a
building supplies store. The rest was Washington
commercial history.

He was quite elderly by the time his name was
being bandied about as one of the first sponsors on
Washington television.

Our studios were out in residential northwest
Washington, at Fortieth and Brandywine streets. He
lived on Massachusetts Avenue only a mile or so
away, but our eccentric early signal leaped over
his apartment building and he couldn't receive the
station on his home set.

So every night his chauffeur drove him to the station to see "his" show. Unassuming as he was, he never announced himself, and he never told his advertising manager what he was doing. He was afraid others would think he simply didn't know how to tune in his set.

Network television assignments began to fall my way, and one of the earliest may still hold the record as the most complicated in the medium's history. It was the coronation of Queen Elizabeth on June 2, 1953. There was tremendous interest in the United States. The story had everything—a beautiful young princess ascending an ancient throne with pageantry unmatched by any other event in the modern world. It was a grand opportunity for the young medium of television to display its ability to bring the world into America's living rooms. The overriding problem was that our abilities were still limited.

We didn't yet have tape on which to record our camera coverage. We were still in the age of film, which had to be developed—a time-consuming process. And most important, we didn't have satellites or any other means by which the pictures could be transmitted across the Atlantic. The challenge was to find a way to fly the film to New York and get it on the air the same day. The crown would be placed on Elizabeth's head in Westminster Abbey shortly after noon, 7 a.m. New York time. The commercial piston planes of those days took fourteen hours, London to Boston. Given the five-hour time difference and a lot of luck, one might get the ceremony on American television by 10 p.m. CBS decided to go all out to beat the opposition with the first pictures on the network and, second, with the first full instant documentary of the historic day. Furthermore, it was prepared to take a real gamble and promise that our first pictures would be seen at 4 p.m. Eastern daylight time, and the full documentary treatment would hit the air at 10. Separate task forces were set up. Don Hewitt would produce the documentary, with Ed Murrow as the commentator. CBS News president Sig Mickelson would produce the quick version, which I would report.

Hewitt's group chartered a Boeing Stratocruiser, among the fastest airliners at the time. They stripped out seats and installed facilities to develop and edit film. Desks and typewriters were provided for writers and researchers. They planned to have their program ready to go when the plane landed at Boston.

Our arrangements were even more complicated. The Canadian Broadcasting Corporation offered its cooperation, and our film would hitchhike across the Atlantic on one of the first military jet aircraft, the Royal Air Force's speedy Canberra bombers. They could cross from London to Labrador in just five hours. The only problem was that the Canadians, naturally, didn't intend to make a detour to New York with their film. The Canberras had to land in Labrador for refueling anyway, so we chartered a World War II P-51 Mustang fighter to fly our film to Boston's Logan Airport, where we would set up transmission facilities just off the tarmac. CBC would dispatch the first Canberra from London immediately after the coronation ceremony in Westminster Abbey.

All we needed now was something to put aboard that bomber. The best coverage of the day's events certainly would be that of the British Broadcasting Corporation, with its scores of cameras at every possible vantage point and its supreme broadcaster, Richard Dimbleby, who, shortly before his death many years later, would be knighted by that same Queen Elizabeth.

We set up a studio and production center in an abandoned tower at the London airport. We had two rapid film developers that could take pictures off the television tube and deliver them in just fifty seconds. And we had a broadcast booth where, watching the BBC coverage, I could cut in at selected times to inject an American angle to the story. Also, using that technique, we could insert my commentary to bridge large and comparatively uninteresting sections of the daylong events to fit CBS's time restraints. A battery of film editors we had brought from the States stood by to cut the unwanted parts of the film and fit in my commentary.

All seemed to be going well enough on the big day until about midmorning, when it was realized that our film editors were falling far behind; there simply weren't enough of them. Practically as the Canberra was warming up for takeoff, Mickelson made a command decision: The cans of still-uncut film reels would be carefully labeled in sequence, and while they were on the way, we would dictate to the Stateside editors just where, second by second, to make the cuts.

We got our film with the full Westminster ceremony onto that Canberra by the skin of our teeth. CBS News went on the air from Logan just as the Mustang appeared on the horizon. Our reporter, Ron Cochran, was on the tarmac excitedly reporting the plane's progress as it taxied up to the ramp by our control center. The pilot, Joe De Bona, handed down the film to our chief engineer, R. G. Thompson. Whatever self-congratulations occurred to Tommy and the rest of our Logan crew at that moment were instantly crushed. The film reels were not in the cans in which they had been shipped—the cans with the identifying numbers, without which there was no way Logan could know the order in which to broadcast them.

The pilot later explained that he had had to take the reels out of their cans because otherwise he couldn't fit them all into the tiny cockpit of his plane. But we were lucky beyond all luck. The engineers reached into that grab bag of reels and selected one to slap on the air. It wasn't in the order that we in London intended, but it happened to be the reel of the coronation ceremony itself, obviously the highlight of the day. As that reel ran, the staff at Logan got the rest of the reels in the proper order with a lot of words of assistance shouted over a less than satisfactory telephone line from London. Our viewers were told that now that they had seen the Queen crowned, we would take them back to the beginning of her day. It seemed as if we had actually planned it that way.

By that fluke, we won the network scramble to be first to show the actual coronation. But we didn't get on the air first with coronation day pictures. We lost by almost ten minutes to NBC and ABC. They both took a feed from the CBC broadcast of Dimbleby's almost undiluted and unedited BBC program as transmitted to them from Montreal, where that Canberra bomber landed a few minutes before our Mustang relay touched down in Boston. But their report started as the Queen's day began, and it was some reels later before they reached the Westminster ceremony.

The Murrow team arrived in New York a little later than planned, but still in time to get on the air as scheduled. Their original, non-BBC film, beautifully edited by Hewitt and beautifully narrated by Murrow, won great public and critical praise.

With daring coverage like that, television was growing up. The coronation broadcasts were a far cry from our first television remote—the return to Washington of General Douglas MacArthur from Korea in 1951. MacArthur, so incredibly arrogant, so clearly disdainful of President Truman's civilian leadership, was openly questioning the White House direction of the war. Truman, on his part, had reason to question MacArthur's military leadership. He had pursued the North Koreans beyond the 38th parallel, up toward China's border on the Yalu River. His headlong chase after another great MacArthurian victory had brought the Chinese into the war. The winter on the Korean front was terrible; the enemy was fierce and the casualties were high.

Truman, firm in his belief that democracy demanded that civilian authority must always prevail over the military, in his gutsy fashion ordered home the great hero of World War II, General of the Armies Douglas MacArthur. The move was highly controversial. MacArthur had millions of supporters, mostly those of a more conservative persuasion. Millions of others supported Truman, mostly those of a liberal bent. Thus, MacArthur's return to Washington's National Airport was a major news event—loaded with emotion, pathos and political significance.

We handled it from the top of a station wagon parked on the tarmac not far from the airplane steps. Our program was probably about as good as that sort of thing went in those early days. The public relations people were not yet concerned about staging such events for television. They did not keep the welcoming crowd of officials and others at a distance great enough to give the cameras a nice, clean look at the principal actor. As a matter of fact, I could barely make him out even from my elevated perch, and my monitor was, most of the time, a blur of crosshatched lines and snow. I'm afraid that my description of MacArthur's historic arrival home was to a large degree imaginary.

Actually, the great man didn't say much at the airport event anyway. He spared us a reprise of his arrival back in the Philippines in World War II. He didn't say: "I have returned." He saved his oratory for an appearance before a joint session of Congress—the speech he constructed as the farewell message of a great military hero martyred and sent into exile by Philistine politicians.

He was a great public speaker, there was no doubt about it. He was really too good—frighteningly good for a man with all his other accomplishments and attributes. His bearing was that of a conquering Caesar. He seemed to tower over men who were actually inches taller than his five feet eleven inches. He made no effort to hide his superior intelligence and sent every possible signal that he did not suffer fools—gladly or any other way. He left no doubt that he knew the way, and, more important, that he knew that his way was the only way.

In every possible respect, Douglas MacArthur was the very picture of a man on a white horse. As such, he scared the hell out of a lot of Americans, even among the huge majority that honored him as a brilliant soldier who had led us to victory in the Pacific and had created, with stern compassion, a democracy in beaten Japan.

His speech to Congress was rather heavy in patriotic bombast and fustian flourishes, but it was also spellbinding. Watching from the House press gallery, I could feel the sense of enthrallment that gripped the chamber even among those many law-

makers who would oppose the political ambition
they felt was laced between the lines of the speech.

And I saw not a few of them sneak a quick wipe
of their cheeks as they rose to give him a rousing
ovation after his closing sentence—delivered, of
course, with perfectly measured cadence, each word
marching proudly erect to the general's command:
"Old soldiers never die, they just fade away."

It was dramatic. It was also just oratorical hyper-
bole. He had no intention of fading away. Powerful
supporters were already pushing him as a Republican presidential contender in the 1952 campaign,
and they were to win him the coveted spot as the
convention's keynote speaker. They were confident
that this hero with the silver tongue would stampede
the convention and then smother the Democrats.

Several things got in the way. For one thing, his
speech wasn't that great. When he dealt with the
issues, his conservatism confirmed the more moderate Republicans' fear of his authoritarian posture.
Further, most of the right had already made a commitment to that wing's longtime leader, Ohio's
Senator Robert Taft. But perhaps the greatest im-
pediment to MacArthur's presidential ambitions
was that the moderate Republicans had found
their own war hero, one less controversial and far
more personable than MacArthur—Dwight David
Eisenhower.

A few years later, sometime in the fifties, when
we were searching Army pictorial service files for a
particular historical picture, we came across some

old footage from the Philippines. The scene had obviously been carefully staged to show MacArthur at his imperial best, working at his desk as U.S. Army commander in Manila in the days before World War II.

The camera travels some distance across the large room to emphasize the grand nature of the commander's surroundings. As it gets into a medium-close shot, from stage right appears an officer, literally bowing as he approaches the Great Man. He places some papers in front of him. Without looking up, MacArthur signs the papers and, still without acknowledging the courier, slides them back to him. The officer picks up the papers and, again bowing, backs out of the picture. The officer was MacArthur's aide, the man later to become the commander of all the armies fighting Hitler in Europe: Dwight Eisenhower.

I wasn't a great admirer of MacArthur's politics, but I'll admit I suffered a twinge of regret when he did actually fade away. You see, if my Grandfather Fritsche hadn't been so darned protective, I might have been Douglas MacArthur, Jr.

When my mother was a teenager growing up in Leavenworth, Kansas, one of her beaux at Fort Leavenworth was the young MacArthur—young, but apparently not young enough.

The family legend goes that MacArthur asked for Mother's hand in marriage. Grandfather accused the young captain of being a dirty old man, far too advanced in years for his daughter, and chased him off the front porch, one of MacArthur's few retreats.

Once, at a large reception, I dared mention the matter to the general.

"Helen Fritsche," he repeated. I thought I detected a slight glint in his eyes.

"Ah yes. Yes."

And he turned to greet another guest.

CHAPTER 8

FAME CAME suddenly—a thunderclap, a bolt from the blue. There had been some limited recognition, mostly among other newspaper people through the United Press bylines from overseas, and among those television viewers who could get WTOP-TV in Washington. Occasionally those local broadcasts in the capital brought a little national attention.

In 1950 *Time* magazine carried a short piece in its medical column reporting what it believed to be the first diagnosis by television. My physician, Dr. John Ball, called me after the broadcast one night to say that I wasn't looking so well, that he feared I might have caught the flu that was going around, and that perhaps I should drop by to see him. This was the same Dr. Ball who had taken my call when I had been felled by appendicitis. An ambulance had rushed me to Suburban Hospital in Bethesda, and the good doctor had inquired whether I wanted a general or a spinal anesthetic.

"A spinal," he explained, "leaves you conscious, but you can feel no pain below your chest. In effect you are paralyzed."

"Could I watch the operation with a spinal?"

Ball said he'd never had such a request before, but

he didn't know why mirrors couldn't be arranged to permit me to witness the proceedings. Whereupon a male attendant arrived in my room to prepare me. He was shaving away when he asked: "You got a hobby, Mr. Crockett?"

Whatever shot they had given me was wearing off. The pain was excruciating.

"No, no, no I haven't," I muttered through clenched teeth.

"You oughtta have a hobby, Mr. Crockett."

"Cronkite."

"Yeah, you oughtta have a hobby. Why don't you take up woodworking?" This was so ridiculous that he was beginning to get my attention.

"I sell woodworking tools on the side. I'm going to leave my card on the bureau here. Give me a call if you want to get some nice tools cheap when you get out. You really oughtta have a hobby."

Now he had aroused my curiosity. How did he happen to be in this interesting sideline, I wanted to know.

"Well, working here at Suburban Hospital, all these guys come in on the weekends with their fingers cut off and all that and I just say, 'Hey, do you want to sell your tools?' and they nearly always do. I got a basement full of the stuff."

It was the punch line as he finished his work. A moment later they were wheeling me to surgery. A large mirror was arranged over the operating table, and with the spinal taking effect, I could watch but not feel as they strapped me to the table, my arms bound to my sides and my head held in a vise. My head was covered and an oxygen mask was fitted to my nose and mouth.

The operation began. It was fascinating. The neat knife thrust, the clamps holding back the flaps of flesh, the exposure of my viscera. The surgeon and his team were working in perfect unison as far as I could tell, scarcely a word between them. Unseen behind me, however, the anesthesiologist and his assistant were engaged in spirited conversation when the crisis hit. Suddenly I could not breathe. My lungs simply wouldn't work. I would later learn that this was shock. Having been told during the war and at other times that people died of shock, I had always assumed it was something like an electrical shock, and I guess that, in a way, it is.

The effect simply is that everything is short-circuited. Bodily functions—most important, the lungs—quit. The blood stops pumping, and within minutes the brain goes dead. This had happened to me—or was happening. I had no means of communicating—my hands were tied down, my head locked in position. Only my eyes were showing and I rolled them frantically in a desperate effort to attract attention.

Oblivious to my plight, the anesthesiologist was telling the nurse, and I remember it word for word: "I saw this little blue beauty out on the lot last Saturday, a neat little two-door for only seven ninety-five. If it's still there, I'm going to pick it up this weekend."

I was dying and he was buying a car. Apparently the surgeon could see my life signs failing as he worked. He looked up in alarm and shouted through his mask: "Oxygen!"

"Whoops," said the anesthesiologist as he turned a valve. As instantly as it had all begun, I was breathing again. I might accredit my numerous mental lapses since then to damage done in that minute or so, but I doubt I could substantiate the claim. The defendants could certainly make a case that these lapses began long before the suspect operation.

This, however, was an extraordinarily vivid demonstration of what I fear occurs too often in our hospitals. People die as a result of such negligence, and the medical personnel, adhering to an unwritten code of mutual protection, draw their wagons into a circle, nod sadly and wisely and tell survivors that the heart of the deceased simply failed under the strain of the operation.

When I got back to my room, none the worse for the operating room ordeal except for the painful incision, a surprise awaited. The television station management had arranged at great effort to deliver a set to my room—this in the days before television sets were portable and before they were standard hospital-room equipment.

As I was wheeled into the room, the nurses, who had gathered to watch a rerun of an old Laurel and Hardy comedy, retreated to their appointed rounds. They left me alone, immobile across the room from the set. I had never been that much of a Laurel and

I arrived at Dr. Grey's Lying-In Hospital in St. Joseph, Missouri, in 1916, born to a young dentist and his bride of one year.

When Dad's Thirty-sixth Division shipped out to France, he was its dental surgeon, and Harry Truman was commanding an artillery battery.

A whole brood of Cronkites: Grandmother and Grandfather with Dad (there on the left) and his brothers and baby sister. Another boy and girl would come along later.

Grandfather Fritsche's original drugstore in Leavenworth, Kansas, was a wonderful place.

Galveston, Texas
September 27 - 1930

Mother and Dad are standing. At fourteen, I'm sitting between grandmother Mathilda Fritsche and grandfather Ed Fritsche.

Fred Birney, an inspiring journalism teacher who influenced the course of my life

WKY offered me a job as football commentator in Oklahoma City.

The Houston Press recruited me from its Austin bureau to work in Houston. That's me in the background behind City Editor Roy Roussel.

My gorgeous
bride—forty-five
minutes late for
our wedding

Here is Betsy,
with Kathy in
her arms, beside
Nancy and
grandmother
Maxwell.

An Air Force public relations man dubbed us civilian war correspondents "the Writing Sixty-ninth." Putting on flying clothes, we were (left to right): Gladwin Hill, William Wade, Robert Post, myself, Homer Bigart and Paul Manning. Andy Rooney missed the photo session.

The press at the Nuremberg Trials was seated perhaps forty feet from the defendants. To my right is *The New York Times'* Drew Middleton; to my left, Dick Clark and Ann Stringer, both of the United Press.

There has never been anything as exhilarating as driving at high speed in competition.

A more family-oriented sport: sailing with my son, Chip

Nancy and Kathy get to meet the Beatles on their first American appearance. Ed Sullivan discovered them through the "Evening News."

In 1950 CBS signed me to do the six o'clock newscast at WTOP-TV in Washington, D.C.

Two years later, Sig Mickelson selected me as the anchor for the convention broadcasts.

The 1952 Democratic and Republican conventions were not only the first time, but also the last, that the American public would have such an opportunity to see our great political conclaves in pure undiluted form.

With "You Are There," we had an extraordinary company of actors eager to learn about the new medium of live television under the direction of Sidney Lumet.

In 1954, CBS decided to produce "The Morning Show." Charlemagne and I discussed the news of the day.

My best friend among that first class of *Mercury* astronauts was a Navy test pilot, Wally Schirra.

I failed first-year physics at the University of Texas. If my professor had heard me explaining orbital mechanics to an audience of trusting millions, I'm afraid he would have spun in his grave.

The back of a station wagon was "broadcast center" for the launch of the first American into space in 1961.

President Kennedy helped us inaugurate network television's first half-hour evening news broadcast in 1963.

"From Dallas, Texas, the flash—apparently official. President Kennedy died at 1 p.m. Central Standard Time—a half-hour ago..." The words stuck in my throat.

Harry Truman was the first president to open the White House to a television tour.

Eisenhower and I made a trip back to the beaches of Normandy to film his reminiscences for the twentieth anniversary of D-Day.

Vietnam was a far different sort of war than what we
senior correspondents had known in World War II.

Lyndon Johnson was quoted as saying, "If I've lost
Cronkite, I've lost middle America." It was just five weeks
after my broadcast that he announced he would not run
for re-election.

The first formal Israeli-Egyptian peace agreement resulted
from the meeting of Anwar Sadat and Menachem Begin
that was brought about, in turn, by the separate interviews
with them on the "Evening News."

To say that Nixon was the most complicated personality
to occupy the Oval Office is barely to touch the surface.

President Carter honored me with the Medal of Freedom in 1981.

DOONESBURY

For Walter Cronkite — for whom we all rise on a special evening —

A champagne toast and a raucous story at the White House with (left to right) President Reagan, Press Secretary Jim Brady behind me, Director of Communcations David Gergen, Attorney General Ed Meese, Vice President George Bush and Chief of Staff Jim Baker, and in the foreground, CBS producer Bud Benjamin

by Garry Trudeau

ALL RISE!

RICK, GO ASK HIM TO MAKE IT STOP RAINING!

SHOULDN'T WE SAVE HIM FOR TURBU- LENCE?

©B Trudeau

admiringly, Garry Trudeau
24 April 1978

Garry Trudeau's take on me in 1978

Enjoying retirement at the wheel of the America's Cup
twelve-meter *Courageous*

Hardy fan, but now they struck me as particularly funny. The first laugh sent a piercing pain up from my new stitches. I rang for the nurse to come turn the set off. This exercise was as useless as usual. She didn't appear. I tried to clamp my jaws to restrain the laugh. Useless. I pressed the pillow against my ears. Useless. Now I was holding the stitches together as each laugh threatened to split them wide.

"Laugh? I thought I'd die." The old phrase had a new, ominous meaning for me. The nurse eventually came, and for the second time in an hour, my life was saved in the nick of time. That television set button that turned off the laughs was as welcome as the valve that had turned on the oxygen. The on/off buttons on a few million television sets across the country would have a life-or-death meaning of a different sort in the years ahead.

The full impact of the career I had chosen began to hit me first with the political conventions of 1952—and not fully until the night that the last of the two major conventions ended. It was in the early predawn hours of the morning, and the usual heat of a Chicago July had beaten its brief daily retreat before the lake's cool breeze wafted across Michigan Boulevard.

Sig Mickelson and I were walking down the nearly deserted boulevard. Sig, as the first president of CBS Television News, was father to much of the medium's development and to TV news as we know it today. In fact, he may have been the first to use the word "anchorman." It was either Sig or our convention producer, Paul Levitan. Each has his partisans. I remember hearing Paul first explain the term as referring to the person on a relay team who runs the key last lap, and then Sig said it referred to the steady anchor that holds a boat in place. In any case, the meaning had been changed forever, and I was the first bearer of it. Sweden was a little slow to adopt the term. There, for some years, anchormen were called "cronkiters."

As Sig and I walked down Michigan Boulevard, I was aware, of course, that our telecasts of the conventions had won some national recognition. *Time* magazine had done a laudatory piece on my work. It said: "Smooth-talking Walter Cronkite delivered the most lucid flow of comment and information." Now Sig was speaking words I would never have expected from a boss.

"Well, Walter, you're famous now. And you are going to want a lot more money. You'd better get an agent."

A newsman with an agent? Agents were an adjunct of the entertainment business, not journalism. The mere thought seemed blasphemous to me. Mickelson patiently explained that any raises would not be a matter decided between him and me, that the television business didn't work that way. He pointed out that CBS News had a business manager chosen because of his skills at negotiating the lowest possible cost for the department's talent. Certainly I should not match my skills against this professional, but instead should have a professional negotiator of my own—an agent.

My misgivings about the sort of business I was in were well founded. This was show business, and as it turned out, down that road lay the perils of the star system and the million-dollar anchors. As for the money Sig was suggesting I would want, I really hadn't given it any thought. Journalists in the days before television didn't gauge each assignment on the basis of the career enhancement and economic reward it might bring. My base salary at CBS was still quite low—below two hundred a week—but the extra fees for sponsored broadcasts brought the total up to a not magnificent but certainly livable wage. Further, the challenge and excitement of anchoring the first full-scale television coverage of a political convention was too appealing to pass up.

As the conventions opened in that year of 1952, I suppose some of my CBS colleagues were envious of the assignment Sig had given me, but most of the best-known radio reporters were still contemptuous, to a degree at least, of this newfangled picture business. They became more interested in television as their own pictures began to appear and public recognition followed.

Fame engulfed all of us whose faces hung out there on the television tube. I watched as it first struck Eric Sevareid. He was one of those exceedingly bright people recruited by Ed Murrow in London at the beginning of the war—including Charles Collingwood and a dozen or so others, a most exceptional group who became known as "the Murrow Boys" and established CBS as *the* news network. All of them were huge successes in radio and at first ridiculed television and its show business glamour as being unworthy of their talents. That is, until occasional appearances shattered their radio anonymity and they began to bask in public recognition.

It came to Eric at the 1952 political conventions. He was in the corridors of the convention hall when a lady approached him. She gushed in adulation. Eric was digging his toe into the floor in an expression of modesty when she asked if he would do her a favor. Eric reached for his pen to give her the autograph he was certain she was seeking, but she said: "My little boy was the Boy Scout who gave the Pledge of Allegiance this morning. He went into the men's room over there several minutes ago and he hasn't come out. Would you go in and see if he's all right?"

The impact of television was immediately apparent to that entire convention. The late great reporter Don Hollenbeck was in line waiting to get into a men's room. He was wearing the man-from-Mars equipment with which CBS had outfitted him—a backpack, earphones, a silly little skullcap with a long antenna rising from it.

The fellow up at the head of the line turned around, peered at Don through alcohol-clouded eyes and cried: "Oh, no, not television in here!"

The presence of television began to influence politics from the beginning. And because it increased the public interest in how politics worked, it inspired Theodore H. White to write *The Making of the President, 1960* about the 1960 election of John Kennedy. He probed inside the machinery of the campaign between Kennedy and Richard Nixon. He exposed all the nuts and bolts and told a fascinated world how the gears meshed and the engine worked, who the real mechanics were and how they tinkered with this part or another to make the machine run better or, at least, differently.

It was a brilliant book and became a best-seller. And it almost ruined political journalism. The journalist pack, previously in pursuit of the issues that presumably had motivated campaigns, skidded to a stop like the Roadrunner. In a cloud of dust it reversed course and went chasing off after technique instead of substance, and thirty years later it was only beginning to get back on the track of substance.

The *1960* book and several similar White volumes on subsequent presidential campaigns were very important additions to our political literature. They brought into the spotlight's bright glare practices that tend to thwart and distort the electoral process. But White himself never suggested that campaign tactics and technique should take precedence over the issues, and it is not his fault that his journalist followers and admirers have concentrated on the sizzle rather than the steak.

In emphasizing political manipulation rather than issues, the press has probably contributed to public cynicism about the political process. It is reasonable to assume that this, in turn, has helped lead to the disquieting decrease in the percentage of our quali-

fied electorate that goes to the polls. That number
has fallen so low as to be an international embarrassment. This vaunted democracy, beacon to the world,
has the lowest voter participation of any major
nation. The number of eligible voters who actually
go to the polls has dropped below 50 percent. Thus,
the majority electing our officeholders may be less
than a quarter of our eligible population. That raises
a question as to whether we qualify as a democracy
at all.

The fault for this lies with all of us—the politicians, the press and the public, which tolerate an
educational system that turns out a population which
in large numbers is too illiterate to participate mean-
ingfully in a democracy. And some fault may be
placed squarely on television—its use, its misuse
and its nonuse. Unfortunately, it is probably more
than a coincidence that as television viewership has
increased, voting participation has decreased.

Politics stuck its toe into the television age at the
party conventions of 1948. Cameras were there, but
the number of stations and sets were so few as to
relegate that pioneering event to a historical footnote. By 1952, however, the nation was tuned in as
politics really entered the television age. Those 1952
conventions were a brief moment of glory in television's infancy before the politicians discovered
its vast potential and set out to master it. For the
first time millions of Americans saw democracy in
action—as it chose its presidential candidates.

On television the public saw the issues, the big
ones and the little ones, debated in platform commit-

tees; they watched the critical battle for delegates waged, not alone on the convention floor but also in the committees; they were taken to the keyholes of the smoke-filled rooms where decisions were being made.

Of course, the public didn't see everything that went on at the conventions, but it certainly got the flavor from television. The Republican nomination hung on the outcome of fights to be seated between opposing sets of delegates from seven states, especially Georgia and Texas, in each case one slate supporting the longtime leader of conservative Republicans, Senator Robert A. Taft of Ohio, and the other supporting the political newcomer but national hero General Dwight D. Eisenhower. Meeting the week before the convention got under way in earnest, the Republican National Committee decided that its debate and vote would take place behind closed doors. So we set up our cameras outside those locked mirrored doors of the Boulevard Room in Chicago's Conrad Hilton Hotel.

Standing outside with microphone in hand, as indignant as the press gets whenever it is locked out of what it considers to be the public's business, I emphasized the secrecy of the deliberations going on behind what I referred to as the "mirrored curtain." For one afternoon, however, I was broadcasting a fund of information about the goings-on inside. The source of those reports baffled both the Republicans and my broadcast opposition. My source was literally "on the inside."

Our chief technician, Orville Sather, had tapped

into the microphones on the committee's podium inside the room. He ran a wire up the outside of the hotel and into a broom closet several floors above. There one of our newspeople listened to the proceedings through earphones and wrote notes that were rushed to me downstairs.

Unfortunately, this didn't last too long. Our man had to go to the rest room, and while he was gone, a reporter for a small out-of-town station became curious about that outside wire and traced it to the closet. He was just putting the earphones to his head when the Republican security people, also tracing the wire, broke in on him. We might never have had to admit that we were the perpetrators of the bugging except that, with good heart, we had to confess in order to get the inquisitive but innocent reporter off the hook.

The National Committee turned the debate over to its Credentials Committee. The attempt to ban television coverage of the Taft-Eisenhower delegate fight brought thousands of protests pouring in from loyal Republicans across the nation demanding to know what the committee was trying to hide. The Credentials Committee saw the wisdom of opening its debate to television.

It voted to seat most of the Taft delegates, but after heated debate, the full convention overrode that decision and gave most of the disputed delegates to Eisenhower. This was the big test vote of the convention, and established Eisenhower as the party's nominee.

The television audience watched that fight, as it did the rest of the proceedings at Chicago's International Amphitheater, as first the Republicans then the Democrats met on the edge of the stockyards. The TV viewers were witness to the only-barely-controlled chaos of proceedings on the convention floor. They heard the open debate and they watched skilled politicians maneuver as the master parliamentarians, the Democrats' Speaker of the House Sam Rayburn and the Republican former and future Speaker Joseph Martin, wielded their gavels with practiced and heavy hands.

Most of the time the podium was crowded with highly placed hangers-on, and the chairmen were almost elbowed from the lectern by party officials offering advice, sought and unsought. With these extemporaneous proceedings, the public got a wonderful sense of participation in the political process, a wonderful civics lesson. It nearly saw, as well, a great tragedy.

With the informality of pretelevision days, there was virtually no decorum on the floor. Most of the delegates were men, and many of them were in shirt-sleeves and suspenders. A perpetual fog of tobacco smoke hung over the assembly. The delegates came and went at will. Frequently there were few delegates on the floor as the speakers droned on. Others sprawled across several of the folding chairs, napping away the previous night's indiscretions. Many read newspapers and tossed them on the floor when they were through.

At the Democratic convention, during one session that had gone on most of the night, the floor was calf deep in paper. Somehow it caught fire, and flames immediately leaped from the floor. Senator James Byrnes, at one time President Truman's Secretary of State, was at the microphone with his South Carolina delegation.

Someone grabbed his microphone and was shouting, in a voice tinged with panic: "Don't panic. Don't panic. Don't panic. It will soon be out. Don't panic!"

Delegates beat at the flames with their coats and stamped at the edges of the blaze. Firefighters arrived to help extinguish the fire. Byrnes resumed talking, opening with a disclaimer that despite the heat of the debate, he had not started the fire.

It was later learned that several of the hall's exit doors had been locked for security reasons. The fire had the makings of a real disaster—a matter that did not escape me when the flames seemed to be gaining the upper hand. There would have been no escape from our broadcast booth, high in the amphitheater's rafters.

That was the convention that nominated as its presidential candidate the reluctant Governor Adlai Stevenson of Illinois. As we waited in the hall for him to arrive, an advance copy of his acceptance speech was passed out to the press. Eric Sevareid was sitting with me at the anchor desk, and we both began poring over the speech. I was deeply impressed by the beauty of Stevenson's language, unmatched by any other politician in my time. Eric and I finished our reading, and as I looked toward that master essayist, expecting to hear a paean of appreciation, he tossed down the Stevenson copy with a look of disgust. And he said: "I'm not sure I'm going to enjoy covering a politician who writes better than I do."

I met with Stevenson several times during the ensuing campaign, and as with most of those who knew him, I became a great admirer of his intellect, his personality, his gentlemanliness. I also decided he would probably not make a good President. He was almost too bright, too humane, too liberal (in the best sense of the word). He saw and understood, it seemed, all sides of all issues.

We who covered the campaign watched him many times sitting on the stage waiting to be introduced, oblivious to the preceding speakers as he reviewed, edited and rewrote portions of his prepared address. Almost always he seemed to be seeking compromise with opposing points of view, watering down his strongest arguments. I feared that this sort of conciliation could wreck his White House.

Although it probably wasn't that important, I was also disappointed on occasion by what appeared to be his arrogance but what I believe was a sign of distraction. He was clearly unhappy with the perennial campaign practice of sending candidates off to small meetings in union halls and church basements simply to satisfy a local politician's ego. Unfortunately, by the short shrift he gave such meetings, he

gave well-wishers who might have waited hours to
see him the impression that he wasn't equally
delighted to see them. I don't think this was the real
Stevenson, and I suspect that he would have been
appalled if any of his advisers had dared bring the
matter to his attention.

Those 1952 conventions were not only the first
but also the last time the American public would
have such an opportunity to see our great political
conclaves in pure, undiluted form. By 1956 the parties had begun to sanitize their proceedings. In time,
platform and credential hearings were moved farther
from the convention (both in time and geography),
in part, it can be assumed, to discourage television
coverage. The list of speakers was limited and carefully screened "to avoid confusion," we were informed; delegates were even told what they should
wear and how to behave so as to present a more dignified appearance.

As much of the convention's business as possible
was done in advance of the meeting, or at least
behind closed doors. Disputes, always the basis of
free debate, were swept under the rug. Delegation
microphones were strictly controlled, turned on or
off at the whim of convention officials. Elaborate
stages were built with projecting platforms where
speakers could perform in splendid and imperial
isolation, not unlike Mussolini orating from his
balcony.

In an effort to please the television cameras, chaos,
to a large degree, was banished from the convention

halls, and so, to a large degree, was democracy. The conventions were reduced to marketing tools. From that day forward, the image on the tube has been the most important aspect of a political campaign, and politics and television have gone skipping hand in hand down this primrose path.

By the 1956 campaign year the public's fascination with television had created a new phenomenon. The people frequently showed more interest in the television reporters than in the candidates. In that year I was one of the few reporters riding Estes Kefauver's bus through Florida in his campaign against Stevenson for the Democratic presidential nomination. He was stopping at what must have been the smallest whistle-stops in the history of American politics. Two old men playing checkers at a country crossroads were enough to command his attention.

If the crowd was larger, however, a problem began to develop. I wasn't our evening anchor yet, but when I got off the bus many of the curious would surround me rather than the candidate. Finally the senator, noting, somewhat wistfully I thought, that he was the candidate, asked me if I would mind getting off the bus last so that he would have a chance to meet the people first.

Kefauver, despite his coonskin hat and country ways, was a smart, sophisticated politician. He may have been the first to bend television to his will by staging what became known as a photo opportunity. At the Democratic convention that year he violated

an old custom that candidates not appear in the convention hall before the nomination roll call was
completed. He caused a stir by showing up to escort
his aged father to a box seat near the podium. Naturally all eyes were on him, including those of the
television cameras. His was perhaps the first political publicity coup deliberately staged for television.

The photo bite was invented before the sound
bite. The politicians learned fast, and early on began
trying to control their television appearances for
maximum advantage. Of course, they ran headlong
into broadcasters intent on transferring to television
the journalistic ethics they had learned as newspaper
reporters.

Our reportorial instincts sometimes ran into broadcasting's tyranny of the clock. Early in 1952 Washington and presumably the rest of the country were
speculating on whether Harry Truman would run for
reelection. He was scheduled to address a Democratic function at Washington's National Guard
Armory, and CBS was the only network to cover it
live. The speech was supposed to run to eleven
o'clock, but as usual for almost any speech, it was
clearly going to run over.

Just as the clock was ticking toward eleven, I
sensed that Truman was about to make the announcement for which we had been waiting. But
through my earphones the director was telling me:
"Okay, give us a good night. We've got to get off."

I had no way of communicating with the control
room, but as I took to the air I said that the President

seemed to be about to make an important statement. The control room either wasn't listening or didn't care. All I heard was: "Cut, cut. We're running over. Get off."

A minute after we left the air, Truman announced he would not seek another term. We'd missed a clear beat.

Early in that pioneering decade of the fifties, the then majority leader of the Senate, Lyndon Baines Johnson of Texas, was finally persuaded to appear on our CBS Sunday morning panel broadcast, which, I believe, we still called "Capitol Cloak Room." Shortly it would become "Face the Nation." Johnson showed up at our studios on schedule for a prebroadcast briefing fifteen minutes before airtime. He sat down with the panel and pulled from his pocket a sheaf of papers. He handed a page to each of us and said: "Boys, here are the questions you'll ask me."

As moderator I thought perhaps I should attempt to moderate. I explained to him that we didn't use prearranged questions, that the guests were never advised as to what they would be asked.

"That's all right with me," he said, and took the papers from each of us and walked out the door. I caught him in the corridor and persuaded him to go on the broadcast, now minutes away, by agreeing that we would limit the questions roughly to the areas he had designated.

Bill Downs asked the first question—a tough fast-ball far afield from any of the Johnson-approved areas. The future President peered at Downs through squinting eyes and finally got his clenched jaws open far enough to say he wouldn't answer the question. The rest of the half hour went like that: monosyllabic answers or none at all from the guest, and an increasingly nervous panel.

Downs later chastised me for making the compromise with Johnson and pointed out that he had not violated the agreement to limit the questioning since he hadn't agreed to it in the first place. It was not exactly television's finest half hour, but historically it may be significant as a harbinger of the relationship that still exists between politics and television: a standoff between an attempt to manipulate the medium and the medium's determination not to be manipulated.

"Capitol Cloak Room" had been on CBS Radio for years, but when we transferred it to television, Larry Spivak, the originator of "Meet the Press," was incensed. He had started his program on NBC Television nearly a year earlier, and he angrily threatened to sue all of us who had anything to do with what he insisted was a CBS "imitation."

I must have had in the back of my mind a particularly vitriolic attack he had made upon me at a cocktail party a few days before, when at the conclusion of the following Sunday's "Capitol Cloak Room" I said: "And thank you, gentlemen, for being on our panel, and thank you, Senator Kerr, for being our guest on 'Meet the Press.' "

I didn't even hear myself say it, and neither the

panel nor Senator Kerr seemed to have either, but as I left the studio our producer, Larry Beckerman, came flying out of the control room in the terminal stage of agitation. Somehow I survived what was one of my larger broadcast gaffes.

The politicians' attempts to control television have led to some unfortunate confrontations. In the Wisconsin primary of 1960 the viability of a Catholic presidential candidate was still being tested. We persuaded John Kennedy to appear on our election night broadcast from Milwaukee, and in the course of the interview I naturally asked his opinion of how the Catholic and non-Catholic vote was going.

He was obviously upset by the question, and only later did I learn that his campaign manager, brother Bobby, claimed he had produced Jack for our broadcast on condition that the Catholic issue would not be raised. I was never informed of such a promise, if indeed one was made by our producers. Like Downs a few years earlier, I would not have agreed to it anyway.

Soon thereafter John Kennedy called on CBS president Frank Stanton to complain about our coverage with a warning whose implication was unmistakable. He reminded Dr. Stanton that if elected president, he would be naming the members of the Federal Communications Commission to which CBS was in many ways beholden. Dr. Stanton courageously stood up to that threat, as he did on so many other occasions in defending television's free press rights.

Apparently Kennedy cooled down in his opinion of me because a few months later he agreed, reluctantly, to appear on an interview program we had devised. Interestingly enough, in this campaign on which Teddy White would base his first *Making of the President* book, issues so dominated television coverage that I sought a way to get behind the candidates' façades, to show their inner personalities.

I proposed a totally unrehearsed, unedited dialogue in which I would ask them some probing personal questions—a formula so standard today that it is strange to think it could ever have been considered radical. Management said I could do the program, but they were highly skeptical that I could get the candidates to appear in that format.

Indeed, Kennedy turned me down at first, but reluctantly agreed to participate after Nixon accepted. Nixon even volunteered to be interviewed first, although clearly the man who appeared in the second week had the considerable advantage of having gotten a taste of what was to come.

Early in the interview I asked Nixon: "Mr. Vice President, I know you must be aware . . . that there are some who would say, 'I don't know what it is, but I just don't like the man; I can't put my finger on it, I just don't like him.' What is it that you think they don't like about you?"

Nixon answered that question as if it had been rehearsed. He thought it was three things: the strident nature of his campaign in California against Jerry Voorhis for the House and Helen Gahagan Douglas for the Senate, his active role in the House

Un-American Activities Committee's Red hunt, and his physiognomy. He said he felt that his appearance was unfavorably affected by his rather low hairline and his heavy blue beard, which was obvious no matter how close he shaved.

Later, of course, it was his contention that the poor makeup job done to soften these features was what defeated him in his debate with John Kennedy, the first televised debate of a presidential campaign. The implication—which the Nixon people did nothing to correct—was that the CBS makeup woman had deliberately sabotaged him. The truth was that they were so suspicious of that happening that they had refused the ministrations of our cosmetician and had provided their own. Unfortunately, the parents of our Frances Arvold, CBS's highly skilled makeup artist, were solidly loyal Republicans who almost disowned her when they read of the Nixon allegations.

In a private conversation at one point during the campaign, former New York Governor Tom Dewey asked me what I really thought of Nixon. I gave my standard answer about not rendering personal opinions on figures in the news.

"But," I added, "I can tell you what I believe a lot of people think. He reminds them of three of the archenemies of our time."

And I named the onetime German heavyweight champion, Max Schmeling; the Nazi leader Rudolf Hess; and the Red-baiting Senator from Wisconsin, Joe McCarthy—all with heavy dark beards and low hairlines.

Dewey grabbed my arm. "You know," he said, "I never thought of Schmeling!"

The attempt by politicians to use television in the early days was frequently thwarted by their own inexperience. On one of our panel broadcasts our guest, Dewey, at one point said that the Kennedy campaign had gone awry and that the Democrats would be unable to put it together again—any better than you could put *that* together again. And he pulled a raw egg from his pocket and smashed it into the ashtray.

The problem with this imaginative visual was that he had failed to tip off our producers and the cameras never panned to the ashtray. All he did was splatter the rest of us with egg and leave a television audience puzzled by the odd expressions on our faces.

As for the rest of the Nixon performance on my interview show, he answered every question for the next half hour as if he were reading the answers from a TelePrompTer. He was so smooth, in fact, that the hoped-for spontaneity of the broadcast was never there. The following week we did Kennedy in his Georgetown home. He seemed somewhat ungracious, a little annoyed by our presence.

The questions, I think, were not as tough as those I had asked Nixon—Kennedy didn't have the political record on which to base very much—and the last question was the same: "What single quality do you think will be the most important that you take to the White House?"

It was such an obvious question that if he had seen our previous program with Nixon or if he had been briefed at all, he would have known it was coming. But he flubbed it, badly. He stumbled around and finally stammered that his particular attribute was "a sense of history." The cameras off, he got up, said a perfunctory good-bye and went upstairs.

I went out to the CBS truck parked in the street. I was looking at the recording of the interview to be played back later that night when our producer, Warren Bush, came by to tell me that Kennedy was insisting on doing the program over. He maintained that because of the way we had positioned him on his divan he appeared slumped over and unattractive, but clearly it was his answers, not his posture, that bothered him.

The producer said that Kennedy had rejected all of his arguments as to why it should not be repeated, primarily that we had made much of the fact that the Nixon program was unrehearsed and unedited, and that, in fairness, we would have to issue an equally prominent disclaimer stating that the Kennedy program had been redone at his request.

So I went up to Kennedy's bedroom to try my hand. The room looked like a college dormitory, down to the Harvard banner on the wall. Kennedy was lying on a twin bed, his jacket and shoes off, his collar undone and his tie pulled down. "Ready to go?" he greeted me.

"No," I said, "I'm ready to argue some more."

And I told him again how unfair I thought it would be and, with the disclaimer, how unfair it would probably appear to others. But he was adamant, said he didn't care about that. At which point I vented my frustration.

"All right," I said, "but I think this is the lousiest bit of sportsmanship I've ever seen."

I was halfway to the door when he called me back.

"Okay," he said, "let it go."

With all of our increased sophistication vis-à-vis the relationship between television and politics, things don't change that much. I thought of that episode years later, when in 1980 Senator Edward Kennedy dared challenge an incumbent President, Jimmy Carter, for their party's nomination. Kennedy badly booted an interview with Roger Mudd when he responded to a question for which he should have been prepared, a question not dissimilar to mine on which John Kennedy had stumbled. Because Mudd was a personal friend of the Kennedys, presumably the Senator thought he was safe in his hands.

Reporters, too, can flunk the interview exam. At the infamous 1968 Democratic convention in Chicago, where the street battles between the police and antiwar demonstrators stole the headlines from the proceedings, the bête noir in most people's minds was the city's powerful Mayor Richard Daley. Not only were his police officers using excessive force in routing the demonstrators (in what the Milton Eisenhower Commission would later call a "police riot"), but he was trying to control the convention inside the hall.

It was never established as fact, but I have always believed that Daley, perhaps acting on a hint or more from Lyndon Johnson, was prepared to try to stampede the convention into drafting Johnson for another term. Although Johnson had said he would not run, he had Air Force One, the presidential plane, standing by as he watched the convention from his Texas ranch. Ostensibly it was there in case he decided to address the convention. But it could also have rushed him to Chicago if a draft had developed.

In the best fashion of machine politics, Daley had stacked the public galleries with stooges ready to follow his every command and prepared to demonstrate popular support for a Johnson draft if any speaker had brought it to the floor. His security forces on the floor were also ready to keep a peace that would best serve Daley's agenda. They manhandled press and delegates alike. When they slugged our Dan Rather in the midst of one melee, my temper and objectivity snapped and I said: "I think we've got a bunch of thugs here, Dan."

Daley had refused any meetings with the press, but I persuaded him to come to our convention booth at some time convenient for him. (He later told me he agreed in order to please his wife, who, he said, was a fan of mine.) He told us he would be there at seven o'clock, just as the evening session began.

Knowing that he was a master at avoiding any direct answers by filibustering until his time was up, I conceived a plan that might have circumvented this. I thought I would ask him one simple question, prefacing it with a short recital of his recent actions and the criticism they had engendered. "In the face of all this, what is your explanation?" I would ask, and then, by not dignifying his answers with further questions, presumably let him hang himself. Of course, as any freshman journalism student might have known, the little plot backfired badly. His answer was smoothly exculpatory, and I looked as if I had just handed him some uncontested network time—which I had.

At Miami Beach that year the Republican convention was almost as interesting, although the demonstrators were kept under control, thanks to the innovative street diplomacy of Rocky Pomerance, an inspired and genial giant from Brooklyn who had worked his way through the ranks to become police chief of Miami Beach. The convention proved that the conservatives, who had dominated the party in 1964, still controlled it despite the overwhelming defeat that year of their candidate, Barry Goldwater.

And despite his defeat in the 1960 presidential race, it nominated Richard Nixon for another run. He chose as his vice presidential running mate Spiro Agnew, proving again the quixotic nature of politics and politicians.

Agnew as Governor of Maryland was a liberal Republican. He was convinced that the party needed to be wrenched back from the conservatives and that the best way to do this was to get behind the candidacy of New York's ambitious Governor Nelson Rockefeller, whom the conservatives had virtually driven from the floor of that '64 convention.

Although Rockefeller was reluctant to make a public declaration of his interest, Agnew worked openly to build support for his nomination. At the 1967 Republican governors' conference in Palm Beach, painfully through a laryngitis-inflamed throat, he outlined to me his plans to develop a cadre of liberals who would hold the line for the New Yorker against the conservative forces trying to lock up the convention for Nixon far in advance of the first gavel. Agnew was adamant that Nixon, if nominated, would lose the election, and that if he should win, his policies would be disastrous. For a year, still without any public declaration by Rockefeller, he worked for his nomination.

Finally, in early '68, Rockefeller scheduled a Saturday news conference in New York City to announce his intentions. It was almost universally accepted that he would run for the nomination. And this, apparently, is what he let Agnew believe, for Agnew called into his office most of Baltimore's influential political writers and a collection of his political allies.

The buffet table was spread with goodies and whiskey flowed. Rockefeller at the last second had changed his mind, however. He announced that he would not run. Not forewarned, Agnew was seriously embarrassed in front of his colleagues and the press. He was so angry that a few days later he telephoned Nixon and offered him any help he needed. He was rewarded with the vice presidential nomination.

Agnew would later lead the administration's campaign against the press, particularly television, before being forced to resign his high post rather than face trial for alleged income tax evasion. He would not be tried on charges of accepting payoffs from contractors, a practice that he allegedly began as Governor and continued as Vice President.

William Scranton suffered a disappointment similar to Agnew's with Rockefeller, but it was not Scranton's gentlemanly style to be vindictive. A former congressman and Governor of Pennsylvania and a liberal Republican, Scranton sought the presidential nomination in 1964. Just two days before the Republican governors' conference in Cleveland that year, he called on Dwight Eisenhower at his Gettysburg retirement home. He knew that Eisenhower had been telling Republican leaders that he felt Goldwater would be a disaster as a candidate, assuring Johnson's reelection. Scranton believed Eisenhower was sympathetic to his candidacy and he left Gettysburg thinking he had the former President's endorsement. He and others figured that the Eisenhower endorsement virtually assured him of the nomination.

I ran into Scranton as he arrived with his wife at their Cleveland hotel. As is the custom at those governors' conferences, they were met at curbside by the hotel manager and a welcoming party of Republicans. They were loaded with flowers and gifts, with other gifts, many quite expensive, waiting in their suite. They invited me to join them upstairs.

The manager accompanied us to the suite carrying a large leather case. As they entered the room, he placed the case on a table and opened it. It was a record player with a record already in place. The manager put the needle on the record and said: "There is a little welcoming speech for you here."

With that a Scranton aide called the Governor to the bedroom for a telephone call. The record in the living room was beginning: "Welcome, Governor, this is Bob Hope. You are going to have a wonderful time in Cleveland!"

But in the bedroom Scranton was listening to an enraged Eisenhower saying that the story of their Gettysburg meeting had been leaked and Scranton had it all wrong anyway, and that he never did intend to endorse him, that he was staying neutral. It turned out that George Humphrey was the operator who pulled the rug out from under Scranton. Humphrey was to be Ike's host in Cleveland. He was a close friend and Ike's former Secretary of the Treasury. And he was a Goldwater supporter.

He telephoned Eisenhower at Gettysburg and said that the popular ex-President and titular leader of his party must not be seen as participating in an anti-Goldwater cabal. I heard, but never confirmed, that Humphrey even told the former President that it would be awkward for him to stay at his Holiday Hill farm if he were backing Scranton. The next day in Cleveland, with Eisenhower a guest at Humphrey's farm, the two men appeared together at a meeting of the Republican governors and Eisenhower left them with the clear impression that he would not object to a Goldwater candidacy.

That 1964 convention in San Francisco was a dandy. Betsy and I took our sixteen-year-old daughter, Nancy, along, with her promise that she would not get involved in any demonstrations or activities that could embarrass us, particularly any that could cast doubt on my impartiality.

Our caution was not unreasonable. We had been blessed with two lovely daughters—and cursed, in that they reached their teens in the terrible sixties. Nancy and her younger sister, Kathy, seemed to enlist in every ugly fad that, according to the standards of their parents, blighted their generation.

I'm sure that in their group I was classified as an old fuddy-duddy. I once told Nancy that and she patted my head and said: "Yes, you are, but you also are a funny daddy."

I loved them, but that was despite my feelings about their general appearance most of the time. One Thanksgiving we persuaded them to dress for the family luncheon. Afterward friends joined them to go out and Nancy disappeared upstairs. She came back down a moment later, out of her Thanksgiving dress and into some indescribable outfit that, as I remember it, looked like—and probably was—from a remnants sale.

I dared a slight witticism: "Are you going to a costume party?"

Nancy shot back: "No, I've just been to one."

We parents were so frightfully ignorant that we thought that at least, thank goodness, they weren't into marijuana or worse.

Kathy's first book was about how children of famous parents coped with their parents' fame. It was written after she herself became a mother. In a clever tour de force, she interviewed her sister. Their revelations of their teen years in New York threw their mother and me into a paroxysm of shock from which I'm not sure we have yet fully recovered.

We did have some hints during those dark days. On one occasion Kathy called us from school to say that her class was going to a concert and she needed an additional five-dollar allowance. How nice, we thought, conjuring up pictures of her absorbing the music of the Boston Pops at Tanglewood. Driving to the country that weekend, we listened to radio reports of a wild gathering of thousands of young people at a place called Woodstock. How terrible, we remarked when we heard accounts of drugs, alcohol and nudity. And then an announcer referred to the affair as a "concert."

"Concert!" we shouted to each other as the truth burst upon us.

I later heard that Kathy had spent most of her time at Woodstock working in a makeshift first-aid center nursing victims of narcotic overdoses. A barely perceptible silver lining in the cloud.

Perhaps the darkest moment during those years

was at Christmas dinner, 1963. We were joined by a cousin, Doug Caldwell, at the table. He was just out of Marine officer training, handsome in his uniform with his new lieutenant's silver bars shining on the epaulets. He and Nancy had gotten along fine in their early years, but at dinner she spent a good deal of the time glaring at him, as if he were somehow responsible for the Vietnam War, to which he proudly said he would soon be going. Soldiers and cops were cut from the same cloth, Nancy asserted—savage, sadistic beasts.

I'm afraid I raised my voice as I challenged her, pointing out that they both put their lives on the line for the rest of us. Her counter challenges grew more irrational until Nancy screamed: "I'd gladly kill a cop!"

That tore it. Now I outscreamed her: If she felt that way, she could get out of our house. She fled to her room and I stormed up to mine. My emotions were tearing me apart. I was enraged at Nancy's statement, but simultaneously I was blaming myself for letting the conversation get out of hand. I was confident that Nancy didn't mean what she said for one minute, that it was intended solely to shock. Nor did I mean that I would kick her out of the house. And I was particularly chagrined that her little brother, Chip, had had to see us in such an angry dispute, and watch his father lose his cool. It wasn't much of a Christmas dinner, one to expunge from the memory book.

The major relief we parents got in those days was

in sharing our concerns. The conversation at every dinner party, sooner rather than later, turned to the behavior of our offspring. The horrors recounted by others sent us home most nights believing that perhaps our kids weren't so difficult after all. (I guess they weren't, really. They all turned out just fine, thank you. We all survived the Vietnam War, including Doug, who served there with distinction.)

At some point during the sixties a revelation came to me. What right, I asked myself, did Betsy and I have talking about our children behind their backs? Simply because they were our children, did they have fewer rights to considerations of privacy than friends, neighbors or office colleagues? We wouldn't talk about friends to others with the sort of criticism and candor we were unloading on our own children. Betsy agreed with me, and for the last half of the decade we sat mute at those dinner tables, and son Chip, seven years younger than Kathy, escaped our semipublic excoriation almost entirely. Actually, he didn't seem to offer as much raw material for serious concern. He reached teenhood just as the sixties faded. Youthful behavior patterns did seem to change then, or perhaps—is it possible?—we parents and society at large were adjusting to life as it would be lived in the late twentieth century.

We still weren't halfway through the desperate decade when the Cronkite family arrived in San Francisco in the summer of 1964 for the Republican convention.

The first morning there, I was in the Mark Hopkins barbershop when a familiar voice came from under the towel covering the face of the fellow in the next chair. It was, unmistakably, Walter Winchell.

"Hey, Walter," he said, "that's the cutest little girl of yours. She was a sensation last night. She stood outside here right in front of Goldwater's rally pushing a big Scranton sign up right under his face. I'm leading my column with it."

Before that incident, the Goldwater people had demanded that the Mark remove us from our suite. It was directly below theirs, and they felt certain we were there deliberately to bug their headquarters. The Mark managed to placate them.

The entire conservative leadership of the Republican party came to San Francisco to play a tough game, and they did. They took every opportunity to embarrass, taunt and humiliate Rockefeller and his supporters. Their speakers not only attacked the liberal Republicans; they scarcely missed an opportunity to attack the press as well. Even Eisenhower joined in this game, including in his speech a paragraph sharply criticizing us: "Let us particularly scorn the divisive efforts of those outside our family, including sensation-seeking columnists and commentators, because, my friends, I assure you that these are people who couldn't care less about the good of our party."

As he read his statement, delegates rose in their chairs and shook their fists toward our booths in the balcony. Eisenhower looked startled by the reaction.

The episode concerned me. I had never heard

Eisenhower express such opinions before. So I went along to his suite at the St. Francis Hotel. He greeted me warmly and we exchanged the usual niceties before I brought up the offensive paragraph. Again Ike seemed surprised, as if he hadn't heard those words before, let alone uttered them. He stumbled around in what seemed to me to be almost an apology. I got the distinct impression that the import of the words had not struck him as he rehearsed his speechwriters' work.

Eisenhower happened to be in the same St. Francis suite where four years earlier I had met Nixon's vice presidential running mate of that year, Massachusetts Senator Henry Cabot Lodge. I caught him there on the campaign trail for one of our candid candidate interviews in the same series that had opened with the Nixon and Kennedy sessions.

We were to follow the same rules: no advance interviews, no meeting beforehand between the candidate and me. On camera I would enter from one side of the room, he from the other, and the entire conversation would be taped, on the record.

We followed the rules, but just as we greeted each other and took our seats, the hotel power failed. While it was being repaired, we were left sitting with each other and conversation could not be avoided. He launched into a sharp criticism of all his previous interviewers. He complained that the press, implicitly drawing a comparison with the lace-curtain Irish Kennedys of Massachusetts, had made too much of his background as a Boston Brahmin, one of that elite upper class so influential in every phase of life in New England. He was indignant, and he expressed his certainty that I was too intelligent to indulge in such foolish persiflage. He did not know that he was speaking of my first question. Once on the air, I asked it anyway:

"You have been described as one of the 'Boston Brahmins.' What is a 'Boston Brahmin'?"

He thundered, or as nearly thundered as his haughty conservatism would permit: "Oh, Walter, now you ought not—I don't know—and nobody in Boston cares about that. We're all intermarried and we don't think in those antiquarian terms at all."

And Lodge asked why I didn't also mention that he was "distantly connected, in a family way, with Senator Kennedy."

How, I wanted to know.

"Well, my daughter-in-law is the cousin of the husband of one of Senator Kennedy's sisters," he answered. "I said 'distantly related'—that describes it accurately."

With the increasing number of Latin Americans, Italians and Jews in elected offices, it seems certain that changes are in the wind, but for our first two hundred years we Americans have picked our Presidents only from among those with unquestionably solid Anglo-Saxon names—and more Anglo than Saxon, at that.

When, in 1992, New York's Governor Mario Cuomo was agonizing over a possible run for the presidency, he publicly mulled over the question of whether his Italian ancestry would affect his chances. He suggested that an American whose name ended in a vowel could never be elected President. Cuomo was a rare combination: an intellectual and a spellbinding orator. I would have bet that he could have won the Democratic nomination and been elected to the presidency. He had electrified the 1984 Democratic convention with his keynote speech, and I never saw him fail to excite those who shared his liberal vision of the American future.

Despite the pollsters and the political operators' contrary opinions, I remain convinced that the public was ready for a leader who could restore that vision after the selfish eighties. I don't believe the public has rejected liberalism; it simply has not heard a candidate persuasively advocate its humane and deeply democratic principles.

It seemed to me that Michael Dukakis blew any chance he had of defeating George Bush in 1988 when he ran from the "L-word," even to the extent of letting Bush get away with accusing him of being a card-carrying member of the American Civil Liberties Union. Dukakis ducked that, too, although Bush had handed him on a silver platter a chance to defend the sort of Americanism that believes that the Constitution protects all of the country's citizens regardless of their appearance or the popularity of their cause or the ugliness of the crimes of which they are accused. As difficult as it may be to swallow some of the ACLU's positions, its courage in defending those for whom there would seem to be no defense is in the highest order of civilized behavior.

The convention with perhaps the most far-

reaching effect on American politics was the Democratic meeting in 1972. George McGovern was nominated as the party's presidential candidate, and his
forces managed a revolutionary change in the party
rules. In an attempt to democratize the presidential
nominating process, they stripped most of the political establishment of its privileges. Officeholders
and state party officials no longer would automatically become delegates to the national convention.
They would have to stand for election in either state
conventions or primaries.

The first to take advantage of this revolutionary
change was Georgia's Governor Jimmy Carter. He
realized that he did not have to gain anybody's
approval to run for the party's presidential nomination. He raised the funds and he beat the bushes and
he won in state conventions and primaries. The party
would never be the same. And with the realization of
their new importance, states across the nation
adopted the primary system.

The McGovern reforms had another effect. A new
responsibility had been loaded upon the press.
Under the old system, the party bosses selected candidates for offices from city councilman to President. They screened the would-be candidates, and
while a noteworthy number of rascals got past them,
the system was reasonably effective.

Deciding on a candidate for Congress, the party
hacks in the smoke-filled room ran through the
possibilities.

"How about Eddie Johnson?" one would suggest.

"Are you crazy?" might come a retort. "Eddie's a damned drunk. You can't run him."

"What about Henry Jones?"

"Come on, man. He's a womanizer. He's slept with every woman in the district. No way."

And thus went the screening process, a process virtually eliminated by the McGovern reform. So it fell to the press to do the screenings, to examine the candidates' peccadilloes, which, if they could possibly affect their performance in office, should be revealed to the voting public.

Candor comes irregularly, if ever, in politics, and an alert press can nudge it along a bit. My nomination for the most candid politician of my time would be Robert Strauss. He is one of the greats on the political scene, a distinguished lawyer in Dallas and Washington, a longtime power in the Democratic National Committee and its chairman from 1970 to 1972. He would later be President Bush's bipartisan Ambassador to the Soviet Union.

Bob is a hail-fellow-well-met with enough charm for a boxcar of politicians, but perhaps his most attractive feature is his occasional bursts of candor. After the Democratic whipping in the off-year congressional election of 1970, there was the usual postmortem speculation among pundits about a dire future, if any, for the Democrats. I took a camera crew around to see Bob, and he detailed a lot of reasons why that speculation was far off the mark. As our crew was packing up to leave and we still sat at his desk, I said: "Bob, you know, you made a few statements just now that I really find hard to believe."

"Walter, boy, you've got to believe me, fully 85 percent of everything I told you today is the absolute truth."

CHAPTER 9

T HERE IS A considerable upside and an almost
inconsiderable downside to television fame.

On the upside, of course, is the certainty of getting a good table in a crowded restaurant. Although
there is a downside to the restaurant's version of a
"good table." Successful restaurant owners have to
be pretty smart operators. They know which tables
you couldn't get the dumbest rube to sit at, and they
establish that these are the preferred locations,
where only their most favored customers are placed.
These tables are frequently right inside the front
door, swept by the cold winds with each new arrival
or departure. Putting the celebrities there not only
gets rid of those terrible tables but puts the "stars"
on display for the other customers.

Another "preferred" location is right by the
kitchen. Nobody except a celebrity would ever
uncomplainingly accept such a table, let alone tip
the headwaiter liberally for putting him there.
Celebrities simply aren't as smart as restaurant
owners.

A downside to celebrity is the autograph seeker
who, getting your signature, turns to a companion
and asks: "Who is he?"

Some years ago I was standing at the back of a political rally during the New Hampshire primary. I was straining to hear the candidate from my dark corner when a young lady shoved a piece of paper at me and asked for my autograph. I was signing when she screamed. I mean screamed—the sort of high, piercing scream that might accompany a rape or a deadly assault. The candidate stopped in mid-sentence (it takes a lot to get a politician to do that) and the crowd turned in their seats. And she yelled at me: "You signed over David Brinkley!"

But mostly it is up, not down. For instance, the benefits of wealth—let's make that "the benefits of being reasonably well off." Like the day I discovered that I could afford a sports car.

From an early age, I had been fascinated by cars, like any American youngster. The car I was driving to high school in Houston at fifteen would have been snatched from me if my parents had known that I raced it against other kids' jalopies on an old abandoned wooden racetrack on the city's outskirts.

In New York after the war I read of the new boom in British sports cars, but I didn't seriously think of buying one until I began noticing them in a used car lot under the elevated Red Bank station, where the train stopped briefly en route to the city. We were summering on the Jersey shore, and I was lounging on the beach when the postman brought the day's delivery. And there was a check for a lecture fee mistakenly sent directly to me instead of my agent. I suggested that day that Betsy take me all the way to the Red Bank station—so "we could spend a little more time together." That wasn't what I sneakily planned on spending.

When we got there, I urged her not to wait for the train. As soon as she drove off, I ran under the tunnel to the used car lot. Clutching my unexpected check in my hand, I said to the salesman, driving my usually hard bargain:

"What sports car have you got for $1,767.50?"

The astonished salesman escorted me to the lot and showed me a dandy little Austin Healy for $1,795.00.

"I'll take it," I said, "if you can sell it to me before the train comes." Later I tried to fathom why I'd made that stipulation: If I was going to have a car, I hardly needed the train. But that was only one of the small oddities surrounding that purchase.

My salesman, now more bemused than astonished, scribbled out a receipt and a temporary title, ordered dealer's plates slapped on the car, handed me the keys and demanded the difference between my $1,767.50 check and $1,795.00. I thought he was going to waive the difference, but since I didn't have it in cash he said he would trust me to bring it in the next day.

I hadn't driven a stick shift since sometime in the early thirties, and my departure from that lot was a little shaky—almost as shaky as my attempt to restart the machine after it stalled at the first toll booth on the Jersey Turnpike. Getting it restarted took the combined talents of, and a few keynote speeches from, a convention of drivers assembled from the cars behind me.

I felt pretty sporty in my new acquisition until, at the Lincoln Tunnel on the way home that night, I found myself in the lane next to a tractor-trailer truck and I realized that if I drove between his wheels my head might just clear the lower side of his rig. Even that couldn't discourage me. A few weeks later that tired four-cylinder Healy was traded in for the newest six-cylinder model. With a shiny new car I set out for a so-called hill climb in the Catskill Mountains. En route along the sun-baked back roads I ran over something that exploded with a strange pop, but the incident didn't seem serious enough to warrant stopping.

When a stop sign brought us to a halt, however, the most obnoxious odor enveloped us. The bottom of the car had been sprayed with either the remains of a long-dead animal or a long-spoiled can of meat. There was nothing for it, though, but to drive on to the Ellenville hotel hosting the sports car meet.

Once there and having checked in, I drove the Healy around to the back, borrowed a hose, cleaned it as thoroughly as possible and parked under a nearby tree. The next morning I found that the tree was a huge mulberry bush and my nice ivory-colored car looked as if it were suffering from a terrible mulberry pox. I borrowed a hose and thoroughly cleaned the car once again.

As Betsy and I tried to drive past the hotel, we found that all the assembled sports cars were lining up for a parade through Ellenville. We were invited to buy a ticket for the concours d'élégance, the cup to go to the handsomest vehicle in the parade, a contest in which were entered magnificently kept, mint-condition antiques. This was hardly for us, but I entered—proceeds to charity and all that.

We watched an exciting hill climb and attended the prize-giving banquet that night. They got to the first prize in the concours d'élégance and, lo and behold, they called my name. The master of ceremonies announced that the committee, having watched my efforts with the borrowed hose, had decided that such eagerness and dedication should be rewarded.

I moved on to racing, and thanks to the tutelage of one of the best, René Dreyfus, the prewar champion of France, I got pretty good at it. René was in Indianapolis for the 1940 race when France was invaded. It would have been dangerous for him to return to his country, so he enlisted in the U.S. Army and thereby gained American citizenship. After the war, with his brother Maurice, he opened a restaurant that catered to the French UN set and also became the New York rendezvous for the international auto racing fraternity.

The skill involved in driving a high-performance race car on road courses in those days before automatic transmissions intrigued me: shifting down and up for maximum speed and power around numerous curves and up and down the occasional hill; touching the toe to the accelerator even while braking with the heel and, with the other foot, depressing the clutch. So delicate was the touch that some of the best drivers wore ballet slippers.

Even on the enclosed oval at Indianapolis I learned by driving test cars that a lot of skill is required; coming into the sharply banked corners high and on the outside, diving for the inside at the bottom of the curve, drifting out and accelerating to straighten out just before the car hits the wall. This was not a sport, as I had always assumed, simply for the heavy of foot.

I cut my racing teeth with the Austin Healy and, with a codriver, won a ten-hour endurance race for economy cars in a Volvo. With my appetite whetted, I joined some other effete types in a group we called Club Lotus USA, for which we bought three used Lotus Club Eleven racing cars.

These extraordinary British racing machines were made of aluminum, so light you could almost lift them. The heaviest component in the car was the driver. The four-cylinder engines were retooled from the wartime fire pumps that stood by at England's emergency water tanks. Those devils had a top speed of 140 miles an hour and handled like the finest race car built.

Their clearance off the ground was barely three inches, and sitting at the wheel was like sitting on the ground—a fact brought home to me in dramatic fashion. Our early races were at a tight, sporty course at Lime Rock, Connecticut. The secret to winning there, as on most courses, was to get into the straightaway at maximum speed. At Lime Rock this meant almost jumping off the brow of a small hill and then drifting down and out of a broad curve before pushing the accelerator to the floor.

I was not doing badly in that exercise when, just as I was reaching maximum speed, I noticed a large terrapin beginning to cross the road. As I went around the next circuit I kept thinking about that terrapin being crushed by a race car. For three circuits he (or she—I never was very good at turtle gender) kept edging farther out into the road until, the last time around, we were looking at each other, eye to eye.

Then it struck me. It wasn't just the terrapin that was in mortal jeopardy; if I hit that beast, my little Lotus would almost certainly flip over. That next circuit was made with considerable apprehension. I went over the hill, slid down the slope and straightened out, thinking more of possible evasive action than of maximum speed.

The terrapin was gone, and he hadn't even left a spot in the road. Some kindly soul had removed him to safer ground—or a soup pot.

We were scheduled to race our Lotuses in the international twelve-hour race of endurance at Sebring, Florida. That was the biggie, then the only U.S. race to attract the world's top drivers. At the last moment, however, Colin Chapman, the Lotus builder, withdrew our entry. Almost simultaneously Lancia, the Italian motor company, decided that Sebring would be the site of a test-drive for a new economy car they were about to introduce. They hired us to drive them and flew the cars and mechanics to Florida just two days before the race.

It rained heavily the day before the race, and we had no time to adequately test the cars. They turned out to be incredibly slow. There we were, plodding along at barely 100 miles an hour, sharing the course with the world champions going at nearly twice that speed. It was very sobering to come into a curve where passing was dangerous at best and find in your rearview mirror the Ferrari or Maserati of Juan Fangio or Phil Hill.

I wasn't nervous, although I did have trouble on my first turn at the wheel. My codriver had started for us, and when he came in after two hours, I leaped into the seat. But the door wouldn't close. I slammed it as hard as I could. Something was blocking it. My mechanic discovered the problem and solved it: He pointed to the leg I had failed to pull into the car after me.

When I came in from my turn, I had to report that the car was making a strange noise on the tightest of Sebring's turns. I tried to explain to my codriver and the mechanics that there was this strange chirping sound as I took that corner. A fellow driver from Chicago was monitoring my performance around the course, studying my lines through the turns. When he came in next, he exulted in the fact that I may have been one of the greatest drivers he had ever seen.

"I've never seen a performance like it," he raved. "Your line through that hairpin was consistent and,

Cronkite, it was unbelievable, every time just so. You lifted that inside rear wheel just a few inches off the ground. I've never seen anything like it."

So that's what the chirping was: the rear wheel bouncing along burning rubber as I quite inadvertently lifted it off the ground. I was going around the corner on three wheels. I wouldn't try that again for a million dollars. I wouldn't have tried it then if I'd only known.

I not only drove in that race, I broadcast it. Between my turns at the wheel I dashed up to our booth and shared the duties with our CBS racing commentator, Art Peck. It was Art who, manning the public-address microphone at Lime Rock, commented on my first race that I had moved, as he called it, "into the silverware department." I was running third, proudly showing off to Betsy, my mother, and Nancy and Kathy, then twelve and ten.

Art's praise had scarcely cleared the airwaves when I shifted badly and went spinning off the course in a great cloud of dust. As Betsy and Mother gnawed at their fists, Nancy uttered the bottom line: "Does this mean Daddy isn't in the silverware department anymore?"

It was the children who brought me back to earth and drew me away from race cars. As they grew up and I spent more of my free weekends at the track, I realized that this wasn't exactly a family sport. I hadn't been under any pressure to quit. Betsy was stoical. So stoical, as a matter of fact, that I decided I must be overinsured. She later confessed that she threw up a lot. She did have one sneaky trick to slow me down. When she timed my practice runs, she told me I was doing better than I was so I wouldn't press too hard.

My emotional reaction to racing was strange. I wondered why I was doing it in the first place, and I came to the conclusion that a lot of us raced for the same reason that others do exhibitionist, dangerous stunts. It sets us apart from the average man; puts us, in our own minds, on a level just a little above the chap who doesn't race.

For me there has never been anything as exhilarating as driving at speed in competition. Part of that exhilaration was attributable to the fear that gripped me before the race. On the Monday before a coming weekend event, I began having qualms. By Wednesday I was looking into the shaving mirror and whispering "damned fool" deprecations at myself. By Thursday sleep had departed and I was beginning to hope that perhaps I would fall, break an arm and have an excuse to withdraw. By Friday I was a blithering idiot, and by Saturday, donning my fireproof driving suit, I seriously considered ripping it off and publicly admitting my cowardice.

But all that changed the minute I pulled on my helmet, slipped behind the wheel and revved up the engine to join the chorus with my competition. There was never another second of fear. Concern, occasional alarm, of course, but not fear. The adrenaline pumped ever faster as the race went on. And as I climbed out of the car, win or lose (and it was mostly lose), I was on a high that lasted through the evening. At dinner I talked too much and too loudly. The excitement simply wouldn't let up.

So it was hard to quit. I got an occasional fix by driving the pace car at the Daytona stock car races and test-driving a Jaguar at Indianapolis, clearly a tribute not to my skills but to the privileges that came with fame. And I believe I made the first televised broadcast from a race car when, for a CBS special, we took the Lotus to Daytona. Cameras weren't miniaturized yet and wouldn't fit in the car, but a big Telephoto lens followed me around the track as I broadcast an audio report of the sensations of speed.

I HAD NEVER been on a sailboat, but I had read more than my share of sea lore. Quite deliberately I decided that sailing was the family-oriented sport that I should substitute for racing.

The club where we summered outside Carmel, New York, had just begun racing the new Sunfish, a small, basically one-person sailboat. People had been urging me to try my hand at one, and now, with my new direction, I agreed. The instructions seemed simple enough: Pull on this string here and it brings the sail in or out to control the speed, and this handle here moves the rudder to turn.

All that had just been explained to me when the time approached for the day's first race. They helped me into a boat with instructions simply to follow their lead and do as they did and that we'd be starting out going down to that mark at the other end of the pond.

Well, for the first time and almost the last time, I was across the starting line first and was headed for the first mark. And I was pulling away from the rest of the fleet. Now what might have been a moderate problem became a first-class crisis. I didn't have the slightest idea how to make that ninety-degree turn around the mark. I did what came naturally. I capsized.

I later learned that the reason I had led the fleet to the first mark was that I was too dumb to know I was going too fast, right at the point of losing control. But I was hooked, and we transferred our sailing to Long Island Sound and began moving up in a succession of bigger and bigger boats. Betsy finally complained: "Doesn't anybody ever buy a smaller boat?"

The answer is: Not if they can help it.

The major problem with sailing was the children, for whom we had launched into this new sport in the first place. Their busy social lives didn't leave the kind of time required for a daylong sail or an extended cruise, and we never had enough room to take along all the friends they wanted to invite. I still dream, however, of ocean voyages with my son, Chip, to find that male bonding that modern life seems to deny us.

Sailing for me, though, has satisfied many urges. For one thing, it feeds the Walter Mitty in me, that inner heroism with which James Thurber endowed his unforgettable character. I never sail from harbor without either having a load of tea for Southampton or orders from the admiral to pursue that villain Long John Silver and his rapacious crew. I love the challenge of the open sea, the business of confronting Mother Nature and learning to live compatibly with her, avoiding if possible her excesses but always being prepared to weather them.

There is nothing more satisfying than dropping anchor in an otherwise deserted cove just before sunset, of pouring that evening libation and, with a freshly roasted bowl of popcorn, lying back as the geese and ducks and loons make your acquaintance and the darkness slowly descends to complement the silence.

The cars, the boats—all made possible by the wages of fame.

On the other hand, the downside. Not the least of which involves the attention of the *National Enquirer*, that supermarket tabloid of hilarious fiction.

The *Enquirer* appeared one week with a big banner headline over the masthead proclaiming the inside story of my encounters with unidentified flying objects. The story's lead was a one-paragraph description of my office and my posture, as, feet on desk, I recited my experiences with UFOs.

The rest of the story was all in quotations; my first-person story of watching a dog being kidnapped from a Caribbean island by little people from a spaceship and a series of other adventures too amazing to repeat here. The story had a byline and was datelined New York, so I called the New York office of the *Enquirer*. A fellow answered with a heavy Australian accent. I detected a little embarrassment as he identified himself as the author of the piece.

I advised him that I didn't recall ever meeting him and that my secretary's log indicated that he had never visited my office. This he acknowledged. The description of the office had come from some of my associates; his personal visitation was a question of literary license.

But we had met, he insisted. The first time was at Gallagher's Steak House, where he said I had been kind to him when he'd introduced himself at the bar one night. No, that wasn't where he interviewed me. That had occurred, he now remembered, at a National Conference of Christians and Jews benefit function where I had been honored one night, the award having been presented by Henry Kissinger.

An interview could not have happened there, I said—that was totally impossible. He said it had taken place as I was leaving the hall. Equally impossible—I had left the hall with Kissinger, who was giving me a ride home. That was just the time of the interview, he said. All of the quotes had been supplied by my good friends who had heard my stories many times, and all he had done while walking down the Pierre Hotel corridor that night was to ask me to confirm them, which he claimed I had done.

The story was a fabrication from beginning to

end. The bylined writer who had concocted the fiction was Robin Leach, who would go on to fame and fortune with further television fables of the rich and famous.

Some years later I told that story on a "60 Minutes" exposé of the *Enquirer*. I said they neither reported nor checked facts, that there was no truth in their accounts. Apparently they set out to prove to me that they could indeed research a story. They must have spent at least a million dollars digging up the full life story of Walter Cronkite. They tracked down elementary school classmates who hardly knew me. They tracked down my high school homeroom teacher. They spied on my son at Brown University.

Of course, the *Enquirer*'s sources were reporting back to me, and I had a pretty good idea of what the rag was up to when I had my grand encounter with one of its so-called reporters. As I was waiting for the puddle jumper that was to take me from LaGuardia Airport to Martha's Vineyard, I noticed a young man engaging in brief conversations with my fellow passengers. I thought at first he might be conducting a poll of some sort, but he wasn't carrying the telltale clipboard or otherwise taking notes.

The mystery was partially solved when he found what he was looking for, and exchanged a number of bills for a passenger's boarding pass. As we lined up to board, he maneuvered to stand right behind me. And when we took our seats, he was able to sit next to me.

We were scarcely off the ground when he said that

he was about to visit the Vineyard for the first time and could I recommend a hotel. An Australian accent again—almost a dead giveaway that he was an *Enquirer* reporter. I confronted him with my certainty that this was his identity, and that he was there to report on me. He cheerfully admitted his affiliation with profuse flattery about my powers of observation and reportorial deduction. He seemed a nice enough chap, except for his choice of employer, and we talked of newspapering.

"Why," I asked at one point, "is it that so many of you reporters on the sleaziest tabloids are Australian?"

He scarcely gave the question a moment's thought. "You know what I think it is, Mr. Cronkite? I think it is because our standards are so much lower than those of you American journalists."

As we disembarked I offered a sort of apology. "You know, I'm about to go to my Edgartown house. It has five bedrooms and only mine will be occupied tonight. If you worked for anybody else in the world, I would invite you to stay. As it is, I'm sure you can find a hotel."

The *Enquirer*'s full-page piece on my private life eventually appeared and, thankfully, offered not one titillating episode. As for my airplane companion, his contribution was a quote allegedly from the bartender at the popular Harborside Inn. He claimed that this gentleman had said that I was there every night, that I was a great guy, and that I regularly picked up the bill for whoever else was at the bar.

My friends knew that this was highly unlikely, and anyway, the truth was that I had been at that bar only twice in the course of my extended stays on the island.

I hate to tempt them to try again, but the *Enquirer* didn't seem to seriously dent my credibility. Hewing to my own personal standards honed by years of the United Press's total objectivity and the exceedingly strict CBS news standards, our "Evening News" broadcast won wide praise for its objectivity, and suddenly I, as its anchor, showed up on various polls, Elmo Roper's and the *U.S. News & World Report*'s annual survey, as the nation's most trusted person. When asked to comment on this phenomenon, I could only suggest that they clearly hadn't polled my wife.

Some years ago, when *Time* magazine was doing a cover story on me, the reporter, remarking that I seemed just too calm, too laid-back, asked if there was anything that bothered me. Betsy's quixotic sense of humor rose to the occasion, and that week's edition, in an otherwise generally laudatory story, reported that my only worry was that I was shrinking.

Up until then I had never for one moment thought about shrinking. But ever since then, researchers, trusting the Time-Life files, have reported in other publications that this is my principal concern. (Actually, there has been a little worry recently. As with most people, the vertebrae seem to be collapsing a bit.)

Betsy so consistently fabricated these little items about me that when a very good but very tough reporter, Oriana Fallaci, was doing a cover story for *Look*, I tried to get away with telling her that I was a widower. Anything to keep her from interviewing Betsy.

Of course, total objectivity doesn't please fringe fanatics. Their concept of objectivity boils down to their own prejudices. I could tell that we were neutral on controversial issues when complaints from the left and the right roughly balanced out. I felt that if we were being shot at from both sides, we must be in the middle of the road.

Among the ideologically committed who had not slipped into fringe lunacy, there was another interpretation of objectivity. Theirs was a simple construction: If you weren't against them, you must be for them. This is how I account for the numerous suggestions from both sides of the political spectrum that I run for public office.

The manner in which I was importuned to run plumbed the depths of cynicism. Individuals and groups, from college students to representatives of powerful political organizations, suggested that I run for offices from City Hall to the White House, and without exception—I repeat, without a single exception—not once did any of them ask where I stood on the issues of the day. Not once.

They all emphasized the ease with which they thought I could be elected; that my prominence was such that campaign expenses would be minimal. It is possible that they mistook my impartiality on the air for approval of their side. I fear, however, that these professionals figured that once I was in office, they could manipulate such an amateur, and that it didn't really matter what my own views were.

One year some students at Vassar said they were starting a movement to draft me for the presidency. They claimed they had put a deposit on a storefront headquarters in Poughkeepsie but would like some assurance that I would run before they put up the full payment.

"I can go Sherman one step further," I wrote them. "Not only if nominated, I would not run, and if elected, I would not serve, but if perchance I did serve, I would be impeached."

There were a couple of brushes with candidacy in which I played an innocent role. One was of little consequence. My name was apparently one of many thrown on the table when the George McGovern forces were desperately searching for a vice presidential candidate at the 1972 Democratic convention. In 1980, when Illinois' Republican Senator John Anderson was planning a third-party bid for the presidency, the story came out of Chicago that his advisers were suggesting me as his running mate.

Morton Kondracke, then with *The New Republic*, was the only reporter who asked for my comment. I thought I made it clear that I wouldn't do it, but I also said that I was honored to be considered. Apparently I misspoke, or Kondracke misheard me. His brief article the next week reported only that I was honored to be considered.

When that was printed I was at sea, bringing my

boat up the Atlantic from Florida to New York. The Cuban boat lift was on and the political campaign was on, and I had promised to keep in touch with the office by shortwave radio. The Kondracke story had been picked up by the wire services, and reports were flying that I had agreed to run with Anderson. CBS, naturally, was frantic. For one thing, they might be losing me. For another, even by expressing interest I had endangered my vaunted objectivity.

Meanwhile I couldn't get a shortwave message out or in. The Cuban boat people had filled every radio channel with their chatter. Six days later, arriving at Morehead City, North Carolina, I called the office and was met by an explosion of demands for explanations and then demands for a denial.

The lesson here was a valuable one: If you ever want to float a trial balloon, launch it and disappear. If you don't puncture it, it may sail on forever.

CHAPTER 10

DURING the Truman administration one of the most popular figures around Washington was George Allen, who was known as the White House jester. He was a traditional Southern Democrat from Mississippi. Heavyset, of medium height and jolly, he was a very successful lawyer and lobbyist and a friend of the powerful in Washington. He was a member of Truman's kitchen cabinet, that group of cronies, most of whom held no office but whom the President carried from the Senate to the White House to join him in a bourbon-and-branch, a bit of poker and conversation that only occasionally took a serious turn.

Allen's principal claim to fame was that he was a superb storyteller with that gift (particularly common among Southern politicians) of endlessly spinning presumably true tales of political peccadilloes.

In the early fifties Allen was seized with a great idea: He would have a television program in which he and another political insider as the weekly guest would trade current stories of the day that would amuse and entertain and might even illuminate some aspect of the goings-on in the nation's capital.

It sounded good to Bill Paley, particularly since

Allen's most succulent bait was a promise that he
could produce his good friend Vice President Alben
Barkley as his first guest on "Man of the Week."
Barkley's reputation as a political raconteur rivaled
and perhaps surpassed Allen's, but the Veep was shy
about public appearances and appeared on television
very rarely and then only in a serious mien appropriate to a public official.

The broadcast was widely publicized and it
certainly sounded like a blockbuster—these two
ultimate insiders sharing their humorous stories
about Washington. Allen, however, only a few days
before the broadcast, got cold feet and suggested
that it might be well if he and his guest had a professional broadcaster as an interlocuter to help things
along.

The selected broadcaster was me. In my naïveté I
saw my role as scarcely more than getting Allen and
the Veep on and off the air. Wrong. Wrong, wrong,
wrong.

I did that part all right. I introduced them and, as
planned, tossed it to George with some such bland
cue as: "Well, George, what's the story of the week
here in the capital?"

George looked at me as if the thought of his
telling a story on television had never before
occurred to him. For most of the half hour he kept
looking at me, just like that.

George finally opened with something like "Well,
Alben, I guess the President got a pretty good laugh
over that story you told him about the education
bill."

The Veep: Yes, I guess he did.

George: That was a pretty good story. I guess you couldn't tell it here?

The Veep: Nope, don't think so.

The exchanges for the remaining thirty minutes hardly rose above that scintillating level. It may have been the longest half hour that the new medium of television had yet produced, and I wouldn't be surprised if it still holds the record today. In reviewing the disaster it was clear what had happened, and it should have been obvious to all of us, including, above all, George.

The problem simply was that the stories that so panicked the President and everyone else in Washington were either profane, obscene or, most likely (since most allegedly were about contemporary politicians), substantially untrue—gross exaggerations built around a mere kernel of fact. They were also frequently racist, although that would not have been considered a deterrent in those days. (At least we have made some progress in that direction.)

None of the stories, in other words, was fit for the television audience—not the television audience at that time, which was still presumed by the networks to need protection from the profane, the obscene and the untrue.

George was delighted to abandon the program within a week or two, as we converted it to the more standard Washington interview presentation. With that format, "Man of the Week" went on for years, finally merging with another similar CBS weekend offering, "Capitol Cloak Room," to become "Face the Nation," which continues today.

When Allen had his brief flirtation with the medium, television had not yet, of course, made its big impact on Washington. The talk shows were gaining attention, but the White House had not yet become a part of the Capitol's electronic loop.

The first TV incursion into the White House was finally arranged, after a lot of initial rejection, with Truman. He acknowledged that the people should be permitted to see their leader's residence since its extensive remodeling—a four-year, $5,761,800 project during which the Trumans had lived in Blair House across Pennsylvania Avenue.

For the broadcast, Truman would guide network correspondents on a personal tour of the house. The three networks would pool the coverage and the broadcast. I was the CBS man, and in our little lottery I drew the ground floor and basement. Frank Bourgholtzer of NBC took the second floor, and ABC's Bryson Rash the third floor.

The broadcast was, of course, live. We didn't yet have tape, and films made off the tube—kinescopes—were of very poor quality. My homework was thorough. By the day of the broadcast I knew the story behind every room, every painting and every stick of furniture on my two floors.

It wouldn't seem that knowledge can be wasted, but it turned out that I needed few of the facts with which I was loaded. And of the facts with which I dared to prompt the President, he either corrected me or topped me. I learned then, firsthand, of the kind of ego that grips a person who has been elected to probably the most powerful job in the whole world.

Examples:

As we entered the main-floor sitting room, I noted that this was the room Dolley Madison had taken such pride in redecorating after the British had played arson with the White House in 1814.

"Most of these decorations Bess has done," the President countered, not about to let Dolley take anything away from his adored wife.

And again, as we went into a rather dungeon-like room with a vaulted ceiling in the basement, I had to spring my knowledge and remark that this was the room from which Franklin Roosevelt had reached out to the people via radio in his effective Fireside Chats.

Naturally, Truman put an asterisk to my note: "Yes, and I've done all my broadcasts from here."

Much of the broadcast went that way, and I thought of the cat, rubbing against its owner's leg, against the chair or its bowl, marking its possessions and its territory with the spoor nature had provided. It dawned on me that, of course, each of the building's occupants must yield to the perfectly rational desire to see history record as unique and distinctive his tenancy of the White House.

Truman was the third President I had a chance to know—although my acquaintance with one, Herbert Hoover, came when he was living in retirement at the Waldorf Towers sometime after his departure from the White House. He had been out of office twenty years and would die a decade later at the age of ninety. We spent an hour or so together, and I thought he was particularly lucid, if a little ponderous and tendentious. I couldn't get him to discuss the past at any length, although I would have liked to hear him reminisce about his star-crossed presidency.

It was ironic, however, that Hoover, who had been brought down by his inability to stem the Great Depression, talked mostly about the current state of the economy under then President Truman. And he still referred to the "radical influences" in Washington, which he blamed for the policies that the Roosevelt administration called progressive. He saw all Democrats as happy inheritors of these policies and damned by the same liberalism.

A few years before, he had completed a monumental work commissioned by President Truman—a study of waste in government. The Hoover Commission's many-volumed report contained hundreds of recommendations for trimming the vast government bureaucracy that Roosevelt's centralization had spawned. Hoover did not seem surprised that there had been no immediate attempt to implement any of the recommendations, nor did he seem disappointed that there was no prospect of that happening. He was too experienced in the ways of Washington to expect anything else. His guide as to how we might achieve some degree of fiscal responsibility might still be useful, but, forgotten, it gathers dust on the government shelves.

My acquaintance with Franklin Delano Roosevelt was not quite as limited as mine with Hoover. Our paths crossed on a few occasions. The first was in 1928 at the Democratic National Convention in Houston, where, in his first major appearance since being paralyzed by polio, he gave a bravado physical performance at the podium to put forward his fellow New Yorker, Al Smith, for the presidential nomination.

To tell you the truth, I was *told* that I had seen Roosevelt there. The Boy Scouts were ushering at the convention and I had accompanied them, and I vividly remember the exciting scene in that convention hall—the band music, the banners and signs, the blaring of the loudspeakers. But when I came home that night I couldn't tell my father who I had actually heard speak. If he had been the type, he might have taken a hairbrush to me. As it was, he advised me that it must have been Roosevelt, for that was the day of his appearance.

By an odd coincidence, I was also at the Republican convention in Kansas City that summer. We had moved from Kansas City to Houston just the year before, and I was back visiting my grandparents. My uncle, like all of my Middle Western kin, an unwavering Republican, took me to a session of the convention. I do not recall seeing anyone of importance there either. I know I was disappointed that President Calvin Coolidge wasn't present.

In 1928 Smith was defeated partly because he wanted to repeal the Eighteenth Amendment's prohibition against alcohol, partly because the country wasn't yet ready for a Roman Catholic President, and at least partly because he pronounced the new wireless phenomenon "raddio." His strong New York accent bothered a lot of the out-country.

Hoover, of course, was elected; the Depression wiped him out and in came Roosevelt. I saw him for the first time (not counting that possible Houston experience) during the 1940 presidential campaign, when he was defying the tradition that chief executives serve a maximum of two terms. On one of his swings through the Middle West, Joe Hearst, the Kansas City bureau chief for the United Press, and I joined the train. Joe was to assist our White House man as far as Denver. As one of the bureau's younger members, I was sort of a human sacrifice to the primitive state of communications then. As nearly as I could make out my assignment, I was to be a human mailbag. At a given point along the route, I was somehow supposed to hang out of the speeding train to be captured by a great hook alongside the track. If I survived, I would then telegraph Joe's copy back to Kansas City.

It didn't turn out to be nearly as adventuresome as I had imagined. I was permitted to alight in a safe, sane and civilized fashion at one of the whistle-stops to pursue my telegraphic chores. What impressed me on that trip was the condition of the President. Although I had of course seen scores upon scores of pictures of him, had edited and written cutlines for many of them, and like everyone else had seen hundreds of feet of newsreel coverage of him, I had no idea of the extent of his disability as a result of poliomyelitis. The press clearly conspired, although I am certain without any formal agreement, to cover up the fact that our President could not walk or even stand without considerable assistance.

I don't believe this conspiracy was the result of political considerations. It scarcely could have been, given the Republican orientation of most of the press at that time, and the extreme distaste with which many publishers viewed the New Deal President. This was a rare show of delicacy on the part of the press. It is doubtful, given the strength of the Roosevelt personality, that the public would have reacted differently to him if it had known the degree of his infirmity, but the silence about it was extraordinary.

I was to see President Roosevelt in slightly more intimate circumstances several times thereafter, when I was briefly in Washington and our White House man would take me along to his informal press conferences. Memory springs a surprise when we recall how comparatively unimportant Washington was in our lives right through the early years of the Roosevelt administration. Before he concentrated power in the national capital, the state capitals made most of the news that had a serious impact on us. The two most important issues were roads and taxes, and the state governments had more to say about them than Washington did—a condition to which Republican Speaker Newt Gingrich's 104th Congress sought to return us.

So, in most of those years of the Roosevelt administration, the White House press corps was but a handful of men (a very, very rare woman, then) who had their desks in a small room just off the reception room in the West Wing of the White House, just around the corner from the President's office. We newsmen lounged in the tired leather chairs and sofas of that unattractive room, chatting in the most casual way with many of the President's important visitors. When the President felt the urge, he'd send the word and the dozen or so newsmen would pile into the Oval Office and stand in a semicircle around his desk. The conversation was a free-for-all—questions and sometimes uninterrupted lengthy answers. Nothing could be attributed to the President unless he gave specific approval.

It was a wonderful system. It gave the press a far better sense of the background of the administration policies than is permitted by the present televised news conferences, with their time limits and huge crowds. There is probably no way to revert to the Roosevelt method. Washington has become too big, too complex, too world-important, with hundreds of reporters from across the globe in residence. Any news conference must be a mass audience. Or must it?

I'll tell you how I would handle the press should my parents' fondest dream ever be miraculously realized. Based on the fact that only the major newspapers, press services and networks keep correspondents regularly at the White House—and that hordes of reporters pile in only for presidential news conferences—I would adopt something akin to the Roosevelt technique. Irregularly but frequently I would send a call out to the White House press room for anybody in attendance to drop in for a little informal, off-the-record (unless otherwise stated) chat. Of course, these impromptu sessions would have to be augmented to take care of the hundreds of others who aren't in regular attendance at the White House, but that could then be done by means of the type of televised news conferences that have become the norm.

This would provide a far better briefing, doing away with the undignified picture of the President shouting cryptic answers to necessarily cryptic questions as he boards his helicopter for Camp David—an innovation of the Reagan administration.

Incidentally, since this ridiculous scene was dictated by the President himself, or at least his advisers, and you can be certain that the press would have liked a more orderly procedure, the media shouldn't be condemned for the apparent rudeness of their questions.

Sam Donaldson was not an apostle of inelegance but an exceptionally smart practitioner of a technique forced upon him and his colleagues in the White House press room. There was neither time nor opportunity for the well-phrased, carefully considered, politely presented question in the environment that the White House itself sponsored under the Reagan and Bush administrations. One can only assume that the Republican White House preferred it that way.

Since Roosevelt, the President who handled the press best was probably John Kennedy, although it should be remembered that he once banned the New York *Herald Tribune* from the White House in a fit of temper over something that had offended him. Some of Kennedy's closest friends were newspeople, noteworthy among them Ben Bradlee, who, when Kennedy was President, was *Newsweek*'s Washington bureau chief and later managing editor of the Washington *Post*.

Various alleged episodes of marital unfaithfulness have surfaced in the decades since Kennedy's death, perhaps none more shocking than a story recounted in a book by Joe Alsop. The columnist and author wrote that on the very night of the inauguration, Kennedy forsook the White House and showed up alone at an informal open house Alsop found himself hosting at his Georgetown home after all the other partying had ended. There, according to Alsop, the man who had been President of the United States a bare twelve hours enjoyed a bedroom tryst with a very attractive young actress.

The version of the Kennedys' inaugural night that I got years later from the by then twice-widowed Jackie Kennedy Onassis—or at least the version I think I heard—was somewhat different. Occasionally we have sailed from our Martha's Vineyard summer home across Nantucket Sound to Hyannis. We drop anchor near the Kennedy compound, and almost always a vivacious and gracious Ethel Kennedy drops by in her sailboat. She insists that we come ashore, play tennis if there is time, and stay for dinner or whatever entertainment the always active Kennedys have planned for the evening. One day she said we had to stay for dinner to help celebrate Jackie's birthday. She would not listen to our protests that we were not dressed for such an event. Just four or five people, she said. Just the family.

It turned out to be so, and I was seated between Ethel and Jackie. It was a nice, intimate time and Jackie was unusually loquacious, although with my hearing and her breathless whisper I was having trouble understanding everything she had to say.

I felt my ears flapping when I heard her telling me of the fun she and Jack had had at the White House on inaugural night. Let me try to reconstruct her story as I heard it—or didn't hear it. "Oh, Walter, Jack was so funny. He insisted that we go into the Lincoln bedroom first, and despite his bad back he wanted to carry me across the threshold like a bride. We got into the bedroom and he dropped me on the bed and . . .

"Oh, we laughed so, but then, Walter, we went over to our bedroom and he picked me up and had trouble getting us both through the door. Then he went over to the bed again and he . . . We laughed so!"

I asked for a repeat at the critical points—I asked

twice, as much as decency would allow, and twice the whisper faded until there was nothing left but my imagination. If Jackie had just talked more and aspirated less, this story might have contributed something to the history of that inaugural night.

The revelations of later years about Kennedy's romantic escapades, even within the White House, have posed justifiable questions about the integrity of the press. Surely, one is entitled to ask, newspeople covering the White House must have known of Kennedy's many liaisons? Why didn't they tell us?

Newsmen, particularly those who are supposed to be expert on their beats, are usually quick to claim inside knowledge of almost any story in their bailiwick that comes up now or forever in the future. Yet it is interesting that none of the White House correspondents I know claimed at the time to have any evidence of John Kennedy's alleged bedroom escapades. Most will tell you today that they knew about the rumors but were never able to come up with enough evidence to go with the story. This alibi represents a denial of responsibility for a gross dereliction of the Fourth Estate's duty.

Certainly the Kennedy-era reporters were operating in a time almost as different from today as were the years of Lincoln or Washington. In the sixties the Washington press, like the media elsewhere, operated on a rule of thumb regarding the morals of our public men. The rule had it that, as long as his outside activities, alcoholic or sexual, did not interfere with or seriously endanger the discharge of his public duties, a man was entitled to his privacy. This pardon was extended to the young President. In the light of later revelations that at least one of his lady friends had close Mafia connections, this pardon was a mistake. If there were newspeople who knew about this and failed to report it, no wonder they are too embarrassed to confess now.

Kennedy seemed as comfortable with the press as Nixon was uncomfortable. Even as at one point Nixon's acolytes, under his spiritual leadership and later his craven protection, tried to manipulate an election by burglarizing the Democrats' Watergate headquarters and stealing their campaign secrets, Nixon engaged in an active conspiracy to destroy the press's credibility. Without credibility, of course, the press cannot be effective in carrying out one of its most important duties in a democracy—monitoring the performance of government. (Of course, the press itself has the principal responsibility in maintaining that credibility.) The Nixon administration policy was based on a simple formula: If it could bring down the press's credibility, it might improve its own.

This was the Nixon, of course, who when defeated for the governorship of California told his concession news conference: "You won't have Dick Nixon to kick around anymore."

My wife, Betsy, had a definitive observation on that. At lunch with some of her Republican lady friends the next day, she heard them say how affected they were as they watched Pat Nixon weeping copiously at her husband's side.

"I felt so sorry for Pat last night," one said.

"I feel sorry for her every night," Betsy declared.

Now, however, as the outstanding political phoenix of our time, Nixon sat in the White House and thought he had the power to get even with the hated press. So he set his deputies on the job, and Vice President Spiro Agnew was named lead dog. He opened the campaign in Des Moines, Iowa, with a speech that was written by White House wordsmith Pat Buchanan, who some years later would be overcome with delusions of presidential grandeur. He identified the network news organizations as the main target in a speech that dripped with vitriol.

The entire attack was predicated on a fundamental belief that there was a press conspiracy against the Nixon administration and all that was right and proper in the conservative world. Buchanan wrote and Agnew said: "A small group of men, numbering perhaps no more than a dozen anchormen, commentators and executive producers, settles upon the twenty minutes or so of film and commentary that is to reach the public. They decide what 40 or 50 million Americans will learn of the day's events."

Buchanan even charged the network commentators with "instant analyses" after presidential speeches, although he had been present when other White House aides briefed reporters and commentators before the speeches were delivered. Buchanan had been a newspaperman before joining Nixon's White House. He was joined in the antipress campaign by another former newsman serving on the Nixon writing staff. Bill Safire was the inventor of catchy phrases that bumper-sticker writers would envy. He called us, for instance, "nattering nabobs of negativism."

I like Bill Safire and I don't have anything personal against Buchanan. I think Safire is one of the best thinkers and writers in journalism today. His column in *The New York Times* is must reading. But when serving Nixon, these two former newsmen, Safire and Buchanan, lied. It has always puzzled me how anyone can put to paper, even in the service of a cause he feels is just, material he knows to be deceitful, if not outright false.

That was the case with this basic tenet of the Agnew proposition. Buchanan and Safire knew perfectly well that, while it is true that a handful of people decided what would be on the three network news broadcasts each evening, there wasn't the slightest—not the slightest—consultation among them. Indeed, their intense rivalry prescribed just the opposite.

What they knew, because they came from the business, is that what goes onto a responsible network broadcast or into a responsible newspaper and how that news is played are determined, with rare exceptions, solely by the story's news value. That news value is put on a scale shared by all professional journalists. A story is newsworthy depending on how many people it affects and how deeply it affects them, and/or how close it happens to home, and/or how aberrational it is.

What Safire and Buchanan chose to ignore was

that the play of stories on front pages across the country was, almost without exception, exactly as it was on the network's evening newscasts. The managing editors of those mostly Republican-owned newspapers weighed the news and came to the same conclusions as the broadcast editors did.

Not only did a considerable segment of the public applaud Agnew but, amazingly, so did some newspaper publishers and editorialists, who must have believed that we network types secretly dictated to their own editors how the news should be played each day. I wanted to answer Agnew, and we found a convenient vehicle to do it. A couple of weeks later I went back to the heartlands he had chosen for his speech, and in my birthplace of St. Joseph, Missouri, before a Chamber of Commerce luncheon, I delivered my defense and answered questions. And CBS used the appearance as a special CBS "60 Minutes" report.

I am sorry to say that my response to Agnew did not bring the Nixon antipress campaign to heel. It was to get even nastier and more dangerous. Potentially the most damaging tactic was an attempt to separate the networks from the generally more conservative local station managements.

Local stations, with their less substantial financial base, are more susceptible to political and economic pressures. Furthermore, their ownership is more likely to be Republican and conservative. Already there was tension between them and the networks over our coverage of the Vietnam War and the home-front protests against it. Many of them felt that, simply by showing the war and the demonstrations, we were somehow condemning the one and supporting the other, and therefore were somehow less than patriotic.

The Nixon administration approach to the network affiliates was overt without the slightest subtlety. The White House head of communications, Clay Whitehead, suggested outright that they did not need to carry the network news broadcasts, that they could do the same job locally simply by reading the wire service dispatches. This not only would give them total control over their broadcasts but would relieve them of having to field complaints from conservative viewers over the network's handling of the news. It would also mean that they could keep all the news revenue at home.

Since the suggestion came from the White House itself, it also presumably implied that the stations would be spared any trouble from the Federal Communications Commission should any protesters suggest that by canceling the national broadcast, they were not living up to their license commitment to public service. For whatever different reasons they may have had, not one station bought the White House suggestion.

At the height of the Nixon antipress crusade I testified at a congressional hearing that there was a White House conspiracy against the press. Some of my colleagues, even those at CBS, thought I had gone too far. They said I had no proof that the campaign was centrally directed and was in fact a conspiracy. I think I used the old duck theory: If it swims, walks and quacks like a duck, it probably is a duck.

At any rate, when the Watergate tapes were released, there was the proof. Indeed, there had been Oval Office talk of the need to get the press; Nixon's own marching orders read clear: "The press is the enemy."

Herb Klein, Nixon's longtime friend and press secretary, admitted years later that he was stunned by the Agnew speech, which he labeled "McCarthy-like." And Safire himself wrote this (also, of course, years later):

"Was there a conspiracy, as Walter Cronkite of CBS once solemnly charged, on the part of the Nixon Administration to discredit and malign the press?

"Was this so-called 'anti-media campaign' encouraged, directed, and urged on by the President himself? . . .

"The answer to those questions is, sadly, yes."

In an odd twist, I got along rather well with Nixon. In fact, I was somewhat embarrassed that I did not make his news media "enemies list," which was part of the campaign. He was quoted somewhere as saying that I was the best of a bad lot. I am not sure I would put that on my escutcheon.

Nixon, either as candidate or as officeholder, did not make many promises to me for interviews, off-the-record chats or the like, but he delivered on whatever promises he made.

Nixon was fundamentally flawed in exercising the social graces. He was stiff, uncomfortable and totally incapable of even halfway sensible small talk. Not that this should be a presidential criterion, but it never hurt.

A classic story was confirmed for me by Abba Eban, the erudite, silver-tongued, Oxford-educated Foreign Minister of Israel under Prime Minister Golda Meir. Mrs. Meir made her first visit to Washington as Prime Minister shortly after Nixon had elevated Henry Kissinger from National Security Adviser to Secretary of State.

As the Prime Minister was presented to the President in the White House foyer, among Nixon's first words were: "Madame Prime Minister, we are both blessed by having Jewish Foreign Ministers."

To which Mrs. Meir replied: "Oh, but Mr. President, I am doubly blessed: Mine speaks perfect English."

Nixon's social awkwardness, possibly induced by his impoverished childhood, was in sharp contrast to the sophistication of the Kennedys. If charisma was the game, Jack and Jackie won it going away. Bobby and Ethel had it too, with a slightly homier, less elegant twist, and so does Teddy.

An image that always will live with me is that of the newly sworn-in President of the United States and his beautiful First Lady sitting in the back of their open limousine as it pulled away from the Capitol for the parade back to the White House. I was at the microphone in an open car immediately in front of them. The President tilted his top hat toward me and Jackie gave me a wave and a dazzling smile, and they wiped away in a second any lingering memories of conflict and confrontation. I have thought since how similar that scene must have been to the one in the back of the open car just before it passed the Texas Book Depository in Dallas not three years later.

Cut short as it was, the Kennedy administration left little that was noteworthy for the history books, but his charm, his style—personal and political— and his rhetoric captured the hearts and the imagination of a generation of Americans to a degree unmatched by any other occupant of the White House in this century, and I'm not forgetting the great popularity of the Roosevelts, Franklin and Theodore.

Making comparative rankings of Presidents is an unnecessary exercise fraught with contention but otherwise relatively harmless. And the results can be surprising. For instance, I think that of the Presidents I have known since Hoover, the best brain was possessed by Jimmy Carter.

I base this not on his political or administrative skills, which clearly were wanting, but on his incredible ability to read complicated material and file and catalog it in his memory so that it could be instantly recalled when needed. This orderliness of mind was evident in his news conferences and other situations where he was speaking extemporaneously. Transcripts of his remarks read like a finely honed and thoroughly edited manuscript—every sentence parsed to the satisfaction of the most meticulous English grammar teacher.

Long before Ross Perot suggested it and Bill Clinton thought of adopting it, CBS and President Carter initiated what was to be a series of radio call-in programs in which citizens across the nation could address the President with their questions or their problems. I fielded the calls as Carter and I sat in a pair of wingback chairs in the Oval Office of the White House. No questions were submitted in advance and none was refused.

There was the usual built-in three-second pause to give monitors the chance to intercept obscenities or otherwise offensive material. Otherwise it was first come, first served as the switchboard lighted up. I had given a lot of thought to how I would handle what we expected to be long-winded questions and the callers who wanted to make speeches of their own—problems with which any public speaker is acquainted. Surprisingly, the problem in that form never arose during the entire two hours of our broadcast. The problem, it turned out, was not with the public but with the President. No matter how far out the question, he had in his head a textbook of knowledge about it.

One lady called in from Wisconsin to ask about milk price supports, and Carter delivered an excruciatingly long dissertation on the history of all agricultural supports with facts and figures relating to every increase in milk prices since World War I.

Despite that, he and we thought the program a

success. It had to be abandoned, however, because the telephone company said it jammed its facilities to a dangerous degree.

Carter's administration was plagued by an unusual problem. He lived up to a campaign promise to turn his back on the Washington bureaucracy. To carry it out, he imported his advisers from Georgia. In most cases, they were perfectly fine people. They just weren't tutored in how to get things done in Washington. They learned the hard way that you don't succeed in the labyrinth of Capitol politics without making a lot of compromises with the entrenched apparatus.

As one of the most skilled and wiliest of all Washington operators, Speaker Sam Rayburn, used to instruct the young congressmen who sat at his feet: "You've got to go along to get along."

Dwight Eisenhower expressed to me his total frustration in dealing with the government bureaucracy. He was appalled that his direct orders had a way of disappearing into thin air without action ever being taken.

Carter was smart, but Nixon may have been the most ardent student to occupy the White House. It is likely he felt inadequate, and in many aspects he deserved his inferiority complex. But he was diligent in his attempts to overcome the holes in his knowledge. His homework paid off and he became exceedingly well informed on issues of the day, particularly in foreign affairs.

This stood him in good stead after he was forced

from office. One of his first speeches as he embarked on a road he hoped would regain for him some measure of popular respect was delivered in a brave appearance at the hotbed of his disgrace, the National Press Club in Washington. It was a brilliant analysis of the national and world situation delivered apparently extemporaneously without a note. It won a standing ovation from a cynical audience. Many of his speeches after that received similar praise for their thoughtful and candid appraisals of current events.

To say that Nixon was the most complicated personality to occupy the Oval Office is to barely touch the surface. At times he actually seemed unbalanced. I was a guest at a state dinner on one occasion when I noticed his eyes fix on the molding at the edge of the ceiling. Then they began following the molding across that side of the room, then across the adjoining side, even to the side behind him, and back along the next wall to the starting place. One would assume that he was following an intrusive beastie in its circumnavigation of the room, but I could see nothing there and a couple of other guests who also noticed this strange behavior likewise saw nothing to attract such presidential attention.

During his 1968 primary campaign one of his aides and a former CBS executive, Frank Shakespeare, invited me to the candidate's hotel room at the end of one of the strenuous days on the hustings.

Nixon was half reclining on the sofa, his stockinged feet on the coffee table. As we sipped our drinks and talked, his language was that of the streets, in the vernacular and sprinkled with profanities. The whole scene was so contrary to the formality, the stiffness I had always seen in the man that I decided it was a setup, that it was a little playlet scripted and directed by Shakespeare to try to establish his candidate as one of the boys, possibly worthy of the press's acceptance, if not its admiration.

The Nixon revealed on the Watergate tapes, however, was the Nixon of that campaign hotel room. Apparently Shakespeare had not engineered Nixon's performance just for me. It was the Nixon who, as Eisenhower's vice presidential running mate, had embraced Senator Joseph McCarthy in the 1952 campaign. The Wisconsin Senator's witch hunt for Communists in government was in full swing, and McCarthyism was a campaign issue. Nixon's early leadership of the infamous House Un-American Activities Committee put him in the same ideological league as McCarthy and his followers.

Eisenhower had sullied his reputation by failing to stand up to McCarthy even when the Senator dared to attack Ike's mentor and sponsor, the nearly impeccable General George Marshall. It can only be assumed that Eisenhower, who was most comfortable with the liberal Republicans of the party's so-called Eastern Establishment, yielded in this case, as he had in others, to pressures from the party's conservative right wing—a problem that has plagued every Republican administration since Hoover's, excepting only Reagan's, which was almost entirely right wing anyway.

Nixon himself was a product of the belief that the right wing needed constant nursing. His selection as a running mate was suggested to Eisenhower to help assuage the right wing, whose candidate, Ohio's Senator Robert Taft, Eisenhower had defeated for the nomination at the Chicago convention in 1952. I never thought that Eisenhower cared much for Nixon. When it was revealed during the closing days of the campaign that Nixon had been involved in some shady fund-raising among wealthy backers, ostensibly to cover office expenses, it briefly appeared that Eisenhower might dump him from the ticket. Eisenhower did not rise to his defense immediately and let him twist in the wind until after the famous television address in which Nixon appealed to the public with a bathetic recital of his humble life. That was the broadcast that featured his wife's "good Republican cloth coat" and his love for his dog, Checkers.

He may have touched Ike's heart, but it is more likely that the party conservatives again came to the rescue and convinced Ike and his advisers that Nixon had to stay.

I spent considerable time with Eisenhower after he left office. We made a trip to Normandy together to film his reminiscences for the twentieth anniversary of D-Day, and I spent a week at his Gettsyburg residence to record thirteen hours of interviews that were the basis for Fred Friendly's three-hour

memoir of his presidency. And during all of that
time I never succeeded in getting him to talk about
Nixon except in the most perfunctory way. There
was scarcely enough faint praise to constitute a
damnation.

The Gettysburg interviews changed my opinion of
Eisenhower as President. Until then I had joined in
the common wisdom shared by most of my Washington correspondent colleagues: that Ike was a lazy
President, more interested in practicing his golf
swings on the lawn outside the Oval Office than in
practicing statecraft at his desk. According to this
view, what command he exercised was accomplished through a staff system that allowed him to
excuse himself from involvement in most of the
decisions that emanated from the White House.

This assessment was supported by Ike's performance at his news conferences. While the reporters
usually understood what he meant, his grammar and
his sentences were so disorganized that it was almost
impossible to make sense of the transcripts. He was
the master of garbled syntax.

Gettysburg was a revelation. Ike was seventy-one
at the time and felt that he was sharpest in the mornings, so he limited our interview sessions to three
hours before noon. Each night before the next day's
meeting we outlined to his son, John, who was acting as his researcher and adviser, the areas we intended to explore the following day. These were so
broad that they would scarcely serve as chapter
headings, and there were so many of them that
it would have been impossible for anyone to re-

search them, let alone absorb the research, before the interview.

Each day as we sat at the desk in his study with the cameras rolling, I had on my knee a pile of notes on the subjects I wanted to cover. Ike did not have a single sheet of paper in front of him. Yet for the entire five days of the interview I did not ask him about a single incident during his eight years in the White House of which he did not have intimate knowledge. Never, except at the very end, did he invoke his privilege of asking us to redo a question. Clearly the common knowledge of the White House press corps was not knowledge at all but wrongful supposition.

Only on one last question did he stumble, and it was a question from left field.

"What are the real powers of the presidency?" I asked.

He asked for a moment to think that one over, and we turned off the cameras. A moment later he was ready and, in a typically rambling three- or four-minute dissertation, he ticked off the various constitutional powers of the presidency. Since in the course of our conversations in the past he had railed against a bureaucracy that he claimed couldn't be moved and wouldn't even respond to a direct order from the President, I was hoping for a more subjective answer as to what he found his *real* powers to be. But I didn't have a chance to press the matter. It was our last day, the President clearly was tiring, and son John indicated that our time was up.

The 1963 trip to England and Normandy with Ike

to prepare a documentary on the twentieth anniversary of D-Day was sheer delight—a lot of hard work but sheer delight.

Ike had not had a chance since the war to really tour the Normandy battlefields where Hitler's forces had suffered the defeat from which they would never recover. He had made two or three previous visits but always in an official capacity, surrounded by officials and troops and bands and thousands of spectators, circumstances hardly conducive to sight-seeing.

Bill Paley, who had been a psychological-warfare colonel on Ike's staff in London during the war, went along, as did Mrs. Eisenhower and Walter Thayer, the publisher who folded the New York *Herald Tribune* for Bill's brother-in-law, Jock Whitney, and an early supporter of Ike for President as well as a personal friend of both Paley and Ike. Mrs. Eisenhower, my Betsy and executive producer Fred Friendly and his staff made up the official party.

We took Ike back to all the scenes of his preparations in England for D-Day, including Winston Churchill's bomb shelter headquarters under the Admiralty buildings off Pall Mall and the briefing room at Southampton, where, after a one-day delay, he defied the terrible weather and ordered the invasion to proceed.

On the beaches of Normandy we stood in the German bunkers as he mused upon what the Wehrmacht lookouts must have thought when, on that morning of June 6, 1944, they saw that great armada of battlewagons and landing craft emerging from the dawn's haze. At one point Friendly planned to have me drive Eisenhower along the sands of Omaha Beach as he pointed out some of the scenes of action there, but then it occurred to Fred that it was Eisenhower who was showing me the area and that he should be driving. Ike willingly climbed behind the wheel. Watching this drama unfold from a little knoll behind the beach were Mamie Eisenhower and Betsy. Mamie gasped and reached over for Betsy's hand. "Betsy, your Walter has never been in greater danger. Ike hasn't driven in thirty years, and he wasn't any good at it then."

As we were filming this scene, along the beach came a nun with a group of uniformed girls, perhaps eight to ten years old. Undoubtedly she was giving them a tour of the battlefield, and she must have been making frequent references to General Eisenhower. But she led her little charges right by us without ever looking our way.

We all were in some real danger flying back to London when our chartered plane developed trouble in one of its two engines. My only thought was that this was a crash in which I would definitely be listed among "those also on board."

Incidentally, there were rumors and even thinly veiled allegations during the war that Mamie overindulged as she waited in their Wardman Park Hotel apartment for Ike's return from duty. One magazine even referred archly to her "sitting tight in the Wardman Park lobby."

If she had any such problem, it didn't raise its

head during our week or so together on the Normandy trip. Only once was there the slightest hint.
Mamie ordered a second cocktail as we waited for
dinner in their Caen hotel suite, and Ike hastily but
firmly suggested that there was no time for another.

Of course, Ike was himself the subject of many
rumors regarding his affair with his British driver,
Kay Summersby. She was always at his side during
the war, and their closeness was apparent to all.
Shortly after the war, as the Summersby story was
getting some circulation and Ike's friends were
becoming concerned that it might seriously tarnish
the hero's reputation, I was with a group of Ike's
generals and his intimates—among them dashing
Rosie O'Donnell of the Air Force and Omar Bradley, the universally admired commander of the First
Army, workhorse of the European victory.

We were simply visiting and drinking in the Waldorf Towers suite of Louis Marx, a toy tycoon who
during the war had taken to adopting generals and
looking after their families and Stateside interests.
He helped them all make some money in business
areas with which they were unfamiliar, and he
named his several sons after them. The matter of
Summersby came up, and one of the generals delivered the wisdom of Solomon as perceived by
returning heroes. "Ike's a damned fool," he said.
"He doesn't understand the first rule. When you get
ready to dump 'em, first get 'em a job."

The judgment was greeted with a chorus of
approval, a chorus in which at this late date I would

not swear that Rosie or Omar joined. At any rate, shortly afterward Summersby was given a job as a fashion coordinator at CBS, the network owned by Ike's good friend Bill Paley.

Generals and Presidents and, I suppose, men of high rank in the world of commerce, industry, labor and, as we know, even the ministry (and, God forgive, just possibly the press) are not immune to the attractions of the opposite sex.

We know at least some of the John Kennedy story. Franklin Roosevelt had his Lucy Mercer, and there were rumors about Lyndon Johnson, although I'm afraid I am quite unable to testify personally to any evidence in this regard.

In all the aspects in which I did see Johnson, however, he lived up to the most frequent of his many sobriquets; indeed, he was bigger than life. He strode through his political life from congressman to President with confident bluster and with his left hand always cocked to snare an opponent's lapels and pull him nose-to-nose for a dose of some old-fashioned Johnson persuasion.

Although I had covered Texas politics and once or twice had seen him in the halls of the state capitol, in Washington I first encountered him in Speaker Sam Rayburn's little hideaway office behind the House of Representatives. There the Speaker presided in the late afternoons and early evenings over what he called his "Board of Education." In attendance by invitation only were a few intimates, including always some of the younger House members in whom he saw promise or perhaps discerned a need for a little coaching in party discipline.

Vice President Truman was at Rayburn's board session when he got the word that Roosevelt had died and he was the new President of the United States. Johnson was frequently in attendance as the Speaker reviewed the day's legislative events with the political sagacity for which he was known and with illustrative and highly informative political anecdotes of which he was a treasured repository. Johnson perched on the radiator cover at one side of the room and, wonder of wonders, remained silent as he absorbed the fascinating lore and advice of the Speaker.

Johnson learned well at Rayburn's tutorials and used his learning to become one of history's most effective Senate majority leaders. He would have had a place in the history books even if he had not made it to the presidency, but he applied Rayburn's lessons and his own natural abilities to maneuver himself onto John Kennedy's 1960 ticket, although perhaps there were never two such opposites crowded into the same harness.

(It was not only Rayburn's lessons that helped Johnson at that 1960 Democratic convention in Los Angeles. As the powerful chairman of the convention and as the hyperpowerful Speaker of the House, with whom any Democratic President would have to get along, Rayburn was a major figure in persuading Kennedy to accept Johnson as his running mate.)

I made my first visit to the LBJ ranch on the

banks of the Pedernales west of Austin to do the campaign interview that was to be part of the series for which I had finally corralled Kennedy and Nixon. It wasn't much of an interview. Johnson wasn't keen to do it in the first place, and he was anything but forthcoming.

Future interviews at the ranch would go far better, when they were at least partly at his own instigation. Each of them offered another insight into the Johnson character. We did a major interview on the future of the space program, a matter in which he had a keen interest, and not just because he had been influential in getting the $60 million space center located outside Houston.

I was wearing a fine Rolex watch that the Swiss president of the company had given me. He had pointed out that this model was not available to the general public and that he presented them only to heads of state. As Johnson and I sat under a spreading oak tree dripping with Spanish moss, I realized that his interest in space seemed to be waning as he stared at my lap. I was tentatively feeling to see if I was unzipped when he practically leaned into my face and demanded: "Where did you get that watch?"

When I told him that the watch was a gift from the Rolex president, he erupted. "That son of a gun told me that he only gave those watches to heads of state and such!"

I had a feeling that up to that moment he suspected me of having filched his.

There was later to be a minor impasse in a major CBS negotiation with the President. We contracted to do his memoirs, and I spent many hours over the course of several visits interviewing him at the ranch. The Johnsons very kindly put me up in one of their guest houses. It was done in what might be called a desert brown, and my producer, Burton Benjamin, decided that I should wear a green suit. Not normally favoring green suits, I had to buy a couple from Brooks Brothers.

During the interview Johnson and I talked of the Kennedy assassination, which had brought him to office. At one point he said: "I can't honestly say that I've ever been completely relieved of the fact that there might have been international connections. I have not completely discounted it."

Try as I might, I could not get him to expand on this tantalizing but incomplete speculation.

Nonetheless, my conviction is that if there had been a conspiracy, some evidence would have emerged by now—secrets involving that many people aren't that easy to keep.

When doing interviews with sitting or past Presidents, we extended a courtesy not offered others. Since Presidents were privy to so many state secrets, and we wanted them to not feel encumbered in speaking freely to us, we recorded an audiotape of the full interview and then gave the Presidents a few days to review their words for security leaks. No questions would be asked if they requested that something be excised, but this privilege expired after a few days. This was to protect us from expensive reediting as the interview's exhibition date drew near.

A couple of weeks after the deadline expired on the Johnson tape, the President decided he wanted that assassination speculation removed. CBS at first refused, and the President and his lawyers grew more and more adamant until they were threatening to withdraw from the remaining interviews in the series. The deadlock continued for weeks—and my green suits hanging in the Johnson guest cottage became hostage to the negotiations. If Johnson sent the suits back to me, it would surely indicate that he was breaking off the negotiations, that there would likely be no more televised memoirs, at least not with CBS. And if I sent for the suits, the Johnson forces could deduce that CBS intended to break off the negotiations.

CBS eventually agreed to cut the offending quotations, but LBJ's views emerged elsewhere later. I always assumed that Johnson's suspicions of a conspiracy were based on the fact that he knew at that time what neither the public nor, far more important, the Warren Commission, which investigated the assassination, knew—that the CIA had plotted the assassination of Fidel Castro, thus providing the motivation for a Cuban plot against Kennedy.

The spread that was the LBJ ranch was, even by Texas standards, an impressive one, and it was LBJ's domain. He was totally comfortable there and he let you know it. On one of our interview visits, the gracious Lady Bird invited our whole production crew to lunch. Johnson was out of the White

House and was on a limited regime, taking frequent naps to rest his ailing heart. He showed up for the lunch with nothing but a robe thrown over his shorts. As he presided at the table with an entertaining fund of stories, his usual arm-waving gesticulations would spread the robe wide, revealing a less-than-attractive hairy torso. There were women on our staff, and Mrs. Johnson, at the other end of the long table, was clearly embarrassed. Whenever she could catch her husband's attention, she would indicate that he might pull the robe together. He would get the signal and peevishly tug on the robe, only to launch into another story for a repeat of the whole performance.

He was on a restricted diet, and we sympathized as he complained about it. With each course, and particularly the dessert, he kept a sharp eye on Lady Bird and, whenever her attention was directed elsewhere, without apology he would sneak a forkful of food from the guests' plates on either side of him.

In the weeks before Nixon's inauguration I spent an evening with Johnson at the White House. I was planning to take Mrs. Johnson's press secretary, the ebullient and witty Liz Carpenter, to dinner, but she announced that the President wanted to buy us a drink first. The three of us gathered in the little private study off the Oval Office. He put the bottle on the table, we poured a drink, and he began talking. It was clear that he was beginning to suffer the severe postpartum symptoms that afflict most leaders who come to that day when they must step down to comparatively powerless obscurity.

Almost wistfully and sometimes almost sotto voce, he mused about his career—about the friends, and the enemies, he had made along the way; about what he considered his successes and his disappointments. I yearned then for a tape recorder, but even now I feel constrained against reconstructing his almost nonstop monologue. It was clearly private time, and it should remain such.

But I feel no constraint about reporting on the interruptions in his recitation, which illustrate that even First Couples in their big house on Pennsylvania Avenue aren't a great deal different from the rest of us. At about eight o'clock the President's phone to his living quarters rang. His end of the conversation went something like "Yes, Bird. Yes, Bird. Well, I'm talking with some folks here and I'll be up in just a minute."

At about eight-thirty, the phone rang again. "Yes, Bird. Of course, Bird. Well, just hold on. I'll be up there in just a minute or two."

At about nine, the phone rang. "Yes, Bird. Yes, I know it. I'll be right up."

At about nine-thirty, the phone rang. "Bird, Walter Cronkite and Liz are here. I'm going to bring them up for dinner."

Lady Bird Johnson happens to be one of my favorite people. She was on the student newspaper at the University of Texas just ahead of me, and although I admired her work, I can't claim to have known her there. But Betsy and I have been privileged to know her well in recent years. She is a wonderful hostess, but her tolerance for husbandly infractions was in no way extraordinary.

Upon arrival at the family dining room, the President and his two guests were greeted (if that is the word) by a First Lady in a robe and slippers, her hair in curlers under a net. The table had been hastily set for four, but the food was already there and apparently had been for some time. What was supposed to be hot, was cold; what was supposed to be cold, was hot.

An embarrassed waiter offered to reheat the dinner. Lady Bird sternly advised him that it would not be necessary. As loquacious as the President had been for the preceding two hours, he now fell into a blue silence. She did nothing to relieve this dark cloud hanging over the table.

THERE WAS never a more inveterate golfer than Ike Eisenhower. He told me once what he thought had induced the heart attack he suffered in Colorado while President. As I can best reconstruct that explanation: "I was having one of the best rounds I had ever had, even though I always was bothered by all those Secret Service fellows standing behind every tree, and their communications cars and all that. I was on the eleventh hole when one of them said Foster [John Foster Dulles, his Secretary of State] was on the phone. And he said it was on the secure line and I would have to go back to the clubhouse to take it.

"I went back and it was Foster worrying about some matter that I don't even remember what it was. I know I didn't think it was all that important. We talked a little while and I finally got back out on the course. I hadn't played one more hole when there was the Secret Service again saying Foster was back on the phone. My game was ruined—and, you know, I think that's what gave me my heart attack."

After the war Scotland gave Ike and Mamie lifetime use of a Scottish castle. Hearing that we were taking the children to Scotland, they offered us the use of it and we had a glorious visit. Upon return to the States, I telephoned the President to report on our trip, convey messages from the castle's staff and thank him for his generosity.

"And how was the fishing?" he inquired.

I knew I was disappointing him when I had to confess that I hadn't gone fishing in his favorite streams, but in a lame attempt to get off the subject, I mentioned our visit to one of the world's great golf courses.

"But we did go over to Edinburgh and spend a couple of days at Gleneagles."

"Wonderful," the President said, "and what 18 did you play?"

Whereupon I had to offer a second confession: I hadn't actually played a round.

With that, and without further conversation, not even a "good-bye," the President simply hung up.

With an idiot like me, what more could be said? I later learned that this was an old military habit of his. He usually did not spend time on the telephone uselessly saying "Hello" and "Good-bye."

One of our more affable, straight-arrow Presidents was the President-by-accident, Gerald Ford. Ford was the only person who served as President without being elected either President or Vice President. Nixon had appointed the party wheelhorse who had long been minority leader of the House to fill the vacancy left by Spiro Agnew's resignation from the vice presidency. When Nixon was himself forced to resign to avoid impeachment after the Watergate scandal, Ford became President.

When Ford sought the nomination for reelection, Ronald Reagan made a run at him at the Kansas City convention and came close to unseating an incumbent, a rare apostasy in party politics. Jimmy Carter defeated Ford in the '76 election but Ford was to play a bizarre role at the 1980 Republican convention in Detroit.

Reagan won the nomination, and the convention was awaiting his choice of a running mate when the hall was swept by an incredible rumor. Some party stalwarts were suggesting that ex-President Ford run for the vice presidency on Reagan's ticket, an unprecedented idea. Negotiations were active and the phone lines were busy between the hotel suites of the Ford partisans and the Reagan headquarters.

With not a lot of hope for success, I invited Ford to come to our convention anchor booth and tell me about it. He came, and for the benefit of our CBS television audience he said he was not seeking the nomination but he was listening. However, he made clear that he would accept the offer only if Reagan promised that he would share with him some of the most important duties of the presidency.

"A sort of copresidency," I suggested, and Ford agreed. That cut it. At both the Reagan and Ford suites the books were slammed shut. No presidential candidate could agree to such a power-sharing deal. Our interview certainly made news; it probably shaped the course of events.

Throughout our interview, unbeknownst to Ford or me, a terrible rumpus had been going on outside our studio door. When Ford first appeared on our air, ABC had dispatched one of its fiercest and most successful correspondents to get him over to their booth. We had to call extra security guards as Barbara Walters literally fought to get inside our studio. They were barely keeping her at bay when the interview concluded and Ford emerged.

At a luncheon that both Barbara and I attended the next day, Ford told the group that he had a sore shoulder, suffered when Barbara twisted his arm to get him onto ABC.

The Fords were among the most friendly occupants of the White House, but Reagan won the affability contest hands down. I had trouble with his political philosophy, particularly his endorsement of laissez-faire trickle-down economics, the concept that if the people and industries at the top are successful, prosperity will somehow be visited on all the rest of us.

He was a strong President who lived up to his campaign promise to reverse Franklin Roosevelt's economic and social revolution. He did so by surrounding himself with the same advisers from the nation's top echelons of business and finance who had engineered his election, and then leaving them alone.

Almost every Oval Office visitor left impressed with the Reagan modus operandi. Before answering questions or introducing new topics, he slid his top desk drawer open enough to read from a set of cards presumably prepared by his staff.

He had one weakness that, while scarcely threatening the democracy, did plague his political opposition and the White House correspondents who were assigned to put his comments into perspective. Reagan would read or hear of some incident that he felt demonstrated the rectitude of his policies or the fallacies of the opposition. Possibly he did not deliberately falsify, but his natural love of a good story frequently led him to stray far from the facts. The stories, often repeated, became part of the political lore, while the press corps and the Democrats found that their corrections never quite caught up.

But, by golly, he was affable. Shortly after his inauguration, I announced that I was stepping down from the "CBS Evening News" anchor desk and I requested a final presidential interview. He granted it readily, although, having been in office only three months, he really had little to say and the interview was hardly a major news maker.

When it was over, however, he invited me into his private office off the Oval Office—the same one of the long night with Lyndon Johnson. And there were several of the top people in his administration whom I had known well: Vice President Bush, Secretary of State Jim Baker, Attorney General Ed Meese, media specialist David Gergen and press secretary Jim Brady, who within a few days would catch a bullet meant for the President and suffer lifelong brain injuries.

The President had a cake and champagne, and we spent possibly two hours there in a hilarious exchange of stories—most of them dirty.

CHAPTER 11

IT IS TOO bad the Vietnam War gave itself such a bad name. It was its own worst enemy.

When the United States got involved, the idea seemed rational enough. President Truman, in accordance with his doctrine, proclaimed on March 12, 1947, that we would take whatever measures were necessary to contain Communism, poured millions into France's effort to hold on to its Indochinese colony, which was seething with the rebellion of independence-seeking natives. The French were driven out but salvaged something in Vietnam by a partition of the country—the Communists in the north and a regime sympathetic to capitalist-democratic principles in the south.

President Eisenhower bought into the emerging "domino theory": that any further revolutionary successes among the old French Indochinese colonies would start a chain reaction and they all would disappear behind the Iron Curtain. So he supported the new South Vietnamese government, not only with funds but also with a significant number of military advisers to help train its new army.

At his inaugural President Kennedy extended the Truman Doctrine with his pledge that this nation would "pay any price, bear any burden, meet any hardship, support any friend, oppose any foe to assure our survival and the success of liberty." With the depredations of the Communist guerrillas growing more serious daily, by the fall of 1963 Kennedy had authorized 18,000 military advisers, up from 685 when he took office in 1961. This was a stretch of his inaugural pledge. It could hardly be said that South Vietnam's ambitious, quarreling, corrupt leaders had established a democratic government. But they maintained that this was their intention, and that was taken by Washington as grounds for hope that Vietnam might provide a toehold for democracy on a subcontinent that Communism threatened to overrun.

There was certainly nothing in our recent foreign policy background to give Washington pause before climbing into bed with unsavory totalitarians as long as they were of a conservative stripe and dedicated anti-Communists. Pursuing our post–World War II program to contain the expansionist ambitions of the Soviet imperialists, we had made alliances with rightist dictators around the globe: the "colonels" in Greece, the Shah in Iran, Franco in Spain, Chiang Kai-shek in Formosa. The excuse was that we needed their friendship and their territory in order to establish the military bases that presumably would deter Stalin's aggression.

With those moves we became at least passive conspirators in the suppression of democratic movements in much of the world. Particularly in the developing world, the rising young leaders who had opposed the colonialism of the past with strong rhetoric and sometimes violent action were viewed by our leadership as radicals dangerous to the established order. A case can be made that many of them saw America as their ideal, only to be disappointed and embittered by its failure to embrace their ambitions for their countries. Robert McNamara, President Kennedy's Defense Secretary, in his revealing book on the Vietnam War, put the North Vietnamese leader, Ho Chi Minh, in that category.

Many were undoubtedly Marxists all along, and it was not our rejection that drove them into the eager arms of Moscow and Beijing. But it seems to this observer that in those early post–World War II years we squandered one of the greatest reservoirs of goodwill any nation ever had. We let the admiration and hopes of the world's people and their leaders drain away through the huge cracks in our idealism. All in the name of self-interest and military expediency. There should be a better definition of those two imperatives of national policy.

If President Kennedy's objectives in Vietnam were as limited as he said they were, they might have served those interests. But by the time Kennedy was in the Oval Office, it may have been too late. The previous administrations of Truman and, especially, Eisenhower had rejected any possibility of dealing with Ho Chi Minh, and had cast our lot with the French colonialists of Southeast Asia.

It is always easier for an affluent society such as

ours, and particularly one linked by heritage and relationship to the cultivated societies of Europe, to side with a regime that seeks to duplicate and preserve the looks and demeanor of our lifestyle, to which we are accustomed, rather than to embrace those whose native culture and appearance are different from our own.

In the years immediately following World War II, American intellectuals were gung ho for the dissolution of the European colonial empires, particularly the strongest of them: that of Great Britain. They applauded lustily when the British, their resources depleted by two world wars in barely a quarter century, had to let go of India and in short order thereafter most of their remaining colonies around the world.

When the French chose to fight to hold on to Indochina, American sympathies for the most part were with the native populations. Admiration was high for the French, who defended to the death their last bastion at Dien Bien Phu, but that admiration was diluted by our strong sense that self-government and independence were the rights of all peoples everywhere. That is why Kennedy was applauded for his inaugural pledge, and why his loan of military advisers to the government of South Vietnam was accepted without noticeable reservations or concern.

That was the way I saw the situation at the time. While most of us knew little about Ho Chi Minh or the nature of his North Vietnamese government, we did realize that it was Communist, and our interest, our policy since World War II and our young President's pledge all agreed that we would defend democracy wherever the Red menace threatened.

From the beginning it was clear that going to South Vietnam's aid, even with only a limited commitment of military advisers, was not exactly defending democracy. The Saigon regimes of Emperor Bao Dai and the successor we nominated, Ngo Dinh Diem, did not fit our definition of democracy. But they did offer the hope that they could be reformed in our democratic image and thus provide a toehold for democracy on a continent that otherwise threatened to disappear behind another Red curtain.

Kennedy acted upon the stern assessment of the situation delivered to him by the Joint Chiefs of Staff in January 1962. "Of equal importance to the immediate loss [of South Vietnam] are the eventualities which could follow the loss of the Southeast Asian mainland," their letter said. "All of the Indonesian archipelago could come under the domination and control of the U.S.S.R. and would become a Communist base posing a threat against Australia and New Zealand. The Sino-Soviet Bloc would have control of the eastern access to the Indian Ocean. The Philippines and Japan could be pressured to assume at best a neutralist role, thus eliminating two of our major bases in the Western Pacific. India's ability to remain neutral would be jeopardized and, as the Bloc meets success, its concurrent stepped-up activities to move into and control Africa can be expected."

The domino theory that if we lost Vietnam the other nations of Southeast Asia would fall in rapid order to Communism seemed reasonable and was widely accepted. Thus, many of us supported President Kennedy's decision to dispatch to Vietnam those few military advisers to protect a little plot of land where democracy might have a chance to grow.

The evidence was clear, and is frequently forgotten today, that early on Kennedy was becoming disillusioned with the prospects of political reform in Saigon and disenchanted therefore with his own policy of support. And I have always believed that if he had lived, he would have withdrawn those advisers from Vietnam, although his Secretary of State, Dean Rusk, later wrote that he had never heard the President mention this possibility.

Barely twelve weeks before he died in Dallas, I interviewed him over the Labor Day holiday at his Hyannis, Massachusetts, home. In that interview he said:

"I don't think that unless a greater effort is made by the [Vietnam] government to win popular support that the war can be won out there. In the final analysis it is their war. They are the ones who have to win it or lose it. We can help them, we can give them equipment, we can send our men out there as advisers, but they have to win it, the people of Vietnam, against the Communists.

"We are prepared to continue to assist them, but I don't think that the war can be won unless the people support the effort, and in my opinion, in the last two months, the government has gotten out of touch with the people."

That scarcely sounds like the statement of a President about to commit more troops to the battle. It clearly was intended instead to send a powerful warning to Diem and his éminence grise, his brother Ngo Dinh Nhu, and Madame Nhu, possessors of a private army in the fine old Oriental tradition. Their nepotistic, pro-Catholic dictatorship had led to serious troubles with the nation's influential Buddhists, and discontent had even spread to some elements of the army. The stability of an ally in whom two American administrations had heavily invested was seriously threatened.

So, unbeknownst to me and the American public at the time, my interview with the President came even as debate was raging within his administration on what should be done with Diem. Just a week before the interview, Kennedy's Vietnam brain trust had sent a message to our Ambassador to Vietnam, Henry Cabot Lodge, that was about as unequivocal as such diplomatic instructions can be:

"U.S. Government cannot tolerate situation in which power lies in Nhu's hands. Diem must be given chance to rid himself of Nhu and his coterie and replace them with best military and political personalities available.

"If in spite of all our efforts, Diem remains obdurate and refuses, then we must face the possibility that Diem himself cannot be preserved."

Actually, the brain trust, which included Under

Secretary of State George Ball and Averell Harriman, drew up the message while three of its key players—Dean Rusk, Robert McNamara and the President himself—were out of town. Rusk recalls that Ball telephoned the text to him and he approved, mistakenly thinking that the President already had. The cable went to Saigon.

When the senior trio returned to Washington, according to Rusk's memoirs, they tried to soften the instructions to Lodge, but in Lodge's hawkish view, their effort came too late. He cabled back: "We are launched on a course from which there is no respectable turning back, the overthrow of the Diem government. There is no turning back because U.S. prestige is already committed to this end in large measure and will become more so as the facts leak out."

What was clearly a warning in Kennedy's remarks to me actually might have been meant as more than that. The President, while using the broadcast to keep up the public pressure on Diem, at the same time might have been trying to disassociate himself from any future charges of American complicity in the coup that his administration's actions had already set in motion. That is speculative—but it is fact that two months after the Kennedy statement, Diem and his brother, Ngo Dinh Nhu, were assassinated in a military coup.

In his memoirs Rusk notes that as the coup got under way he instructed Lodge to offer Diem arrangements to get him out of the country. "But in hopes of finding military units that would support him," Rusk wrote, "Diem rebuffed this offer, was captured and killed. Had we been as actively involved in the coup as others suggest, we could at least have prevented Diem's death." Note the former Secretary's qualifying word "actively."

At any rate, those thorns were out of the American side, although a succession of Vietnamese governments thereafter, with their authoritarianism and actual or suspected corruption, never succeeded much better than Diem in gaining widespread public approval. And the inside story of that interview of mine adds an other shadowy element to the story, with evidence buttressing my suspicions that the President hoped to use our broadcast to prepare a defense if, as Lodge so bluntly put it, "the facts leak out."

Kennedy had granted me the interview to help us inaugurate network television's first half-hour evening news broadcast. These daily showcases of broadcast journalism had all been a short fifteen minutes before then, in the pattern of the radio news programs. A quarter of an hour on radio was adequate to tell the news of the day, and even to add a couple of minutes of commentary at the end. But it had proved totally inadequate when pictures were added.

Television had an impact far greater (in most but not all cases) than that of the spoken word alone, but the pictures were time-consumers. The news departments had been lobbying the network managements for years for the half-hour broadcast, and while the networks were willing, their affiliated stations were opposed. They had their own fifteen-minute local newscasts, which together with the network offerings made a neat half-hour package, and they were opposed to any tampering with this successful early evening formula.

The imperatives of the half-hour network program were so strong, however, that under the leadership of Dick Salant, the management team of Paley and Stanton took the bit in their teeth and simply announced to the affiliates that on September 2, 1963, the "CBS Evening News with Walter Cronkite" would become a half-hour broadcast—take it or leave it.

Station after station threatened to leave it, but, failing to bluff CBS, by the time the big day came they fell into line almost without exception. NBC was able to follow suit just a week later.

(It might be noted here that the network news departments a few years later understood how desperately they needed a full hour to do even adequate credit to each day's news flow. The affiliates put up the same resistance, and although at one time or another either CBS or NBC set a date to go for the full hour, on these occasions it was the networks that crumpled. Today the half hour is still the norm, although recognized as inadequate by every network newsperson.)

So it was to mark that first half-hour broadcast that I arrived in Hyannis to meet the following morning with the President of the United States. As I drove up to the motel where the White House press

corps stayed, our veteran correspondent Robert Pier-
point was waiting at the steps. He lit into me in a
show of daring disrespect for the anchorman.

"Listen," he practically shouted, "if you're going
to break a big story, it seems like the least you could
do is tell your own White House man about it."

"What big story?" I asked.

"That the President is going to make a major
statement on Vietnam on your broadcast tomorrow
night. It's all over the AP."

This idea was offensive in several ways, appreci-
ated perhaps only by a professional journalist. In the
first place, it indicated at the least that Kennedy
intended to use my interview to plant a statement to
suit his purposes, and no respectable newsperson
wishes to be thought of as a conduit for official
announcements, even ones by the President. It also
suggested that Kennedy had been advised in advance of the questions I was going to ask, perhaps
had even approved them in advance. There are some
newspeople who will promise such prior approval in
order to obtain an interview with a hard-to-get subject, but the practice was strictly prohibited by our
CBS guidelines and was definitely against my own
code. And further, I thought it was impossibly pre-
sumptuous of the President's press secretary, the
affable Pierre Salinger, a close friend of most of us
newspeople, to leak to anybody something he hoped
would come up in the next day's interview, and
Salinger was almost certainly the source of AP's
story.

I was angry. I found Salinger at the bar and let him have it.

"And I promise you this, Pierre," I told him, jabbing an index finger into his chest. "I promise you, I'm not going to even bring up Vietnam when I talk to the President tomorrow. I'm not even going to bring it up!"

As incredible as it seems today, or would have seemed even a month later, that would not have been a serious omission. Our involvement in Vietnam at that early stage was still mostly political in nature, and the concern was not so much the commitment of American troops but whether or not we would continue to support the Diem regime there.

Salinger took me aside and then followed me to my room, arguing for the Vietnam question. I would be passing up a chance to really make news, this was an important matter, if I didn't get into it the President would make the statement elsewhere and I would look foolish for having passed it up.

Nothing would sway me. He was picking me up at eight the next morning to drive to the President's residence, and as he left I promised him once more that I could only allay the embarrassment his leak had caused me by not bringing up Vietnam—that the embarrassment would be turned back on him and my honor would be avenged. In the car on the way to the Kennedy compound the next morning, Pierre spent the entire time arguing his case. I remained adamant, and I meant it at the time.

But as I sat there on the lawn of his Hyannis home

with the President, I had calmed down enough to realize that, since the interview would have to be edited for time anyway, nothing would be lost in asking the Vietnam question of the moment. If he indeed had something newsworthy to say, we could use it; if not, we could drop it.

And I realized, too, that in my anger I had forgotten what Pierre knew all along: The subject has more control over a news interview than the reporter. At any time he wanted, the President could inject a statement on Vietnam whether I posed the question or not. I did at least torment Pierre by not asking the question until deep into the interview.

The President's answer was important, and did indeed make headlines. He effectively pulled the rug out from under Diem and changed the course of events in Vietnam. Naturally the statement that I had said I had no interest in eliciting led our program and was an auspicious opening for the first network half-hour evening newscast.

There was a sequel to this story. After Kennedy's tragic death, those who served Camelot attempted in several instances to revise history to protect his image or burnish it, and one of Salinger's efforts was directed at the effect of that Hyannis interview. In *The New York Times Magazine* and a subsequent book, he wrote that we had distorted Kennedy's comments by leaving out material that qualified and considerably softened his bald statement regarding Diem. We did indeed edit the President's comments for length, but the substance was unaffected.

He did say at one point, "I admire what the President has done," but he also said: "And the people will not support the effort if the government continues to follow the policy of the past two months. I hope that'll be clear to the government."

My assumption is that Salinger was preparing a preemptive defense should history, as it has since, uncover the American part in the anti-Diem coup. If there is any mitigating factor in the American plotting, it is that the administration never planned that Diem and Nhu should die.

Whatever Kennedy had in mind about the future of the Vietnam War, however, became moot in those terrible seconds in Dallas. His successor, Lyndon Johnson, was a superb politician and an effective administrator and therefore would become a powerful President, but his weakness was foreign policy.

It was not a matter that had interested him and so, in those first months of his presidency, he was at the mercy of his advisers from the State and Defense departments, and the military buildup in Vietnam accelerated. The United States manipulated, to the extent we could, the makeup of the Vietnam government, and the war became ours. A reluctant Congress was brought along with Johnson's vast exaggeration of the Tonkin Gulf incident, the alleged but never fully substantiated attack by North Vietnamese vessels on two American destroyers.

Although by that time we were already deeply involved on the ground, with almost 20,000 troops in Vietnam and a casualty list of more than 200 killed and wounded, somehow this shadowy naval action was represented by Johnson as the step beyond which the North Vietnamese could not go. And he persuaded Congress to give him a virtual blank check to conduct a full-scale war without ever declaring one.

It may have been the only war ever started by a flatulent whale. Sonar operators told CBS "60 Minutes" producer Joe Wershba years later that they had great difficulty distinguishing enemy torpedoes from occasional emissions from gaseous whales. The possibility here for historical revision is mind-boggling.

There were two basic mistakes in the Johnson administration's handling of the war. The first was the President's guns-and-butter policy of trying to shield the American economy from the consequences of the war. The people at home were not asked to share in the costs of the war—there were no material shortages or rationing, as in World War II, and taxes were not raised to pay for it. This not only was disastrous economic policy, creating a debt with which generations yet unborn will still be burdened, but it increased the frightful inequity of sacrifice: The lives of draftees were sacrificed, or at least disrupted, while life on the home front was scarcely disturbed.

The other administration mistake was far more insidious. Perhaps himself misled by a military either greatly overoptimistic or incredibly duplicitous, Johnson never leveled with the American people about the nature or likely extent of the war, although his secret briefings with congressional leaders were fairly straightforward.

Congress was led, by rapidly increasing increments, into the commitment of vast forces. It was suspicious and attempted to control the extent of our involvement, but under pressure from the military experts it was apparently powerless to stop the escalation.

We were in the early stages of this buildup and were beginning to take our first casualties when I made my first trip to Vietnam. At this stage, Vietcong bombs were exploding with some frequency and with devastating results in the Saigon restaurants frequented by Americans. But the danger I had elected to face seemed to begin before I ever reached Saigon. As I boarded the Vietnamese airliner at Hong Kong, I was impressed by the efficiency of the boarding procedure and the cleanliness of the plane, but mostly by the beauty and charm of the stewardesses. Far from the hell of war, this was heaven.

Before takeoff one of the smiling, long-haired beauties handed me a copy of Saigon's English-language newspaper. A very black headline summarized the day's leading story: "Air Vietnam Stewardess Held in Airplane Bombing."

Was my stewardess's smile the smile of the cobra?

The flight was less relaxing than it had promised to be only a moment ago—and I learned the first, the fundamental, the elementary lesson about the Vietnam of the 1960s: One could not depend on things being what they seemed to be.

Saigon still retained some of the old French colonial charm that would soon disappear in the dust and smog of thousands of military vehicles crowding its once lovely tree-lined boulevards. The Caravelle Hotel, designated as press headquarters, was filling with correspondents and news bureaus, but many of us still stayed at the less modern and hence more gracious Continental Hotel across the square.

The roof garden of the Caravelle provided a box seat for the war. We watched the nightly bombing raids and gunship counterattacks on the city's outskirts, some nights more intense than others. One night, over to the northwest, five, six, maybe seven miles away, was a brilliant display of flares, lighting the countryside around. Tracers from unseen helicopters poured fire below, accompanied by the clump of mortars and the occasional bump and concussion of 500-pound bombs. The next morning Armed Forces Radio said that the U.S. command had reported there had been no important activity in Vietnam the night before.

A caste, or class, system that has always, I suppose, been applied to war correspondents to one degree or another has become more evident and more offensive with the growth of television. There are the grunts—the real battle reporters, cameramen and field producers who spend much of their time and risk their lives alongside the soldiers in the foxholes. Also there are the equivalents of the rear echelon troops—the bureau managers, broadcast producers, expediters—who man the base camp and seldom if ever see the real action. And then there are the anchorpeople, or, in the case of the writing press, the columnists, who spend a few days dipping their feet in the waters of war but who never suffer total immersion.

The members of this latter caste, influential as they are thought to be, are almost certainly going to be invited to dine with the generals and to have audiences with high officials in the host country. They are going to be offered escorted tours of the war—any war, whatever the war—and hence see a somewhat different war than those sharing the foxholes.

The danger is that they may believe this official version of events rather than what they are told by their own colleagues in the field. One can try to avoid falling into this trap, but it is not easy when duties on the home front necessarily limit one's visits to the war zones and thus one's exposure to the facts.

The damage can be limited by the VIP correspondent's own awareness of the problem, by his or her experience in previous or similar conflicts and by his or her determination to visit the foxholes and at least momentarily share the truth that is revealed with startling clarity out where the bullets fly.

Like most of us, I would rather have the approval of my colleagues than that of any other jury. That was particularly true with respect to our superb correspondents in Vietnam—and there were a legion

of reporters, cameramen, soundmen and producers
who risked their necks to get the story for CBS. I
have some idea of what they thought of the visits of
the 800-pound gorilla. As a young correspondent I
held the same opinion of other gorillas in other wars.
I would like to think that I conducted myself in
Vietnam in such a way as to win at least some measure of approval from them.

I took advantage of the generals' dinners and the
high-level political interviews, but I also made brief
forays into what passed for the front lines in a war
that had none. On that first visit I went out with the
helicopter-borne 173rd Airborne Brigade, the first
unit to be sent to Vietnam after the escalation from
the military-observer stage. I rode with them into the
jungle not far outside Saigon as they sought out the
Vietcong to provide some sense of security for a city
on whose outskirts, in those early days, the enemy
appeared almost nightly. On subsequent visits I flew
with the air support helicopters as they swept low
over the jungle's treetops, machine-gunning whatever was under that green canopy, and I flew with
the Air Force as it bombed that same jungle, where
concentrations of the enemy were reported to be.

In the field and back in Saigon I heard the tales of
the pacification officers who were working in the
villages to win the hearts and minds of the people.
While they acknowledged that they were not
encountering much enthusiasm for democracy, as
they had hoped, most of them had not yet sunk into
the slough of cynical pessimism that would come
later.

I was still impressed with our effort—impressed enough, as a matter of fact, to view with some embarrassment the performance of much of the press at the military's daily evening news briefing. While most of the older hands and experienced war correspondents appeared to be attempting in a rational way to extract the facts from the military and make sense of the daily communiqués, the younger reporters seemed to be engaged in a contest among themselves to determine who was the most cynical, who the most confrontational in their rude challenges to the appointed spokesmen. They struck me as attempting to defend the truth by branding every military statement as a lie.

I was not yet prepared to grasp the fact that Vietnam was no ordinary war as some of us senior correspondents had known it in World War II. This was no routine meeting of press and authority. I was not prepared for the ultimate truth: These hapless spokesmen were charged with explaining a war that had no explanation, and both they and the press knew this to be the awful truth. The press named the evening news briefing "the five o'clock follies." It could have been the name for the war.

Despite all this, I returned from that first trip to Vietnam with the feeling that the evidence in the field seemed to support the contention of the high command and the administration in Washington that we were making progress.

But then came the revelation of Cam Ranh Bay. That big open body of water was ringed by perhaps one of the most beautiful beaches in the world. The green forested hills wore the wide fine sands like a necklace. It was so perfect that many of us cynics suggested that it would be the postwar site of a chain of hotels—with casinos, of course.

That would have been a kind fate compared with that which fortune dealt the bay. The United States built a huge naval base there. Its roads and docks and warehouses, which covered almost 100 square miles, not only ruined the landscape; they provided the first physical evidence that perhaps the military didn't themselves believe the optimistic reports they were giving the administration and the country.

The building of that base was ordered in April 1965, when the administration had led congressional leaders to believe that our ultimate commitment of troops would be no more than 200,000. Yet the base was designed to service the other end of a pipeline that could handle many times that many troops. With Cam Ranh Bay my disillusionment began. That and the increasing reports from the military and the political foxholes of Vietnam that neither the battle to subjugate the Vietcong nor that to win over the Vietnamese villagers was meeting with any tangible success.

Additionally, there was something distinctly uncomfortable about a war in which it was impossible for even the most optimistic military spokesmen to claim that we were liberating and holding any sizable parts of the territory of South Vietnam. The criterion for success that our military adopted was the body count. The only way to measure victory, it seemed, was in terms of how many Vietcong we could kill. That was scarcely uplifting, scarcely inspiring, scarcely calculated to build the morale of either the fighting forces or the home front. It became increasingly difficult to justify the war as the terrible cost to ourselves in blood and material grew and the supply of Vietcong needing to be killed appeared inexhaustible.

At home my growing disillusionment was fed by the performance of President Johnson. He had long since made it his war. He adopted it officially when he invented or accepted that exaggerated version of the Gulf of Tonkin incident and with blustering indignation forced through Congress the Tonkin Gulf resolution. It gave him authority to conduct the war as he saw fit, and was, in effect, a formalization of the reality that the United States had taken over the conflict. For Johnson it was a personal challenge, almost a personal vendetta against the enemy. George Bush would later exhibit a similar trait in his military action against Noriega in Panama and Hussein in Iraq.

The extent of Johnson's personal involvement was brought home to me one night at the White House. There was some sort of late afternoon reception at which I was surprised to see Allan Shivers, a former Governor of Texas and not infrequent political adversary of the President's. The President came over to me at one point and said that Shivers was staying for dinner in the private quarters and he and Mrs. Johnson would like to have me stay as well.

There were just the four of us for dinner. The President was his most gracious to Shivers, and we had a pleasant time both before and after dinner sitting on the second-floor south porch that Truman had built despite a storm of architectural controversy. We talked—that is, *they* talked—mostly about Texas politics, which had fascinated me ever since I was a young cub reporter at the state capitol in Austin. Also, Shivers and Lady Bird Johnson had been just ahead of me at the state university there and we had much in common.

There was no doubt that Johnson was laying on his old enemy a pretty thick accounting of his duties, performance, prerogatives and powers as President. And then Vietnam came up.

As his hands drew in the air a picture of the action, I heard him say: "I'm going to bring my ships in here, and then, with my airplanes up here, I'm going to send my troops in." *His* ships, *his* planes, *his* troops. Maybe it was just a little braggadocio, one Texan to another, but what an astounding if unconscious revelation of his view of the conflict.

My disillusionment was keeping pace with that of growing numbers of the American people. And then in 1968 came Tet.

The huge North Vietnamese–Vietcong offensive kicked off on the Asian New Year's Day, in violation of a holiday truce. Within days it had swept through every important city in South Vietnam except the big Marine base of Danang and Saigon itself. Even in

Saigon the Communists were in the streets in some corners of town and had mounted a frightening suicide assault on the American Embassy in the heart of the city. According to reports, in scores of villages that we had considered pacified, the hearts and minds of the peasants had turned back to the Vietcong.

All of this even on the heels of more assertions from our military that the end of the Vietnam War was in sight, that they could clearly see the light at the end of the tunnel. Polls showed that the number of Americans who had sickened of the war and no longer had faith in the administration or the military that served it had become the majority. Demonstrations against the war spread from the campuses to middle-class communities across the nation as the Tet offensive brought public confidence to a new low.

I was proud of the degree to which we had kept our evening newscast free of bias, although on a subject as controversial as the war, we did not get credit from either side for doing so. The conservatives and government supporters thought we had joined the wild-eyed, "unpatriotic" liberals. The students and other war opponents branded us as mouthpieces for the establishment. I tried to keep our reports impartial but personally I tilted largely toward the dissidents because of the stridency of some of the conservatives in branding as unpatriotic those who opposed the war. Patriotism simply cannot be defined. Many of those against the war protested with the most dedicated patriotism—in the total conviction that the war was not a just one and was besmirching the image of a nation they loved.

In a misguided attempt to convince the administration leadership of the impartiality of CBS News, company president Arthur Taylor invited then Secretary of Defense James Schlesinger to a private luncheon with me in his office. The love feast collapsed before we had our first martini when Schlesinger invoked the need for patriotism on all fronts and I was unable to resist a probably too vociferous attack on the whole philosophy.

"It is not the journalist's job to be patriotic," I recall saying. "How can patriotism be determined anyway? Is patriotism simply agreeing unquestioningly with every action of one's government? Or might we define patriotism as having the courage to speak and act on those principles one thinks are best for the country, whether they are in accordance with the wishes of the government or not?

"It is everyone's duty to obey the laws of the land, but I think your definition of patriotism, Mr. Secretary, would preclude our listening to and reporting upon the opinions of those who believe your policies are inimical to the best interests of our nation. Perhaps these dissidents are the patriotic ones. At least they have the right to believe that their love of country is as sincere as yours, and that they have a right under our Constitution to speak their beliefs. And it is no breach of patriotism when we report on their half of a historic dialogue."

Taylor was moving toward the thirty-fifth-floor windows. He seemed to be contemplating jumping. Schlesinger was slack-jawed. He is a man of considerable learning who does not look kindly on those of lesser intelligence. It took him only a moment to recover his usual arrogance, and the lunch went on in the atmosphere he preferred—total dominance.

At the time of the Tet offensive, this was only part of the debate that was rending the American people. With the new uncertainties created by the Tet offensive, it seemed to me that perhaps we should put on the line that high level of trust which polls showed the people had in our broadcast. Perhaps, I proposed to our news president, Dick Salant, I should go to Vietnam as quickly as possible (the Tet offensive was still in full swing) and try to present an assessment of the situation as one who had not previously taken a public position on the war. Salant agreed, and that same night I was off for Asia.

Back at the box seat to war on the roof of the Caravelle Hotel, I watched the helicopter gunships and bombers attacking suspected Vietcong concentrations on the city's outskirts and saw fires blossom on the docks downriver. I drove the several blocks from the city center to the Chinese section, which the Vietcong had penetrated, and I stood in the still-smoldering ruins they had left behind.

With producer Jeff Gralnick, cameraman Jimmy Wilson and soundman Bob Funk I flew and trucked with GI reinforcements into the ancient city of Hue, where the Marines were fighting house-to-house and

where incoming artillery shook the command headquarters. It turned out to be harder to get out of Hue
than to get in. Ambushes had closed the roads. We
shared a helicopter out with the bags holding twelve
Marines whose war had ended that day at Hue. I
thought about them as, back in Saigon, I was assured
by our leaders that now we had the enemy just
where we wanted him, and with just a few more
troops, 150,000 or 200,000, we could finish the job.

Tell that to the Marines, I thought—the Marines
in the body bags on that helicopter. To me it sounded
like more of the old siren song.

The official version: We had dealt the enemy a
terrible blow, his offensive had failed and he was in
retreat (although the cost to us and our South Vietnamese allies indeed had been extremely high in
terms of men and materiel), and those once-pacified
South Vietnam villages whose hearts and minds had
proved so fickle were only being expedient in welcoming the Communists back—they would be back
with us as soon as the areas were cleared.

As Tet wound down, I spent an evening up-
country at the Phu Bai headquarters of General
Creighton W. Abrams, Jr., the military's number two
man in Vietnam, whom I had last seen in the World
War II Battle of the Bulge as he fought to relieve the
airborne troops in Bastogne. He was remarkably
candid in admitting that the Tet attack had come as a
surprise, and the serious extent of the damage, in
casualties, materiel and morale. His officers joined
us for a soft drink and their conversation brought

home the nature of modern war as even the experience of battle itself had not. It was a highly and brutally technical discussion of fire power and kill ratios and the like. How, in effect, we could kill more Vietnamese. I wanted us to win the war, but this emotionless professionalism was hard to take.

But most incredible was the claim from on high at our Saigon headquarters that all we needed now was a few tens of thousands more men and we could finish the job. As it was, General William Westmoreland after Tet asked Johnson for another 206,000 troops. That would have meant 750,000 in Vietnam, three quarters of a million. Johnson said no, in effect closing the book on Lyndon Johnson's war. It would soon become Richard Nixon's war.

My decision was not difficult to reach. It had been taking shape, I realized, since Cam Ranh Bay. There was no way that this war could be justified any longer—a war whose purpose had never been adequately explained to the American people, to a people whose conscience burned because of the terribly, the fatally unequal sacrifice of the troops and the home front.

So I flew home and did a special report on the Tet offensive. It was as factual as we at CBS News could make it. But I ended it with a clearly labeled editorial. This was a radical departure from our normal practice. I had only once or twice stepped out of my role as an impartial newscaster, and on both those occasions I was defending freedom of the press on the theory that if we members of the press did not speak up for this democratic essential, no one else would.

As we discussed the broadcast, Salant warned that I was placing my reputation, as well as CBS's, on the line and that we were putting ourselves in jeopardy; that given the delicate state of the bitterly divided American public opinion, we might well lose a substantial part of our audience. I had no problem making my decision. Salant, as courageous as ever, agreed, although he was more aware than anyone else could have been of the troubles that might soon tumble around his head from disturbed, less courageous affiliated stations and thus perhaps his own management.

In the broadcast I made it clear that my subsequent words represented my own opinion and that this was an extraordinary affair. I said: "To say that we are closer to victory today is to believe, in the face of the evidence, the optimists who have been wrong in the past. To suggest we are on the edge of defeat is to yield to unreasonable pessimism. To say that we are mired in stalemate seems the only realistic, yet unsatisfactory, conclusion. . . . It is increasingly clear to this reporter that the only rational way out, then, will be to negotiate, not as victors, but as an honorable people who lived up to their pledge to defend democracy, and did the best they could."

The reaction to the broadcast was not at all what we expected. Although there were the usual letters of complaint from those who disagreed, they were not in unusual numbers. The newspaper editorials around the country reflected the previous views of their publishers.

There was no reaction from the administration, official or unofficial. I did not hear of, and I do not believe there were, any complaints from the White House to the CBS management, although in the past Lyndon Johnson had been quick to telephone me, and other anchorpeople, to complain of coverage to which he objected, and he was never shy about mentioning this to management.

The explanation came many months later, when we learned that the President was actually stunned by the broadcast. George Christian, the President's news secretary, and his assistant Bill Moyers, later to win fame on television, were present as the President and some of his staff watched the broadcast. "The President flipped off the set," Moyers recalled, "and said: 'If I've lost Cronkite, I've lost middle America.' "

I think it is possible that the President shared my opinion, and that, in effect, I had confirmed it for him. He probably had as much difficulty as I had in accepting the military's continued optimism in the face of the Tet setback.

The broadcast, I believe, was just one more straw in the increasing burden of Vietnam, and as such it added that much more weight to the decision which was forming in Lyndon Johnson's mind not to risk defeat in the forthcoming election. It was just five weeks after the broadcast that he announced that he would not be a candidate for reelection. David Halberstam would eventually write in his book *The Powers That Be* that it was the first time in history that an anchorman had declared a war over.

Of course, I was not through with Vietnam. None of us were, not until that last helicopter lifted off from the Embassy roof to complete our ignominious flight from Saigon as the Communists came sweeping in.

Shortly after the post-Tet broadcast, Robert Kennedy invited me to lunch at his Senate office. It was just the two of us and he wanted to explore my views on the conflict further. When he expressed his strong belief in the necessity of extricating ourselves from Vietnam, I gratuitously suggested that he ought to take his argument to the people by entering the presidential primaries that spring. The press had been speculating on the possibility that he might challenge Johnson for the presidency.

"Give me three reasons why I should run," he countered, "and I'll give you three reasons why I shouldn't."

He saved me from having to play that game by continuing: "Let me ask you one. Where are you registered to vote—in Connecticut?"

No, New York, I told him.

"Then you aren't registered as a Democrat?" He had clearly been checking the rolls.

"I'm registered as an independent," I said.

"Well, that doesn't matter. We want you to run for the Senate this year."

He filled the void of my speechlessness by outlining the sort of support I could expect from the party. At the first pause I told him why I had eschewed politics up to that time and planned to continue to do so—namely, my concern that once a prominent network anchor ran for public office, the people might suspect all news anchors of doctoring the news to satisfy secret political ambitions. The subject was left at that.

When I got back to our Washington news office, the bureau manager, Bill Small, was eager to know what Kennedy had said about running for the presidency. I told him of our limited conversation on the subject.

"What did he tell you about the weekend meeting at Hickory Hill [his Virginia residence]?"

He hadn't mentioned it.

"Roger [Mudd] has the whole story. The old Kennedy brain trust is in town, and they are going to decide this weekend whether Bobby should run."

It was a top story from one of the best political reporters ever to work the capital scene. Obviously it had to go on our air that night. But it presented me with a terrible problem and underlined once again the danger of off-the-record meetings with news sources. My lunch with Kennedy had been off-the-record. Now, when we put the Mudd story on the air, it would appear to his intimates and perhaps to Kennedy himself that I had violated his confidence to develop the story of the weekend meeting.

I called the Kennedy office to explain the situation to him. His press aide Frank Mankiewicz said he was on the Senate floor and couldn't be reached. Air time was approaching so I asked if Frank could take a message to the Senator. Frank was obviously a little miffed that he hadn't been included in the luncheon, but he was professionally cooperative.

So I said: "Tell him that Roger has the story of the Hickory Hill meeting and that he got it entirely independent of our luncheon, and would the Senator please give me a quotation I could use about the meeting and his intentions to enter the race."

Mankiewicz called me back an hour or so later.

"I reached the Senator on the floor and he gave me a message to read to you. He said you could use it only if you use it in full. I don't know what it means, but here it is: 'Senator Kennedy said that he was contemplating running for the presidency just as Walter Cronkite is contemplating running for the Senate from New York.' "

Bingo!

A week or so later Frank Stanton commanded an immediate appearance in his office, an unprecedented order. He sternly faced me across his desk and demanded to know if I had urged Senator Kennedy to run against President Johnson. I repeated the luncheon conversation as accurately as I could and said I didn't think that my offhand remark could be interpreted as "urging." And I pointed out that the meeting had not been at my instigation.

"I appreciate your explanation," he said. "President Johnson is upset about it. I'll tell him what you said."

So much for off-the-record conversations. But at least this matter never came up again in any of my many future meetings with President Johnson.

Incidentally, just to keep the record clear, one of those who was closest to President Johnson does not agree that our CBS Tet broadcast helped persuade the President not to run for reelection. In an oral history he did for the LBJ Library in Austin, George Christian, responding to a suggestion that the broadcast was pivotal, simply replied: "Well, I don't buy that. It didn't quite happen that way."

I missed the dramatic last days of the American stay in Vietnam—the terrible helicopter flights from the roof of the Saigon Embassy. That is, I was not in Saigon. But I was determined not to miss the end of one of the biggest stories of my news career.

I had suffered a back injury as the end was approaching in Vietnam, and when the Communists were closing in on the capital I was flat on my back at home. We ordered up an ambulance and a particularly strong brace, and with my doctor in attendance, I did the story of the fall of Saigon and the end of the line for American intervention there literally strapped to my chair at the CBS anchor desk.

Of course, the story was far from over. Hanoi still held an uncounted number of our prisoners and finally agreed to release the first group. A few of us correspondents had gathered in Laos, each with his own scheme for getting into neighboring North Vietnam to cover the release. As those things usually do, it ended up with Hanoi arranging a plane and letting us all in. Hanoi had clearly taken a beating from our bombing. Hundreds, perhaps thousands, of small, individual shelters, about the size of a sewer pipe, pockmarked the sidewalks. But the people seemed remarkably cheerful. They waved as our bus passed by. I have no idea whether they were aware that we were Americans, but we clearly were "big noses" (as many Asians call those of us of European heritage) and I cannot imagine what other conclusion they might have drawn.

We were taken to the infamous "Hanoi Hilton," from which this first batch of prisoners would be freed. The prisoners were standing outside their prison cells, small two-man rooms that looked like horse stables. They were thin but not emaciated, and wore a nondescript collection of loose clothing. It was immediately apparent that they did not know what was going on. In a final bit of unnecessary cruelty, their Vietnamese guards had not told them they were about to be released. Suddenly they were confronted with a busload of newspeople.

We were permitted to talk to them but were warned that we were not to discuss details of their release. Actually, we had no details except that they were being flown out that afternoon. We asked the usual questions about treatment, food, conditions of their capture, length of their imprisonment and so on. Still unconvinced about their immediate fate, most of them were very cautious and, before answering the simplest question, would cast an apprehensive look at the guard in each cell.

I hit on a way to spread the word. Without addressing the prisoners, I would say to my camera-man: "Say, we've got to move along. These men are supposed to be catching their plane home this afternoon."

Grins split their faces. But there was a telltale indication of the severity of punishment they had received in their prison. Not one of them let out a sound to celebrate the great news.

Years later, in 1985, we took Senator John Mc-Cain of Arizona back to Vietnam to film his personal story. A Navy pilot, he had been shot down directly over Hanoi and had parachuted into the lake in the city's center. He suffered a broken arm that, thanks to the lack of attention, has never quite properly healed.

McCain spent most of six years in the Hanoi Hilton. Now it was an army photography center but physically it looked about as it had during the war. Our Vietnamese escorts took us into the same little office where they had tortured the American fliers for information, and McCain gritted his teeth as we were forced to sit there at the same green baize table for a propaganda talk on how well the prisoners had been treated.

As we toured the site some minutes later, McCain looked from outside into the room that had been his cell, but nothing our producer or photographer said could persuade him to step inside.

The Vietnamese had erected a small monument on the banks of the lake where McCain had been dragged ashore. We photographed him beside it as our translator read the comparatively straight-forward version of his capture. At that hour of the day the area was virtually deserted, but as we stood there a small family approached to watch us. The toothless grandfather hobbled on a cane. His daughter, I judged, held one small girl by the hand and another in her arms.

Our translator told them that this nice-looking gray-haired American was the pilot whose story was told by the plaque on the monument. They were beside themselves. You would have thought they had been introduced to a movie star. They told us they had been bombed out early in the war and that the son and husband was missing. This was reported matter-of-factly as they stared at McCain and patted him in what appeared to be genuine admiration. How do you figure?

Hanoi was a mess, as flat a postwar economy as I've ever seen, including that of Germany or Russia. There were few motorized vehicles, and even the ubiquitous bicycles didn't look as though they had many more miles in them. Almost as many were being pushed with flat tires as were being ridden.

We drove down to Haiphong, North Vietnam's principal port. It had been severely bombed, but goods were being ferried ashore from dozens of vessels in the harbor. The sixty-mile road to Hanoi, the country's main thoroughfare of commerce, normally heavy with truck traffic, had also been reduced in many places to a single lane. Repairing it were literally thousands of workers digging and tamping with primitive tools, many of which looked homemade.

The principal bridge along that route had been destroyed by our bombs. The Vietnamese had thrown a rickety one-lane military bridge across the river. To control the traffic, an officer in a watchtower signaled to an ancient fellow below who, on his instructions, pulled on a string attached to a tattered piece of aluminum that might well have come from an unlucky American bomber. The red paint on one side presumably signaled "stop." The other side wasn't painted. That seemed to mean "go."

It struck us as remarkable that under the regime of the victorious Communists, while the North Vietnamese capital of Hanoi struggled for survival, Saigon was close to its old, glorious, graceful colonial self—this despite its tedious new name of Ho Chi Minh City. The pretty girls with their long dark locks and colorful robes were just as enticing as ever as they pedaled through the crowded streets, and there seemed to be certain signs of prosperity in the shops and among the people.

The saddest sight in Saigon were the street children. Of mixed parentage, many with GI fathers, they were either forced into harsh orphanages or shunned on the streets. They lived as primitively and hopelessly as the homeless everywhere. Speaking a form of pidgin English, they begged outside the hotels and preyed on American sympathy by asking that visitors either help them get to America or,

when they got home, help them find their fathers.
Their conversations were furtive as they kept a
lookout for the police, who would wield their clubs
with abandon to beat them away.

They represented just a part of the dregs of war
that have been exploited by some unscrupulous
American fund-raisers. I have long been concerned
with the organizations that keep alive the hopes of
many Americans that their missing sons, husbands
and fathers might still be living and in the hands of
the Vietnamese.

While the Vietnamese government has not been as
candid as we would wish in accounting for the
missing, the "evidence" that there are any American
servicemen alive in Vietnam, excepting a few
deserters, is simply not credible. Yet it is understandable, if one had a close relative missing there, that
one would want to make a donation to anyone who
claimed to be working on their behalf. It would
almost seem unlucky and, indeed, sacrilegious, not
to donate.

I was chairman of a committee that spent considerable money and effort trying to learn the fate of
more than twenty newsmen missing in Southeast
Asia, many of them in Cambodia. We uncovered
many leads, none of which ever panned out, and
it beggared imagination why the former enemy
would want to be bothered with such reluctant
and conspicuous prisoners. Surely they would be
more trouble than they were worth, and the threat of
international scandal if they were eventually dis-

covered would give pause to the most belligerent government.

The Vietnam War left us another legacy from which we still seek escape. A generation of officers later, there still lurks in the Pentagon the belief that the media lost the war. We could have won, they insist, if the press had not shown those pictures of naked, napalmed Vietnamese girls fleeing our bombing, of prisoners being shot in the head, of burning hooches, of wounded GIs. Television brought the war into our living rooms at home and destroyed our will to fight, their theory goes.

It was put succinctly by a Marine major writing in *Military Review*, the official journal of the U.S. Army. The underlining and italics are his: "The power and impact of television was <u>the</u> deciding factor in turning American public opinion from one of supporting the U.S. defense of South Vietnam to one of opposing it.

"More than any other factor, it was the television camera that brought home the reality of war that shocked the nation and broke its will.

"What we need, contrary to the wide-open and unrestricted policies of Vietnam, is not freedom of press, but freedom <u>from</u> the press, more specifically, freedom from the television camera and its interference.

"In the next war, the television cameras must stay home!"

Wait a minute, a little voice says, isn't there something called the First Amendment that might be affected by this? No problem for the major: "Much is made of the 'public's right to know.' This is not a legal right, but is a concept invented by the news media to ensure their access, not the public's, to newsworthy events."

A quote from the brave new world order, as viewed through tinted military goggles.

Our TV cameras did record some—not all, but some—of the misery that the war brought to Vietnam. As I recall, we also reported some other disillusioning things about that war, things the major didn't see fit to recall in his article:

A corrupt, incompetent, unpopular government that we were committed to support.

An allied army that often preferred not to fight.

A resourceful, dedicated enemy, resolved to struggle on regardless of casualties.

And the thoroughly reported lies and mistakes of our own leaders, whose political survival depended on making a war look good even as it turned bad.

For more than four years Barry Zorthian was the official U.S. spokesman in Vietnam. In Zorthian's view, the idea that the news media lost the Vietnam War is a "canard." And in the Army's own *official* history of military and media relations in the war, we read: "What alienated the American public, in both the Korean and Vietnam wars, was not news coverage, but casualties. Public support for each war dropped inexorably by 15 percentage points whenever total U.S. casualties increased by a factor of ten."

A "canard" can have a long life if enough people,

including those in high office, believe it. The Pentagon was electrified and heartened in 1982 by the conduct of the Falkland Islands war by Britain's tough Prime Minister Margaret Thatcher. There British forces severely limited reporters' access, kept TV cameras away from the fighting, censored dispatches, provided poor communication facilities and, on occasion, misled newsmen. And Thatcher got away with it.

That may explain what happened a year later, when Thatcher's fawning admirer President Ronald Reagan decided that Fidel Castro's Cuban Communists had gone too far on the island of Grenada. The American tradition of giving journalists open access to the battlefield, a tradition at least a century and a half old, came to an abrupt end. When U.S. forces landed on Grenada, newsmen were excluded for the first two days of the operation, until it was virtually over. The official explanation for keeping them out: preserving secrecy and protecting them from harm.

The safety angle won't wash. Safety is not usually the first concern of the press, and at any rate, it is their, not the military's, responsibility. Newspeople have always been willing to go where danger is, and it is an insult to the many who have died on foreign battlefields to bring the American people the truth, to suggest that theirs was a foolhardy adventure.

The Grenada operation's commander, Admiral Joseph Metcalf, was a little more candid later. He admitted: "I did not want the press around where they would start second-guessing what I was doing."

Restricted access kept newsmen from correcting many false impressions that the government put out about Grenada, some of which still color the public's memory. We were told there were 1,100 Cubans on the island, all "well-trained professional soldiers," preparing to take it over. Later officials admitted there were under 800 Cubans there, only 100 of them combatants.

We were first told that the American students in Grenada were in danger of being taken hostage and that the airport had been closed by the Communists so they couldn't fly out. We later learned that the airport was open, and, for what it was worth, the Grenadians and the Cubans had assured the United States that the students were free to leave at any time.

We were first told that because our forces acted with surgical precision, there were no civilian casualties. It was later revealed that a U.S. Navy plane accidentally bombed a mental hospital, killing at least seventeen persons. And so on.

With this record of misinformation perpetrated by the Reagan administration, we are entitled to harbor other doubts. For instance, to back its claim of Cuba's military intentions, our military, when it finally let correspondents into Grenada, three days after the invasion, showed the newspeople a warehouse at the airport filled with boxes of Soviet-made armaments.

There is no evidence that I know of to suggest that this was anything other than what our military said it was. But for three days huge Air Force transport planes had shuttled to the island from Barbados and the United States in far greater numbers than resupply of our forces would seem to have demanded.

Is it possible—is it *just* possible—that our forces actually had not found evidence of heavy Cuban military activity and so had planted it for the benefit of the correspondents in order to justify the invasion?

Now, that is far-fetched—I hope. I really don't want to believe that our government could have been that Machiavellian. But historians in the future might well raise that possibility, and there is no independent information to disprove it, such as that which might have been supplied if our free press had been able to attest that the arms really were there when our troops first arrived. Thus is illustrated the kind of mischief, of the birth of rumor, that a lack of trust—and a lack of evidence collected by a free press—invites.

In the face of the strong press reaction to the Grenada blackout, Secretary of Defense Caspar Weinberger called three or four of us old World War II correspondents to a couple of dinners at his Pentagon office. Our complaints and our suggestions led him to appoint a commission under Major General Winant Sidle, a veteran of the Vietnam public relations war. Sidle's report addressed the most vital needs of the press in case of a future military engagement. It provided for a standby pool of reporters, with records of responsibility, that would accompany our troops in any future action.

The first test of the system was Panama—and the Pentagon failed miserably to live up to its own promises. A new Secretary of Defense, Richard Cheney, delayed the press call-up "with full knowledge," as he put it, until it was too late to cover the critical first hours of the invasion. Further, he vetoed the creation of a pool of American correspondents, a number of whom were already in Panama reporting on its government crisis.

When the Washington-based pool did arrive, it was kept from the action until the fighting was almost over, along with some five hundred other newspeople who got there on their own. Pentagon spokesman Pete Williams laid the problem to "incompetence"—an "incompetence," we might note, that very conveniently hid whatever it was the military and/or the administration might have wished to hide.

Once again, as in Grenada, the military hoisted itself with its own petard.

The absence of newsmen has clouded an important part of the Panama story—the wisdom of our troops in engaging the enemy in the densely populated neighborhood of El Chorrillo. The official U.S. version is that 100 to 200 civilians died there, but many Panamanians, with support from some U.S. civilians in a position to know, insist that thousands of casualties were buried in mass graves. Again, we don't know the truth and we may never learn it.

Rumor has fertile ground in which to grow and to poison our future relations with Panama, because there were no impartial observers there.

Our government simply must not shy away from sharing with the people the unpleasant results of war. All aspects of such foreign adventures must be exposed, and discussed, in a free society.

Take a look at Germany. After World War II most of the German people protested that they did not know what had gone on in the heinous Nazi concentration camps. It is just possible that many of them did not.

But this claim of ignorance does not absolve the Nazi-era generation of Germans from blame for Hitler's atrocities. And why not? Because they complacently permitted Hitler to do his dirty business in the dark. They raised few objections (most even applauded) when he closed their newspapers, sent into exile (or worse) dissident writers and editors and clamped down on free speech. When the German people accepted that, when they agreed by default that they had such faith in their government and their leaders that they trusted them to act in their name without their knowledge, they became responsible for what their government later did in their name.

It is drummed into us and we take pride in the fact that when we face military action, these are "our boys (and girls)," "our troops," "our forces." We felt those sweet pangs of patriotism again when they went flying off to the Persian Gulf. It was "our war," and indeed our elected representatives in Congress gave our elected President permission to wage it. Well, we certainly were entitled to know what they were doing in our name—not only entitled, it was our right as citizens of a democracy to know. And yet, we didn't. Because of onerous, unnecessary rules, concocted for the most part for political reasons, the American people were not permitted to see and hear the full story of what their military forces did in an action that will reverberate long into the nation's future.

After Panama the Defense Department's own official review of press relations—the so-called Hoffman Report—criticized Secretary Cheney and other officials for "an excessive concern for secrecy." That chastisement apparently fell on deaf ears. For the Pentagon came right back in the Persian Gulf with the toughest press restrictions ever—a set of regulations intended to prevent free access of correspondents to the troops, not only in combat but back in bivouac areas. They even banned any unauthorized conversations with military personnel met by newspeople in chance encounters, and they prevented any reference to religious services for U.S. troops for fear of offending the devout Moslem Saudis. Those two ridiculous restrictions were later lifted.

There were other hobbling restrictions, and the briefings were not always as informative as they should have been. Why wouldn't they tell us the location of the bridges that our planes were supposedly hitting? Didn't the Iraqis know? Or were we missing those bridges and the Air Force was reluctant to speak of them at all?

As a matter of fact, the Army's permission for the networks to televise live those briefings was perhaps the most diabolical move in their entire public relations offensive—whether it was deliberate or not. From their Vietnam experience they realized that some of the reporters' questions display an abysmal ignorance of military strategy and tactics, easy prey for a skilled briefer. They also knew that with the large number of reporters in Saudi Arabia who had never been in combat situations before, this percentage of the ignorant was bound to be overwhelming. Put these ambitious neophytes on the air and the press would be exposed as the ignoramuses that some of them indeed are. The ploy worked far more successfully than even the Pentagon could have dreamed.

But the most serious restriction, the one that denied us our history, was that which set a limit on the number and the movement of correspondents who could visit the troops in the field and accompany them into action. Pools were formed of selected correspondents, but they were put under such restrictive escort that they could not talk freely to the troops and, most important, were not permitted to join forward forces in General Norman Schwarzkopf's dash across the desert.

There will be official military film, but should we be asked to trust a record kept by those most interested in telling only one side of the story? We have again been denied an impartial, uncensored history of our troops in action, in all their glory, with all their mistakes. The Pentagon in its press relations in the Persian Gulf acted with an arrogance foreign to the democratic system. It trampled on the right to know of the people it serves.

Let's be clear. There must be military censorship in time of war. Strategy, tactics, size of forces, success of operations are all legitimate secrets that the military must not disclose. And the demands of television news executives for live coverage of the battlefield are ridiculous. Can we imagine giving the enemy headquarters the advantage of watching American television pictures from behind our lines?

But access to the battlefield and the troops must be permitted so that an impartial history can be recorded for eventual release. Censorship must be imposed only as long as military exigency demands it. Furthermore, as in World War II, there must be an appeal procedure by which the press can argue the case for release of its dispatches and pictures. This is neither too much for a free press to ask, nor too much for the army of a democracy to give.

CHAPTER 12

O F ALL humankind's achievements in the twentieth century—and all our gargantuan peccadilloes as well, for that matter—the one event that will
dominate the history books a half a millennium from
now will be our escape from our earthly environment and landing on the moon.

The fifteenth century wasn't exactly without noteworthy events: Gutenberg's invention of the printing
press, Leonardo da Vinci, Joan of Arc. But what is
the one date and event we remember? October 12,
1492, when, we were told in school, Christopher Co-
lumbus discovered the New World.

In books, or on computer disks, or whatever
people are using to record their past, the future residents of the universe will learn of the primitive but
courageous voyage of a tiny spaceship called the
Eagle to the surface of the moon and of men's first
steps on a celestial body other than their own. They
won't fully appreciate the trials and tribulations,
the humor and the drama that gripped the world as
humans first undertook flight in space and then extended their range to the moon itself.

I just happened to see the forerunner of all that—
rocket flights of destruction rather than discovery.

While the American inventor Robert Goddard was a pioneer in rocketry, the Germans, under the pressures of war, were the first to build long-range high-altitude rockets. They unleashed their so-called V-2s on London during the last days of World War II. The launch site was in Wassenaar, a suburb of The Hague in western Holland. From our airborne landing zone on the other side of the Netherlands we could watch the plumes of smoke turning into contrails that traced the rockets' pattern as they climbed to altitude before plunging, faster than the speed of sound, into London.

It would be a long time before we could watch American rockets rise into space on their fiery columns. At the war's conclusion the Russians and the Americans raced to capture the German rocket scientists based, for the most part, on the Baltic coast at Peenemünde. We got our share, including the Germans' brilliant leader Wernher von Braun.

The American test site was set up on a remote, snake-infested swamp called Cape Canaveral on the Florida coast east of Orlando. As the test site grew, so did the nearby villages of Cocoa, Cocoa Beach and Titusville, until they replicated every boomtown in every bad movie ever made—cheap hotels, bars, girlie joints, their wares proclaimed in gaudy neon.

This was the environment into which reporters lucky enough to be assigned the space beat plunged, but the background cacophony was drowned out by the melody of the great enterprise to which the area was dedicated. A spirit of high adventure permeated the place. While the eyes of the rest of our population might have been downcast as the nation dealt with a succession of problems—civil rights, assassinations, Vietnam—it seemed that everyone at the Cape was looking up, up into the skies that invited their conquering touch.

Those early days, however, were marked by battles with the military for at least a tiny modicum of information as to what was going on at the Cape. The space program was being run by the Air Force, whose first priority was to develop rockets as weapons. Naturally it considered that top-secret. We were not told when a launch was planned, nor were we given access to the Cape. The nearest public point from which our cameras could get at least a Telephoto look at a launch was a jetty at the Cape's southern edge on the outskirts of Cocoa Beach.

Most of the launches were at night, and the bright searchlights that illuminated the launchpad were our tip-off that a launch was imminent. We equipped ourselves with adequate food and drink and heavy coats against the night chill and fought for the most comfortable of the great granite rocks that formed the jetty.

The cameramen had it tough, as cameramen usually do. Once set up, they had to keep their eyes pretty close to their viewfinders should the rocket suddenly blast off with that spectacular burst of fire. And they had to follow it closely because, not infrequently, they went off course and exploded with apocalyptic intensity.

Our problem was that, because of the Air Force secrecy and the fact that the searchlights usually stayed on, scrub or no, we had no way of knowing when a launch had been canceled. To our rescue rode a genial innkeeper from one of the better motels, a onetime Nazi concentration camp inmate named Henry Landwirth. When the bar at Henry's motel began filling up with the engineers back from the Cape, he sent a messenger to the jetty with the word that the mission had been postponed. He may have saved some of us from pneumonia. He saved all of us from death by boredom.

As with all trades, we had our little tricks to play on the fledglings who joined us for the first time on the jetty. Among the launching gantries on the Cape stood an ancient lighthouse. At night the lights upon it could be mistaken by the unknowing for another launchpad. It was standard initiation procedure to direct a newcomer's attention not to the real launch-pad but to the lighthouse to await its launch.

When it was decided that the country should plan for manned flight as well as the perfection of ballistic missiles, it was also wisely conceded that such an expensive program was going to need public support and that this would be hard to get in an atmosphere of secrecy. Hence the National Aeronautics and Space Administration was born and the program, in most phases, opened to the press.

Now we were told when tests were planned and were provided with some primitive facilities among the snakes and mosquitoes some miles from the launchpads.

I had become particularly friendly with B. G. Mac-Nabb, Consolidated Vultee's tough *Atlas* project engineer. *Atlas* was the rocket that would carry the first Americans into orbit. MacNabb thought more of his *Atlas*es than he did of NASA's bureaucracy, and he suggested that if I'd get my crew onto the Cape before prelaunch secrecy closed the roads, he would see that we got a box seat for the launch atop the six-story *Atlas* hangar, almost overlooking the pad.

We had a little trouble getting to the roof with the camera equipment. The only access was by way of a vertical ladder that ran up the side of the building from the third floor and that terminated at the roof in a handhold that was very tricky to navigate. Finally, safely in place, we awaited nightfall and the launch.

Just before dusk there was some turmoil below, and there climbing up the ladder was the vanguard of a congressional delegation that NASA was escorting to the *Atlas* rooftop. Our floor director, David Fox, a little London Cockney with a highly developed, disrespectful and unorthodox sense of humor, stood at the top of the ladder awaiting the first congressman. As that gentleman puffed to the top rung and studied with terror how to hold the ladder and swing his legs over the parapet, Fox demanded to see his credentials.

The numerous passes required for various areas of the space complex hung on a chain around the congressman's neck. He gestured toward them with his chin. "I can't see them from here," Fox said, "and the rules say I can't touch them."

Faced with the daunting prospect of letting go of

the ladder with even a single hand to present his credentials, the congressman froze. Eventually he
recovered enough to tremulously begin his descent,
the column of congressmen arrayed under him following suit back to the third floor and a conference
with their NASA escort, who led the next ascent and
exposed Fox's gambit.

The visitors finally made it up the ladder and over
the parapet. We stayed, sharing an uneasy cama-
raderie with the congressman and suffering an
embittered silence from NASA. MacNabb shrugged
off his mild chastisement.

Many of us were skeptical and deeply concerned
about NASA's plan to launch the Navy astronaut
Alan Shepard on what would be our first space
flight. We knew, as did the world, that it was a comparatively feeble attempt to begin to catch up with
the Soviets, who it seemed had won the space race
by sending Yuri Gagarin in orbit around the earth.
The United States wasn't ready for orbital flight, but
NASA considered it essential that they at least put a
man into space, even if that space was only 116
miles up and the flight would be a short ballistic tra-
jectory of just 302 miles and lasting only fifteen
minutes.

Shepard would ride the tiny one-man *Mercury*
capsule on top of a *Redstone* rocket, a mere fire-
cracker compared with the rockets that would follow, and we had watched *Redstone*s blow up on the
pad or, tumbling wildly out of control, be destroyed
shortly after launch by range safety officers. We

feared that Shepard's flight was premature and that NASA was taking a terrible risk. I watched that launch with greater trepidation than any of the many space flights I would see in the years to come.

My best friend among that first class of *Mercury* astronauts was another Navy test pilot, Wally Schirra. He inherited a great wit (too frequently warped by terrible puns) from his father, a World War I Army pilot, and his mother. They had toured the air circuses popular between the wars, Pop flying an old Curtis biplane and Mom walking the wings. After Wally's first *Mercury* flight, he made all the proper public relations statements about it being just another test flight, that there had been nothing to fear thanks to NASA's constant and vigilant monitoring and the safety features built into the craft.

Over a beer one night, I promised never to tell if, off the record, he would level with me about what he had really been thinking in the last minutes before his rocket blasted off. And Wally said: "Well, I was lying there looking up at all the dials and buttons and toggle switches on the control panel and I thought to myself: 'Good God, just think, this thing was built by the lowest bidder.'"

As our program progressed to the huge *Saturn* moon rockets, with a hundred times the power of those first *Redstone*s, Schirra would save one of the first of the *Saturn*s and the lives of his crew in a heart-stopping moment on the launchpad. The engines had just received the signal to start, a point at which there is little chance of recall, when a malfunction alarm rang through the cockpit and the control center. Within a microsecond Schirra took every action for which he had been trained. The engine shut down and the rocket, just beginning to stir toward liftoff, settled safely back on the pad.

Some of the early drama of the space program was unnecessary. There is a critical point in space travel when the vehicle plunges back into the earth's atmosphere. The friction creates a temperature of up to 5,000 degrees Fahrenheit. The spaceship is protected by a nose shield that is not effective if the craft isn't lined up perfectly for the reentry. As the heat builds, all communications are blacked out. Until the spacecraft emerges from this blackout three to five minutes later, ground control has no indication as to whether the flight has survived the reentry.

The drama of John Glenn's flight reached its pitch as, for the first time in the American space experience, we awaited that fiery return into the atmosphere. As he came out of the blackout, Mission Control piped his voice to us in the press stands and the broadcast booths and a nation cheered.

Scott Carpenter was the astronaut on the next orbiting mission after Glenn's pioneer flight. As the seconds of blackout ticked away, we heard nothing from him. What we heard was a clearly strained voice from Mission Control saying that they were trying to reestablish communication with the astronaut. All the indicators were ominous, but with no confirmation of his fate and intent upon not unduly alarming the public, in our broadcast we danced delicately around the possibilities.

This uncertainty went on for fifty-three minutes before Mission Control announced that an unharmed astronaut had been picked up by the *Atlantic* rescue craft. The delay in the announcement of his recovery, it was explained, was because he had landed several miles away from the planned point.

Only later did we learn that, right on schedule as the capsule emerged from blackout, Mission Control had all the telemetry, the digital messages, from the spacecraft indicating that everything was normal aboard. All that had failed was the voice link. But the public relations man charged with keeping the press advised neglected to give us that little detail and left us, and the world's audience, uninformed for most of an hour. It was inexcusable incompetency.

Sometimes the idiocy seemed to be on the part of the public.

After Mercury, the next phase of our space flights were the two-man trips in the larger *Gemini* capsules. On the *Gemini 8* flight the controls locked and the ship began tumbling violently. Gyrating like that, there was no hope of it returning safely to earth—of lining up that heat shield for the fiery reentry into the atmosphere. It appeared that we were about to suffer our first space tragedy. We went on the air immediately, of course, interrupting the program in progress. It was a dramatic broadcast as we listened in on the apparently doomed astronauts and Mission Control desperately fighting to solve the problem.

Meanwhile, however, telephone switchboards at CBS stations around the country lit up as angry viewers called in to complain that the program they were watching had been interrupted. The program they had been watching? A futuristic adventure serial: "Lost in Space."

Astronauts Neil Armstrong and David Scott did beat the problem and *Gemini 8* made it safely home. The first tragedy of the American space program was to be *Apollo 1*, the spacecraft designed to go to the moon. When they were running some early tests on the pad, a single spark ignited the almost explosive atmosphere of pure oxygen in the spacecraft, and within a couple of horrible last minutes, three astronauts were incinerated.

Not until the *Challenger* disaster on January 28, 1986, would we lose another astronaut, and then seven would go, including the civilian teacher from New Hampshire, Christa McAuliffe. Instead of her, it might have been a journalist. In 1983 NASA finally inaugurated a civilian-in-space program and planned for a journalist to be the first one to go. However, President Reagan, in a campaign speech attempting to lure support from a teachers' union, promised that a teacher would have that honor.

While McAuliffe underwent her extensive training, NASA began the process of selecting the journalist who would be next. There were more than a thousand applicants when the screening began. They got the list down to forty of us and were preparing to make the next cut when the *Challenger* exploded and the civilian-in-space program was canceled.

I was frequently asked if I still wanted to go into space after *Challenger*. My answer was that I did but feared that my plumbing would go before NASA fixed theirs. Actually, I would still like to go. I know, however, that I would see the glass as half empty rather than half full. An orbital flight would be the most exciting thing I can imagine—except the flight I would like above all others to make: the trip to the moon. It would be great to see Planet Earth from that vast distance, to observe as our lucky astronauts have, this great blue orb, this one spot of color in the dark expanse of space—to revel in the mystery of our existence here.

That first landing on the moon was, indeed, the most extraordinary story of our time and almost as remarkable a feat for television as the space flight itself. To see Neil Armstrong, 240,000 miles out there, as he took that giant step for mankind onto the moon's surface, was a thrill beyond all the other thrills of that flight. All those thrills tumbled over each other so quickly that the goose pimples from one merged into the goose pimples from the next.

When Neil emerged from the *Eagle* I almost had regained my composure, which I'd lost completely when the *Eagle* had settled gently on the moon's surface. I had just as long as NASA had to prepare for that moment, and yet, when it came, I was speechless.

"Oh, boy! Whew! Boy!" These were my first words, profundity to be recorded for the ages. They were all I could utter.

I would cover all the remaining moon shots, but this was the apogee of my quarter of a century reporting the space adventure. It was a life of some exciting moments: experiencing, in a whirling centrifuge, the heavy pressures of a rocket takeoff and, in a transport plane in parabolic flight, the weird sensation of weightlessness. I operated the simulators on which the astronauts trained. I landed the mockup of the lunar lander and drove the little *Lunar Rover*, the moon-crawling vehicle, and I had a great time at the controls of the shuttle.

The shuttle simulator was like the real thing except, of course, it was earthbound, in this case in the Houston space center. John Young was my pilot. We had just made one of our pretend landings and were still rolling down the runway when the phone patch from Mission Control said: "We've got an indication of a fire in here!"

John, with some exasperation, said to me that this was a puzzling thing: Why would they want to practice that sort of emergency when we were just doing an exhibition ride? And he noted that he hadn't even brought along the manuals that would tell him what action he should take. Control came in, insistently: "John, we've got an indication of a fire in here."

"I know, I know," John answered. "I'm working on the problem."

"Oh, not in the simulation. In the building here. You and Cronkite get the hell out of there."

One of the more exciting moments of early space coverage came with the first liftoff of the giant new *Saturn* rocket, the power that would send the *Apollo* spacecraft to the moon. We had long since been promoted from the back of the station wagon from which we covered the Shepard flight. Now the networks broadcast from permanent two-story structures at the press center near Mission Control.

My desk was behind a large window, probably 100 square feet, that stretched across the front of our studio. NASA had supplied the specifications of the blast it would have to withstand. But when *Saturn* erupted on its stand, three miles from us, the shock waves hit us like a hurricane. The building shook, acoustical tiles in our ceiling bounced out of their frames, soft drink bottles walked off the desk, and that window vibrated and bulged and threatened to explode like an umbrella in a gale.

I tried to dampen the vibration by pressing my hands against that window with all the force I could muster. As the shock waves receded, I was accepting congratulations for saving the day and perhaps the lives of our studio personnel when the glass company representatives came dashing in. Didn't anyone tell us, they demanded, that we were never, never to touch the glass, that it was meant to vibrate and that interfering with that vibration dangerously weakened it?

I particularly admired the work of the astronauts. That first class of the seven *Mercury* astronauts set a tough example to follow. They worked hard. Test pilots all, they had learned well their difficult,

demanding and dangerous craft of flying airplanes
that no one had ever flown before. Now, besides
mastering all the complicated technology of these
new space machines, they were put through a gru-
eling routine of physical fitness, of extended field
trips learning survival techniques in all terrains from
deserts to mountains, of intense classroom study of
orbital physics, astronomy and geology, and the
geography of both the earth and the moon.

Most of them played as hard as they worked, but
this in no way diminished their dedication to the job
for which they had been selected. Tom Wolfe captured their personalities in his excellent book *The
Right Stuff*, but the movie version of the book was an
abomination that I felt libeled them and everyone
around them.

They enjoyed life and got the most out of it with
just a touch of the pilots' wartime creed of "live it up
today, for tomorrow we die." But they were by
no means residents of the monkey house that the
movie made the space program out to be. Nor, as the
movie suggested, was President Lyndon Johnson's
support of the program a mere effort to bask in
others' glory. Nor, certainly, were the German rocket
scientists all vaudeville-inspired dialect comedians.
Nor were the reporters the insensitive louts the
movie depicted.

As a matter of fact, covering the space program
presented a challenge to us all. There was a great
deal we had to learn about the mechanics of space
flight and the idiosyncrasies of the physics of mov-

ing bodies in the weightlessness and atmosphere-free environment of space. One of the little oddities that had to be understood in order to explain space-craft maneuvers was that the spacecraft, in relation to the earth, slowed down by speeding up, and vice versa. By accelerating, the craft moved higher, away from earth, and thus took longer to orbit the earth—in effect, slowing down. But by actually slowing down, it fell closer to earth, thus speeding around it faster.

I have often wondered if my late University of Texas physics professor, wherever he resides in his immortal reward, was aware of my CBS space broadcasts. It was that same Professor Boner who failed me in first-year physics because, among other things, I couldn't understand why a pulley works. If he heard me explaining orbital mechanics to an audience of trusting millions, I'm afraid the good professor would spin in his grave.

Covering the space program gave me an opportunity to meet some interesting people. The shy hero of the first solo airplane flight across the Atlantic, back in 1927, Charles Lindbergh, came with his wife to visit the Cape for the first time to see the first moon launch. He wanted no publicity, no receptions, no press conferences. NASA persuaded him, how-ever, to attend a brief cocktail party for a few of its top officials. Having had to do my broadcast first, I arrived a little late and was immediately taken to meet Colonel Lindbergh, interrupting his conver-sation with a group of a half dozen men.

I told him that I had just been diving on an interesting under-water habitat experiment with his son, Jon. That grabbed his attention. He wanted to know all about it. As I finished, he asked if I would mind telling the story to Anne, Mrs. Lindbergh, and he led me, proud as punch, over toward another group in which she was the center of attention. Just before we reached them, Lindbergh slowed a bit and asked: "Tell me, what is your name again?"

Some of the acquaintances I found most interesting were in the space program itself. One of the *Atlas* chief engineers was the visionary Krafft Ehricke. Krafft had been at Peenemünde with Wernher von Braun. He was a grandfatherly character, almost in a Santa Claus mold with pink cheeks, a hearty laugh and a German accent that had a certain charm. We had known each other for some time and I enjoyed his company immensely. As with all Germans of his generation, I wanted to know what he thought of Hitler. Or I thought I wanted to know. I was somewhat afraid of asking, lest he turn out to be a confirmed Nazi. On the other hand, that seemed highly unlikely.

One day we were at the bar near the Convair plant in San Diego and I steeled myself to ask the question.

"Ach, I hated Hitler," he said, turning almost purple. And he raved about how he couldn't stand Hitler, repeating over and over that he hated him. The denial was far too fervid. It was phony, I felt. I was shocked, terribly disappointed.

"Don't you understand, Walter?" Krafft continued. "If he had been just a little bit smarter, he would have given our rocket program a lot more help. If he had really supported us, we would have been so far ahead that even I might have gone to the moon. I hated him."

So Krafft in this respect was totally apolitical, his vision narrowed as with so many dreamers by a single commitment that blocked out all other considerations.

I suffered some criticism for my coverage of the space program. I was accused of having failed to observe the first journalistic precept of impartiality, of having unabashedly been a NASA booster. I believe my critics were wrong. I know that I did not try to suppress my excitement about the technical achievements and the grand adventure of space flight, but I also disagreed sharply with some aspects of the space program. NASA didn't bestow any medals upon me.

Our government's greatest mistake, to my mind, came at the beginning of the program. We abandoned the early development of a very high-altitude aircraft, the *X-15* rocket plane, that held the promise of flights into space and a return to landing fields on earth long before we could perfect the expendable rockets on which both we and the Soviets based our programs—rockets that were really giant firecrackers depending for power on controlled explosions and that were good for just a single flight.

The conquest of space was our great achievement, but there were other scientific/technological stories that were grist for television's mill. Some, however, were difficult to cover because of a lack of unanimity among scientists as to their meaning or their importance.

A noteworthy case of scientific uncertainty was the reaction to the leak at the Three Mile Island nuclear plant in Pennsylvania, on March 28, 1979. The possibility of catastrophe, in one form or another, seemed great—the possibility of a meltdown or a terrible explosion spreading radioactive waste over vast areas of the eastern United States and downwind no telling how far; the possibility of leakage of nuclear waste into the Susquehanna River, poisoning forevermore the Chesapeake Bay and all the rich lands along its shore.

These were only two of a dozen scenarios, some far less frightening, put forward by various equally authoritative and distinguished scientists. Our viewers wanted instant answers, of course—warnings or assurances—but, clearly lacking any knowledge of our own, we could only report the different conclusions of the scientists. Later we were accused of broadcasting confusing reports that fed public alarm. We did, but the confusion wasn't ours, it was that of our learned sources.

Perhaps even more important than space exploration for our immediate future is our examination of the earth's oceans. They cover 71 percent of the earth and we still know so little about them and what lies at their bottom. It is generally believed that there are vast mineral riches to be mined there when we learn to extract them without environmental danger and can make the political decision as to whom they belong. The development of deep-diving miniature submarines and lightweight scuba gear has begun to open up for man these great riches. That other world below the surface is one of pure magic.

In 1982 I rode the Woods Hole Oceanographic Institution's three-man *Alvin* 8,500 feet down to the thermal rifts southeast of Mexico's Cabo San Lucas. This was the second trip following the discovery of these volcanic vents and the scientifically shattering fact that there were animals down there—great worms, spiny crabs and huge clams—that lived by chemosynthesis, their energy supplied by chemicals rather than a food chain sustained by the sun. The discovery may lead to entirely new theories on the origin of life on earth as well as point to the possibility of life in the deep oceans of which we have never dreamed.

Most exploration involves some danger and there was some of that on the *Alvin* dive. Besides the fact that at the time there was not another *Alvin* to dive so deep should mechanical failure trap the crew, the thermal vents emitted gases hot enough to melt the plastic windows of the submarine. Some of the vents were invisible, and the danger of drifting over one of them was ever-present.

At least the *Alvin* had some power of its own to try to avoid trouble and to speed its return to the surface—although from 8,500 feet the trip still took more than three hours. My maiden dive, some years earlier, was on the first of the American-built miniature subs: the Westinghouse *Deep Star*. It was a diving saucer along the lines of Jacques Cousteau's first effort. It had a very small electric motor to drive it slowly across the bottom, but no power for descending or ascending. A small series of weights like those on a commercial scale pulled it down as it sank slowly in wide graceful curves, falling like a leaf.

To ascend, the saucer depended on a device far too simple for my taste. The operator pulled a lever that released the weights. If that worked, the saucer again rose of its own buoyancy, very slowly and again in sweeping curves. If the lever didn't work, there was no way to release those weights and the submarine and its crew would be doomed to remain forever on the ocean's bottom.

That trip 4,800 feet deep off Point Loma, California, offered two surprises. There was the almost microscopic bioluminescent plankton that arranged itself into the most intricate geometrical shapes, like the most artistic and complex chandeliers, suspended in the dark of the depths just beyond our portholes. And on the bottom of what I had assumed up to then were our pristine ocean depths we found an occasional paint can or a piece of crockery bearing the insignia of the U.S. Navy, jettisoned by warships en route to the big base at San Diego.

Incidentally, the Scripps Institution of Oceanography, studying the bioluminescence of the oceans, solved a World War II mystery. Occasionally when our forces searched captured Japanese patrols they found vials of a greenish powder they believed was a mild narcotic. The Scripps lab discovered that it had a different use. It was dried and powdered bioluminescent plants. The Japanese soldiers on night patrol dusted the powder into their hands and spit on it. By briskly rubbing their hands together, they could produce enough light to read a map.

On a grant from the U.S. Navy, Scripps was studying animals and sea plants that provide their own light. It had discovered that satellite photos of warm waters, like the Indian Ocean, clearly showed the track of vessels which were moving under cover of night. The tracks were the disturbed bioluminescent creatures that are heavy in those waters. Since the time of Aristotle, fireflies and bright watery creatures have intrigued man, but not until they became a factor in national defense did anyone consider spending much money to investigate them.

The same is true of the northern lights, the aurora borealis. These, too, have spawned centuries of speculation, but it took a military consideration to properly finance the study of them. I flew with a specially equipped transport plane that the U.S. Air Force sent almost nightly up around the North Pole. If lucky, the plane flew directly under the incredibly beautiful cascade of multicolored ions apparently tumbling like a Niagara from somewhere above.

The study became a matter of urgency when fears arose that these severe electrical disturbances could alter the course of intercontinental missiles crossing the northern reaches. The fears extended to the pos-

sibility that should the Russians be better at pre-
dicting when these heavenly tempests would occur,
they could launch their missiles while our detection
gear was temporarily incapacitated.

It is a shame that we are not curious enough about
the world around us to finance such research except
when the results have a military application. Our
willingness to be ignorant seems to know no bounds.
Take this matter of pollution. Can you explain to me
our total lack of reaction to those little boxes on the
front pages of most of our newspapers that report,
day after day, that the air quality in our town is
unhealthful? Wouldn't you think that, upon reading
that we are breathing air that is dangerous to our
health, we would all march on City Hall and demand
immediate remedy? But we do nothing—we just sit
there and fill our lungs with bad air.

Wouldn't you think that seeing the evidence on
the ground or watching the occasional television
report that our trees are dying from poisoned air, that
our streams, rivers and lakes are so denuded of
oxygen and poisoned by industrial fallout that fish
can't live there—wouldn't you think that we would
demand that those responsible stop it or that our
government shut them down?

One of the accomplishments of which I am
proudest during my almost twenty years as managing editor and anchor of the "CBS Evening News"
was a series that we ran occasionally over several
years called "Can the World Be Saved?" We conceived it shortly after reading Rachel Carson's semi-

nal book, *Silent Spring*. While she dealt mostly with the murderous effects of the then popular insecticide DDT, it awakened us to all the forms of pollution threatening our atmosphere and our very lives.

Each part of our series, produced by Ron Bonn, exposed a different threat. We launched the programs just in time to be in the vanguard of the not-yet-named Decade of the Environment. We were grateful for the impact we had and the awards we received—with as much modesty as we could muster.

One of our interviews was perhaps the most provocative of my career. René Dubos was an internationally respected microbiologist at the Rockefeller Institute and one of the first to become seriously concerned about the poisons that were being introduced into our foodstuffs as pesticides, fertilizers and preservatives.

He explained to me that such poisons first affect, but very slowly, the muscles. And, he noted, the brain is a muscle. What alarmed him was that these poisons might be eroding our ability to think our way out of our problems. The day could come, he forecast, when we would pass the point of no return—our brains would be so crippled that we couldn't solve our problems but we would be unable to recognize our disability. Yes, he repeated, the day could come, and he looked out his window and, with that professorial sotto voce, added: "Or maybe we already have passed that point."

When we look at the problems that threaten our

existence on earth—overpopulation, pollution, nuclear proliferation, to name just three of the more ominous—and we look at our puny, impractical, overpoliticized efforts to solve them, we must conclude that Dr. Dubos' doomsday scenario may not be far off the mark.

Many of my more adventurous excursions were for a series called "Walter Cronkite's Universe," produced by Jon Ward. Some of the deep dives were part of that series, as were trips into the Amazon, to the Army's City Under the Ice on the Greenland ice cap, up the Gambia River to visit a chimpanzee rescue team, and to a climbers' base camp on the slopes of Alaska's Mount McKinley.

That latter excursion was in a beat-up old plane with snow skids owned and piloted by Lowell Thomas, Jr., the son of the famous adventurer, writer, lecturer and broadcaster. He ran the base camp and regularly flew climbers and supplies to it. He dodged the clouds and found our way around and through the mountain peaks, sometimes through passes that appeared narrower than the span of the plane's wings. As we approached an impossibly narrow draw, Lowell casually mentioned that this one was called "One Chance Pass."

I asked him why, since he was not exactly impoverished, he didn't buy a new plane to replace this one, which was literally, even as the Alaskan bush pilot stories had it, patched together with gaffer's tape and tied together with baling wire. He replied that he would like a new plane, but they didn't build one slow enough for him to find his way through the mountains. That was good enough for me.

His landings were wonderful. Uphill, right up the mountainside. When he got to the point where the plane was about to slide back down the hill, eager hands rushed out from the camp and held it in place. The takeoff was played in reverse. The helpers turned him around and held him until, with a quick wave of his hand, he ordered their release. The plane slid downhill, gaining near-takeoff momentum by its own weight. Finally a little boost from the engine and we were up and away.

My other airborne trip to a formidable mountain was in Pakistan, and the mountain was part of the High Himalayas. Pakistan and China had accomplished what appeared to be the impossible. They had pushed a road across the Karakoram Pass, at 18,290 feet the world's highest road, but it had not yet been used. It would not be for years, until the scores of landslides that blocked it finally subsided and were stabilized.

But when, during an interview, I expressed to President Zia ul Haq my desire to be the first Westerner to go there, he said it could be arranged. He laid on a series of flights by the Pakistani Air Force—a World War II vintage DC-3 to a base at the foothills, another DC-3 to a base perhaps halfway to the pass and then a little helicopter to the pass itself. The helicopter was built for two, but the pilot agreed to crowd my cameraman, Tom Aspell, and producer, Harry Radliffe, into the small space behind our seats. The trip to the top was spectacular. In those rugged mountains the farmers miraculously have terraced the steep hillsides and subsist on their crops, sheep and goats. There are no roads to most areas and they live in isolation.

On our way up, our English-educated pilot spoke highly of his aircraft. The French-built Alouette, he explained, was the only helicopter capable of reaching the heights of the pass, and the pass was at the extreme limit of its capability. My interest in this fact was considerably accentuated when he added— rather matter-of-factly, it seemed to me—that he hoped we didn't have any trouble there. The Pakistan Air Force had only two Alouettes, the other was down for repairs, and there wasn't any other way they could rescue us if ours somehow failed.

With that we were settling down on the tiny plateau where, somewhere under the snow, presumably was the road. As we got out, our pilot warned us not to move quickly, that we might pass out from the sparsity of oxygen at that great altitude, almost three and a half miles up. To spare us further exertion, my cameraman set up near the plane. As I prepared to record my impressions of this incredible mountainscape—the Soviet Union visible right over there, China over there, India and Pakistan back there—I shouted to the pilot to please shut down the engine.

His head shook violently. Oh, no, he replied—at this altitude he could not restart the engine. He must keep it running. This was not exactly heartening, but, in for a penny, in for a pound, the cameraman and I worked our way a little farther from the aircraft, over to the edge of the peak.

Just as we got there, the engine coughed. It coughed again. We looked in horror as the rotor blades barely turned in fits and starts and our pilot jabbed and pulled at various knobs on his dashboard.

We didn't need any oxygen to beat a hasty retreat, shouting, as we ran, for the pilot to prepare for takeoff. The fact that I am writing this is proof that we made it, and perhaps explains why we didn't bring back any footage of significance. Furthermore, I found out somewhat later that I had not been the first Westerner there. Seymour Topping of *The New York Times*, an old subcontinent hand, had been there shortly before but had not yet written about it. Successful reporting is often a matter of timing.

The trip into the Amazon with a team from World Wildlife was a cinch by comparison. Scarcely any drama except for the surprising discovery that it is not the animals that threaten survival in the jungle but the falling trees. In the thin soil of the Amazon just beyond Manaus, the trees grow tall, muscling their neighbors to reach the sun, but there is little root structure to support them. So, night and day in a constant bombardment, they come crashing down. Their fall, fortunately, is partly broken by the thick growth, but slinging one's hammock under an already fallen tree is recommended procedure, a sort of natural bomb shelter.

I also was assured that one can swim among flesh-eating piranhas at midday, when they aren't hungry. I dared to test the proposition, but only long enough to say I had done it.

The more interesting fish in the Amazon's side waters is the tambaqui. At spring floodtide it lurks under the Brazil-nut trees whose branches hang over the swollen streams. The Brazil nut has a husk that, when ripe and still on the tree, bursts open, propelling the nut on a wide arc toward the water. The fish leap for the nuts, catch them before they hit the water, and, with one bite of their powerful jaws and their teeth—all molars—crush them.

Considering my hopeless attempts to open Brazil nuts, I have great admiration for the tambaqui. And incidentally, the fish, prestuffed with Brazil nuts, are delicious.

CHAPTER 13

O NE OF THE biggest stories of our century was the multifront engagement to gain civil rights for all Americans. From the moment on December 1, 1955, that Rosa Parks dared to sit down in the "whites only" front of a Montgomery, Alabama, bus, it was an unfolding story of a struggle for the soul of a country. The question that seemed so simple was awesome in its complexity: Could the people of the United States begin to live up to their credo that "all men are created equal" and establish that this was indeed "one nation indivisible"?

There in Montgomery black women supporters of Mrs. Parks vowed to boycott the Montgomery buses until segregated seating was abolished. And to lead their cause, they chose a quiet, dignified, relatively unknown Baptist minister from a local church. His name was Martin Luther King, Jr.

While the struggle they began has not been fully resolved even as we enter a new century, most of the Twentieth's highlights fell on my watch as managing editor of the "Evening News." I felt heavily my responsibility to be sure that our stories, while reflecting the deep emotions of the conflict, were not themselves emotional, that they were as calm, as factual, as impartial as good journalists can make them.

This may have been the most severe test of my own journalistic integrity since World War II. We were all on the same side then, and most of us newsmen abandoned any thought of impartiality as we reported on the heroism of our boys and the bestiality of the hated Nazis. This civil rights struggle that was tearing at our nation was of a vastly different order, an order of much greater magnitude in terms of the demands for neutrality in our reporting.

My natural sympathy was with the blacks. I am not sure what my father's attitude toward them was before that incident on the dentist's front porch in Houston, but I had frequent reminders of what it was *after* that young delivery boy was smashed in the face. From the time I was ten until I went away to college, I heard him rail almost nightly against some racial injustice he had witnessed that day. His testimony was a litany of incidents to which my mother added each evening from her catalog of experiences with "the help." Dad's indignation in the evening clashed with my schoolboy life in the daytime. If anyone in Houston was daring to advocate integration of the races, their words certainly weren't echoing in the halls of San Jacinto High School or any other of the environs I inhabited. There was no suggestion, either inside or outside the halls of academe, that there was anything wrong with the segregation we scrupulously observed in study and play, or that anything needed to be done about it. My brief career sharing drugstore delivery duties with blacks threatened my standing in my social set— such standing as I was permitted as a "Yankee." A father of one young lady of whom I was enamored opened up the subject as we shared a root beer one evening on their family porch.

"Anne tells me you all are delivering for the drugstore." This seemed to be a question, so I gave an affirmative answer.

"Nigger boys deliver for them, don't they?" I affirmed this as well.

"I don't know your folks, young man," opined this distinguished Houston lawyer, "but, I swear, I don't know how in the Lord they could let you do such a thing."

Having thus placed the blame for this social breach upon my parents, he spared the child and permitted me to continue seeing his daughter despite the possibility that I might spread the plague he feared, a plague he would call "nigger-loving."

He would have been right to have suspected that I carried the germ of racial "tolerance." (It would be several more years before I learned that "tolerance" is a stage of development unacceptably short of total commitment to undiluted equal rights for all.) My father had planted the seeds that would grow to full awareness of the fact that one class of Americans—a class to which we, by birth, belonged—were intent upon keeping in servitude another class—a class condemned by birth.

While this conviction was growing within me, I

had no trouble bridging the gap between my views and the attitude held by my friends. While early on I found their opinions of the blacks distasteful, I didn't have the courage to challenge this over- whelming majority, to become the odd man out of their circle. As I got older, my embarrassment grew over my participation in spreading the ethnic jokes that were—and are—the staple of humor around the world.

In those high school years I accepted the fact that my friends were inheritors of a culture built on slavery as an economic reality—a proposition over which their grandfathers had fought a bloody war barely sixty-five years before. We were taught in school that the conflict was not a "Civil War" but "the War Between the States." My pals mastered the rebel yell and displayed the Confederate flag with a touch of defiance. Their views have moderated with the passage of another sixty-five years, but it was only a few years ago that, at a reunion of my Texas University fraternity, I heard a prominent doctor, then teaching at a major medical school, argue that the blacks' brains were smaller and that they did not have the intellectual capacity of the whites.

I would not know socially a single black until well after World War II. Except for servants or employees barely beyond the status of servants, there were no blacks in high school, none at the Uni- versity of Texas, none in the Texas legislature or the Texas government, none in those parts of the mili- tary with which I was attached, none among the

Americans at the Nuremberg war crimes trial, none in the American Embassy in Moscow.

While my assignments did not bring me into contact with them, thousands upon thousands of blacks were of course drafted for service in World War II, but with few exceptions, they were assigned to serve in support positions. Many died trying valiantly to fulfill their mission of driving supply trucks to the front lines.

We all know from our history lessons that the Founding Fathers, while proclaiming the right of equality for all, actually didn't intend to include blacks, Indians or women. However, by the middle of the twentieth century the irony of segregating men called to die for their country so offended President Harry Truman that he integrated the military. The high brass and a large part of the citizenry bitterly opposed the move. They said the military couldn't function if black and white men were ordered to share the same living facilities. They have been proved wrong.

Truman's daring edict strengthened the 1950s move toward civil rights. It gave blacks reason to believe that their cause was not a hopeless one. By the mid-1950s—after the Supreme Court's unanimous and historic decision outlawing segregation in public schools—Rosa Parks was encouraged to act. And I and a few hundred other reporters and editors were forced to put our journalistic ethics to the test against our own emotions.

Our executive producers carrying the load and

calling the shots through that difficult period were the steadiest hands television has known: Bud Benjamin, Russ Bensley, Ernie Leiser, Les Midgley, Paul Greenberg and Sandy Socolow, and out on the street, on the sometimes dangerous front lines, were splendid correspondents like Betsy Aaron, Nelson Benton, Murray Fromson, John Hart, Charles Kuralt, Robert Schakne, Howard K. Smith, Dan Rather and Larry Pomeroy.

And there were cameramen like the inestimable Laurens Pierce, who was a few feet from Alabama's George Wallace when he was shot in Laurel, Maryland. The would-be assassin fired almost over Pierce's shoulder even as his camera was focused on the Governor. The film showed scarcely a flutter as Laurens followed the stricken Governor to the ground and then swung around to see the crowd capturing the assassin.

I regret that the nature of the story and the technological restrictions of the time—before it was easy, and therefore routine, for the anchor to travel—kept me off the streets to experience firsthand the intensity of those now historic moments of crisis: the sit-ins in Atlanta, the march at Selma, the rally at the Lincoln Memorial.

I did fly to Los Angeles as the first riot wracked the small residential district known as Watts. It was practically over by the time I got there and was introduced to a "slum" of private houses, green lawns and palm trees. This required some readjustment of my thinking about the underlying problems of racial segregation and injustice. As aware as my southern boyhood had made me of the insults heaped at every turn upon the blacks, I thought that the principal cause of their unhappiness was economic, that it was bred in the rat-infested big-city ghettos in which segregation forced them to live. I missed at first what I now believe to be true—that important as the economic considerations are, the fundamental motivation which brings most blacks to the barricades is the desire to live in dignity. That aspiration takes many forms, but it is clearly at the foundation of all fights for social justice.

Trying to tell the story of that quest in the sixties' battles put our reporters in considerable jeopardy. Many whites, in the North as well as the South, saw them as part of the problem, agents provocateurs stirring up the blacks, helping them stage demonstrations for our cameras and clearly favoring them in their reporting.

With few exceptions, wherever our reporter-camera teams appeared they were surrounded by a crowd of angry whites who assaulted them with threats. And there were many occasions when the whites carried out their threats of violence. Cameramen were not infrequently pelted with stones, and their cameras were pushed into their faces. Sometimes the police joined in the harrassment, suggesting in language as violent as their looks that our newspeople had better get out before those threats were carried out. Seldom did the police, particularly in the South, offer the crews the protection they deserved.

Our correspondent Robert Schakne could have

suffered serious injury from the bottle that hit him in the head in Birmingham. A National Guardsman aimed his rifle butt at the back of Dan Rather's head. Fortunately, he missed his head, but the blow to his shoulder sent Dan to the ground. NBC's Richard Valeriani was hit in the back of the head by an ax handle that left a nasty gash. Our Betsy Aaron was knocked down by Georgia Ku Klux Klansmen, causing a painful knee injury.

One of the more serious threats to our coverage came not in the streets but in the white-collar confines of our affiliate stations in the South. Acting either on their own sentiments or under pressure from local advertisers, and most probably both, the stations complained of our coverage to the CBS management. They maintained that our reports were biased in favor of the blacks and that they distorted the position of the whites by suggesting that all white Southerners were as violence-prone as those we pictured on television. Some of those station owners even threatened to withdraw their affiliation from CBS, an action that, if widely followed, could have shut down the network. Many of the stations, embarrassed to make an issue of civil rights, simply stepped up their equally vehement protest over our Vietnam coverage.

One of our affiliates in Mississippi took the most serious measure against our coverage. It denied us the use of its facilities to transmit our reports back to New York and onto the network. It cost us time and money to charter flights to get our film down to New Orleans or Miami, where we could relay it—time and money we could have spent to improve and expand our coverage. The station failed in its duty to serve the people's right to a free press. CBS network executives expressed their concern to CBS News management, but I was not aware, during my time, of the slightest interference with our coverage.

The critics of our coverage were not limited to the segregationists of the South. Many of those of the other persuasion across the nation, including the South, felt that television did not go far enough in exposing the inequities between the races in this country.

Martin Luther King, Jr., had elevated the civil rights struggle from a mostly sectional concern to a national cause with his 1963 rally and oratory at the Lincoln Memorial in Washington. Two hundred thousand blacks and whites were there that day and millions more heard on television his powerful "I have a dream" speech:

"I have a dream that my four little children will one day live in a nation where they will not be judged by the color of their skin but by the content of their character. I have a dream today. . . . I have a dream that this nation will rise up and live out the true meaning of its creed, 'We hold these truths to be self-evident; that all men are created equal' . . . I have a dream."

Whether they shared his dream or not, he galvanized a nation—black and white, integrationist and segregationist—and moved the struggle for equality to a new plateau.

We did our evening broadcast from Washington

on April 4, 1968, the night that King was slain. The bulletin came from Memphis when we were on the air, and we pumped out as many details as we had before time ran out. That night I was awakened by the sirens and the red glow in my hotel room as, a few blocks away, Washington's downtown black district was set ablaze. That conflagration turned out to be a fire bell in the night, herald of the many urban riots that would char our national conscience.

In those critical years the civil rights movement found an unexpected ally in Lyndon Johnson. As President of the United States he rose above the sectionalism he had served as a Senator from Texas and, with his legislative skills, pushed through the Civil Rights Act of 1964. Of all his achievements, he seemed proudest of that one, and he should have been.

We have made huge strides in thirty years. Compared to the blatant segregation in the South and the latent segregation in the North in those days, today we mingle easily in public places, in our offices and schools, and deep friendships are possible. But, of course, we have a long way to go.

Perhaps the most severe of all our problems is the great economic divide that is condemning too many of our minority populations to the hopelessness of the ghetto and, sin of all sins, denying to their progeny the education that could give their generation some hope. One of the great inconsistencies of the welfare "reformers" of recent years has been their insistence that welfare mothers go to work while simultaneously opposing the child care facilities that would make that possible. But their greater failing may be the inadequate funding for programs such as Head Start that give the children of the inner-city slums a chance at education.

While turning our backs on our own deep racial problems, we spent a number of decades in mid-century condemning the segregationist policies of South Africa. Those policies came to an abrupt end in 1991.

Not until a masterful white leader, F. W. de Klerk, appeared on the scene, freed the black leader Nelson Mandela and took the courageous steps toward ending apartheid did there seem to be any really serious effort among South Africa's white ruling classes to end the unconscionable servitude in which they held the blacks.

The whites had built what was, for them, an idyllic society on the backs of the blacks. With a huge force of cheap labor, they lived well in a country of great natural beauty, rich in natural resources and of strategic importance geographically.

Life in South Africa before the reforms began in the last decade of this century was almost a mirror image of life in our states of the old South before the civil rights legislation of the 1950s and 1960s. American blacks lived mostly in communities entirely segregated from the whites. If welcome at all in public facilities, they were separated from whites. Although our Constitution guaranteed them the vote, they were effectively denied it by the southern stratagem of the poll tax—a payment for the right to vote that few blacks could afford. They were also terrorized into staying away from the polls by white racists.

South Africa didn't even pretend that blacks had the right to vote, and this became the rallying point and the principal source of debate for the reforms to come. Dinner parties and luncheon meetings there in the middle of the century were not unlike those in the American South at about the same time. Etiquette practically demanded that race relations was a subject to be avoided, even as politics and religion were. Except, of course, when the group was known to be clearly on, or approximately on, the same side of the issue. Thus, liberals could indulge in healthy, although sometimes heated, discussion of tactics for ending apartheid even as conservatives argued over the pace of what many of them saw as a tragically inevitable move toward some sort of limited democracy for the blacks.

It was in this atmosphere that I made my first trip to South Africa in 1976. I went there at the beginning of the revolution that would, fifteen years later, sweep the blacks into power. The blacks had become unruly. Under a daredevil leadership of remarkable courage, they assumed a new militancy and, on June 16, 1976, rioted against their white masters in the sprawling ghetto of Soweto, 800,000 blacks in a suburb of Johannesburg. The immediate cause was a government decision that some Soweto classes would be taught in Afrikaans, the dying language of

South Africa's original white settlers. It was a calculated insult, but tensions were so high that any spark would have set off the explosion.

The uprising was put down, of course. Seven hundred blacks died there and in subsequent riots over the next two years. Large sections of Soweto were burned out.

Soweto was a turning point. Many previously conservative whites were frightened into an understanding that the old ways could not long survive, and liberals who had held their tongues were emboldened to speak out for reform. In this environment the South African Journalists Association did the heretofore unthinkable. It nominated a black photographer for the country's most prestigious journalism award. The citation was for several pictures Peter Magubane had taken during the Soweto uprising, including one played on front pages around the world of a white policeman beating a black demonstrator.

The South African police, naturally, had picked up Magubane a few days after the photo appeared. He was already a favorite target of theirs. In the mid-sixties they had held him in solitary confinement without charges for 586 days—almost twenty months—and then had issued an order that the South Africans called "banning." The ban on Magubane permitted him to speak to only one person at a time and forbade him to leave his small local region or to work as a photojournalist. The ban lasted five years before being lifted by the Minister of Justice. Magubane returned to work at the Rand *Daily Mail.*

Now, disturbed by his graphic Soweto pictures, the authorities threw him into jail again, and again without filing any charges. He was still imprisoned, four months later, when he was nominated for the Stellenbosch Award, South Africa's equivalent of the Pulitzer Prize for journalism. The authorities threatened not to let him out to receive the reward, but then changed their minds and released him two months before the grand presentation banquet.

I was invited to go to Johannesburg to make the principal speech at the banquet. Seriously concerned about the country's limitations on free speech, I doubted that I should go. First, I queried as closely as I could the association people. I had in mind the speech I would like to make. I told them that I would not presume to pose as an expert on their situation but that I would attempt an analysis of how South Africa's limitations on free press and speech looked to the outside world—most notably, of course, to us Americans. They maintained that this was exactly the sort of speech they would like to hear.

Still uncertain, I took the precaution of conferring with one of the most prominent of South Africa's white political exiles, Donald Woods, the longtime, highly respected editor of the East London *Daily Dispatch.* He had finally fled to London when the government's threats seriously constrained his freedom.

Given the assurances of the association that I was

going to be permitted to deliver my planned speech, Woods thought I should go; that, indeed, some good might conceivably come of it since many of the unreservedly conservative leaders from the government and its lackey press would be in the audience.

Considering the speech I planned, it was with some audacity that I also requested an interview with Prime Minister Balthazar Vorster during my visit. It was granted for the day after my speech, at the Prime Minister's summer office in Capetown.

The evening of the awards the government information office threw a small cocktail party for us. Minister of Information Dr. Connie Mulder was there, as was the chief of national security, Minister of Justice Jimmy Kruger, and, of course, some of the editors and other officials of the Stellenbosch group. In the social atmosphere of the occasion, there seemed to be a jolly relationship among them. Kruger apparently even intended as humorous his remarks about the possibility of an award for Magubane.

"Well, if he wins," he said, laughing, "I'll help him hang his award on the wall when I take him back to his cell." Perhaps no one in that room, except the Minister himself, knew whether he intended to follow through on that threat. But none would have been surprised if he had.

Magubane did win the award, and he was not returned to his cell. He returned to the *Daily Mail* and later became a valuable member of *Time* magazine's South African staff.

At the dinner that night I spoke on freedom of the press, pointing out that a free press is as vital in keeping various branches of government informed of each other's doings as it is in educating the public. I said:

"It is this free access to information, not alone among the population but within the government itself, that the Russian system, for instance, prevents . . . and it is far the weaker for it.

"I might mention in passing that, as restrictive as is the Soviet system, we [at CBS] have a resident correspondent there and frequently we can shoot film there, although under some restraint. I'm sorry to say that we are not now permitted to have a resident correspondent here: Our requests for visas are largely denied."

What proved to be the contentious part of my statement was the next line:

"It is hard for us to understand why working conditions for us should be freer in the Union of Soviet Socialist Republics than in the Republic of South Africa."

The speech seemed to be well received by most of the dinner guests and particularly by the Stellenbosch officials who had urged my attendance.

The next day I was off by early plane to my appointment with the Prime Minister. Dr. Eschel Rhoodie, the deputy minister of information, accompanied my producer, Bud Benjamin, and me up to Vorster's large, airy but sparsely furnished office in a second-floor corner of the government's summer headquarters. As I crossed the parquet floor toward his desk, Vorster rose, a large, somewhat beefy chap. He greeted us with a rather grim smile and a very simple "How do you do?" gesturing simultaneously for us to sit in two straight-backed chairs adjoining his desk.

He resumed his seat and, folding his hands across his ample midriff, said: "Do you wish to apologize?"

"For what, Mr. Prime Minister?"

"Surely you must know that you have insulted my nation, my people and me," he retorted.

I told him I didn't have the slightest idea what he was speaking about.

"You seriously believe, do you, that it is not an insult to compare the Union of South Africa with the Union of the Soviet Republics?"

For a moment I drew a blank. In the face of his challenge, I honestly could not recall my comparison of the two nations' censorship practices. It did come to me, but before I could respond Vorster unrelentingly pressed on.

"Perhaps you have come to apologize. I am willing to accept your apology."

"Sir," I recall responding to the Prime Minister, "I regret it very much if you feel I have insulted you or your country, but I scarcely could apologize for a statement which I know to be the truth."

Vorster sat impassively staring at me. An almost breathless Dr. Rhoodie tried to put the interview back on track.

"Mr. Prime Minister, I know that Mr. Cronkite

would like to talk to you of affairs in South Africa and the world, and we in the Information Office will deal with the matter of his speech last night."

I rose to perhaps one of my proudest moments. I stood up and said: "Mr. Prime Minister, given the atmosphere in which this meeting began, I think there would be nothing to be gained by continuing the interview. Good day, sir."

I extended my hand. Vorster rose to grasp it, and I detected a smile in his eyes as he bade me farewell. I like to believe he was saying to himself: "Well, it takes one stubborn Dutchman to put down another."

The speech, Vorster's reaction and the abortive interview all became grist for the unpublished underground rumor mill in Capetown and Johannesburg, and I enjoyed a hero's welcome at the remaining social events on our limited schedule—including a very pleasant dinner at the home of Harry Oppenheimer, the diamond king, who, along with his wife, had been walking a narrow path of moderation among the country's industrial leaders.

There were no further repercussions until five years later, when I sought to return to South Africa. I intended to join one of our most purposeful and tenacious CBS producers, Brian Ellis, who had been working for months on a documentary film that we called *Children of Apartheid.*

The South Africans refused me a visa as a working journalist, but after some brief to-and-fro, they agreed that I could have a two-week tourist visa that would carry a prohibition against any work. This sort of thing has happened to many newspeople in many dictatorships and I, like them, intended to carry on filming and interviewing until they caught me and threw me out. But I also hoped that, by personal appeal, I might get the government to give me much more freedom to work.

I called on the Minister of Home Security, Stoffel Botha, the man with the ultimate control over visas. His press secretary warned before I came that Mr. Botha "was about to go home ill with the flu and is in as foul a mood as I've ever seen him."

Not a very auspicious start, but I found Botha scarcely more dour than most of his fellow cabinet members. He found it possible to keep a straight face as he explained why I could not have a working permit.

"Your reputation has proceeded you here, Mr. Cronkite. We know you are a workaholic. And since you applied for a tourist visa, we didn't want in any way to tempt you to ruin your vacation by working."

Despite the flu, he then delivered almost a two-hour dissertation on South African affairs, spending most of that time in an attack on the trade sanctions that the United States and others had imposed on the South African government. He maintained that his ruling National Party had been moving ahead with reforms that now were handicapped by the sanctions. They slowed progress toward integration, he insisted, by denying the nation funds to do the job. Their reform plans included providing blacks equal but separate education as well as such measures (on which first steps had already been taken) as the elimination of passes for blacks to enter white neighborhoods and permission for interracial marriage and black trade unions.

He said that although the international sanctions had increased the pressure from his party's indignant right wing opposed to any liberalization, the leadership planned to take to the electorate "principles" of sharing power with the blacks. He emphasized, however, that this would never be extended to one-man, one-vote because of the huge black majority. Black communities would be granted self-government with the right to send delegates to a central authority, and he acknowledged that this would formalize a continuation of the segregation of the blacks.

He concluded his lecture by asserting that the international sanctions fit the Communist master plan to weaken South Africa's economy, thus slowing reforms and leading to further unrest.

Deputy Information Minister Stoffel van der Merwe emphasized that South African national pride was adversely affected by the sanctions. He likened them to the demands of terrorists. "You cannot give in to them, permitting them to dictate internal policy," he said. (He also noted that the press had to be censored to keep the revolutionaries from getting the publicity vital to their cause.)

Botha's dissertation was not what I had expected when I called on him, but it turned out to be the most succinct presentation that I was to get of the position of the last South African conservative government before the coming of President de Klerk and the white surrender to reality.

Again during that period in South Africa just before the transition, I was personal witness to the internal arguments that too frequently weaken liberal, reform causes. I had the privilege one night in Johannesburg of sitting at dinner between Helen Suzman and Helen Joseph. They were among the most courageous of South Africa's liberal leaders, but the paths they had taken in resisting apartheid were diametrically opposed.

Helen Suzman worked within the establishment. She was long the only liberal member of Parliament, an outspoken and well-spoken challenge to the conservative government and its dictatorial ways.

Helen Joseph was a revolutionary, in philosophy and in manner. While Suzman was laying down the rationale for reform in the halls of government, Joseph was at the barricades, defying social convention as well as the law to associate with blacks and encourage their cause.

At dinner their common distaste for, and common indignation over, the present government was obvious, but it was hard to discern empathy between them. Their disagreement over tactics, over the best way to proceed toward reform, was profound. In the presence of Joseph, it seemed to me, Suzman felt required to defend her conviction that the best way was to work within the system. From them both, however, I got the feeling that the revolutionaries,

within or without the system, were getting just a
little panicky that the limited reforms proposed by
the Botha government might work and block the real
reforms that they had long espoused.

Of course, they were spared this eventuality when
the Botha reform proposals proved unacceptable to
nearly all sides and the de Klerk government came
in with meaningful moves for a truly democratic
government elected through universal suffrage.

Mandela won that election, and de Klerk served
two years as his Vice President. With the new government well launched, de Klerk resigned, declaring
that it was time for his party to stand again in opposition, although, he promised, it was still committed
to making integration work.

The arguments of the reformers around Johannesburg's dinner tables reminded me of those debates in
other countries that, alternating between idealism,
naïveté, cynicism and skepticism, identify the turmoil that marks all great social and political change.

Just before the Communists took over their
country in 1948, Czech liberals argued long and
hard over how to accommodate the Communists'
demands for a share of government. They believed
that the strong minority showing of the Communists
at the polls entitled them to some representation in
government, and nearly all seemed to believe that
the Communists could be given cabinet roles and
still be safely contained. The argument was only
over how far the government should go about meeting their demands—whether they should get both
the interior and the defense ministries, for instance.

In many a late night argument I and others who had seen the Communists in action elsewhere failed to convince our Czech friends that, with their foot in the door, the Communists would exploit the opening until power, all power, was in their hands.

The naïveté of the Czechs and their search for fair, liberal solutions to power-sharing brought them down.

CHAPTER 14

I N TELEVISION news there are three categories of
"biggest stories" that live in our memories.

There are those major events, usually catastro-
phes, that we all covered and in which we shared our
experiences—wars, earthquakes, floods and the occasional "good" ones like the conquest of space and
disease. Then there are those stories that we developed ourselves and that proved to have some importance. And then there are the much rarer stories
that we initiated but that developed a historic life of
their own.

The assassination of John Fitzgerald Kennedy
falls into the first category. Our invaluable "Evening
News" editor, Ed Bliss, a longtime Murrow writer
and editor, was close by the United Press teletype
machine in our CBS newsroom when the first bulletin came over the UPI wire from Dallas.

"Three shots were fired at President Kennedy's
motorcade in downtown Dallas."

Almost immediately another UPI lead said it
appeared that President Kennedy had been "seriously wounded, perhaps fatally wounded" in the
shooting and that the motorcade had broken from
its intended route and seemed to be on the way to a
hospital.

Ed shouted the flashes to me and I shouted to the whole newsroom: "Kennedy's been shot! Let's get on the air!"

But it turned out we couldn't get on the air immediately. The cameras hadn't yet been put in place for our "Evening News" program, and it would take another twenty minutes to warm them up. I headed for a radio booth in the next room, and from there broadcast the first television announcement of the assassination attempt.

Our flash was heard over the "CBS News Bulletin" slide and interrupted the soap opera "As the World Turns." We beat NBC onto the air by almost a minute.

As soon as the cameras were set up, I moved back to our news desk, where I would spend most of the next four days.

Our staff was quickly mobilized both in New York and Dallas. The hero correspondent was Eddie Barker, news chief of our Dallas affiliate, KRLD, whose news sources among the police and hospital personnel were invaluable. He fed information to Dan Rather, our White House correspondent who was on the scene at Parkland Hospital, and that team kept us informed of developments, much of the time, ahead of the opposition.

For the first hour, a shocked nation hung on the sketchy details from the hospital as it became clear that the President was in critical condition. And then came the Barker-Rather report from outside the emergency room that they had learned the President was dead. We were still debating in New York whether we should put such a portentous but unofficial announcement on the air when, within minutes, the hospital issued a bulletin confirming the news. It fell to me to make the announcement.

It is an interesting thing about us newspeople. We are much like doctors and nurses and firemen and police. In the midst of tragedy, our professional drive takes over and dominates our emotions. We move almost like automatons to get the job done. The time for an emotional reaction must wait.

I was doing fine in that department until it was necessary to pronounce the words: "From Dallas, Texas, the flash—apparently official. President Kennedy died at 1 p.m. Central Standard Time—a half hour ago [pause] . . ."

The words stuck in my throat. A sob wanted to replace them. A gulp or two quashed the sob, which metamorphosed into tears forming in the corners of my eyes. I fought back the emotion and regained my professionalism, but it was touch and go there for a few seconds before I could continue: "Vice President Johnson has left the hospital in Dallas, but we do not know to where he has proceeded. Presumably, he will be taking the oath of office shortly, and become the thirty-sixth President of the United States."

I was on the air for six hours when our producer, Don Hewitt, said Charles Collingwood was there to relieve me briefly. As I got up from my chair, I realized for the first time that I was still in my shirtsleeves, my tie loosened at the collar, far more informal than I would normally appear on the air. My secretary had slipped my jacket onto the back of my chair but I had not noticed, and so intense were those hours that no one else even mentioned my dishabille.

I went into my glass-walled office off the newsroom intending to call Betsy. I needed an intimate moment to share emotions. Millions of Americans were doing the same. All afternoon I had been reporting that telephone lines were jammed and switchboards clogged across the nation. I had not thought that this would create a problem for me, but on my desk all twelve of my incoming lines were lit.

As I stared, one of them blinked dark and I grabbed it hoping to get an outside line. Instead there was somebody already there. And she was saying with all the broad "a"s that pass for culture in America:

"Hello, hello, hello. Is this CBS?"

I confirmed that it was.

"Well," she said, "I'd like to speak to someone in charge of the news."

I reported that she had reached our newsroom.

"I want to complain," she complained, "of your having that Walter Cronkite on the air at a time like this, crying his crocodile tears when we all know he hated Jack Kennedy."

I was in no mood to listen to such unfair and distorted reasoning. I asked the lady's name and it was, as her accent indicated it might be, hyphenated. Something like Mrs. Constance Llewellyn-Arbuthnot. She also threw in her Park Avenue address for full measure of her importance.

With all the outraged dignity I could muster, I told her: "Mrs. Llewellyn-Arbuthnot, you are speaking to Walter Cronkite, and you, madam, are a damned idiot."

If she had a retort to that definitive statement, it is known only to herself and God. By the time she delivered it, my phone had long since been returned to its cradle.

The dramatic and emotional scenes over the next three days would wring us all dry. Every appearance of the young President's widow was a tearjerker, and none more than the picture of three-year-old son John-John saluting his father's casket as the cortege passed.

The drama soon faded into the long-drawn-out inquiry into the murder. President Johnson appointed Chief Justice Earl Warren to head a blue-ribbon panel to investigate the crime. It met for ten months and delivered its conclusion that it could find no evidence of a conspiracy and that Lee Harvey Oswald was probably the lone gunman.

This opinion was not universally accepted. The larger conclusion depended on many minor conclusions based on what many felt was skimpy or downright doubtful evidence. At CBS News we set out to examine each of the questions of evidence that bothered us all. Producer Les Midgley spent the almost-unheard-of sum of a half-million dollars to test every possible thesis. We built a firing range duplicating the view Oswald had from his perch in the

Texas School Book Depository window, complete with the various obstructions to his vision as the Kennedy car passed along the street below. From that position experts fired a rifle identical to the one Oswald had allegedly used, and proved to many doubters that it could indeed have been fired three times while Oswald had the President in his sights.

We established that an echo effect could have led Texas Governor John Connally, wounded as he rode with the President, to believe that one of the shots was fired from in front of the car, and not from behind the car, where Oswald was.

And on and on, through the whole list of doubtful evidence, until we had to announce our conclusion that the Warren Commission had delivered the only finding possible. As a news story, this was actually a disappointment for us. We would have had a far better story, a real world-smasher, if we could have disproved the Warren Commission finding.

What neither we nor the Warren Commission knew at that time was that there was a motive for a Cuban plot against the President, one of the conspiracy theories that had been proposed. The CIA did not level with the commission and failed to reveal that it had plotted against Castro's life. What difference that information might have made to the Warren Commission can only be a matter of conjecture.

The most significant mystery of our time, of course, led to the growth of an entire industry of conspiracy theorists. All their speculations were

WALTER CRONKITE

based on a heavy structure of imagination seasoned with a pinch of unprovable and distorted "facts."

As wild as was the wildest of these conjectures, they were all topped by the moviemaker Oliver Stone in his film *JFK*. He mixed the most sensational of them and brought forth a poisonous concoction. In his formulation, the Cubans and the Mafia, a band of homosexuals and even President Johnson himself were involved in plotting Kennedy's death, and the hero of his fantasy was the self-promoting district attorney in New Orleans who prosecuted an innocent citizen in pursuit of headlines.

It was suspected among the knowledgeable in New Orleans that Jim Garrison had persecuted Clay Shaw, a homosexual businessman and art connoisseur, because he was jealous of Shaw's acceptance in the rarefied stratosphere of New Orleans' society.

Stone's slick movie was seen by millions of people who were not old enough to have lived through the Kennedy assassination and were not familiar with its details. Its documentary style must have led many to believe they were seeing an authentic historical reconstruction of the tragedy. That is a tragedy in itself.

It is generally accepted that movies built on novels depicting ancient history beyond the reach of this generation's researchers for the most part reflect their producer's interpretation of the past and cannot be viewed otherwise. But any so-called docudramas produced in times contemporary with the events they pretend to depict must be suspect. It is a dangerous cinematic form. Present and future generations are likely to assume that the film reflects thorough, factual, journalistic reporting of current events. They are likely to ignore the idea that the film is only the producer's interpretation of events—an interpretation that is frequently afflicted with paid propaganda, special pleading or commercial theatrical hype. It is a great way to distort, and a very poor way to teach, history.

Critics of this contention of mine like to point out that I was the host of a very successful program originally broadcast in the mid-1950s called "You Are There." It was a reconstruction of historical events as if CBS News had actually covered them. The presence of the CBS correspondents interviewing historical characters indubitably injected authenticity into our theatrical version of events.

But our series proves rather than challenges my points about docudramas. With the rarest of exceptions, the events had occurred long before any motion picture cameras could have recorded them. A great stamp across each frame of film could not have proclaimed more clearly that our accounts were reconstructions.

That fact was brought home by a serious miscalculation in the production of a contemporary story, one of the rare exceptions to our norm. The story was the burning of the great German zeppelin *Hindenburg* as it attempted to land at Lakehurst, New Jersey, after its maiden transatlantic crossing. My

role was that of a news anchor in a modern newsroom taking you back to historic events. My anchor
desk was set up in a corner of the large studio in
which the rest of the drama was staged. The final
scene was of the *Hindenburg*'s bridge as it was
swept by fire, and the stagehands set off large
smoke pots.

Unfortunately, my anchor desk, supposedly in
midtown Manhattan far from the scene of action,
was actually only a few feet from the burning *Hindenburg*. As the reporter at Lakehurst threw it back
to me "in the CBS newsroom" for the summing up,
smoke totally enveloped my desk. The cameras
could hardly see me, and my final lines were delivered with a mighty crescendo of coughing.

Those were the days of live television, before the
development of tape, and each production had all
the excitement of an opening night. And many of the
mishaps.

To seal the fate of the defenders of the Alamo, a
final cannon shot was supposed to bring the fort wall
crashing down on one of the last survivors, Jim
Bowie. We saw the Mexicans pull the lanyard. We
saw the fire belch from their cannon's mouth.
We saw the Alamo's wall shudder with the impact of
the cannonball. We saw Bowie, lying there taking a
final shot at the Mexicans. What we did not see was
the wall collapse. Not until, that is, we saw a broom
handle, wielded by an alert stagehand, appear in the
lower left corner of the screen to give it a shove. The
wall fell, Bowie was duly buried beneath it, and we
could switch to my final line: "What sort of day was

it? A day like all days, filled with those events that alter and illuminate our times. And you were there."

"You Are There" was an exciting show to do. It was presented on Sunday evenings, when most Broadway theaters were dark, and it gave a chance for older actors and ingenues alike to try their hand at this new thing called television. E. G. Marshall, Shepperd Strudwick, Lorne Greene, Ray Walston, Kim Stanley, Paul Newman and Joanne Woodward were all part of what we came to know as Sidney Lumet's Players.

Sidney was our director, and he was to go vaulting to Hollywood to become one of the industry's most talented and successful moviemakers. He and our producer, Charles Russell, would become Hollywood heroes when, long after the fact and when it was again safe to speak out, it was revealed that throughout the long run of "You Are There" they had employed several of the screenwriters who had been blacklisted in the fifties' anti-Communist hysteria. They all operated under the names of less talented writers who courageously agreed to the conspiracy. The whole plot was almost exposed when one of the "names" succumbed to delusions of grandeur and demanded the right to edit and coproduce "his" programs. Naturally his demand was refused, and only extraordinary diplomacy and pressure from Sidney and Charles kept him quiet and prevented the threatened exposure, which probably would have ended the career of everybody connected with the show.

This was during the era of Wisconsin Senator Joe

McCarthy's insult to democracy that he tried to camouflage as a search for Reds in government. I had
covered some of his activities and Senate hearings
when I found myself in a New York hotel elevator
late one night with the Senator and his attractive
wife. As usual, he had been drinking.

I nodded a hello, which he returned, but we did
not speak. But as they left the elevator, I heard her
say to him as if they had just been speaking of me:
"*That's* Walter Cronkite."

We lived with such paranoia in those difficult
days that I was certain I was about to be pilloried by
McCarthy demagoguery. Happily, nothing happened, and thanks in part to Ed Murrow's television
exposure of the man, McCarthy would soon be only
a blot on our history.

It was another of Washington's aberrations that
produced an example of the memorable story in
which the journalistic perpetrator can take particular
pride. Mine concerned the Watergate scandal.

Ever since the burglars employed by one of
Richard Nixon's reelection campaign committees
had been caught breaking into the Democratic election headquarters, the story had sporadically hit the
front pages. It got a particularly big play in the early
summer, when the Washington *Post*'s Bob Woodward and Carl Bernstein began digging up details
that exposed it as a serious plot, probably involving
the White House, as opposed to the "boys'-night-out
caper" that administration spokesmen tried to make
of it.

Their first reports came in rather rapid succession, but then the revelations began coming more slowly. The stories appeared with less regularity in the papers across the country. They moved off the front pages and back toward the classifieds and, in many cases, eventually dropped from the papers entirely. With the newer developments growing more complex, and depending as they did on knowledge of the intricacies revealed earlier, the follow-up reports were getting harder to understand.

It occurred to me that it was time to try to pull this important story together in a comprehensive and coherent review that would keep it from slipping into limbo—a simple ABC of the plot and the people involved, the trail from the burglars to the White House. This we did in a detailed but easy-to-follow report prepared by producer Stanhope Gould, who had been our Watergate man from the beginning.

What I did not know at the time was the amount of pressure that the White House, having caught its second wind, was putting on the Washington *Post* to drop the story. It was threatening its advertisers and the *Post* itself with subtle reminders that the *Post*'s broadcasting empire was subject to government licensing.

Our broadcast revived public interest, the *Post* was bolstered in its determination to press on, and the Watergate case brought Richard Nixon and his White House cohorts to the bars of justice. Of course, they did not go down without a fight. Within minutes of the broadcast of the first installment of our scheduled two-part presentation, one of Nixon's factotums, Charles "Chuck" Colson, was on the phone with a forceful complaint to our CBS chairman, Bill Paley. Paley was shaken enough to pass along his concern to our news boss, Dick Salant.

Salant was a highly principled man who strongly believed in a chain of command and responsibility. He did not let us know that Paley was disturbed. Instead he represented as his idea that we had put undue emphasis on the story by the length of time we gave it. He suggested that we trim the next installment.

Our review was scheduled for two days, and the first installment ran an unprecedented fourteen minutes out of the twenty-four minutes of news time allotted to us in each thirty-minute broadcast. Since Salant had not revealed that political pressure was involved, I saw no problem in acceding to his request. We had made the impression we wanted with the first piece, there was a lot of duplication in the second, and I felt we could shorten it without damage. This enabled Salant, without my knowledge, of course, to go back to Paley and inform him that he could tell the White House that we were shortening the second story. This may not have been fully satisfactory to either Paley or Colson, but it served to placate the Nixon people and we escaped further White House retribution.

I did not find out for months that the White House, via Paley, had applied the pressure to which

Salant responded. He took full responsibility, partly because that was his creed but also, in all probability, because he knew that if I thought he was responding to White House pressure, he might not be able to control the eruption.

As it was, I am sorry that it happened. Up until that time, and ever since, except for this single failure, I have been able to claim that CBS management never brought any pressure on the "Evening News" to satisfy either political considerations or advertisers' demands. That there were such attempts by politicians and advertisers, I don't doubt, but they were blocked in the executive suites and never reached the newsroom.

Our contribution went widely unrecognized, except by the Washington *Post* management, but Gould, my other colleagues and I can take a lot of credit for keeping that Watergate story alive until its denouement in Nixon's resignation.

IN SHARP contrast, I did not deserve the praise and glory heaped upon me for bringing Egypt's President Anwar Sadat and Israel's Prime Minister Menachem Begin together and setting off the chain of events that would lead to the first formal peace between Israel and an Arab neighbor. That story is an example of newsgathering enterprise that develops a life of its own.

When the Egyptian dictator Gamal Abdel Nasser died, his political heir was Colonel Anwar Sadat, who, it was generally thought in Cairo, would be a mere caretaker until the ruling group of army colonels chose a permanent successor.

After three or four months in which it seemed that Sadat was consolidating his power, I obtained the first television interview granted to a Western correspondent. We sat and smoked our pipes under a vast, spreading banyan tree at The Barrage, the President's country residence on the banks of the Nile. The interview was as tepid as the afternoon was hot. Sadat droned on about his hopes and plans for Egypt's future as I fought to stay awake. Suddenly he brought me bolt upright. I was sure that I had heard him say he intended to go to Jerusalem.

Yes, he assured me, he would go to Jerusalem—just as soon as there was peace, a peace that would depend upon the Israelis meeting all of the conditions that Egypt had put on the table practically since the founding of the Jewish state—for openers, the return of the Sinai to Egypt, the Golan Heights to Syria, and Jerusalem to Jordan. So his statement appeared to be merely a metaphor for his optimism that peace would come in his lifetime and permit him to visit Jerusalem.

We didn't even use the quote in the brief report I was able to extract from that long, dull interview. In ensuing years I became an admiring friend of Sadat's. His political and personal courage put him at or near the top of my list of political leaders. And on more than one occasion I heard him repeat his statement about going to Jerusalem.

Too late for our "Evening News" broadcast, the news wires from Tel Aviv on Friday night, November 11, 1977, reported a rumor that Sadat might visit Israel. Its source was a Canadian parliamentary delegation that, before visiting Israel, had been to Cairo and had heard Sadat, addressing his Parliament, state that he would go to Jerusalem.

So over Saturday and Sunday, my days off, I waited for the rumor to be knocked down by Sadat in response to the inquiry of some enterprising reporter. By Sunday night there was still no comment from Cairo and the rumor was continuing its rounds in the Middle East.

As my "Evening News" producer, Burton Benjamin, and I discussed the next day's report, we agreed we should try to get Sadat on a satellite interview so that, under my questioning, he could make his intentions clear.

So on Monday morning I had him on the satellite.

"Good morning, Walter, and how is Barbara?" was his greeting. He was fond of Barbara Walters and somehow we were linked in his mind. He began every conversation with me by asking how Barbara was. Barbara is a friend of mine, but unless she falls ill— pray not—her health is not a burning issue with me.

After we got our Barbara preliminaries out of the way, I asked if he had any plans to go to Jerusalem. He would like to go very much, he said, and I asked what I knew would be the definitive question: What are your conditions for going? Whereupon he went into the usual litany of Egyptian demands on

Israel—withdrawal from the Sinai and the Golan Heights, and on and on.

"And those are your conditions for going to Israel?" I asked, just to tie a ribbon around the denial.

"Oh, no, no, Walter," he replied. "Those are my conditions for peace. The only condition is that I want to discuss the whole situation with the 120 members of the Knesset and put the full picture and detail of the situation from our point of view."

Suddenly I was trying to put the ribbon around a much bigger story.

What would he need to go, I asked, and he said all he needed was an invitation. And how soon could he go?

"In the earliest time possible."

Let's pin that one down, I thought. Such promising initiatives in the past have collapsed as politicians, yielding to various special interests, wrangled over the agenda for a meeting. An early date might stymie opponents in both Cairo and Tel Aviv.

"That could be, say, within a week?" I suggested.

"You can say that, yes."

By the time I had told him good-bye, Benjamin was on the phone to Tel Aviv. Get Begin!

The bureau arranged to set up a temporary studio in a room adjoining the hall at the Tel Aviv Hilton where he was scheduled to speak that night. He had been told of Sadat's statement, and he agreed to my interview by satellite. He was clearly prepared. He took with considerable aplomb my report that

Sadat was ready to come, that all he needed was an invitation.

"Tell him he's got an invitation," Begin said. I pressed him for details. He said he would make a statement to the Knesset the following day and then would talk to the American Ambassador, presumably about forwarding the invitation.

"But I can assure you," he said, "as we really want the visit of President Sadat, we really want to negotiate the peace, to establish permanent peace in the Middle East, I will not hesitate to send such a letter."

I had a feeling he didn't believe this was all for real. I think he envisioned the long series of diplomatic negotiations that any such visit would require, realizing that there was a great distance between this dialogue with an American correspondent and any possibility of Sadat really coming. My report to him that Sadat said he would be prepared to appear within a week jarred him out of any such complacency. He backed and filled.

"Very good news," he said, but quickly added: "Well, if President Sadat is ready to come next week—if he tells me that he will come next week, I will have to postpone my trip to Britain because I am supposed to go next Sunday to London at the invitation of Prime Minister Callaghan."

If that was the beginning of an excuse to postpone the meeting, he instantly thought better of it. "But I suppose that Prime Minister Callaghan will also be agreeable, rather, to postpone that meeting for a

week, and rather have President Sadat in Jerusalem
because it gives hope to have peace in the Middle
East."

Then, apparently, his political instincts told him
this left him no maneuvering room to further consider the advisability of this visit. "But if President
Sadat would come after my return from Europe, I
will come back home next Friday, after my visit to
London and to Geneva, and then he may come the
other Monday [sic]."

He may have heard warning bells that this might
be interpreted as a stall. The onus for any failure
now of a meeting must not be placed around his
neck. "But anyhow, anytime, any day he's prepared
to come, I will receive him cordially at the airport,
go together with him to Jerusalem, also present him
to the Knesset and let him make his speech to our
Parliament. I will follow him onto the platform,
greet him, receive him."

Begin would live up to that promise to the letter.
But he concluded the statement to me by putting
squarely onto Sadat the blame should the meeting
not take place. "I think it's now up to President
Sadat to carry out his, I should say promise, or bring
into fruition his readiness to come to Jerusalem."

The rest is history, as they say, except for a couple
of sidebars.

Sadat flew to Israel five days later. The world
press descended on Tel Aviv. On Friday night at the
TWA lounge at Kennedy Airport, it seemed that all
of our competitors were there. They were booked on

a flight to Israel, and they assumed the same of us. But Bud Benjamin and I were booked on a flight at about the same time to Cairo. I had arranged with Sadat for us to fly into Israel with him. Our immediate chore was to protect that exclusive by letting our opposition board that Tel Aviv flight before they discovered our secret.

Fortunately, the Tel Aviv flight was called first, so Bud and I fell in with the others en route to the gate. Except we kept falling farther behind the crowd. I don't think they missed us until they were airborne.

It looked like a clean beat. But we hadn't figured on Barbara Walters, a serious mistake. She had taken an earlier plane via a different route to Tel Aviv. When ABC learned of our Cairo ploy, they intercepted her and got her a charter to Cairo the next morning.

Just as we were boarding Sadat's plane, along she came, running across the field with hand upraised like a substitute entering a sporting contest. Sadat invited her aboard, and her enterprise robbed us of our exclusive.

Sadat did invite me up to share his private quarters for much of the flight, and as we crossed into Israel two fighters of the Israeli Air Force appeared off our wings as escorts. One of the pilots brought his plane so close that even through his visor we could see his broad grin as he waved a greeting to the Egyptian President.

The greeting from the long line of Israeli digni-

taries at the airport was warm. As Sadat got to Golda
Meir, until recently the Prime Minister, she grabbed
his hand and with that schoolmarm air of hers said:
"Why didn't you tell me you wanted to come to
Israel?"

One can only speculate about what might have
developed in Egyptian-Israeli relations if the more
liberal Meir had been in charge. Begin was never
overwhelmed with the peace accord and his Agricul-
ture Minister, General Ariel Sharon, did everything
to scuttle it by building more Israeli settlements in
the disputed territories.

It was later suggested by some critics that I had
overstepped the bounds of journalistic propriety by
trying to negotiate an Israeli-Egyptian détente. They
did not know the full story—that my initial journalistic intention was to knock down the speculation
over the visit.

And anyway, journalists from time immemorial
have affected the course of events by asking judi-
cious questions and conducting timely interviews. In
the past some correspondents did, on occasion, try to
help friendly officials by floating a trial balloon in
their dispatches. In those cases they crossed the jour-
nalist-source dividing line. This was not the case
with our Sadat-Begin interviews.

THE RESULTS achieved by any given story may
differ considerably from the expectations of the
reporter, writer, editor or producer. Take the case of

Jimmy Hoffa and his Teamsters Union. We did a particularly revealing investigative report on the strong-arm tactics the union used in its organizing drives. We focused on its effort to enlist independent cleaning establishments. We detailed the threats against the owners and their families, the bombings and arson of reluctant shops and, in particularly difficult cases, even murder.

Our daring cameramen even got shots showing one of their tactics. The Teamster goons kept targeted cleaners in a constant state of alarm by parking outside their homes and businesses big limousines with a couple of dangerous-looking thugs aboard.

I interviewed law enforcement officials and union bosses, including Hoffa himself. Hoffa and his gang were unfailingly cordial, but, of course, not exactly forthcoming regarding their operations. It was a hard-hitting piece. Because of the Teamsters' reputation for violence, CBS provided me with bodyguards the night the show hit the air and for days thereafter. They also escorted the children to and from school. The morning after the broadcast my secretary stuck an ashen face into my office. "Jimmy Hoffa's on the phone," she gasped.

I told her to listen in as I picked up the phone. Hoffa couldn't have been more friendly. Like a longtime fan, he praised the show. Great, he said, and all the boys at headquarters thought so too. He just wanted me to know, and let's have lunch at Duke Ziebert's the next time I'm in Washington.

My producers and reporters and researchers spent the day pondering the Hoffa reaction. We examined all the possibilities, including that he might be trying to lure me into letting down my guard before administering the hit. And then it came to us. We had given Hoffa a few million dollars' worth of publicity. His Teamsters ruled by terror. Our "exposé" was an hour-long commercial that graphically warned their targets of the punishment that awaited them if they resisted Teamster "organization."

A small problem that resulted from the story was the middle-of-the-night calls we got from various neighbors reporting that mysterious men were sitting in a car double-parked in front of our house. Our bodyguards!

WE HAD A little better luck, at least in terms of disturbing the culprits, with our undercover report on corruption in the Boston police department. Our program, called "Biography of a Bookie Joint," produced by Jay McMullen, used cameras hidden in lunch boxes and long-range listening devices, to record police patronizing and guarding a number of bookies.

We received several threatening calls from Boston and at the annual policemen's ball just a couple of nights after the broadcast, Richard Cardinal Cushing roundly lambasted us for having cast aspersions on "Boston's finest—our boys in blue." When I called the cardinal's office to get more details on his complaint, his assistant tried to assuage me.

"I wouldn't worry about it," he said. "His Eminence didn't see the program."

I hope I sounded as astounded as I was when I asked what, then, he was complaining about.

"Oh, you know how it is," he replied. "He had to say something to buck up the lads' morale."

A few weeks later I flew to Boston to speak at a National Safety Council conference. There was an unmarked car at the bottom of the plane ramp and two rather hefty men standing by it. As I reached the last step, they each took me by an elbow and escorted me to the car.

"We're Boston police," one of them said. "We're taking care of you."

I wasn't at all sure what "taking care" of me consisted of. There were a couple of terrifyingly silent blocks until one of them spoke up. They had been sent by the conference, he said, to get me safely to the hotel. With the ice broken, we settled into a nice friendly relationship. They didn't volunteer any comment on the program, so I thought I'd test the water by asking how things were going in the police department. That didn't flush out anything. The answer was:

"They're going better now that we've got the kah de kah." I hadn't heard of a kah de kah. My inquiry brought disbelief.

"You know the kah de kahs. Your boys in New York have had 'em for years. Most departments have had them. We've finally got them."

Not a clue. I tried, fruitlessly I'm sure, to explain my ignorance.

"The kah de kahs. You know, all the kahs have radios so we can talk kah de kah."

Well, it beat talking about the news media and bookie joints. The Boston police are a wonderful part of the mosaic that is America.

AMERICA itself was the star of the greatest show I was ever privileged to attend: the bicentennial of our Declaration of Independence, July 4, 1976.

The success of that great day was built on failure. The federal government, under President Nixon and his appointed bicentennial director, John Warner, simply failed to get a grip on the occasion. As across the country the realization dawned that Washington didn't have a clue, village after village, town after town, city after city, state after state planned their own observances.

Each had its own version of the meaning of the Declaration; each had its own sense of what its own community and its own ethnic population had contributed to make this country what it is. The variety and the spontaneity and the spirit of their celebrations across the land offered an extraordinary look into the heart of a great nation.

Without any idea of how successful the day would be as television drama, we at CBS planned to spend the holiday touring America with dozens of remotes in places large and small. The centerpiece, to which we would frequently return, was the great parade of tall ships in New York Harbor and, to cap the evening, the annual Boston Pops Independence Day concert with its incomparable fireworks display culminating in the *1812 Overture* with real cannon fire.

An unconscious bit of symbolism testifying to the fact that this was indeed a people's celebration befitting the Declaration itself was that (if memory serves me correctly) we went to Washington only once, and then to show in a guarded corner of the National Archives that precious paper we honor as the Declaration of the United States of America.

I was our anchor for the broadcast, the success of which depended not at all on words but on detailed planning, superb engineering logistics and a team of very cool producers. While our executive producer, Ernie Leiser, knew that the mostly unscheduled nature of events rendered the exercise nearly hopeless, he assigned a team of writers to prepare copy for various bridges during the day and particularly the grand opening.

Our control center was in Madison Square Garden because we already had facilities there for the Democratic political convention coming up shortly. I took my place at the anchor desk just before 6 a.m., the Leiser script in front of me. But as the red light came on, the exuberance of the day overwhelmed me. I didn't read "Good morning from CBS News." I blurted out: "Up, up, up, everybody! It's your birthday!"

Leiser damned near fainted. Instead he uttered a short oath, said something about Cronkite blowing the opening, not using the script, where do we go next.

The frisky spirit lasted, though, right through a

most wonderful day. Some of the remotes were not as good as others, of course, but they all exuded an enthusiastic amateurism.

The only news of the day with which we dared to break into our own broadcast was the stirring account of the raid by Israeli commandos on the airport at Entebbe, Uganda. They rescued 103 hostages, most of them Israelis, held by pro-Palestinian hijackers of an Air France plane.

After eighteen hours of unprecedented and unparalleled television, we left the air at midnight.

Betsy and I joined the millions still celebrating on the streets and in the bars of New York, and we watched the sun rise on another year of our country's glorious history.

ACCOMPANYING the President of the United States on a trip abroad sounds like a glamorous assignment, but it rarely is. It involves a lot of hard work, lengthy hours, torturous travel, a succession of public relations handouts and a story that does not lend itself to much individual enterprise.

An airport reception upon arrival, a speeding trip through what might be exotic streets now hidden behind either crowds of welcoming citizenry or a shoulder-to-shoulder wall of troops. While the official party has a little "downtime" to rest, the reporter pounds out his copy or does a standup television piece posed in front of some national monument.

The reception and dinner that night: If you are

lucky they keep you outside and you can lounge around awaiting the evening communiqué. You might have a chance to slip into a nearby bistro. You are there just in case anything untoward happens. If you are incredibly unlucky, you might be selected as the "pool" reporter representing your colleagues lucky enough to be outside. You will get to sit through a boring dinner with boring speeches and, usually, a boring exhibition of the native dance.

Occasionally there are exceptions, and one was President Nixon's historic trip to China. It opened up our relations with the Communist regime that had been at a cold arm's length since Mao Tse-tung's long march drove our imperialist ally Chiang Kai-shek to his island retreat on Formosa, now called Taiwan.

Nixon, regardless of whatever other opinions people had of him, deserved great credit for his studious approach to foreign policy. And he should be recognized for the move toward reconciliation with China that he initiated when most of the powerful members of the Republican party hierarchy were deeply opposed. It was an act of great political courage.

When we flew to China, the country was just emerging from the so-called Cultural Revolution during which fanatical Red Guards, in their zeal to enforce Mao Tse-tung's version of ideological purity, reduced hundreds of thousands of intellectuals to menial work. It almost certainly was the cruelest policy imposed on a regime's own people since

Stalin's mass execution of thousands of his country-
men whom he suspected of disloyalty.

Beijing, as a matter of fact, reminded me in many
ways of Moscow immediately after the war. It was a
city in gray. The buildings were gray, shading
toward black, darkened by the choking smog made
up of equal parts coal smoke and grit blown in from
China's distant western reaches. The people were
gray, their quilted jackets and pants a perfect camouflage against the dull buildings past which they
unsmilingly plodded. Their numbers were a reminder of the "Ripley's Believe It or Not" claim that
the Chinese people, marching four abreast, would
pass a given spot forever.

Our convoy of limousines through Beijing's
broad streets and the vast plaza of Tiananmen
Square, of later drama and disrepute, attracted little
attention from the people despite the U.S. flags
flying from the fenders. The regime had not promoted our visit. The canny Mao and his sidekick
Chou En-lai would see how things developed first.

They developed well. The ground had been prepared by the secret visits to Beijing of Henry
Kissinger, the President's National Security Adviser.
No hitches developed, and Nixon, after the formal
visits and interminable speechmaking, was able to
announce a new relationship of better understanding
between our countries.

The press wasn't there for Nixon's historic
meeting with the ailing Mao, but we were all invited
to the Chinese and U.S. state banquets held in the

Great Hall of the People—a great hall indeed, on the Square. The speeches were as soporific as usual, but the food was marvelous. We sat at large tables for ten with Chinese officials sprinkled among us. An army of waiters kept a huge turntable at the center of the table loaded with course after course. There is a Chinese tradition according to which hosts serve a number of courses equaling the number of guests, and I believe they were trying to match the hundreds of us those nights in the Great Hall. Chopsticks were, of course, de rigueur, and I don't do badly with them. However, I will reveal a secret, closely held until now.

About mid-dinner the table approximately in the center of the hall was startled by an olive that seemed to drop from the ceiling. I know they were startled because I had followed the course of that olive from my chopsticks on its slow arc over at least three other tables before it reached its destination. The well-oiled olive, when squeezed by my chopsticks, had taken off as if shot from a cannon.

Embarrassment was to pay me another visit when we all went to the Great Wall. Forewarned about China's cold, I had purchased a pair of socks that could be warmed by a battery inserted at the top. As we left the bus at the wall, I dropped in the battery. I put it in wrong side up, and every time I took a step, my right foot got an electric shock.

I thought the little jig I performed before getting the battery rearranged was worthy of a better reception than I got from the frozen-faced guards and my

press companions, so intent on racing for the wall
that they paid no heed to my distress. My delay in
getting to the wall and my separation from my press
colleagues yielded a serendipitous dividend. As they
were herded a short distance up the wall and then
back to the base to await Nixon's arrival, I wandered
some distance up the wall, unimpeded by the guards
stationed every few feet along the way.

From that point up that steep slope, I saw the
President's entourage arriving. I turned to hasten
back to the press area. Now the guards closed ranks
against my progress. I was stuck, perhaps a quarter
of a mile up that damned wall. But there, just ahead
of me, also hurrying down, was the President's aide
H. R. "Bob" Haldeman. He heeded my call for help
and used his White House pass to escort me down.
Because of the delay, I now found myself on the
other side of Nixon from the press assembled below.
Practically one of his party, I made the rest of the
wall tour almost at his elbow as my colleagues pondered this intrusion and glared a lot.

Pat Nixon was off on her own sightseeing tours
each day. They were of no substance but provided
pretty pictures, and we always sent a cameraman
along. One day, for some reason, Barbara Walters
decided to accompany Mrs. Nixon's party. As they
looked over some flower garden or such, she worked
her way up to the First Lady's side and found her
willing to talk.

Barbara frantically turned and called for a microphone. The NBC cameraman was somewhere else at
the moment, but our man was standing near, so he

handed her his microphone, which, by odd coincidence, had no identification on it.

Later that day, close to airtime, Barbara returned to the NBC News hotel suite to ask what they were doing with her exclusive. They knew nothing of such an exclusive; they had seen no such tape. The NBC cameraman had dropped off some pretty pictures of Mrs. Nixon and her Chinese hosts at the flower garden, but no Walters interview. The puzzled NBC producer began calling the other networks. At CBS the fact that an NBC interview had been recorded by us provided an afternoon of jollity. Now our producer, Russ Bensley, drew out the joke just a little further by denying that we had the Walters tape. The fun ended soon after, as Bensley's sense of fairness overcame his sense of humor and he surrendered the tape that CBS had shot—just in time for the NBC evening feed to New York.

At one of the dinners I asked a Chinese official what had impressed him most about the American visit. Without hesitation he answered: "How young your American leaders are."

It was true. At the receptions it was remarkable to see the Americans, clearly healthy and fit and with only a rare grayhead, pass down the line of Chinese hierarchy, gray and bent and often toothless. Chou En-lai seemed the most vital among them and certainly was the most outgoing in his conversations with the U.S. delegation, including those of us in the press who were in his presence on one or two occasions.

We were kept under close escort at all times,

always on the limited itinerary they had planned for us except for such minor excursions as we might be able to talk our so-called hosts from the Foreign Office into. A big deal was a three-block diversion from the approved route.

Security was intense. There were guards on each floor of our hotels, and the staffs clearly had been inoculated with the fear of God should anything be discovered missing from any of our rooms. This defied throwing anything away. Our room boys screened the trash, and anything that seemed possibly useful would show up again carefully laid out on the dresser—paper clips, used carbon paper, toothpaste or shaving cream tubes not fully squashed.

We were in the loaded buses ready to leave our Beijing hotel when one of the floor boys came running toward us waving a pair of panty hose. Diane Sawyer, later of justified television fame, but then a White House press secretary, had made one last desperate attempt to discard them—clearly to no avail.

Although the trappings of the police state had worn heavy, I went to sleep our last night relieved that there had been no incidents. But in the middle of the night there was a brief pounding at the door before it was opened by the floor boy. In the light from the hall, all I could see was army uniforms.

An officer, apparently high in rank, and an aide stepped in. In the half-light, he made what sounded like a most bellicose announcement. I think I was quaking as I got out of bed and into my clothes for what seemed like imminent incarceration. With that, his aide stepped back into the hall and returned with a huge box of candy. The officer saluted smartly and withdrew. It turned out that this odd ceremony had been repeated throughout the hotel. They may have meant well, but the Chinese water torture came to mind.

SOME OF OUR more interesting stories during the cold war came from the other side of the Iron Curtain. Marshal Tito, the tough Communist guerrilla of World War II, by his steely rule kept the constantly quarreling regions of Yugoslavia together after the war. I interviewed Tito twice, the first time in the so-called White House outside Belgrade, the President's country residence on a hill overlooking the Danube River. Tito had founded the concept of the Third World, those mostly underdeveloped nations that did not fall in either the Western or the Soviet sphere.

We spent an hour or so talking about the Third World and its relative power and political expectations. We barely touched on Yugoslavia itself. The year was 1971 and there was no serious challenge to Tito's grip on the country.

I would not see him again until his last visit to the United States in 1978. He was ill, and rising regional leaders were beginning to circle the campfire. His natural ebullience was gone. We talked now not of Third World power and Yugoslavia's promising economy but of succession. He outlined for me his plan—a revolving executive with leaders of each of the twelve ethnic groups in Yugoslavia serving a turn as the country's President.

He recited this from rote, with no hint of enthusiasm. This man knew that none of those pretenders or any other successor could hold a country of such bitter regional rivalries together. He had done it with a dictator's determination and no qualms against the most ruthless suppression of his enemies. Even as he was about to promulgate his plan for succession, he was already going like a slave to the dungeon where he would await the failure he knew was inevitable. Our farewell was a sad one.

Another dictator, Fidel Castro, I met at the height of his power, a few years before the collapse of the Soviet Union pulled the economic rug out from under him. Our appointment was for ten o'clock at his residence, a fashionable dinner hour in Latin America. Bud Benjamin was my producer, and our wives were along on our Cuban visit. They had been invited to our meeting with Castro.

The dictator, in casual military dress, could not have been more gracious as he greeted us in his living room. He bade me sit with him on the sofa. Cigars were passed and the conversation began. Eleven o'clock came, and twelve, and one, and the big hand was moving toward two before he wound down and we said our good nights. Although he chain-smoked them, he never offered another cigar or a bite of food. The wives were looking a little wan as we led them out of the residence.

Our long conversation included my answers to his searching and detailed questions about my World War II experiences. He seemed as fascinated as a child with the most trivial of war stories. As to substance, his long soliloquies were not unlike those heard many times by anyone who has paid attention to his public speeches—except for one answer to a question of mine. I told him of my two years in Moscow and travels through other countries of postwar Eastern Europe and that I had noted that in none of the Communist countries, including his, did the governments seem to pay attention to maintenance. Buildings were left unpainted and unrepaired inside and out, and they quickly fell into utter dilapidation. Why was this, I wanted to know.

It was because, he said, when the Communists won power, the first need of the working class was adequate housing. So they spent all their limited resources on building new apartments for the people and had little left over for proper maintenance of the older, capitalist structures.

But then, he added, it was something else, too: Under Communism, when people didn't own things, they somehow didn't seem to take care of them. And, having delivered this astounding admission, he stroked his beard and relit his cigar.

FROM Communist palaces and workers' hovels to the royal chambers is a small step for the journalist. I had a couple of pleasant, eye-opening meetings with Queen Elizabeth's consort, the Duke of Edinburgh.

The first was in Scotland at a 1968 meeting of the English-Speaking Union. He was listed as honorary chairman of the Union and the chairman of the convention.

I expected the usual royal performance—a reception, a brief speech read from copy prepared by a palace scribe, and farewell. Not with the Duke. He presided at the opening banquet at which I was the speaker. In introducing me he spoke without notes and gave a quite flattering résumé of my career. Later, with just a few notes but no speech, he delivered an excellent presentation on the importance of the Union, followed by a list detailing what he expected from each of the meeting's committees. He announced he would meet with each of them on the following day and by the next night he expected a presentation of their findings and recommendations. Clearly the Duke knew what he was about.

Our next meeting was at Windsor Castle, where he had consented to an interview to discuss the environment in his role as honorary chairman of the World Wildlife Fund. Again he proved to be extremely knowledgeable on the subject of animal conservation. I came away feeling sorry for him and for England. He appeared to be a highly capable, charismatic individual who was denied a chance at real leadership solely because of the traditional constraints on the British monarchy.

Incidentally, our friendship led to a tour of the private quarters at Buckingham Palace. They were somewhat less ornate than I had expected although not without the royal trappings, a motif of crowns throughout the other decorations. The big surprise, however, was the front hall leading out onto the great lawn behind the castle. Tumbled together there were baby carriages, small bicycles and a wagon— just like home.

ONE OF nature's real noblemen is the author James Michener. I had the privilege of accompanying him to Papeete on his first trip there since World War II (his naval tour of duty in that region inspired his first great book, *Tales of the South Pacific*). Jim was a foundling brought up in Pennsylvania with no knowledge of his real family lineage. He became a Quaker and as such lives a nearly spartan existence and gives his fortune away as rapidly as he earns it.

His Japanese-American wife, Mari Sabusawa, was a perfect companion. Primarily to satisfy her love of fine things, they bought expensive art pieces, enjoyed them for a brief while, then donated them to responsible institutions. For the year or two Jim spent researching each of his books, they bought homes in the areas where the stories were set. They had houses on the Chesapeake, in Colorado, Alaska, Hawaii, Florida, Texas and Maine and goodness knows where else.

Our trip was a sheer delight. Jim tried for anonymity, but when he began his inquiries about Bloody Mary and others on whom he had based his characters, the secret was out. Betsy and I and the Micheners were traveling with the Art Buchwalds, the Bob Considines, the San Diego *Union* editor Neil Morgan and his wife and Dick Barkle of Pan Am Airways. We were witness to the joyful greetings the islanders extended to an obviously beloved man who had made them famous.

Jim and I were the only avid sailors in our group, and we slipped away for a couple of days of marvelous sailing around the islands. Perhaps Jim's biggest success was as a Frisbee player. Chip, our son, then aged twelve, was along, as was his Frisbee. He hooked Jim on the sport, and at every airport stop they gave a demonstration for the natives to wild applause and extemporaneous native dances. Jim and Chip came close to being run in by the Singapore gendarmes for obstructing traffic in the airport parking lot with their performance.

A few years ago, when Jim was living on the Eastern Shore of Maryland, having just registered another publishing success with *Chesapeake*, we were sailing in my yawl from St. Michaels to Annapolis when we were hit by a sudden and violent squall. Betsy and Mari Michener went below, Chip and I sailed the boat, and Jim, refusing all of our entreaties to get out of the driving rain, sat stoically by me at the helm.

When we got to Annapolis he looked like the king of the Golden River. He was soaked through. After we dried him off, I chastised him once more for not going below.

"Walter," Jim replied, "last week they made me

an Honorary Admiral of the Chesapeake. What would they think if anyone saw me taking refuge from a little storm like that?"

A FELLOW who didn't care much for the water was Mafia boss Frank Costello. We became friends as producer Les Midgley and I tried, obviously unsuccessfully, to talk him into telling me his life story for television. Costello and I lunched a few times, but he never dropped a hint about the workings of the mob. Some of his peripheral stories were memorable, though.

He liked to talk about his major hobby, the raising of roses. No gardener myself, I was lost in his detailed description of various roses he had grown and that his wife had successfully exhibited at flower shows. He asked me about my hobbies, and I mentioned sailing. It was typical of his curiosity that he pressed for my reasons for liking boats, finally firmly declaring that he had no use for them. In a voice that squeaked from some persistent ailment, he spoke of Frank Erickson, a major bookie:

"You know, Frankie likes boats. He's got this big, long black job out on the Island [a description that fits a Prohibition-era rum runner] and he kept trying to get me on it. I kept telling him I couldn't get away from my business that long, and he told me he had a telephone aboard and there'd be no problem.

"So one day I go out there and we start from Port Jefferson and we're going out somewhere, I don't know, Montauk or somewhere. As soon as I get aboard, I ask Frankie about the telephone and he shows me this thing that I've got to keep holding down a button and only one of us can talk at a time, and all that.

"Well, I used it all day and I want to tell you, I never took such a licking in my life. Every damned bet I made, the whole country climbed on and drove the odds down to nothing. I couldn't make a dime. I didn't find out for years that that telephone of Frankie's was a radio and everybody on Long Island was listening in on my bets."

FRANK SINATRA became a friend over the years, and I was delighted when Don Hewitt, our producer, arranged a long interview with him that would be the centerpiece of a special on his life. The interview was at his home in Palm Springs, and we were getting along famously when Don leaned over and whispered to me not to forget to ask him about the Mafia. My question was simply how he responded to charges that he had Mafia connections.

Sinatra's lips tightened to a tiny line. He gave me a piercing look through narrowing eyes.

"That's it," he said, practically leaping up from his chair and waving his sidekick, Jilly Rizzo, and Hewitt back to his bedroom. I wasn't invited to the private conference, which featured the great voice raised to a level seldom used in the concert hall. The only coherent phrase I picked up was a charge that

Hewitt had promised him that the Mafia question would not be raised.

They worked out a compromise that I never would have thought possible, and Sinatra came back to answer the question. It was not illogical, he said, that he crossed paths and posed for pictures with the many characters who ran the nightclubs and other joints in which he sang. Their affiliations with the mob, if any, he said he had no way of knowing, and he didn't care whether anyone believed that or not.

Sinatra was an interesting man. His public persona, offstage, could be nasty and brutal. His treatment of reporters and photographers was occasionally beyond the pale. But in person he could be as docile and, yes, sweet as a man could be. And it is legend that "if you really want to know what a great friend Frank can be, break your leg." He anonymously cared for untold numbers of show business people and others who were down on their luck. And the slightest special occasion among his friends brought forth a bounty of usually expensive gifts.

ALSO IN OUR pantheon of memorable news stories are those that had a slightly undercover tone to them.

On the basis of some information developed by a U.S. Marine lieutenant colonel, we at CBS found the man who had spied on Pearl Harbor. He was Takeo Yoshikawa, a very successful fuel distributor in northern Japan who, eternally fearful of American retribution, had done his best to fade quietly into civilian life. Eventually Bud Benjamin convinced him that he would be safe if he came as our guest to Honolulu.

He was a slight, mousy, unassuming man who, although a graduate of Japan's Annapolis, cut nothing of a military figure. During the war, in the guise of a member of the consular staff, he had been sent to Honolulu to get what information he could about the American fleet.

Without emotion he told us his story in singsong Japanese. When first in Honolulu, he tried an audacious frontal attack. He tried to get a job at the naval base, but his English was too poor. With no fallback plan and no ideas, he was getting desperate when he visited a Japanese teahouse in the hills behind Honolulu. Lo and behold, down below him, laid out like they were on a game board, were Pearl Harbor and the Navy base.

His visits to the teahouse became part of his daily routine, and he soon had down pat the movement of the fleet units in and out of their berths. He discovered, of course, that the fleet left on Monday mornings for maneuvers and returned on Friday evening for a weekend off. All that remained for him to do was simply to inform Tokyo by diplomatic code that the big ships were all there for the weekend of December 6 and 7.

He recited his story for our cameraman, Wade Bingham, from the site of the teahouse and from a boat we hired that took us among the wrecks still lying as memorials on the harbor's bottom. Eerily he identified each hulk without help from our guide.

We were fully aware that feelings still ran high in Hawaii about the Japanese attack, and we were as secretive as we could manage about Yoshikawa's presence there. We felt that he, and we, would be safest if he were in a small Japanese hotel, and our plan was to be there early every morning and practically tuck him in at night. What we had not counted on was Yoshikawa's thirst for the strong stuff.

Although we thought we had seen him to bed, his morning headaches and certain details he let drop about the previous night shook our confidence. While he was enjoying his stay in Honolulu immensely, we were anxious to get him back on the plane for Tokyo. As we deposited him at his hotel that last evening, he announced that he had decided to stay on for a few days. We suggested that this was a poor idea, but went off to discuss it among ourselves. When we got to our hotel, we were greeted by the evening newspaper with a banner headline: "Pearl Harbor Spy in Honolulu." The story was accurate as far as it went. A CBS crew had brought the spy back, had secreted him away and was shooting his story. Speed was of the essence. We had to get our guest out of Hawaii on the first plane. Benjamin booked him on a Pan Am flight leaving in a couple of hours, and took off for his hotel. He was on a stool, slumped over the bar, already in an advanced state of inebriation. He loudly resisted Bud's entreaties while members of our crew packed his belongings. They physically loaded him into a cab for the airport.

There was a new problem. Pan Am refused to take

him. There was a Japan Air flight soon thereafter. Bud was his most persuasive in pointing out to the Japanese manager that their citizen was in grave danger of imminent imprisonment or worse if the aroused citizenry got to him. The manager reluctantly agreed to take him, and we were able to secrete him in their baggage area until Yoshikawa, small for a man but huge for a duffel, was loaded aboard. We got out of town the next morning, with the Honolulu press close on our tails. The papers were not kind to CBS for having spirited the spy among them and letting him go again.

SPEAKING of being undercover, an extreme example was a visit to the city under the ice above the Arctic Circle, Camp Century, a hundred miles above Thule on the Greenland ice cap. This expensive military exercise was to see if the Army could build facilities in which American troops could live through the bitter Arctic winter to man a defense line against any Soviet incursions across the Pole, by missiles or troops.

The habitat was to be a city, complete with barracks, dining and recreation areas, stores and all the support facilities, and powered by atomic energy. It was literally being carved out of the ice cap. Great bulldozers were scraping streets twenty feet deep in the ice. They would be covered by corrugated metal and covered again by the ice.

Getting there was half the fun. Powered snow

sleds made the trek from Thule in a daylong trip, made longer by the necessity of feeling one's way to avoid tumbling into an ice rift, virtually invisible on the glaring white plain. The timing of our arrival was such that none of the military had moved in yet and we were the first occupants of the first city ever constructed under the polar ice cap. The Guinness people haven't called me yet about including this amazing feat in their record book.

Our home was a trailer equipped with bunks. Not too uncomfortable, except that I suffered an attack of claustrophobia—only my second ever. I attribute it to the warning we received before we were left alone there. Under no circumstances were we to leave the tunnel. The danger was so-called white-outs, about which we had been warned earlier in the day. Between each facility on the base (except to the new tunnel) wires had been run with small flags on them to guide the personnel. When the snows come and blot out the sun, the horizon disappears in a sea of white and human beings can suffer such total dis-orientation that they lose their sense of balance and cannot stand up. Immobility in the snow and ice of the Arctic can in short order become fatal.

It is one thing to remember the precaution during normal daytime activities, but at night, when you are stuck in a tunnel under the ice, the danger above hangs there like a great red flag between you and a chance of getting a breath of fresh air aboveground. A prescription for claustrophobia.

My other bout with claustrophobia was during a

dive in a two-man submarine to an underwater habitat in the Bahamas. In that case, it was a sudden drop in the sub's oxygen supply that affected me. I was talking with Jon Lindbergh, a veteran diver, when I suddenly felt that I had to get out of there. As unmanly as it seems, I wanted to scream. Jon recognized the symptoms and turned up the oxygen, and instantly I was fine.

I have wondered since if it isn't lack of oxygen that feeds claustrophobia—the closed room, the crowded elevator, the tunnel, a city under the ice. At any rate, it was a long night there in Greenland.

An interesting sidelight at Camp Century was the water supply. It came from a pair of pipes sunk into the ice cap. Fresh water was poured down one pipe. It was warm enough to thaw a small pool from which other water was piped back up. This perpetual motion continued as the pipes were sunk a little deeper each day.

Scientists were keeping a close watch on the new water. Since the below-freezing cold is capable of keeping germs in suspended animation for centuries, they checked for all the germs known to have caused the great plagues among mankind in case they might have been carried by strong winds to the far north. They were just about to order the engineers to start a new well. Their problem was that the present pipes had reached a level of ice laid down at about the time of the death of the mammoths a few million years ago. And since they didn't know what had killed those great beasts, they wouldn't know what deadly bacteria to look for in the new ice melt.

Men are brought together in their ad hoc fraternities by strange combinations of circumstances. The Arctic workers were of a type. They went from job to job in the Arctic or the Antarctic, wherever the ice was thick and perennial. Time spent in more livable climates, to their minds, was simply wasted, time out of their lives. Through their friendly conversation, across lit pipes and steins of beer, they seemed to have wiped from their memories whatever life they had led "in the outside world." They clearly enjoyed the isolation of their existence, a tight friendship with a few men of similar personalities, a small band of adventurers.

ONE OF OUR exciting adventures was in pursuit of a news maker on the lam: Daniel Ellsberg, the man who stole the Pentagon Papers. He had worked on the Pentagon's detailed history of our involvement in the Vietnam War. He became so incensed over what he considered the dirty secrets therein that he made off with the hundreds of pages of papers and offered them to the news media. I wanted an interview, but the FBI was hot on his trail and Ellsberg was somewhere in hiding.

It happened that Ellsberg was married to Patricia Marx, the daughter of a close friend of mine, David Marx, a prominent toy manufacturer. The FBI was hot on Ellsberg's trail, and they were in hiding. I called David and asked him to ask her, when she next contacted him, to get Ellsberg to give us an interview.

I was doing a story at Lake Placid at the time, and I told Marx that if she couldn't reach me, she should phone our CBS News vice president Gordon Manning. That night Manning got a call from a mysterious voice who identified himself as "Mr. Boston." He said the interview might be possible and, to discuss details, Manning should meet him in the dark of the next night at the Old Library Building on the Harvard campus.

Manning, a longtime UPI and *Newsweek* correspondent, was one of the sharpest, most aggressive newsmen I had ever known. This was just his meat. The next night he was standing outside the library when a figure jumped from the bushes.

"Are you Manning?" the apparition demanded. Manning identified himself.

"I'm Mr. Boston."

Mr. Boston turned out to be a college-aged youth who clearly was enjoying to the hilt his role in the conspiracy. He drove Manning along a tortuous roundabout route to a cottage in Cambridge. The tour was presumably meant to throw off any federal agents on the trail, and to prevent Manning from identifying the location of the house.

Inside were Ellsberg, Pat, three young members of the conspiracy—and piles of brown paper packages wrapped with string. They were the Pentagon Papers.

Ellsberg immediately demanded that we pledge to read all the thousands of pages of the papers over the network; otherwise there would be no interview.

That was clearly impossible. I'd still be reading those papers today.

Manning stalled on making the pledge but got Ellsberg's agreement to the interview. Thus began another merry-go-round of mysterious phone calls from anonymous conspirators. It was finally arranged that I should fly the next day to Cambridge. I was to go at a certain hour to the lobby of the Commander Hotel. A young man would meet me and escort me to Ellsberg. If I was followed at any point, I was to break off the attempt and return to New York.

There were many amateurish aspects to the plot, but the most obvious never occurred to any of us. It turned out to be pretty difficult for the anchorperson of the most popular television news broadcast in America to go incognito.

I sauntered into the Commander lobby, carefully studied a couple of people sitting there, and waited to be approached. Nobody came. The lobby is not a particularly large one, and loitering strangers are rather obvious. I was contemplating the next move when a fellow came over and introduced himself as the hotel manager and, with a politeness bordering on servility, asked how, Mr. Cronkite, he could be of help.

My cover blown, I had no idea how he could be of help. I lamely said I was looking for the telephone. He offered the phone in his office. No, no, I needed privacy. In that case, there was a booth on the basement floor next to the men's room. I could miss my rendezvous if I was buried in the basement, and if I stayed upstairs more explanations might be required. Obviously time was running out.

As I came back upstairs from a brief visit to the telephone, there was a young man halfway up the walk to the hotel's front door shooting quick looks in every direction. He spotted me and walked up toward the door, then turned abruptly and walked back toward the street. I judged he meant that I should follow. At the curb he paused just long enough for a broken-down sedan to swing alongside, and he invited me in.

He and the driver immediately apologized for being late but said they had had to evade a car they were certain was following them. The rest of their conversation was larded with what I gathered, and I think they believed, was the language of the archconspirator.

We did the circuitous routing bit, and when we reached our destination the conspirators drove three times around the block checking for "bogeymen"— that is, I assumed, federal agents. Not uncovering any, we finally parked and hustled up to and through the front door of a nondescript frame house in a middle-class residential area of Cambridge. Ellsberg was moving to a different location each night.

Inside were Manning; our producer, Stanhope Gould; two CBS film crews; and Daniel Ellsberg, certainly at that moment the FBI's target number one. And the cache of Pentagon Papers. Standing guard were three or four young men of college age with looks as severe as they could muster, looks meant to be threatening but falling somewhat short.

Ellsberg was sharp-featured and of moderate height with only a slight strain in his voice indicating any tension. It turned out that he and Manning were in the midst of a contretemps. He wanted that pledge that we would read the entire file of Pentagon Papers on the air. Manning had promised that we would do justice to their true portent with the specials we would do. A master negotiator, he carried the day and Ellsberg gave us the interview. Of course, Ellsberg justified taking the papers and expressed his feeling that his own future was unimportant compared to the necessity for the people to know the depth of what he considered the conspiracy to commit war in Vietnam. He felt that these startling revelations would surely bring the war to an end.

He was spirited away from the cottage before we were permitted to leave. We dashed to our Boston station and put our scoop on the air that evening. The FBI was surprisingly complacent about our escapade. When Manning and I refused to give details or locate the house for them, they dropped their inquiry. If Ellsberg had not surrendered a few days later, thus saving the FBI further embarrassment, I'm not certain that our future would have been as bright.

Manning in his everyday life never quit thinking of ways to beat the opposition. He scribbled notes to himself on matchbooks, paper napkins, the inside of cigarette packages, all to be relayed the next day to his staff, who referred to these suggestions as "Gor-dograms." His intensity was masked by an extraor-dinary wit. When he had to return hurriedly from a trip to India, he could only get a coach seat on Air India. A concerned staff greeted him in London. The trip wasn't so bad, he reported. But how was the food?

"Oh, the coach food isn't bad on Air India," he answered. "They give you an alms bowl and send you up to first class."

Chapter 15

I visualize the TV industry as a huge building dedicated to the business of entertainment. Journalism is in an attached annex next door. In that door between them is a huge vacuum that runs twenty-four hours a day threatening to suck into the larger building anyone who comes too close.

The pressure has become more subtle, but no less real, in recent years. In the pioneer days, it was blatant.

In 1954 CBS decided to produce "The Morning Show," a two-hour variety presentation that would run from seven to nine in most markets. The format had been introduced a year earlier by NBC with its "Today" show, featuring one of television's early talk show stars, Dave Garroway. In CBS's executive suites there was some tension between the entertainment side and the news division concerning who should produce the program. The news department won and I was its selection to play host.

My role, it turned out, was to duplicate as nearly as possible the Garroway performance, including the delivery of an occasional commercial. CBS, as it should have, strictly forbade any connection between news personnel and advertisers. Doing commercials for a newsman was considered the ultimate violation of journalistic principle.

But now CBS, in making a grand exception for "The Morning Show," was endorsing this heresy. It may have been part of the pioneering spirit, following new wagon tracks just to see where they would lead, but if there was any extended discussion of this change in the upper reaches of CBS, I was unaware of them. It simply was accepted that I would improvise an occasional commercial, again imitating Garroway by doing them in my own, it was hoped, inimitable fashion, based on a story line furnished by the sponsoring ad agency.

In its final form, our program would consist of now almost routine ingredients. Each half hour we would have a news portion, a weather forecast, a feature story that frequently would come from outside the studio, and a musical presentation by the Bil Baird Puppets. While I was the master-of-ceremonies headliner, my role consisted solely of interviewing the newsworthy guests and mulling over the news of the day with a puppet lion, Charlemagne.

Our show received reasonably satisfactory reviews, in which none of the critics reacted as I had expected to my doing commercials. This may have been partly because my national reputation as a newsman was still based primarily on the coverage not quite two years before of the presidential conventions and elections. It may also have been because the number of commercials I actually did was so limited as to fade quickly even from a critic's memory.

The first sponsor was the R. J. Reynolds Tobacco Company, which bought time to introduce a new cigarette, Winston. I spent some time in their boardroom meeting the executives and even more time in the ad agency's conference room being briefed on the great assets and selling points of the product. Presumably I would become so immersed in the facts that my ad-lib commercials would almost be rote—but sounding, of course, as if they came from the heart.

The day for my first commercial came shortly after our show's debut. I lit up a Winston, grinned with feigned satisfaction and delivered the ad campaign's slogan: "Ah, Winston tastes good as a cigarette should."

The program was barely over when I was hustled into a meeting with embarrassed CBS brass and unhappy ad agency and tobacco company people. You would have thought that I had set off a nuclear weapon that had wiped out all of central Manhattan and more particularly, as far as they were concerned, the entire broadcasting, tobacco and advertising industries.

The slogan, they informed me, was "Winston tastes good *like* a cigarette should." I pointed out that this was not grammatical. There was a moment of silence that I erroneously interpreted as a sign of chagrin on the part of those who had perpetrated this faulty construction. As the reaction came crashing down around my head, I realized that the moment of silence was more like an advance memorial to my early departure as the Winston spokesman on "The Morning Show."

It was also noted by the executives that I didn't seem to inhale as I "enjoyed" my on-air Winston. I was forced to admit that I didn't regularly smoke cigarettes. They looked at me with genuine puzzlement, as if I were some strange species discovered by their powerful microscopes. It didn't help the cause, if there had been any cause left. The cautious CBS sales department thereafter steered advertising accounts away from me, and the problem of my doing commercials didn't arise again.

Actually, we had a darned good show. Our producer was Paul Levitan, an energetic young fellow who defied producer stereotype by actually wanting to be liked. He succeeded more often than he failed. He was the son of a violinist in the CBS staff orchestra, and had worked his way up from the then popular entry-level job of studio page. Paul had a keen imagination, a sense of showmanship, and a fearless willingness to attempt the innovative in television broadcasting. He managed to drag television cable to places it had never been, and in order to reach those locations to which cable would not stretch, he improvised a combination of radio and long-lens photography.

By that technique, we brought the public the voice of Ezio Pinza from the top of the Statue of Liberty on the Fourth of July. Celebrities still traveled by luxury liner, and we regularly beat the opposition by hours in getting the interviews with them. We took a tug alongside the incoming ship. From its deck our long-lens cameras photographed the celebrities while I interviewed them by radio. Using a similar technique we traveled alongside on the Hudson River as the inventor of water skis gave us the first televised demonstration of his creation.

Paul had an inability to understand that few people were as all-consumed by their work as he— that 3 a.m. phone calls to their homes didn't inspire the same excitement he felt. This was the basis of an incident that led him close to the lyncher's noose.

It was seven years after "The Morning Show," and Paul was producer of our coverage of John Kennedy's inauguration as President. One of Washington's worst blizzards struck on the inaugural eve. Our crews worked through the night salvaging the cables they had laid earlier along the Pennsylvania Avenue parade route, installing and protecting new ones where needed and building shelters at our reporters' anchor positions. Sometime in the middle of the night an urgent message from Paul went out ordering all CBS personnel to report to our headquarters hotel at 5:30 a.m.

Bleary-eyed correspondents who had covered the previous night's festivities and those technical crews who had worked through the night to assure our coverage despite the blizzard stumbled into the conference hall. Paul's first words from the lectern were "This meeting doesn't concern most of you." Paul was probably saved by the fact that the mob was too fatigued to get out the rope.

Paul was also not particularly well-read. This led to some unconscionable teasing in our "Morning Show" production meetings, particularly by Jack McGiffert, a gifted young writer. Paul had developed a method of keeping track of the various elements for all forthcoming shows. On a wall were marked the various show dates and times, and three-by-five index cards were posted when the time slots were filled. Every morning Paul would go down each column and ask for more information on newly posted elements.

One morning he came upon an entry: "Great Auk." Whose idea was it, and what was it?

McGiffert answered: "It's an animal act, Paul."

"Great, great. We haven't had an animal act for quite a while. What does this animal look like? What does it do?"

As the rest of us began the difficult task of suppressing our laughter, McGiffert came right back with "Well, Paul, this is a sort of bird, but we do have a little problem—we're still trying to find one."

Paul went off on a familiar tirade. We were not to put things on the board until we had absolutely nailed down their appearance, date and time, as the board indicated.

And there was the day that Paul found on the board "Judge Joseph F. Crater." This again turned out to have been a McGiffert inspiration. Crater was the New York Supreme Court judge who had disappeared in August of 1930, never to be heard from again.

To Paul's demands for more information, McGiffert explained: "He is, or was, a judge in New York."

"Is it an interview?" Paul queried.

"It ought to be a terrific one," Jack persisted.

"And what's he going to talk about?"

"His travels," said Jack.

"And where's he been?"

"Well, we don't know. One thing, Paul, not only are we not sure where he's been, but this may be a remote."

"Dammit, McGiffert," Paul yelled, "I want to emphasize this again for all of you: Do not put remotes on that board until you clear it with me first. I've got to know where it's going to be. I've got to know what the costs of the lines are going to be before you put it on the board. Talk those over with me first. Now, McGiffert, where is this going to come from?"

"I'm not sure . . . ," Jack began.

"Jack, that's impossible. How can I plan something you don't even know where it is?" And the contretemps ended with another skin on McGiffert's belt.

Our "Morning Show" produced by the news department lived an uncomfortable life as the dominant entertainment department sniped at our show and pleaded in the executive suites for the airtime to be returned to them. We were aware, of course, of the pressure, but there was no hint of any imminent changes when, in our fifth month, they executed their coup and I learned what it was like to be in the entertainment business.

I was at my host's position preparing for the morning broadcast when Charles Collingwood arrived at his news desk in the studio. He looked extremely pale, and actually ill. To my worried inquiry, he insisted he was able to go on air but said he had something to tell me afterward.

When the show was over he came to my desk and handed me a copy of a Broadway gossip column that would be distributed that morning to various clients of the Hearst feature syndicate. It was by Jack O'Brian, a McCarthyite Red-baiter who had the distinction, as far as we at CBS News were concerned, of having hounded to a suicide's grave one of our most distinguished reporters, Don Hollenbeck. He had interpreted Hollenbeck's liberalism as pro-Communism.

The column's lead item: "CBS has finally gotten wise and is replacing Walter Cronkite on 'The Morning Show' with that brilliant young West Coast comic, Jack Paar." I had never heard of Paar, but I soon learned that he was a protégé of Jack Benny's and that Benny had urged Bill Paley to find him a place on the network. By the time I got back to my office above the studio, my secretary was already amassing a list of calls from radio and TV reporters and columnists. Levitan was as dumbfounded as I, and I was about to learn that the networks instantly confer pariah status on any talent to whom the emperor has given a thumbs-down.

Not one single CBS executive, all so friendly and accessible the day before, was available to take my calls. One was fishing in Florida; another was at our West Coast offices and couldn't be reached; a third was lost somewhere in the Maine north woods. To this day I think as a newsman, not as a celebrity, thinks, and I am constitutionally unable to refuse to respond to legitimate inquiries by my press colleagues. It seemed to me that they had a legitimate reason to seek my response to O'Brian. But I had nothing to tell them except how ignorant I was of the situation, an answer that might appear suspect, at least, but would certainly make CBS look bad.

I called Mike Foster, the exceedingly able, straight-shooting head of CBS publicity. I told him that I was going to talk to the press at noon and that I planned to tell them just what I knew. If CBS wanted to give me some information that might make the network brass look a little better, I would be glad to relay it, but it was up to Foster to get one of them to talk to me.

Within a few minutes one of the executives was on the phone with a lame explanation that the program department would be taking over the broadcast, that it would be more of an entertainment than an informational program, that the Paar deal was not wrapped up, that they had intended to tell me right away, ad nauseam.

It was clear that they had been caught unprepared by O'Brian's premature item. It turned out it was all true, but networks and broadcast stations generally, I also learned, like to fire on-air personalities without

giving them a chance to appear again on their programs. They fear that disgruntled performers will
use their waning airtime to castigate their em-
ployers—probably not an unreasonable concern.

In this case, we dragged on for another week or so
until Jack took the reins of "The Morning Show"
and the office next to mine. Not many days after that
transition, I found among my fan mail a postcard
from Indianapolis. It said: "Tell CBS that they have
made a terrible mistake putting Jack Paar on instead
of Walter Cronkite. Mr. Cronkite is the perfect personality for a morning broadcast. Jack's comedy
would be better on a nighttime program."

The signature was that of Jack's mother, Lillian. I
took it next door to Jack's office, only to discover
that his sense of humor had certain limits. He didn't
think the card was particularly amusing.

All that endures of my connection with CBS's
first morning show in the memories of television
critics old enough to have such memories, or among
those to whom the lore has been passed down, is that
I conversed with a puppet. This is meant to be a
scathing observation, suggesting a rivalry, perhaps,
with Shari Lewis or Edgar Bergen, something
undignified for a newsman. What the puppet and I
talked about has been forgotten.

Actually, Bil Baird, as Charlemagne, was a witty,
erudite and acerbic critic of the daily scene. In our
two- to three-minute spot, I led Charlemagne into a
totally ad-lib discussion of the day's news that was
remarkable for its depth. A puppet can render opin-

ions on people and things that a human commentator would not feel free to utter. It was one of the highlights of our show, and I was, and am, proud of it.

I was to make another appearance on "The Morning Show." The entertainment people couldn't seem to get it quite right either. Up to this writing, although it has long since been back in the news department's hands, it still hasn't climbed out of last place in the ratings. As a matter of fact, its best competitive rating against NBC's "Today" was in those first five months of its existence, back in 1954, forty-two years ago.

After Paar couldn't make it work, they went through a series of hosts. Will Rogers, Jr., had a brief turn, and country singer Jimmy Dean an even briefer one. And they came up with a young man who apparently had been a big hit on some local shows back in his home state of North Carolina: Dick Van Dyke.

He exuded a lovely naïve charm from every pore, was graceful as a gazelle in a sort of home-choreographed *pas d'un*, and could sing. All this, and he could tell some funny stories. But, having been given this big chance so early in his career, he was clearly almost frozen with fright at the prospect of having to carry this two-hour show alone.

The powers figured he needed someone to talk to—to "play against," as they put it. Would I perhaps come back as the news presenter and also do a little ad-lib joking with Van Dyke? I was reluctant to get up at that hour of the morning again for any pro-

gram, and particularly to play straight man to a personality filling a job from which I had been so
recently fired. But reluctance, as so frequently happens, faded before gold.

Dick and I got along fine, although the sparkling
repartee that the front office expected never quite
developed. We had our cordial little exchanges, but
the extemporaneous dialogue was rather lame. Perhaps my openings were a little heavy, but Dick's
responses didn't really take us anywhere either.

The show had been on only a few weeks when
one day Dick and I searched for a few laughs by
recounting our experiences of getting up at such an
early hour. Something prompted Dick to say:
"Walter, I think I'll live and die on 'The Morning
Show.' "

"Dick," I noted, "maybe you already have."

Dick laughed, and danced away from my desk to
make the next introduction. The show ended, and as
we left the studio, he commented on what a good
show he thought we had done that day.

Scarcely was I back in my office when I found on
my phone Louis Cowan, CBS president of CBS
Television, whose responsibilities, besides "The Morning Show," included our highly successful quiz shows,
such as "The $64,000 Question." He himself would
later be a scapegoat, unfairly forced out of CBS
during the investigation of the quiz show scandals.

"What in the world did you say to Dick Van Dyke
this morning?" he demanded. "Charlie Andrews [the
show's producer] just called to say Van Dyke wants

to quit, that he is very upset, that he is sick over your comment."

I didn't have the slightest idea what he could be referring to, and he didn't seem too clear on it either. He called time-out while he got back to Andrews. It turned out that it was the "live and die" comment. Cowan called an immediate emergency meeting in his office to face this terrible crisis.

Andrews gave us a graphic description of Van Dyke's angst. It sounded as though he was so distraught as to perhaps be facing imminent hospitalization. Cowan, a magisterial figure highly respected as an intellectual among the entertainment pygmies, looked over his fingers clasped in prayer and pronounced the obvious impossibility of my continuing on the program with Van Dyke. He promised, however, to pay me for my full contract. I liked Van Dyke and, considering our parting just an hour or two before, could not understand this deep hurt I had allegedly inflicted. But I had no incentive to fight. I definitely did not care for the hours or the job and was happy to be out of it.

So I called for a lunch with my friend and agent, Tuck Stix, and we had our usual table in the center of Louis & Armand's. I had hardly completed giving Stix the morning play-by-play when Van Dyke appeared. He came directly to the table with a big greeting, an enthusiastic comment about how well he thought we were working together, and another reference to how much he liked the show that morning. And he had no complaints about that morning's show? None at all, he said, smiling, and moved along to his table.

This puzzle was solved after a little one-man sleuthing and some keen deduction. It turned out that just the day before, Andrews and others had decided they were going to let Van Dyke go. Of course, they being loyal to the mores of television, he hadn't been told. When Andrews heard my faux insult on the next morning's show, he jumped to the conclusion that I knew of the decision. Fearing that I might indulge in other banter dealing with the secret decision and perhaps might even inform Van Dyke, he took a typically show business route out—he eliminated me.

For the ultimate news entrapment in television entertainment we can go to 1957, when Mike Todd produced an extravaganza at Madison Square Garden, *Around the World in 90 Minutes*. He proclaimed that it would be the circus spectacular of all time, with every star that could be spared from Hollywood's soundstages performing in featured acts. The CBS entertainment department agreed to carry it as a major special and, for some unknown reason, as a "news" event. So they requested and got from the news department a news anchor—me.

I began assembling my research on the main events: Where would they be getting the ballyhooed one hundred elephants from? What exactly was the regular role of the mounted contingent of the Texas Rangers that was coming? What were the acts in which the movie stars would be featured? The Todd office kept assuring me that the material was on the way. Somehow it always seemed to get lost on the four-block trek to my office.

I finally solicited the help of our CBS News president, Sig Mickelson. He went to the head of CBS Television, Merle Jones. Jones was surprised that I'd be going to this trouble but promised to help. I got nothing except some prepared copy introducing the acts—great for a ringmaster but hardly the stuff of a news report.

To the desperate appeals of a frantic newsman, the Todd production office suggested that I come along to a meeting where I could get all the information I needed. I was there that night for the great eye-opener. Todd presided in a small smoke-filled room with apparently all his associates attending—the orchestra leaders, the animal man, the costume lady. The meeting opened and closed with Todd asking if anybody had any problems. Everybody did, and they all compounded my big dilemma of reporting this great spectacular.

The animal man had timed out the repainting of the elephants for the grand opening and they couldn't get them repainted and back out as fast as they'd hoped. Before my very eyes, the one hundred elephants faded to a dozen or so, each of which, after making its circuit of the arena, would return backstage to be redecorated as another elephant and led back to take its part in the "endless" parade.

There was some trouble with one of the principal elements of the Texas Rangers. A New Jersey riding club that was taking part hadn't yet received their "genuine" Texas Rangers costumes, and another of the "Ranger" groups from Connecticut needed another horse van.

The "acts" by the Hollywood contingent, not too surprisingly, consisted mostly of riding those elephants in the grand entry and grand finale.

In the midst of these revelations, Mike Todd's recently betrothed, Elizabeth Taylor, came to the door. She waved off invitations to enter and stood leaning in the doorway for some time as Todd dismissed one problem after another as insignificant. The moment arrived when she drew her own curtain on the proceedings. She flipped away her cigarette, loudly proclaimed her critical opinion with a four-letter word at that point still not accepted in society and stormed away. Todd paid as little attention to her departure as he did to what I, by that time, considered the imminent disaster at the Garden.

I reported my concerns to Mickelson. He made a useless effort to get his news department and me extricated from the production. Between us we agreed that I would not make a great exposé out of the broadcast, but would discard the purple prose of the show's "writers" and repeat none of the extravagant show business falsehoods. So the number of elephants was never mentioned and the Texas Rangers were identified as "simulated." I thought I'd hear from Todd, but there was nothing, and I can only assume he never saw the television version.

In these beginning "golden days" of television

and of television news, the rules were bent as we found our way. Even the exalted Ed Murrow did an entertainment program called "Person to Person" in which the bored Murrow embarrassedly read through a series of questions to invite prepared answers from celebrity guests. Murrow even appeared in a full-page ad in *Life* magazine endorsing Colombian coffee.

In those early days I was invited to appear as myself on a couple of quiz shows, to which the news department didn't object. I was a panelist on a show called "It's News to Me" in which contestants vied to identify items, pictures, songs and whatnot from news stories of the week.

On another I was the "expert" who judged the accuracy of answers on a rather intellectual program called "Two for the Money." An erudite Rutgers University professor had preceded me in that role, and I don't know why in the world the producer, Mark Goodson, thought I could do the job. They found they had to wire me with a secret earpiece through which some real experts backstage could relay to me the required information.

They didn't have to fire me; the show folded. I was prepared. By then I had found that the fired in television are not infrequently the fall guys for the guilty. For instance, the 1964 political conventions. Our team had six conventions under our belt by the time preparations were under way to go to San Francisco for the Republican conclave that summer. We intended to set up our anchor studio, control room, remote control with the floor correspondents and so on in the usual way, using a procedure we had perfected.

I flew out to San Francisco three days before the opening gavel and was met at the airport by Fred Friendly, Murrow's talented television producer who a few months before had been named the new president of CBS News. On the way to the hotel he said we would be stopping at the convention hall so he could show me our anchor setup. There had been a few "improvements" he was sure I would like. When he opened the door to my new booth, I was appalled. There were none of the facilities with which I was used to working.

The anchor desk sat in solitary splendor at one side of the room. There was a second chair there for a commentator who he hoped would be Eric Sevareid. There were virtually no communications to the desk at all. The anchor desk assistant—who in the past was always within arm's reach to pass notes from the control room, information from our correspondents, wire service copy—would be across the room with no means of reaching me except during commercials.

Any cues I needed, Friendly confidently explained, would be given by the floor director or through my headphones directly from the producer in the control room. We had learned in the previous conventions that control room cues through headphones invariably led to almost constant chatter from that location. The babble blocked out the proceedings on the floor upon which I depended to guide our coverage.

Friendly presented all this change as another great advance in convention coverage. I called it retrogression and was outraged that it had been set up without any consultation with me about my needs. Clearly it was meant to eliminate them. During the previous conventions it became obvious that I was the only person in the chain of command who had a sense of the running story from both the convention floor and the headquarters of various candidates and special interests.

It was not intended that way and it wasn't my choice. The problem was the chaos in the control room. Producers were in constant shouting conferences with correspondents and remote producers and cameramen on what stories were developing elsewhere, the movement of candidates, the next camera shots they should take, how much of a coming speech they should use. All of that created such confusion that no one in the control room had a coherent idea of the convention's running story. Sitting in my splendid isolation at the anchor desk, I did. I listened to the speeches from the podium and the offerings of our floor reporters. I also had access to important items and leads culled from the news wires by an assistant at my elbow.

As a matter of fact, it was this that gave me a reputation I have always felt, with some unhappiness, was undeserved. Colleagues called me a "lens hog," claiming that I was reluctant to share airtime with them. It is true that on occasion I advised the control room not to take the offerings of correspondents on the floor or at remote locations, but these judgments were based solely on the fact that I knew and they did not that their reports at that moment would disrupt the flow of the running story. I thought that a smooth report on the convention proceedings was our principal task.

I believe that Friendly, in discarding the previous plans for anchor coverage, was essentially trying to regain control of the broadcast for the producer—himself—in the control room. By the time he sprang the new setup on me, it was too late to change it.

Our convention coverage was the shambles I expected it to be, and I certainly contributed by sinking into a slough of hopelessness as the week developed.

It seemed appropriate that I got the word that I was fired from the upcoming Democratic convention while vacationing with my family at Disneyland. Friendly never was one to duck his responsibilities, and I give him credit for making the effort to fly to Anaheim to give me the word in person. To a calliope background, he imparted the bad news. And he urged that I stay on as anchor of the "Evening News," although we both knew that if he developed successful anchors at the convention, the temptation would be almost irresistible to try them on the daily broadcast.

The Democratic convention was in Atlantic City. Friendly was surprised when I said I intended to broadcast the "Evening News" from there. He agreed, although his assumption had apparently been that I would stay in New York, quietly licking my wounds.

The first morning of the convention I found myself in my hotel elevator descending only with Bob Kintner, the head of NBC News. By the time we reached the ground floor, we had hatched a scheme. The lobby, as we knew it would be, was crowded with politicians, newspeople and the usual convention hangers-on. We walked through the lobby with arms linked, breaking our intense conversation only briefly to acknowledge the greetings of our friends. Our conversation was by Lewis Carroll—absolute gobbledygook—but by the time I reached the convention hall, three blocks down the boardwalk, Don Hewitt, our producer, ran out of the hall shouting: "What's this about your going to NBC?"

Kintner and I had planted a delicious rumor.

Inside the hall, a television crew from a local station buttonholed me. They turned on their lights. Now, one crew's lights attract other crews like moths to the flame. In short order there were at least four crews around me, pummeling me with questions about my feelings, my attitude toward CBS, and all the usual meaningless junk.

And along came a fifth crew, shouting and shoving its way to the front of the crowd. Its efforts came to a sudden halt as it broke into the front row. It was from CBS News, which obviously had no interest in broadcasting my feelings about not being in the anchor booth.

Under management's confused direction, the new anchor team of Roger Mudd and Bob Trout, two of the most skilled political correspondents in the business, had no better chance than I, and by 1968 I was back in the convention anchor job to stay until my retirement from the "Evening News" in 1981.

During those years some of my colleagues complained in print, although anonymously, that I "played it safe" and carefully avoided taking positions on the major issues of our time. They admired Murrow and Sevareid for a very good reason— strong editorialists who called the shots as they saw them. They were powerful and important commentators who made a major difference in the great national dialogues. But neither chose to assume the stewardship of a daily television news program.

I saw my job as quite different from theirs. They were the editorial page; I was the front page. My job was to try as hard as I could to remove every trace of opinion from the broadcast. If people knew how I felt on an issue, or thought they could discern from me some ideological position of the Columbia Broadcasting System, I had failed in my mission.

I also had a daily five-minute radio commentary for most of the years that I was the CBS television anchor. With an assist from two excellent writers, Bob Blum and Dale Minor, I did a hard-hitting opinion piece every day. When Friendly became CBS News president, he suggested that I do a similar commentary at the end of each "Evening News" telecast.

I turned him down. I argued that the overlap between my radio and television audiences was probably small, and most important was preserving the reality and appearance of objectivity for the larger television audience. While the commentary would be clearly labeled as such, we could not expect the audience to be so sophisticated as to believe what we knew to be the fact: A skilled journalist is perfectly capable of laying prejudices aside and writing a straight report at one moment and at the next moment putting on the other hat and writing a strong editorial on the same subject. I believed the public would have branded the whole broadcast as biased based on the commentary that ended it. So we didn't do it.

My departure from the "Evening News" has been widely misinterpreted to suggest that I was forced out by Dan Rather. An understandable interpretation, given the general principles that guide network mores, but simply not true.

I had told CBS management at least two years in advance that I intended to step down from the "Evening News" when I turned sixty-five—in November 1981. They didn't hear me; they couldn't believe that any person in good health would voluntarily leave a job of such international prominence as the one I held. They didn't even pay attention when my intentions were revealed in an interview in *TV Guide*.

Just before we entered the fateful year of 1981, I reminded our then CBS News president, Bill Leonard, of my intentions. I did not know that at that very moment Dan Rather's agent was playing a high-stakes game with ABC and CBS for his client's services. CBS, I gather, had to face the dilemma of figuring out how they could justify the huge salary Dan was demanding until the time I stepped down. Until Leonard remembered our conversation.

He called me in and wanted to know if I was serious. I told him I was. He offered to try to talk me out of it. No way. Whereupon he revealed that if negotiations were successful, Dan would be in the wings. This, I only learned later, was accepted by CBS management only after Charles Kuralt fled from Leonard's efforts to enlist him for the job. Similar exertions by Leonard to put together a dual anchor team of Roger Mudd and Rather fell flat, with neither man interested in sharing the big chair.

By mutual agreement, my retirement schedule was slightly accelerated to bridge my normal summer hiatus, and CBS, having announced its deal, was anxious to get started building up the new man. So I stepped down in March instead of November.

That summer hiatus, by the way, may have kept me from entering the history books as the first million-dollar anchor person. With my remuneration already climbing to what I considered a nearly obscene number, I had entered our contract negotiations in 1973 with a single demand. I did not want a raise, but I wanted three months off a year. This sort of absence by a newsperson was unprecedented, and the negotiations were long and arduous until we reached agreement.

The contract sent my friend Johnny Carson and me off on a jocund race to see how much time we could take off and still hold our jobs. He won.

If I had played for different results, I just might have made that million-dollar figure before ABC hired Barbara Walters to coanchor its evening news as the networks' first female in that role. There was intense press interest in that announcement and, naturally, I was polled about whether I thought Barbara was worth it. My answer: "Compared to what? Compared to a high school teacher? Of course not—no way. But compared to a rock-and-roll singer with whom she will share ABC's airwaves, of course she is—every penny of it and a lot more." That's still my basic feeling today, in the era of multimillion-dollar contracts for the top network newspeople. Let the law of supply and demand apply.

There are some aspects of the situation that I do regret. Something is seriously out of balance when the top people receive such huge wages while the networks drastically cut their staffs to meet grossly reduced budgets. Of course, this is in keeping with today's basic business philosophy of vast rewards for a few at the top while layoffs are ordered below.

Also, it does seem to me that these gigantic multi-million-dollar incomes must remove the anchor-people from any pretense of association with or even understanding of the average person. There was a day not far distant, just before World War II, when nearly all of us newspeople, although perhaps white collar by profession, earned blue-collar salaries. We were part of the "common people." We drank in our corner bars with our friends, the cops and firemen, the political hacks from City Hall, the shoe salesmen and the ribbon clerks. We suffered the same budgetary restraints, the same bureaucratic indignities, waited in the same lines. We could identify with the average man because we were him.

That perhaps still exists at some levels of journalism and in some communities, but certainly in Washington and the major cities the press today is elitist. Reporters are far better educated as a class than they have ever been before. Many hold advanced degrees. Their incomes elevate them to the upper strata of political and business society, where their friends are among the rich and the powerful.

The press cynicism that has been much criticized in the mid-1990s very likely is a result of intellectual snobbishness as well as a natural side effect of superior education. Among this new generation of better-educated journalists, there is an urge to break out of the reportorial straitjacket by slipping a point of view into a supposedly impartial item. I think the new press cynicism is a fad that fast will fade. As the practice unleashed a storm of criticism, I could see self-correction coming across the horizon.

Despite that blip on the graph of news integrity, newspapers today are, in general, more unbiased, more impartial, more factual and accurate than they have ever been. Newspapers are a far cry from those in the days before World War II, when a much smaller percentage of reporters were well educated. And they are a much farther cry from those in the days before World War I, when publishers practiced personal journalism and shamelessly shaped their news columns to reflect their own views.

Among the Fourth Estate elite there are none more elite than the television anchorpeople. Their— I should say, our—highly publicized salaries have given them—us—a royal status in the public's mind, and perhaps occasionally in our own minds.

The anchors do have tremendous power. Never in the history of journalism have single voices reached so many people on a daily basis. They can include or exclude an item, almost on a whim, in their broadcasts. By their presence at an event, they accentuate—perhaps even, on occasion, distort—its importance.

Their power, however, is not unlimited. They are constrained by a series of checks and balances of which even our Founding Fathers could not have conceived. An anchor's attempt to skew the news in order to peddle a particular point of view would run against, first, the ethics of the program's writers and producers and, if their questions weren't brake enough, then the news department's front office and, finally, the network executives.

Their most frequently cited power is that of selecting the agenda of items for public consideration each day, but even that power is circumscribed by the fact that no one anchor has a monopoly and the agenda will be set by the consensus of all television and the press.

Despite the know-nothing accusations of Spiro Agnew and his ideological confederates, there is no conspiracy among members of the press. What confuses the public and, sometimes, the politicians is that the press inadvertently sets the agenda simply by the way it defines news. As long as most journalists, in print or broadcasting, believe that news is that which affects the most people, either intellectually or emotionally—in their minds, their pocketbooks or their hearts—they are going to play the same stories roughly the same way.

A problem with the anchor's exalted position is the tendency for her or him to slide from observer to player. Sometimes this is the unintended result of a purely journalistic exercise, such as our Sadat-Begin interviews. We at CBS News are still cited, erroneously, for having deliberately dabbled in diplomacy with those broadcasts, but our role in bringing about their historic meeting was purely serendipitous. Certainly it was not part of any preconceived plan of ours.

Other critics suggested that there must have been something in the air regarding such a meeting, which I just stumbled into. That is possible. One Egyptian source told me that Sadat was seriously talking within his inner circle of going to Jerusalem four months before we broke the story. However, the important point is that television journalism, in this case at least, speeded up the process, brought it into the open, removed a lot of possibly obstructionist middlemen, and made it difficult for the principals to renege on their very public agreement.

Foreign correspondents frequently and eagerly floated trial balloons in the old days of slow communication by cable and telegraph and slower production of newspapers. Days went by after the filing of the first dispatch before it was answered by all affected parties, and armies could be marching or governments falling in that time. Today this connivance between press and politics is almost passé. Instant communications by satellite have made the trial balloon a slow bird liable to be shot down before it rises above the corn rows.

In the early stages of the Iraq crisis there were rumors around Washington that Baghdad was talking up some possible points for negotiations. That evening Dan Rather in his noteworthy interview asked Saddam Hussein about that and Hussein said there was nothing to it. The same afternoon the President's National Security Adviser, Brent Scowcroft, reacted similarly at the White House. TV brought a quick end to a possible trial balloon floated by some interested party.

Television as a means of communication between heads of state outside the stodgy bureaucratic channels may be one of its great contributions. Professional diplomats may differ because it is their ox that is being gored. There are indeed dangers in instant diplomacy, with instant agreements instantly arrived at. But there are far more advantages in heads of state dealing one-on-one to negotiate compromise without the pressures of special interests or even the input of the professionals who too often are rigidly frozen into the glacier-like movement of any bureaucracy.

One who was concerned about the dangers of international television was Charles de Gaulle. For a long time he withheld permission to put a ground station in France to receive transmissions from the first Atlantic satellite. He finally relented when he was assured that foreign government leaders were unlikely to use it to speak over his head directly to the French citizenry.

His confidence was betrayed. The very day the satellite became available, President Lyndon Johnson ordered himself on it to address the French people. His "glad we could get together by this television miracle" speech was innocuous enough, but it must have had de Gaulle grinding his teeth.

The modern-day advantages of instantaneous communication, not only by television but by satellite telephone, were demonstrated for us one evening at President Bush's Kennebunkport home during the late summer of 1991. We were having a small private dinner—the Bush family and four of us off our boat—when a phone call came through to the President. He took the call in the dining room but transferred it to a more private phone.

When he returned to the table, he was exultant. He revealed that the call had been from Mikhail Gorbachev. The Soviet President had been on vacation with his family in the Crimea on the Black Sea coast when a group of hard-line Communists surrounded the house and, in effect, placed him under arrest. The conspirators—military, KGB, political enemies—were opposed to Gorbachev's liberalization policies. It was touch and go whether they might execute him.

The conspiracy collapsed when Boris Yeltsin, the President of the Russian Republic, defied their attempt to take over Moscow's Parliament building. It was in that crisis atmosphere that the call had come through to Bush.

A beaming President Bush reported that Gorbachev had just called him to say that he had made a deal with Yeltsin and would be returning to Moscow the following day. The President clearly preferred Gorbachev to Yeltsin, but he was to be disappointed as Yeltsin prevailed, forcing Gorbachev's resignation and assuming power himself. Bush had bet on Gorbachev, and the outcome in Moscow was a setback for a President who had recently won a lot of foreign policy points with his handling of the Persian Gulf crisis.

The Persian Gulf War again raised the question about whether anchorpeople should be "parachuted in," as some have termed it, to every major story around the globe. The television staff correspondent with presumed access to a major American network is clearly a force in both domestic and foreign politics, but his power is diminished by the uncertainty as to whether his reports will be given airtime.

With far greater clout, therefore, is the anchor-

person who carries an almost irrevocable guarantee
of airtime, and probably more of it than the staff correspondent would ever command on precisely the
same story. Foreign and domestic news sources
understand this. The anchor is also likely to be given
more and better transportation and communication facilities by a government or a political campaign hoping to curry favorable treatment. There
is clearly an advantage, as well, in having the anchor, upon returning to his desk, familiar with the
scene of a long-running story—Iraq or a campaign
whistle-stop.

"Big-footing," it has come to be called, this business of an anchor moving in to take a story away
from correspondents already in the field. This is
scarcely an invention of television. The newspaper
or press service "star reporter" has always played
such a preemptive role.

Thus, the anchor's presence on the scene of a
breaking story is justifiable for a number of reasons.
What is not justifiable is the dispatching of anchorpeople hither and thither across the face of the earth
for the primary purpose of generating publicity. Under such circumstances there is a danger that the
anchor's mere presence may distort the importance of
an otherwise comparatively insignificant event.

A further and more serious problem: The considerable expense of sending their anchors and all the
support personnel and equipment (producers, writers
and, almost always, at least one extra film crew)
scurrying around the world, plus the additional satel-

lite time they are likely to command, strains the budgets of news departments already suffering from financial cutbacks. Strained budgets have caused the networks to severely reduce the number of capitals in which they maintain full-time correspondents. There are but a handful today.

But the peripatetic anchor is no substitute—except for those peripheral reasons already enumerated—for a resident correspondent who knows the ins and outs of local politics and has a long list of sources he knows he can trust. The part-time correspondents that the networks now depend on in foreign capitals frequently work for broadcast stations or newspapers with strong political affiliations. When the big story breaks, how can they be depended upon to produce impartial reports, or even to direct to impartial sources the network man who rushes to the scene at the last minute?

The full-time network correspondent, supported by a strong bureau, also has the advantage of detailed knowledge that gives him a sixth sense when stories are about to break—an advantage no distant newsman is likely to have.

A case could be made that if the networks had had foreign correspondents stationed in Baghdad, the Kuwait invasion might not have taken place at all. *The New York Times* was reporting the buildup on the border, but television gave the story slight attention.

Suppose network correspondents in Baghdad had been urging their evening news programs to put them on the air with reports on the growing danger. Suppose also that they had reported the confused signals that it appears our Embassy was sending Hussein. Isn't there a good chance that all of Washington would have been alerted and that influential voices outside the State Department would have urged that a strong warning be sent to Hussein, with a different result altogether?

Without an adequate number of correspondents in the field, the network news programs are not the news intelligence sources they should be. And the notion that anchormen can cover the world like a city-desk beat, along with the resultant savings, is contributing to that unfortunate state of affairs.

I was not happy about the course of events at CBS News after my departure from the anchor desk. Within weeks of my departure from the "Evening News" the entire news division was reorganized. The veteran president, Bill Leonard, was removed, and into his place went ambitious Van Gordon Sauter, who was playing the company's executive chairs. He believed his job was to build Rather's reputation at whatever cost, and he seemed to be aiming to climb on Rather's back to the presidency of CBS Television.

The first order of business was to clear CBS News of all the veterans who had helped create its reputation but who now might stand in the way of his plans and, worse, perhaps share any credit for the success he anticipated. He and his assistant, Ed Joyce, rode through the newsroom with scythes swinging. They went down like tenpins, the real geniuses of our business. The handwriting was on the wall when two veteran newspapermen who had brought their high standards to electronic journalism, producers Les Midgley and Ernie Leiser, found the new CBS atmosphere to be dangerous to their health and quit.

At CBS News the new look was one of neon lights and whirling mirrors. Sauter was not satisfied with information. Infotainment was his game. None of his ideas for grabbing and holding a television audience were revolutionary or even new. In essence they were the rules by which the tabloids had lived since Bernarr Macfadden founded the New York *Daily Graphic* a few decades before.

There was nothing wrong with the formula, except that it wasn't right for CBS. Our viewers—and we had been first in the ratings for years—expected us to be *The New York Times* of television news, not the *Daily Graphic*. The Sauter plan was for the "Evening News" to concentrate on a few stories that would be covered as often as possible with first-person recitations by the persons involved.

If the few stories on which the program concentrated had been important ones, imparting greater depth and understanding to major news of the day, Sauter might have had something. I had long been concerned that our formula in my days might be failing in its mission. We were essentially a headline service attempting to give our audience an overview of the day, leaning (perhaps erroneously) on the hope that we would inspire them to consult their

newspapers for fuller details. This had its serious lia-
bilities, of which the most critical was that, by trying
to compress so much information into so little time,
we ran the risk of doing what you do when you compress any gas: By failing to explore a story's com-
plexities, we might be creating more heat than light.
But the Sauter failing was that the important stories
were too often ignored for features with a light
touch. They had thrown the old CBS News out with
the bathwater. CBS News under Sauter and his successors made no attempt to live up to their contract
with me. I got a nice raise, but a promised thirteen-
week annual series never came about. The existing
successful "Walter Cronkite's Universe," a summer
replacement program, was canceled, and not once
was I ever called in for a special news assignment.

The strange dichotomy of my existence was that
CBS had given me a lavish office in our headquarters building, the magnificent Eero Saarinen
creation called, for its almost luminescent dark
color, "Black Rock," and, at Bill Paley's suggestion,
had put me on the corporate board. Meanwhile I was
being treated by Sauter and his minions like a leper.

Although I thought of the CBS News building as
my natural home, visits became uncomfortable. As I
tried to talk in the hall with my old friends, they
looked over their shoulders as if they expected to be
reported for breaking the rules. This could well have
been advanced paranoia on my part, but nothing that
Sauter did helped relieve that feeling.

I felt that I had been driven from the temple where

for nineteen years, along with other believers, I had worshiped the great god News on a daily basis. Our ritual was strictly observed, but on some days our faith was tested by extraordinary challenges. One of those challenges was not the kind usually confronted by most news organizations. In 1964 CBS News moved to an old horse barn down by the docks on New York's West Side. It had long since been abandoned by all but uncounted squadrons of horseflies. It took a couple of years before powerful insecticides, probably poisonous to birds and humans, routed the beasts. Meanwhile stagehands patrolled the studios with flyswatters at the ready to try to intercept those particularly daring insects intent on landing on the noses of those of us on camera.

The flyswatting patrol was not assigned to those who worked behind the cameras, so, as usual, those legions were condemned to suffer. This is an unfortunate situation that television news inherited from the show business with which it shares the tube. The star system crept into our daily operations despite the discomfort of all of us, including me, its presumed beneficiary. I did not help matters any by my insistence that I be recognized as the managing editor of the broadcast, with shared authority and responsibility for it. This was a revolutionary departure from the then prevalent system, under which the executive producer carried the full authority and responsibility alone and the anchorman was primarily a reader of the copy presented to him.

Douglas Edwards was the newscaster, as it was

then called, of CBS's first network television news broadcast, with Don Hewitt as producer and director. The broadcast began in 1948. Edwards had been with CBS Radio since the war years, and much of his day was still spent writing and broadcasting regular radio newscasts. Since a great deal of television newswriting in those days involved writing to film, a very demanding and time-consuming technique that required fitting the words to the flitting scenes on the screen, others prepared most of Edwards' television copy.

Hewitt, Edwards and one of Edwards' principal writers, the exceedingly talented Alice Weel, had to be athletes as well as television pioneers. The broadcast was prepared in the Grand Central Terminal building, but it was broadcast from CBS studios in the old Leiderkranz Hall a dozen blocks away. Always delayed by the exigencies of the news business, they daily made a belated dash from the newsroom to a freight elevator whose operator was tipped handsomely to stand by for them. With the film and the script in hand, the three of them, waving frantically for a cab, exploded from the elevator into the rush hour traffic on Park Avenue. On those many occasions when there were no cabs to be had, they hailed any passing vehicle. Cars temporarily stopped at traffic lights were their particular targets. On one famous occasion Don and Doug crowded onto the back of a motorcycle whose kindly driver apparently gave them the thrill ride of their lives.

Edwards survived fourteen years as anchor. Since

such matters are obscured by dozens of unreliable rumors, I don't know the exact reason why management decided on a change, but the day came when I was called into Dick Salant's office and told that I was to be the anchorman of the "CBS Evening News." It was a Friday and, in the manner of such things in television, I was to start on Monday. I was advised that Doug had just been told. I went straight to his office to try to assure him that I had not lobbied for his job and that the change had surprised me as much as I assumed it had surprised him. He must have been in shock, but he greeted me without the slightest touch of rancor. We had a short chat and parted with a sincere handshake. In this as in all things, Doug showed class. He was a true gentleman. He stayed with CBS until his retirement as one of its best and most popular radio newscasters.

The bestowing of the managing editor title on me caused repercussions in newsrooms nationwide. Across the country, local news readers with few if any journalistic credentials negotiated similar on-air credits, considerably debasing the title. The practice continues today, thirty-five years later. The concept we adopted was that I would have full control over all the words that I spoke on the air, and that the executive producer and I would share the role of selecting what news items would be included and what position they would have in the broadcast. The heaviest burden by far fell upon the executive producer. His was a twenty-four-hour-a-day job, most of it spent with at least one phone glued to an ear.

Not infrequently the other ear also was engaged as he negotiated assignments and logistics. In most of my days on the "Evening News," before videotape and satellites considerably simplified the logistics, the daily scenario might well have gone like this:

The story might be a terrible earthquake in a remote area of Turkey. Let's say the executive producer was Ernie Jones (a pseudonym for all the great producers with whom I had the privilege of working). Jones is on one phone to the Rome bureau trying to get a correspondent and camera crew en route to the disaster, and on the other phone he's talking to Istanbul and our part-time resident correspondent there. The latter is suggesting ways in which the Rome crew can get to the scene—the nearest international airport, the possibility of a charter flight from there, the fastest way to get film from the scene back to Istanbul or Athens for transfer to London. With those details on the way to being nailed down, Jones will phone London with details of when it might expect the film. Film editors there will be alerted to when they will be needed. Jones will later make a decision about whether we can get the film on the air faster by editing in London or in New York.

All this is taking place in the executive producer's office, which was the nerve center of the "Evening News" and which we called the fishbowl because it was a glass-enclosed corner of the newsroom. My office was behind a glass wall in another corner of the room. I divided my time between my office and my chair at the center of the horseshoe-shaped desk, around the rim of which worked our three writers and our editor.

That earthquake story would first have come to us, as did the great majority of all our news, via the press service teletype machines. I would be alerted at the same time Jones was, and we would confer during the rest of the day on what kind of film coverage we could expect. Meanwhile, at the news desk, the editor or I would have assigned one of the writers to the story. His duty was to fill in whatever details the correspondent on the scene did not, or could not, get. If we didn't succeed in obtaining any film, he would have to be prepared to write the story as a "tell" item. His resources would be the press service material and research sources from which he could background the story with a description of the area and its people and perhaps something about previous earthquakes in the area.

Tell items were all those stories for which we did not have film reports. Our daily quota usually ran five or six minutes for the tell stories. The staff began referring to this as the day's "magic number." I suspect that the term contained just a touch of reproach. My determination that regardless of how much compression was needed, we should try to cover all the day's major stories with at least a head-line, constantly ran afoul of the opinion of a majority of our producers that a good film story should take precedence over tell items. I learned years later that some of my colleagues whose stories hadn't made it onto the "Evening News" felt that I protected my "magic number" only to get my face on camera. I'm sorry about that and I wish, even now, I could convince them otherwise, because I think it's a bum rap.

Unless one has had to do the job, it is impossible to grasp how difficult it is to decide what should go into a news broadcast and what must be left out. The rule of thumb for all news operations is that stories are assigned their importance on the basis of what affects or interests the greatest number of one's readers or viewers. Depending upon the nature of the newspaper or broadcast, the balance between what "affects" and what "interests" is quite different. The first criterion of a responsible newspaper such as *The New York Times* is going to be that which their readers need to know about their world that day—those developments that in one way or another might affect their health, their pocketbooks, the future of themselves and their children. The first criterion of the tabloid is that which "interests" its readers—gossip, sex, scandal.

Of the thirty minutes of our broadcast, almost a third was eaten up by commercials and the necessary "lead-ins" and "lead-outs"—the opening of the broadcast, the good night, and the bridges into and out of the commercials. I'm afraid I added a full four seconds to that burden with my signature line: "And that's the way it is . . ." and the date. I had come up with the phrase when the "Evening News" went from a quarter hour to a half hour in 1963. I naïvely thought that by doubling the length of the program I would have time for a short feature story at the end, little two- or three-paragraph items that at UP we had called "travesty of fate" stories. Depending on the story, I could then cap it with my line, which, depending on whether I recited it with humor, or sadness, or irony, became a six-word commentary on life's foibles.

Dick Salant hated the line from the beginning. He argued that it arrogantly implied an unerring accuracy, of which we were not capable and which we did not claim. It turned out that we didn't have time for the feature stories and the line served no purpose. Within days, however, the public seemed to have embraced the sign-off as they had Lowell Thomas' "So long until tomorrow" and Ed Murrow's "Good night and good luck." So I stuck with it. I began to think Dick was right, but I was too stubborn to drop it.

After accounting for the commercials and lead-ins, we had to pack all the news of importance from around the world and from our own complicated and diverse nation into twenty-two or twenty-three minutes. It was a formidable, even impossible, job.

Our producer, pseudonymous Ernie Jones, each night checked with the CBS news desk to find out what stories had broken and what assignments had been or should be made for the next day's coverage. He repeated the process when he arrived in our newsroom the next morning. He talked with the bureaus that were working on already assigned stories. At that point I got into the mix, possibly suggesting angles I felt should be included in those stories and occasionally offering a suggestion that we might look into an unassigned development which interested me. We also conferred with the news editor about anything he had discovered on the press service wires that we had somehow missed. And he frequently had his own ideas about what we should cover.

Based on all this input, Jones did our "one-star" lineup—the list of the items we expected to cover in their order of priority. That one-star would undergo a lot of changes as it proceeded through the day to a four- or five-star edition. As new stories broke, we had to decide whether they should assume a place in the lineup, displacing others. During the rest of the day he rode herd on the bureaus where reports were being produced, conferring with the correspondents and their producers, ensuring that the piece met our needs and would be transmitted to us in time.

The deadline was a tough one for the "CBS Evening News" staff—far more difficult than at the other networks, which preferred to lock up their programs at least an hour or so before broadcast time. In fact, they had to do so since their broadcast studios were several floors away from their newsrooms. Their anchormen had to have time to get from one to the other. I had insisted that our newsroom *be* our studio because only then could I enforce my philosophy—namely, that we were a medium that should pride itself on our technical ability to get on the air instantly, whenever news broke. Therefore, I required that the deadline for our broadcast not be when we went *on* the air but when we went *off* the air. In other words, we should be able to change anything in our lineup, tell story or tape, even while the program was being broadcast.

This was a hangover from my long years with the United Press. The wire service had thousands of client newspapers around the globe, and our mantra was that we had a deadline every minute—that somewhere one of our client newspapers would be on deadline every minute of the day and night. Our fierce competition with the AP and INS meant that speed was everything, almost nosing out accuracy at the finish line. If we could do it at the UP, why shouldn't we do it at CBS? So if we got a late film or tape story at a distant bureau, I expected us to break our necks to get it into the broadcast. And if a news story came over the AP or UP wires, I expected our editor to slip the copy to me for a quick look when we were in the midst of a commercial or a tape piece. If I decided it should be in the broadcast, I had three choices: I could ad-lib it using the press service copy, I could toss it to a writer to whip into shape, or I could spin around to the typewriter behind me and knock it out myself during the next commercial or tape piece.

Anyway I did it, I threw the fishbowl and the director in the control booth into a panic—controlled panic, but panic all the same. The timing of the broadcast was critical. We had to abide by network rules and get off the air at the precise second.

Each piece of film and each item of my tell copy was timed to the second. If we dropped a new piece of film into the program, another had to go. With the maneuver, the entire broadcast's timing was, of course, thrown out of kilter. My tell copy was the accordion that had to expand or contract to meet the new, extemporaneous lineup. I could ad-lib additional facts on one story or another to fill time, or I could much more easily drop tell stories if necessary. These last-minute amendments in the program schedule created massive difficulties for the producers and the control booth. The director had a particular problem. His rundown instantly became obsolete; the producer was shouting new instructions over their intercom; and all the time the poor director had to watch a wall full of monitors and call out to the technical director the shots he wanted.

Every time this happened, the director complained to the producer and insisted that the producer had to tell me that this wasn't any way to do a broadcast and that my deadline every minute was a philosophy which endangered not only the broadcast but the health of the staff as well. The several producers I had over those nineteen years told the directors that if they wanted me to be so chastised, they would have to do the chastising themselves. They never did—again, the 800-pound-gorilla star system at work.

Our flexibility, comfortable or not, served us magnificently on one noteworthy occasion. We were in the midst of the last commercial when my secretary came over to the desk and said that a Mr. Tom Johnson in Austin, Texas, was on the phone insisting that I would want to be interrupted, on the air, to take his call. An old friend, Tom had been a longtime assistant to President Johnson (no relation) and was manager of his television station. He knew news and he knew that if I got the message that he'd said I should be interrupted on the air, I would be interrupted. I took his call.

"Walter," Tom said, "the President died a few minutes ago. It was a heart attack."

Just then we came out of the commercial. The director knew I was talking on the phone, but he had nowhere else to go. The floor director waved at me and pointed at the camera's red light to let me know I was back on the air.

"Tom, just a moment," I said, and, turning to the camera, reported that former President Johnson had just died of a heart attack and that I was getting further details even then from his office in Austin. For the next minute or so until I had to say good night and get off the air, I relayed details as they were fed to me by Tom. We had a clear beat, and thanks to a staff that was well practiced in handling the unexpected, it was broadcast as smoothly as if it had been scripted.

Tom Johnson, who would go on to become publisher of the Los Angeles *Times* and later president of CNN, had better luck getting through to me when I was on the air than had Lyndon Johnson. The President watched all three of the network news pro-

grams in the evening, turning up the sound whenever he sensed that one was about to report on him
or his administration. It was not at all unusual for an
aide to call me after a broadcast with the almost routine opening: "Some of us around the White House
were watching your broadcast and we feel you ought
to know . . ."

This was a little game. The caller knew, and knew
that I knew, that he was speaking for the President of
the United States in delivering that day's complaint
about our reporting. On a couple of occasions the
President himself called after the broadcast. And
then there was the evening that he became so
incensed about something that he phoned while I
was still on the air. His secretary insisted that the
President should be put through to me immediately.
The poor woman had probably never had to face
anyone who refused a call from the President or,
worse, had to tell the President that his call had been
refused. But that's what our staff did, confident that
his call was far more likely to be confrontational
than informational. When I phoned back after the
broadcast, an aide relayed a complaint so trivial that
by now I have forgotten the subject.

In broadcasting, the clock is the ever-present evil.
Perhaps I liked living dangerously, but I was
inclined to crowd more into the day than the day
could accommodate. Although I conferred frequently with the editor and the producer, I spent
most of the time in my office, taking phone calls,
placating affiliates, fending off speech requests and

researching future special events like space shots and political conventions. Additionally, just as anchors are today, I was diverted from the attention I should have been giving the daily broadcast by the network penchant for getting the most value out of their "stars." There was constant pressure to appear on other news broadcasts such as "The Morning Show," or to make a speech for an affiliate station or for a cause particularly dear to a major sponsor.

Some days I would not get out to the news desk until a bare hour before the broadcast. My three writers were excellent, but I frequently had questions about their stories that I hoped they could answer before airtime. I edited their copy to suit myself and occasionally rewrote their efforts. Their versions were probably better than mine most of the time, but my ego ruled—all 800 pounds of it. This last-minute effort meant that the whole news team was forced to operate in a state of high hysteria as they watched the clock hand work its inexorable way toward the moment when the red light would go on and we would be on the air—ready or not. They held their collective breath as my secretary brought my jacket to the desk, I buttoned my collar, tightened my tie and slipped into the jacket, and the makeup woman, with no time left to do the work my physiognomy demanded, gave the face a quick dusting of powder. She ducked out of camera range just as the red light of the cameras blinked on.

I apologize now if I forced our staff to suffer unnecessary tension, but I think they were all proud that we put on one of the best newscasts ever. I can't believe that any news broadcasters today can possibly enjoy the work as much as we did. The smell of that excitement still permeated the newsroom, at least for a short while, after the new Van Gordon Sauter bunch took it over. I regretted that the banishment they seemed to have ordered for me kept me from at least sniffing a little of it.

After finding that my concerns about the course of CBS News had fallen on deaf ears among our executives, I began going public in the many speeches I made to professional associations and university journalism groups. The press picked up some of this, and no doubt the burr was getting unpleasant under Sauter's saddle.

He called me to lunch with Howard Stringer, the "Evening News" producer, and David Fuchs, chief of the news department's business side. It turned out that Sauter was trying to silence my criticism by offering to let me do an occasional documentary program. I must say that he gave me carte blanche in producing the program, but given the lack of management enthusiasm for it, there was simply no joy there and we killed it after a few episodes.

At that lunch Sauter admitted that he was deliberately keeping me off the air because he felt that it would be easier to build up Dan's audience if I wasn't around as a distraction. As Dan presumably became comfortable in the anchor chair, Sauter's successors thought it best not to tamper with the successful exclusionary formula.

Paley must have asked me at least once a month

for a half dozen years why I wasn't on the air. I told him I was ready if anybody asked. He would mumble something about having been told by news management that I didn't want to work—a gross canard. Then he'd lose interest in the matter for another several weeks.

Meanwhile the CBS board had become interesting. Ted Turner made a run at the company. His visionary Cable News Network was just getting off the ground, and the general attitude in the industry was that a twenty-four-hour news service was simply too expensive ever to be a financial success. The board went into heavy debt to buy back our own stock and defeat his takeover attempt.

But the company had been "put into play," as they say on Wall Street, and there were other unfriendly bidders around. That paved the way for eventual disaster. It came riding in on a white horse. Larry Tisch, hotel operator, insurance mogul and tobacco company owner, began acquiring CBS stock in large quantities. He kept assuring our management that he had no intention of trying to secure a controlling position, that his purchases were purely an investment. That was the first of a series of Tisch statements that apparently were misunderstood by everybody but him.

Within weeks he held more stock than Bill Paley, and he moved in. He was elected to the board and, protesting all the while that he didn't intend to become involved in management, maneuvered himself into the chairman's seat.

Paley had been removed from that position two

years earlier in a truly sad boardroom drama. His main problem in his last decade was that he could not bear to share authority over his precious broadcasting company. In 1966 his trusted sidekick, the man who had largely created the CBS image of taste and integrity, Frank Stanton, was scheduled to move into the chairmanship when Paley reached the mandatory retirement age of sixty-five.

As they walked to the board meeting at which Paley was to hand over the gavel, Paley told Stanton that he had changed his mind, that he wasn't retiring after all. A stunned Stanton, in a gentlemanly response typical of him, stayed on as the company president but announced that he intended to respect the sixty-five-year-old retirement age and step down, as he did, in 1973.

Thus began a game of musical chairs. Over the next fourteen years Paley hired four presidents for the company, only to find cause to dismiss three of them when they began to exercise real leadership and demand the authority they needed. The fourth died before the seemingly inevitable confrontation with Paley.

In 1983 the board was happy with Paley's latest president, Tom Wyman, former vice chairman of the Pillsbury Company, a big, handsome and highly capable man. But as had happened with so many presidents before, Paley turned down Wyman's request for the authority he had been promised. Wyman came to the board with a threat to resign. The board had been handpicked by Paley and included some of his closest friends. They all recognized, however, that the time had come to deny the aging boss his whim, that one more dismissed president would give the company a permanent black eye and increase the difficulty of finding a replacement.

There was no one in the boardroom who did not realize what the decision meant. It was time for William Paley, the founder of the company, one of the major figures in the history of broadcasting, to be told that he must vacate his throne. No voice was raised in the eleven-person board in Paley's defense as the matter went to a solemn vote. In the funereal atmosphere that followed, the board faced the terrible dilemma: Who would carry the message to Caesar? The agony was short-lived. Benno C. Schmidt, his authoritative voice diminished to a near whisper, volunteered. Benno had served on the board longer than any other member; he was a partner of Jock Whitney, Paley's brother-in-law and perhaps his closest friend, and had been a loyal friend of Paley's for almost a half century.

Schmidt left the room. He returned in twenty minutes and, grim but businesslike, reported that the chairman had asked that his lawyers work out certain details of his "retirement" and had confirmed that he would continue as "chairman emeritus." The deed had been done.

Paley, his health rapidly failing, became the gray eminence at the board table. Wyman was in charge, but he ran into problems. With only a few of the board members in his confidence, he negotiated a possible sale of the company to Coca-Cola. The secrecy of the operation offended the majority of the board, and the deal was voted down—in effect a vote of no confidence in Wyman. He was forced to resign. There was now a new crisis in the leadership.

Tisch moved in. He and Paley together held enough stock to control the company. He made a deal with Paley to restore him as chairman with Tisch as chief executive officer. Tisch had CBS, just fifteen months after his solemn pronouncement that he had no designs on the company.

With Wyman out, Paley too ill to protest and a board that seemed incapable of standing against him, Tisch, with no broadcast experience, proceeded to dismantle the company in order to increase the cash equity for his stockholders and himself. Various divisions went under the hammer, most disastrously CBS Records. Understandably unable to get along with its volcanic president, Walter Yetnikoff, Tisch peddled the company to Sony for far less than it turned out to have been worth.

The board briefly resisted this one, but yielded when Tisch made a sober promise that the entire proceeds would be used to acquire broadcast properties to bolster what he constantly identified as "CBS's core business." Not a single major property was acquired with the Sony money.

Depending upon one's personal proclivities, the move of the record division out of CBS headquarters had a serious consequence of either good or bad dimensions. Riding the elevators could expose one to the possibility of passive drug addiction when the doors opened on a CBS Records floor. The heavy, sweet odor of marijuana was pervasive.

Tisch seemed to have no vision of a CBS role in the future of the rapidly changing communications, news and entertainment world. Cable was a case in point. ABC and then NBC were beginning to get involved in this new means of distribution. Finally, in answer to many board inquiries, Tisch ordered his assistant, Jay Kriegel, to make a study of the cable potential.

Kriegel eventually produced a report in which he confirmed Tisch's judgment that there was no opportunity for CBS in cable.

While refusing to prepare CBS for the future, Tisch downsized and downgraded the remaining company. The news department was a patsy for the sacrificial table. It had grown fat in the halcyon years and needed some toughening up. But the Tisch knives cut away the fat, then started on the muscle and finally reached the bone. Staffs were reduced and bureaus closed, most disastrously overseas, where it is most important that American-trained correspondents keep an eye on our potential enemies and our supposed friends.

I protested these cuts to no avail. Sometimes I would get a faint "hear, hear" from board members, but none stood up against Tisch as he glared at me. We suffered a phony stockholders' suit at one point, and during a deposition hearing I was told by the plaintiff's Philadelphia lawyer that Tisch, under deposition, had testified that he supposed I was a good newsman but that I didn't understand business. Fortunately, I was not asked to comment, for my answer would have been: I certainly didn't understand business the way Larry Tisch conducted it.

While Wyman was still with us, and shortly after I went on the board, I was protesting the way Sauter was running the news department. I said that it was "irresponsible" to permit this debasement of a great institution. As I went on with my little speech, Wyman sank lower and lower in his chair. When I finished, he came charging at me in a verbal fury. He cited his executive experience and said that never, never, never in his life had he been accused of being irresponsible. My effort to amend my remarks, pointing out that I wasn't charging him personally with irresponsibility, fell short, I'm afraid, of mollifying Wyman, and the episode undoubtedly weakened my future effectiveness in standing up for the news department before the board.

Tisch, by another of his adroit maneuvers, managed to get rid of his three less enthusiastic board members in one move. It was agreed that board members should serve only until the age of seventy. That provided the plank for Roswell Gilpatric, Marietta Tree and me to walk.

Dissidents anywhere have an interesting time, but particularly on boards of directors. I shall never forget the awe that greeted a suggestion of mine at one point that some new labor contract negotiations smacked of union-busting.

One of my major disappointments was that the CBS board, made up of some top-notch business, financial and industrial leaders, was concerned only with the company's finances and paid no attention to its programming. We never discussed violence or children's programming or permissible language or the frequency or suitability of commercials.

Each spring the entertainment executives would show a sampling of the next season's new programs. The board members frowned and grimaced at the sitcoms. They laughed, but only at what were supposed to be the serious dramas. As the lights came up, the members shook their heads, grinned embarrassed grins at each other and went about the business of the next financial report.

CHAPTER 16

A CAREER can be called a success if one can look back and say: "I made a difference." I don't feel I can do that.

All of us in those early days of television felt, I'm sure, that we were establishing a set of standards that would be observed by, or at least have an influence on, generations of news professionals to come. How easily these were dismissed by the Van Gordon Sauters and those who felt they had to imitate to compete.

The infotainment trend has been exacerbated in recent years by the network fight to hang on to a viable share of a shrinking pie. Cable, the increasingly important independent stations and video recordings have reduced the total network audience to barely half of what it once was. The news departments have moved from the loss leaders of my years to profit centers, and management now considers ratings more important than prestige.

I don't envy those many serious broadcast journalists on both sides of the microphone who must live in this environment. The lack of respect in which they are held by their network managers is rubbed in their noses every day when the network-owned stations put the trashy syndicated tabloid "news" shows on in the preferred evening hours once occupied by the genuine news programs. That is a discouraging message from the executive suites to the newsrooms of the tastes, preferences and sense of responsibility of network brass.

Newspapers, under similar pressure of falling circulation, are also guilty today of trivializing the news. Much of the news is featurized, and a lot of it is condensed into "What Happened Today" columns. This led in the mid-nineties to a spate of criticism of the press, but most of it was misdirected, aimed as it was at the journalists. Basically, the problem is, again, the bottom line.

The shame is that most of our newspapers, for a variety of understandable reasons (not the least of which is confiscatory inheritance taxes), have passed from the hands of individual publishers to large chains. These corporate behemoths are forced by their stockholders and the "get mine" mores of the nineties to seek constantly expanding profits. Adequate profits are obviously necessary to the survival of any institution, but stockholder greed now demands super profits, their "maximization."

Newspapers and broadcasting, insofar as journalism goes, are public services essential to the successful working of our democracy. It is a travesty that they should be required to pay off like any other stock-market investment.

To play the downsizing game, the boards and their executives deny to their news managers enough funding to pay for the minimum coverage necessary to serve their consumers well. They reduce the amount of expensive newsprint available until editors do not have enough space for the news they need to cover. Good reporters, writers and editors are spread so thin that they cannot spend the necessary time developing the stories that the public needs and deserves. A more responsible press depends not upon individual journalists but upon more responsible owners. That is the real bottom line.

The future is cloudy in this area. The profits for the networks and the other big players may be further fragmented in the new communications era. How willing will they be then to finance the news and public affairs programming which the public expects, to which it is entitled, and which is fundamental to the nation's welfare?

As for the hundreds of special interests that in the future will supply programming for the multitude of satellite or cable channels or news sites on the Internet, it is unlikely that they will have the resources or the will to provide highly expensive, well-rounded, comprehensive news services. The big question is whether the major players in the new alignment—the entertainment and industrial giants— with no background in news and their focus primarily on profits from other sources, will be willing to underwrite the budget-bending business of serious news reporting. Will they continue even the level of reduced news and public affairs programming that their networks are providing today?

Will the journalism center hold in the changed economic environment of the future? In the last decade the networks have cut back news budgets while supporting in syndication the emergence of tabloid news shows, travesties of genuine news presentations. They bear the same relationship to the network news broadcasts as the *Enquirer* does to *The New York Times*.

Unfortunately, by targeting the lowest common denominator among the potential viewership, these schlock broadcasts lure audiences and make money. Financially hard-pressed network and local station executives, with their substantial budgets for legitimate news gathering, must look at the size of the audience for the tabloids with a gleam of jealousy and wonder if this might be the way to go. The danger, of course, is that the profitable bad has a way of driving out the unprofitable or marginally profitable good.

The major problem is simply that television news is an inadequate substitute for a good newspaper. It is not too far a stretch to say that the public's dependence on television for the bulk of its news endangers our democratic system. While television puts all other media in the shade in its ability to present in moving pictures the people and the places that make our news, it simultaneously fails in outlining and explaining the more complicated issues of our day.

For those who either cannot or will not read—equally shameful in a modern society—television lifts the floor of knowledge and understanding of the world around them. But for the others, through its limited exploration of the difficult issues, it lowers the ceiling of knowledge. Thus, television news provides a very narrow intellectual crawl space between its floor and ceiling.

The sheer volume of television news is ridiculously small. The number of words spoken in a half-hour broadcast barely equals the number of words on two thirds of a standard newspaper page. That is not enough to cover the day's major events at home and overseas. Hypercompression of facts, foreshortened arguments, the elimination of extenuating explanation—all are dictated by television's restrictive time frame and all distort to some degree the news available on television.

The TV correspondent as well as his subjects is a victim of this time compression, something that has come to be known as "sound-bite journalism." With inadequate time to present a coherent report, the correspondent seeks to craft a final summary sentence that might make some sense of the preceding gibberish. This is hard to do without coming to a single point of view—and a one-line editorial is born. Similarly, a story of alleged misdeeds frequently ends with one sentence: "A spokesman denied the charges." No further explanation.

Television frequently repeats a newspaper story that is based on "informed sources." The newspaper may have carefully hedged the story with numerous qualifiers, but the time-shy newscast does not. More distortion.

The greatest victim in all this is our political

process, and in my view this is one of the greatest blots on the recent record of television news. Sound-bite journalism simply isn't good enough to serve the people in our national elections. Studies have shown that in 1988 the average bloc of uninterrupted speech by a presidential candidate on the network newscasts was 9.8 seconds. Nine point eight seconds! The networks faithfully promised to do better in 1992. The average sound bite that year was just 8.2 seconds. The networks promised to do better in 1996.

It took me just seven seconds to read those last two sentences. Clearly no meaningful explanation of issues is possible in that sort of oratorical burst, which occasionally does not even include a noun or verb. Further, figures compiled by Harvard researcher Dr. Kiku Adatto showed that in 1988 there was not a single instance where a candidate was given as much as one minute of uninterrupted time on an evening newscast.

Compare these figures with those pertaining to the newscasts of 1968. Then the average sound bite was 42.3 seconds, more than five times as long as the average in the 1992 campaign, and 21 percent of the sound bites by presidential candidates ran at least a minute.

(Dr. Adatto, in what may have been an unintentional commentary on the twisted values of our hyped-up world, adds a note that "the 1968 style of coverage enabled not only the candidates but partisans and advocates from across the political spectrum to speak in their own voice, to develop an argument on the nightly news." What an indictment it is of today's abridged reporting that we can consider the days of forty-two-second sound bites the golden era of rational political argument.)

Naturally, nothing of any significance is going to be said in seven seconds, but this seems to work to the advantage of many politicians. They are not required to say anything of significance, and issues can be avoided rather than confronted. Furthermore, the politicians have long since learned that in the days of television, pictures are more important than words. Image is everything. So, along with providing the sound bite, a major imperative of the campaign is to provide each day the so-called photo opportunity—the photo bite—which will show the candidate in the most favorable light and has a good chance of making the evening news.

It seems to be impossible for television to beat the politician at this game. Lesley Stahl did a CBS report in 1984 meant to show that the Reagan campaign's skillful use of visuals, sound and photo bites was a cynical manipulation of television. She used numerous examples from previous television coverage. The White House loved the piece. As they told Lesley, the replay of pictures of Reagan at his best far outweighed her critical words.

Besides the evening news broadcasts, the other important points of interface between the campaigns and television today are the debates and the commercial spot advertisements. Politicians approach these forums with abject cynicism, which results, I submit, in increasingly serious damage to their credibility with the public.

Debates are to be avoided if possible. If not avoidable, they are to be minimized. Substance is to be avoided if possible. Image is to be maximized. The debates are a part of the fraud that our political campaigns have become, and it is a wonder that the networks continue to cooperate in their presentation. Since they clearly require the candidates' approval, the networks must agree to the debate formula that the candidates dictate. There has grown up a belief on the part of the sponsoring groups and the networks that it is worth any compromise with the candidates in order to get them on the air together at all. This is highly questionable.

There was marked improvement in 1992, when the candidates and the networks agreed on a single moderator instead of the inchoate panel of journalists that had prevailed in the past. With this improvement, hope was raised that in the future we may get truly meaningful debate and that television will be used as it should be used to inform and educate our citizenry.

Twin evil to the debates are the twenty- or thirty-second or one-minute commercials. They are misused to sell the candidate with slogans and, even worse, to permit others to scurrilously attack the opponent while sparing their candidate that unsavory role.

The photo opportunity, the manipulation of the

sound bite, the control of the so-called debates, the
barrage of expensive negative commercials—all are
instrumental in turning political campaigns into
political theater to be played out on television's
home screens.

The producers, directors and stage managers of
the spectacle are the candidates' managers, their
handlers, the political consultants. Many have become so prominent, and so arrogant, that, without
shame, they have moved onstage themselves. They
have become television personalities in their own
right, and they frequently appear on air to brag about
their contributions, going so far as to claim author-
ship of some of the candidate's best ad-libs. They
can twist a fact with such speed and dexterity that
they have come to be known as "spin doctors."

Can a potential voter really take a campaign seriously after he or she has been escorted by television
backstage to be shown how the managers transform
their candidates into actors? Certainly if that is the
way the political game is going to be played, we citizens had better know about it. But the healthy skepticism that the television coverage invites can soon
give rise to unhealthy, potentially mortal, public
cynicism about government.

Television news competition being what it is
today, its editors are unable to ignore such theater.
So they do the next best thing. In the interest of journalistic integrity, they make sure that the audience
knows that they know that they are being used.

News editors have become fairly good at this.

During recent campaigns, reporters following the candidates have pointed out the carefully arranged management of the events—the advance teams, the recruitment and preparation of "spontaneous" crowds, the care and feeding of the candidate. Mention was openly made of "photo opportunities" and "sound bites." "Reality checks" regularly tested candidates' commercials against the known facts.

It was a noble effort, but it was flawed. In order to be effective critics of this political theater, the television reporters frequently had to replay the offensive material, thus giving it more exposure and greater attention than it deserved. Thus, like Bush's Willie Horton ad against Dukakis in 1988, the defamatory commercials got so many free replays on the news programs as to become almost a cliché in themselves. Candidates learned early on that to respond to a negative commercial or statement was only to invite its being repeated on the evening news.

Dr. Adatto's research found that the networks showed 125 excerpts from candidates' commercial spots in 1988. Interestingly, there were no such excerpts shown in 1968. The lesson to the campaign managers seems clear: The more outrageous the commercial, the greater the possibility of frequent free reruns and the more attention it will draw. The political reporter's accompanying criticism rolls off the political manager's back. The managers have adopted a version of the Barnum and Bailey credo: "I don't care what you say about me as long as you show my candidate's picture." An already skeptical public might gather from this that nothing succeeds in our increasingly immoral world like excess, and, in politics, like dissembling.

All of the failings of television news are lumped together as grist for the mill of those special interests, political or private, that would like to do their business in the dark by dimming the bright searchlight of press freedom. I am baffled by the blindness of businesspeople who scream bloody murder when the press probes their operations. They themselves depend upon the free press to advise them of problems with their customers, their suppliers or their competitors. They could not do business without this intelligence.

Press freedom is essential to our democracy, but the press must not abuse this license. We must be careful with our power. We must avoid, where possible, publicity circuses that make the right of fair trial a right difficult to uphold. We must avoid unwarranted intrusions upon people's privacy. Liberty and, no less, one's reputation in the community are terribly precious things, and they must not be dealt with lightly or endangered by capricious claims of special privilege.

Above all else, however, the press itself must unwaveringly guard the First Amendment guarantees of a free press. The free press, after all, is the central nervous system of a democratic society. No true democracy, as we understand the term, can exist without it. The press may be irresponsible at times, obstreperous, arrogant, even cruel when innocent individuals are caught in the riptide of damaging publicity. But a free, unintimidated and unregulated press is democracy's early-warning system against both the dangers of democracy's own excesses and the approach of tyranny. And inevitably, one of the first signs of tyranny's approach is its heavy footstep on the threshold of press freedom.

The secret of our past success as a nation may be traced to the fact that we have been a free people, free to discuss ideas and alternatives, free to teach and learn, free to report and to hear, free to challenge the most venerable institutions without fear of reprisal. The First Amendment, with its guarantees of free speech and a free press, has been at the heart of the American success story. It must be guarded zealously if we are to gird for the challenges of the new century ahead.

The public seems to sense all this, but does it really understand? The preservation of our liberties depends on an enlightened citizenry. Those who get most of their news from television probably are not getting enough information to intelligently exercise their voting franchise in a democratic system. As Thomas Jefferson said, the nation that expects to be ignorant and free expects what never can and never will be. We can bring that up-to-date and amplify it a bit: The nation whose population depends on the explosively compressed headline service of television news can expect to be exploited by the demagogues and dictators who prey upon the semi-informed.

In the future the situation could get worse. Today the person seeking only the football scores or the couch potato looking for entertainment-world chit-

chat is usually exposed to some general news headlines while thumbing through the paper or waiting
out the evening news broadcast. But when there are
cable and other high-tech channels to which they
can go directly for their sports or entertainment
news or other specialties, even that limited exposure
will end.

The answer to this informational dilemma in
a free society is not immediately apparent but
probably lies in two areas. The first is long-range but
desirable in any case. We must better educate our
young people to become discriminating newspaper
readers, television viewers and computer users. We
must teach them that, to be fully informed, one must
go to good newspapers, weekly newsmagazines,
opinion journals, books and, increasingly, the Internet, as well as television.

By recognizing the advantages and limitations of
each medium, this educated public would go multi-
media seeking to slake its thirst for more information, and it would demand a better product to satisfy
that thirst. Thus, in a market-oriented economy,
demand would raise the quality of both print and
broadcast news.

The second part of the answer to our future information dilemma rests with advertisers and their
agencies. Big business must accept some public
responsibility to, first, support government programs
to improve education, and, second, support those
quality newspapers and/or broadcast programs that
genuinely strive to keep the people informed. Too

often we ignore the advertisers'—that is, industry's—role in supporting responsible journalism.

This public service has its own reward, for the prosperity of any economy depends on the growth of an educated public. This has particular application in the quality of entertainment programming. Although I must say I don't know how in the world quality is to be judged. How does one set standards for quality? Different educational, social and economic strata would undoubtedly define it differently. As desirable as it might be to uplift our television programming generally, this difference in standards is the bog into which sinks any attempt to establish basic criteria. And who are to be the judges we would entrust with the task of monitoring quality? Their judgment would have to be subjective and intuitive rather than objective. What sins of moral righteousness that would involve.

Quality really comes down to a matter of taste, and that might be a little difficult to legislate. Attempts to do so by a small panel, no matter how educated, brilliant and fair its members, come down to the ugly matter of censorship. I cannot imagine a society retaining its intellectual and, yes, even economic vitality under such constraints. We have seen the stultification of whole countries where taste is a government monopoly.

Our anachronistically named Radio Act provides only that broadcasters should operate "for the public convenience and necessity"—an old line borrowed from the attempt to regulate railroads in the last century. The Federal Communications Commission, which was set up under that act, has never successfully interpreted that vague directive as far as entertainment programming goes.

Our laissez-faire broadcasting hasn't produced what one might call a plethora of quality. There is a powerful lot of junk on our airwaves. Personally I abhor the violence—they'd rewrite Exodus to include a car chase—and I don't think the use of gutter language is doing anything to improve our culture.

But along with the trash, there is a lot that is good. The mix may not exactly be what most of us would like, but that is the nature of the marketplace. I wonder if sometimes our discontent is not the result of expectations raised beyond any possibility of realization. Why have we come to expect that *every* television program should be a masterpiece— entertaining and uplifting and to be savored forever in our memories? Why is more expected of television than of the publishing business or the theater? Of the thousands of magazine articles and books, how many are worth clipping or worth putting on the shelf as great pieces of literature? Only a few of our stage productions will be remembered as superb theater.

The fact is that television devours talent at a greater rate than it can be produced. With a gestation period of nine months and twenty more years for some measure of intellectual growth, the human assembly line simply isn't moving fast enough.

Still, in a free market the major objective in programming for the masses is profit, and it is whistling past the graveyard to assume that very much product is going to come over the airwaves that isn't aimed at improving the bottom line. The most dedicated of broadcasters can produce intellectually satisfying programs, and perhaps even occasionally take a loss on one or two, but it is suicidal to get too far ahead of the parade.

Why indeed, we might ask, should television be expected to reverse the people's preference in entertainment? Opera and ballet have been around for quite a long time, and for the most part they still require subsidy from governments or institutions.

None of this is to suggest that I believe that broadcasters should not make every effort to improve their product and to ensure as nearly as it is humanly possible the presentation of quality entertainment. And I want them to make huge profits in the entertainment area—because I want them to pour a sizable share of those profits back into news and public affairs.

Meanwhile television will continue to play a major role in writing history. It has already had an impact on the tide of events. Once television signals from the West breached the Iron Curtain and showed to those locked behind it the benefits of a free society, public uprisings against the Communist status quo were probably inevitable. The daily coverage of the Vietnamese battlefield helped convince the American public that the carnage was not worth the candle. The Israeli-Egyptian peace resulted from the meeting of Anwar Sadat and Menachem

Begin that was partly brought about by the separate interviews with them on the "CBS Evening News."

The Internet and programming on demand and all the rest of the new high-tech stuff promise all sorts of new ways that we might be looking at our world in the next century. They are all bound to depend on pictures and words, and thus, except perhaps with respect to means of delivery, they will resemble the television of my time.

And what stories the new media are going to have to tell. In just the latter half of this remarkable century we have swept into at least six simultaneous eras, any one of which, by itself, would be enough to reshape our world. We have been present at the birth of the nuclear age, the computer age, the space age, the petrochemical age, the telecommunications age, the DNA age. Together at their confluence flows a great river of change, unlike anything history has encountered before.

As we approach the new century, we are living through a technological revolution potentially more profound in its impact—socially, politically, economically—than the industrial revolution of the last century. We have scarcely begun to identify its implications and adapt our institutions to change, although the first massive repercussions already have been felt with industrial downsizing. Hundreds of thousands of workers suffer unemployment or downsized reemployment or the fear of job insecurity. We are finding it as difficult to cope as a society as we are as individuals. We are all a little overwhelmed.

Flowing into that mainstream of technological change have been our generation's economic and political revolutions. They have been propelled by growth and rising expectations, but have frequently been blocked by finite resources and an inadequate education system. Meeting these problems and satisfying the needs of the disadvantaged is the challenge of our time.

The new technologies give proof of the human being's intellectual capacity. Can we really believe that we are incapable of applying that same intellectual power to solving the great problems the world faces, overpopulation, pollution and poverty chief among them?

Can we believe that the beleaguered peoples of the world will long be tolerant of those who possess the tools but who can't make them work for the good of humankind everywhere?

There is going to be social and political and economic evolution, which will explode with such suddenness as to have the character of revolution. The revolutionary forces are already at work today, and they have humankind's dreams on their side. We don't want to be on the other side. It is up to us to assume leadership of that revolution, to channel it in a direction that will ensure freedom's future.

I expect to watch all of this from a perch yet to be determined. I just hope that wherever that is, folks will still stop me, as they do today, and ask: "Didn't you used to be Walter Cronkite?"

A NOTE ABOUT THE AUTHOR

Walter Cronkite was born in St. Joseph, Missouri, on November 4, 1916. He began his career in journalism as a campus correspondent at the Houston *Post* and also worked as a sports announcer for a local radio station in Oklahoma City. In 1937 he joined the United Press and remained there for eleven years, covering World War II and then serving as chief correspondent in Moscow from 1946 to 1948.

In 1950 Mr. Cronkite joined CBS News in Washington as a correspondent, and on April 16, 1962, he assumed his duties on the "CBS Evening News." Nineteen years later, he stepped down as anchorman and managing editor to become a special correspondent for CBS. He also has hosted many public affairs and cultural programs for PBS and for syndication and, in 1993, formed the Cronkite Ward Company to produce documentaries for the Discovery Channel, PBS and other networks.

The recipient of numerous awards and citations for his journalistic achievements, Mr. Cronkite was presented with the Presidential Medal of Freedom by Jimmy Carter in 1981. Arizona State University named its communications school after him in 1984.

Mr. Cronkite and his wife of fifty-six years live in New York City.

(continued)

Grimes, Martha, *Rainbow's End*
Grimes, Martha, *Hotel Paradise*
Hepburn, Katharine, *Me*
James, P. D., *Original Sin*
Koontz, Dean, *Dark Rivers of the Heart*
Koontz, Dean, *Intensity*
Krantz, Judith, *Lovers*
Krantz, Judith, *Spring Collection*
Landers, Ann, *Wake Up and Smell the Coffee!*
Lindbergh, Anne Morrow, *Gift from the Sea*
Mayle, Peter, *Anything Considered*
McCarthy, Cormac, *The Crossing*
Michener, James A., *Mexico*
Michener, James A., *Miracle in Seville*
Michener, James A., *Recessional*
Mother Teresa, *A Simple Path*
Patterson, Richard North, *Eyes of a Child*
Patterson, Richard North, *The Final Judgment*
Phillips, Louis, editor, *The Random House Large Print Treasury of Best-Loved Poems*
Pope John Paul II, *Crossing the Threshold of Hope*
Pope John Paul II, *The Gospel of Life*
Powell, Colin with Joseph E. Persico, *My American Journey*
Rendell, Ruth, *Simisola*
Rooney, Andy, *My War*
Shaara, Jeff, *Gods and Generals*
Truman, Margaret, *Murder at the National Gallery*
Tyler, Anne, *Ladder of Years*
Tyler, Anne, *Saint Maybe*

1997